Optimize Your SAP® ERP Financials Controlling Implementation

 **PRESS**

SAP PRESS is a joint initiative of SAP and Galileo Press. The know-how offered by SAP specialists combined with the expertise of the publishing house Galileo Press offers the reader expert books in the field. SAP PRESS features first-hand information and expert advice, and provides useful skills for professional decision-making.

SAP PRESS offers a variety of books on technical and business related topics for the SAP user. For further information, please visit our website: *www.sap-press.com*.

Nowak, David; Hurst, Quentin
SAP ERP Financials Controlling: The Complete Resource
2009, app. 625 pp.
978-1-59229-204-2

Hurst, Quentin; Nowak, David
SAP ERP Financial Accounting: The Complete Resource
2009, app. 650 pp.
978-1-59229-203-5

Korkmaz, Aylin
Financial Reporting with SAP
2008, 668 pp.
978-1-59229-179-3

Jarré, Sönke; Lövenich, Reinhold; Martin, Andreas; Müller, Klaus
SAP Treasury and Risk Management
2008, 745 pp.
978-1-59229-149-6

Shivesh Sharma

Optimize Your SAP® ERP Financials Controlling Implementation

Galileo Press

Bonn • Boston

ISBN 978-1-59229-219-6

© 2009 by Galileo Press Inc., Boston (MA)

1st Edition 2009

Galileo Press is named after the Italian physicist, mathematician and philosopher Galileo Galilei (1564–1642). He is known as one of the founders of modern science and an advocate of our contemporary, heliocentric worldview. His words *Eppur si muove* (And yet it moves) have become legendary. The Galileo Press logo depicts Jupiter orbited by the four Galilean moons, which were discovered by Galileo in 1610.

Editor   Stephen Solomon
Developmental Editor   Jutta VanStean
Copy Editor   Julie McNamee
Cover Design   Tyler Creative
Layout Design   Vera Brauner
Production   Iris Warkus
Typesetting   Publishers' Design and Production Services, Inc.
Printed and bound in Canada

Contents at a Glance

Contents

PART I Foundation

5   Optimizing Cost Element Accounting, Cost Center Accounting, Profit Center Accounting, and Internal Order Accounting 119

PART III Budgeting

PART IV Product Costing

8   Optimizing Product Costing Decisions using Product Cost Controlling 301

PART V Reporting

"Total truth is necessary. You must live by what you say."
—*Sant Sri Neem Karoli Baba*

Acknowledgments

Writing a technical book is always an exhilarating and exhausting process that allows you to look back on your experiences and ponder the key learning points of your career. And, it provides you an opportunity to thank all those who were part of your learning and growth.

First of all, I would like to thank God, my parents, and my family who have believed in all of my endeavors. Also, this book is a testament to the support and sacrifice of my wife for enduring my writing during weekends and nights. Without her constant support and encouragement, this book and my previous book would not have been possible.

I would also like to express my gratitude to my editors Stephen Solomon, Jutta VanStean, and Jawahara Saidullah, and everybody from SAP PRESS, for their support and guidance in developing this publication. Their critical analysis helped me improve the content and kept me focused throughout the process of writing.

I would also like to thank all my customer engagements for providing me an opportunity to solve their complex problems. I have learned a lot from my experiences with extremely knowledgeable clients, and this book highlights my experiences of implementing SAP ERP Financials for them.

SAP ERP consulting is a small community of people who feed on each other's ideas, so I would also like to thank all of my terrific colleagues that I met and continue to meet during my employment with IBM (ex PwC Consulting), CSC, and Fujitsu Consulting. They have constantly provided me an opportunity to develop my thought processes by sharing their valuable insights. This has allowed me to build on these nuggets of wisdom and develop my own constructs, which I will be sharing in this book.

Shivesh Sharma

"Money is the opposite of the weather. Nobody talks about it, but everybody does something about it."
— *Rebecca Johnson*

Preface

In this book, which is in many ways a continuation of my earlier book published by SAP PRESS, *Optimize Your SAP ERP Financials Implementation*, you will learn all about the SAP ERP Financials Controlling component. This component was previously known as CO, but is now an integrated part of SAP ERP Financials. An additional focus of this book is on management reporting, and how you can implement SAP components to optimize your Controlling functions.

This book is based on SAP ERP 2005, ECC version 6.0, which is the latest version and the one SAP AG suggests for new implementations and upgrades. In this book, however, you will also learn about the differences between the previous versions (4.7/4.6C) and the new version wherever applicable. Differences to versions prior to 4.6C have not been detailed because these do not provide the kind of functionality that today's organizations need to build their future.

SAP ERP Controlling: Process Orientation

This book helps you understand the typical SAP ERP Financials Controlling processes and why you would implement a particular Controlling functionality. Questions such as: "What business benefit will a particular process provide?" and "How can we achieve the efficiencies that were promised when we decided to implement SAP ERP?" are also answered.

You will not only gain an understanding of the Controlling processes but also how you can update your business processes if they are inefficient. To that end, individual Controlling components provide you with integrated management reporting and analytics you can use to identify key decision-making metrics. For example, whether you should manufacture or buy a product can be analyzed using various product-costing tools.

Thus, one of the core themes of this book is walking you through the various business processes, such as procure to pay, order to cash, and so on, as well as explaining the Controlling system as a result of these business processes. This allows you to configure your management reporting around your core business processes, which in turn leads to a better understanding of these processes and how you can optimize them.

Seeing finance and controlling as part of your business processes is very important for you to improve and optimize the financial and controlling business processes. It allows you to construct the framework in which you are operating and then visualize how you can make this process better in terms of reduced timelines or reduced operating costs. This leads us to the next theme, which is the primary focus of this book: optimization.

Controlling in SAP ERP Financials: The Need for Optimization

Optimization essentially means trying to extract the maximum benefit under a given set of constraints. This book walks you through the entire spectrum of management reporting solutions available in SAP ERP Financials so you can then pick the one that best meets your requirement. For example, if you are a software company, implementing product costing does not make sense because the product cost is the cost of R&D, which is a one-time expense. On the other hand, if you are a manufacturing company, you may want to implement product costing to analyze the overall product cost structure and to decide whether you should make or buy a component. Thus, it is very important to choose the components that make sense for your business and within your industry.

How This Book Is Organized

This book is organized into five parts, as shown in Figure 1 and as explained here:

► **Part I: Foundation**: Introduction to SAP ERP, the structure of SAP ERP Controlling, and the SAP ERP enterprise structure (Chapters 1, 2, and 3)

- **Part II: Basic Controlling Processes**: Business process view of Controlling and basic controlling concepts (Chapters 4 and 5)

- **Part III: Budgeting**: Investment Management and Funds Management (Chapters 6 and 7)

- **Part IV: Product Costing**: Product Cost Planning, Cost Object Controlling, and Actual Costing/Material Ledger (Chapter 8)

- **Part V: Reporting**: Profitability Analysis and Reporting in Financials and Controlling (Chapters 9 and 10)

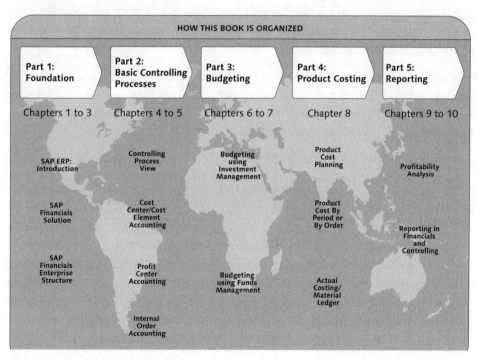

Figure 1 How this book is organized

Let's take a brief look at these parts before we proceed further.

Part I

Made up of Chapters 1, 2, and 3, Part I of this book explores the SAP ERP architecture, implementation methodologies, structure, value proposition, and business case outline. Then we provide a detailed exploration of SAP ERP Financials and the various application components within Financials and Controlling.

After you understand the depth and breadth of the solution landscape, you are introduced to the SAP ERP enterprise structure of Financials and Controlling. You also learn about the pros and cons of selecting organizational entities and mapping them per SAP Best Practices.

Part II

Part II is comprised of Chapters 4 and 5, which cover the basic Controlling processes and how you can achieve significant improvements in your management reporting using the Controlling component of SAP ERP Financials.

In this part, you are first introduced to the Controlling functions and processes in an organization. Next, you learn about global settings that need to be configured for Controlling. Then, you are introduced to cost center accounting, cost element accounting, profit center accounting, and internal order accounting.

Once you understand the Controlling processes, you are then ready to learn about the extended processes in controlling, which we cover in Part III.

Part III

In Part III, which is comprised of Chapters 6 and 7, you will learn about advanced topics of Controlling and how you can optimize your budgeting implementation to suit your business requirements. Specifically, you will learn about budgeting processes, including Investment Management in Chapter 6 and Funds Management in Chapter 7 (Funds Management is the SAP solution for public-sector companies to manage their year-to-year expenditure per budgetary outlays).

Part IV

Consisting only of Chapter 8, this part describes the product costing decisions that help you understand your product costs and make key management decisions. You will learn about the three SAP Controlling solutions: product cost controlling, cost object controlling, and material ledger. You will also become familiar with the rationale and features of each of these subcomponents, as well as understand how to implement them and in what sequence.

Part V

This part is comprised of Chapters 9 and 10. In Chapter 9, you will learn about the implementation and processes in Profitability Analysis from a financial perspective. With the advent of SAP NetWeaver Business Intelligence (SAP NetWeaver BI), most of the Profitability Analysis reporting is moving to the business warehousing platform. However, it is important for you to understand the source structure in ECC for you to understand the reporting structure in SAP NetWeaver BI. It lays the foundation on which the extraction of SAP NetWeaver BI InfoCubes is based.

In Chapter 10, you will learn about the reporting capabilities of the Financials and Controlling components, and how you can use the Report Painter component to customize reporting.

Tip
Each of these five parts covers different aspects of Controlling and builds on each preceding part. Thus, it makes sense to read this book in sequence. However, if you need details about a particular topic and are already aware about the basics, you can start from the beginning of any of the individual parts.

At the beginning of each chapter, we identify a learning path, which helps you keep track of your learning. This is especially important when you are trying to understand the configuration steps for each individual SAP ERP Financials component detailed in a given chapter. The learning path allows you to visualize the importance of a specific configuration step in the overall scheme of things.

Summary

This book, together with my other SAP PRESS book *Optimize Your SAP ERP Financials Implementation*, covers the entire spectrum of the SAP ERP solutions available for Financials and Controlling. However, it is important to understand that an ERP implementation is no magic bullet that can help you change your organization in one go. You need to first build a core enterprise foundation and then keep improving the system to meet any new needs of your organization. You need to understand the current business processes and to try to change them to come as close to SAP Best Practices as possible. If instead, for example, you implement your existing legacy system in SAP ERP, you will not get any real benefit.

So let your journey of learning and adventure with SAP ERP Controlling begin with Chapter 1, where you will be introduced to the SAP ERP solution and the direction in which SAP AG is moving to support the new realities of the marketplace. This chapter also helps you identify the business benefits for your SAP ERP implementation by following the value engineering roadmap offering.

PART I
Foundation

This chapter introduces you to SAP ERP projects, the philosophy of an SAP ERP project, and the typical methodologies used in the industry for SAP ERP implementations.

1   SAP ERP Implementation

SAP provides one of the most comprehensive enterprise-wide business software solutions. In this chapter, we introduce the SAP ERP solution focusing on the key aspects of the implementation rationale, the approach, and some of the key issues. This chapter is a building block for the next chapter, where you will learn more about the SAP ERP Financials solution.

This chapter broadly describes the following:

- The reasons for SAP ERP implementations
- The types of SAP ERP implementations
- The implementation methodologies (e.g., ASAP, ValueSAP, Solution Manager, and other industry Best Practices) and project lifecycle (project preparation to post go-live support phases)
- The use of SAP Best Practices to accelerate your implementation
- The role of SAP ERP Controlling consultants in SAP ERP implementations

The process of implementing SAP ERP has been defined and documented in various publications. The implementation approach has different nuances depending on whom you talk to, but the overall theme is conceptually the same. So let's begin by exploring the reasons for SAP ERP implementations.

1.1   Reasons for Implementing SAP ERP

At a very high level, SAP ERP, or any IT system for that matter, is implemented to achieve a business goal that is important in the minds of the sponsor or executive management. For example, a CFO might realize that the financial reporting is extremely complex, and it takes significant amounts of manual effort to close the books. So instead of working on financial analysis and decision making, the financial organization is trying to get the financial books closed. And, there is always some confusion about the final numbers because there are too many systems of record with conflicting numbers.

The business goal then trickles down to the IT department in terms of business requirements; IT then identifies the *roadmap* to achieve the business goal. The goal helps structure and formalize the overall value proposition of the IT enterprise resource planning (ERP) project. This results in a detailed analysis of the options available for the ERP implementation. At this point, the organization looks at the various tools available that meet the desired objective. So a CFO might look at SAP ERP Financials and Oracle Financials as possible solutions for the organization. Based on a detailed analysis of the organizational needs and goal assessment, the organization chooses a particular software product and signs a contract with the software provider.

Note About SAP AG

Founded in 1972, SAP AG is the industry leader in providing collaborative business solutions for all major industry sectors and markets. SAP AG has an installation base of 41,200 customers and has a significant presence in more than 50 countries.

After an organization chooses SAP as its software vendor, a more detailed level analysis is done to evaluate the components of the SAP architecture that should be implemented and when, which leads us to the next section where we will discuss the SAP ERP roadmap.

1.2   The SAP ERP Solution Stack

At the beginning of your SAP ERP implementation, you have to define how you plan to transition from legacy systems to the SAP ERP application. Or, you might already have an SAP system installed but want to implement additional components or simplify your current architectural landscape. This is also called your *SAP ERP implementation roadmap*. For you to define the roadmap, it is important to first understand the current SAP offerings. We will discuss this next, and then you will learn about the factors that influence the roadmap.

SAP ERP has evolved continuously with each year from its initial release in 1972 (then called SAP R/3), to a broader offering as shown in Figure 1.1. The release shown in the figure is SAP ERP 2005, with add-on components. SAP plans to release the next level of ERP every five years to align better with the customers' upgrade cycles. Thus, the next release is scheduled to be available in 2010.

Figure 1.1 and Figure 1.2 show the SAP ERP landscape, and the SAP ERP solution stack.

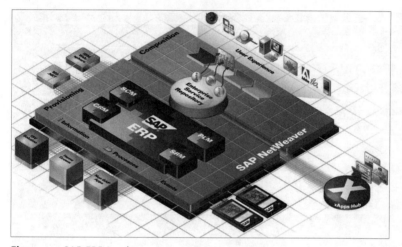

Figure 1.1 SAP ERP Landscape

Specifically, Figure 1.1 illustrates the SAP ERP landscape along with the other available components that integrate with SAP ERP. **SAP ERP** is the core enterprise business application, which can be integrated with SAP Supply Chain Management (**SCM**), SAP Customer Relationship Management (**CRM**), SAP Supplier Relationship Management (**SRM**) and SAP Product Lifecycle Management (**PLM**). All of these components sit on the **SAP NetWeaver** platform, which allows you to also integrate disparate custom and other non-SAP systems in one unified system. You can also connect additional platforms seamlessly such as IBM Websphere, Microsoft's .NET, SAP Executive Search, and SAP BI Accelerator.

All of these can also be used to feed the **Enterprise Service Repository**, which allows you to tailor the user experience into multiple content delivery models.

You can also integrate the *cross application tools*, which allow you to further enrich the user experience.

Figure 1.2 shows you the SAP ERP solution stack in more detail with component-level stacks such as **Analytics, Financials, Human Capital Management, Procurement and Logistics Execution, Product Development and Manufacturing, Sales and Service,** and **Corporate Services**. These can then be further subdivided into individual components.

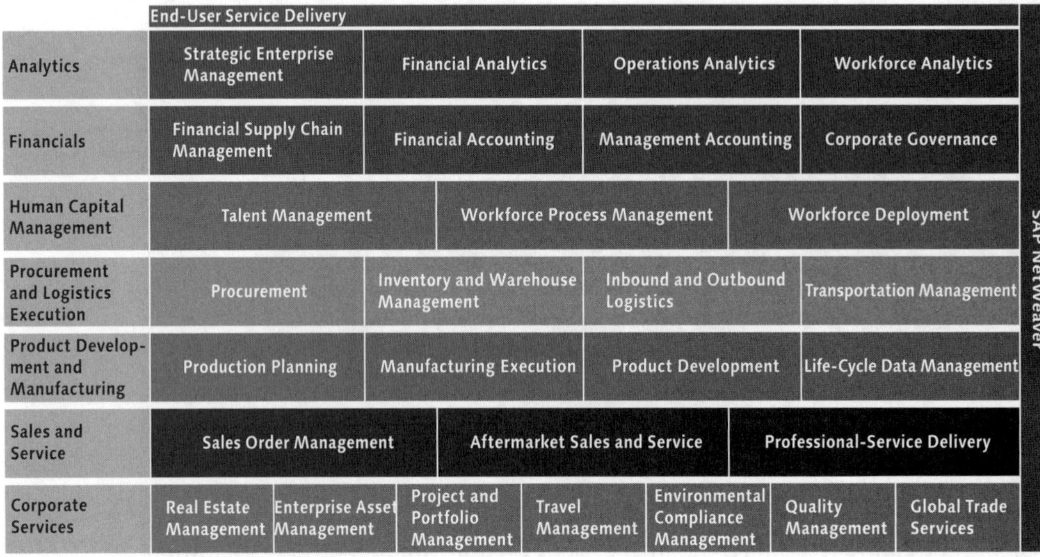

End-User Service Delivery					
Analytics	Strategic Enterprise Management	Financial Analytics	Operations Analytics	Workforce Analytics	
Financials	Financial Supply Chain Management	Financial Accounting	Management Accounting	Corporate Governance	
Human Capital Management	Talent Management	Workforce Process Management		Workforce Deployment	
Procurement and Logistics Execution	Procurement	Inventory and Warehouse Management	Inbound and Outbound Logistics	Transportation Management	
Product Development and Manufacturing	Production Planning	Manufacturing Execution	Product Development	Life-Cycle Data Management	
Sales and Service	Sales Order Management	Aftermarket Sales and Service		Professional-Service Delivery	
Corporate Services	Real Estate Management / Enterprise Asset Management	Project and Portfolio Management / Travel Management	Environmental Compliance Management	Quality Management	Global Trade Services

SAP NetWeaver

Figure 1.2 SAP ERP Solution Stack

Let's take a detailed look at (SAP ERP) **Financials**. This stack can be segregated into **Financial Supply Chain Management, Financial Accounting, Managerial Accounting,** and **Corporate Governance**. Within Financial Accounting, you have multiple options, such as Accounts Receivable, Accounts Payable, Asset Accounting, new General Ledger (GL), and so on. In addition to the SAP ERP reporting stack for SAP ERP Financials, you can also implement SAP Strategic Enterprise Management and use SAP ERP Financials Analytics.

With this many options, it is very important to arrive at the *preferred roadmap* for your organization or your client's organization. For more details about the SAP roadmap analysis offering, refer to my other SAP PRESS book *Optimize Your SAP ERP Financials Implementation*.

In the next section, you will learn more about the various types of implementation that are possible in SAP ERP.

1.3   Types of SAP Implementations

As you saw earlier, the SAP landscape and evolving business requirements necessitate that you tailor your implementation to meet the requirements that make the most sense. In this section, you will learn about the different SAP implementation types and the approach needed in each of the scenarios. Depending on the business requirements you have and the stage of maturity your company's SAP system is in, you can implement the following types of SAP ERP implementations:

▶ **Providing production support**
Typically, companies' use of SAP software matures after two to three years when most of the basic functionality has been implemented. At that point, you need to establish production support processes for the current SAP ERP functionality, which requires only minor tweaks to the existing components. Production support is the most common form of SAP ERP project that you will be involved in, and this aspect of the business is typically managed mostly by internal IT staff. Typical production support activities include a series of checklists that need to be performed at month end and year end as part of the closing process. In addition, you might be asked to create a new financial report that includes an additional level of detail for analysis.

▶ **Enhancing an existing SAP ERP implementation**
Enhancing an existing SAP ERP implementation is a little bit more involved than ongoing production support. It requires you to implement additional functionality within your existing system to meet changing needs, which can involve implementing new components or re-configuring existing components. External SAP ERP consultants who have done the same type of work before and are more familiar with the processes are typically required to be involved. For this scenario, you need to carefully create a mapping of the desired SAP ERP landscape versus the existing SAP ERP landscape before starting small enhancements because this keeps things in perspective. For example, if you acquired a new company with different financial accounting needs from a revenue recognition perspective, you might need to implement revenue recognition using SAP. However, you would also have to make sure that all of the processes are

standardized and also account for the impact to the existing business processes of revenue recognition.

▶ **Upgrading SAP ERP to a new version**
As you learned earlier, going forward, SAP plans to release a new version of SAP ERP core functionality every five years. The SAP ERP release strategy from 2005 through 2010 is shown in Figure 1.3.

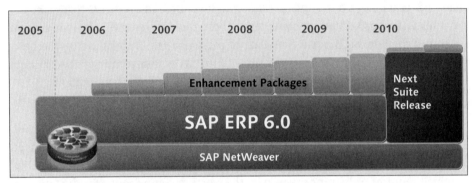

Figure 1.3 SAP Release Strategy for SAP ERP

This means that every five years, your organization will need to make an upgrade-related decision. The key aspects you need to consider are your support agreement with SAP, the licensing agreement, and other organizational factors, as these influence the overall return on investment (ROI) for your SAP ERP investment.

In addition, SAP will provide enhancement packages, such as Financial Shared Services and Banking Relationship Management, which you can decide to implement in between major releases if those packages drive your business benefit realization.

Another decision that an organization has to make when thinking about upgrading SAP ERP is whether to perform a technical upgrade, a technical and functional upgrade, or a strategic upgrade. A strategic upgrade focuses on increasing revenue, whereas a technical upgrade focuses more on reducing costs. A functional upgrade is somewhere in between, with a mixture of increasing revenues and reducing costs. These approaches and some of their benefits are shown in Figure 1.4.

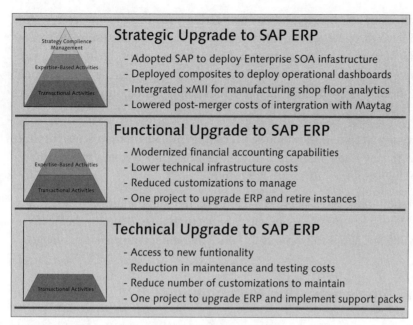

Strategic Upgrade to SAP ERP

- Adopted SAP to deploy Enterprise SOA infastructure
- Deployed composites to deploy operational dashboards
- Intergrated xMII for manufacturing shop floor analytics
- Lowered post-merger costs of intergration with Maytag

Functional Upgrade to SAP ERP

- Modernized financial accounting capabilities
- Lower technical infrastructure costs
- Reduced customizations to manage
- One project to upgrade ERP and retire instances

Technical Upgrade to SAP ERP

- Access to new funtionality
- Reduction in maintenance and testing costs
- Reduce number of customizations to maintain
- One project to upgrade ERP and implement support packs

Figure 1.4 Methods of Upgrading with Business Benefits

Additional goals of a technical upgrade include the following:

▶ Cleanse master data

▶ Remove redundant and unwanted configuration

▶ Harmonize business processes

▶ Enhance performance of the SAP ERP application

Typically, risk-averse organizations perform a technical upgrade followed by a functional enhancement and then a strategic upgrade. This helps reduce the risk and disruption to the business processes because the existing business processes continue to execute, and the user interface changes are minimal (unless you are upgrading from a version lesser than 4.6C). However, most upgrade projects will fall into the category of functional upgrades because organizations will also implement some additional functionality to justify the business case for the upgrade.

▶ **Performing a new implementation**
This involves implementing SAP ERP from scratch in a new SAP ERP landscape. New implementations allow you to discard previous practices and incorporate

Best Practices by modifying and re-engineering your business processes. This can be due to the new functionality that is available in the system as well as due to an increased understanding of new business realities. In some cases, companies with an existing SAP ERP system might also decide to implement SAP ERP from scratch because the previous implementation does not reflect current realities.

As you move from top to bottom in the preceding implementation types (production support to new implementation), the implementation becomes more complex and demanding from the business perspective.

These different implementation types have very different timelines and very different requirements in terms of implementation methodology. Thus, in the next section, you will learn about the various SAP ERP implementation methodologies.

1.4   SAP Implementation Methodologies

As you saw earlier, SAP ERP projects are performed for a multitude of business reasons and require varying levels of skill. Nonetheless, it is important to follow the same set of rules while implementing an SAP ERP project, regardless of its type. This set of rules is called the *implementation methodology*. Implementation methodologies help structure implementations in a way that helps you achieve business objectives. They involve taking on a more method-oriented perspective that translates to a toolkit or a roadmap that helps you get there.

Next we will identify the typical implementation methodologies used globally to implement SAP ERP.

1.4.1   Evolution from ASAP to ValueSAP to Solution Manager

Over the years, SAP has continuously evolved the approach to implementing the SAP suite of applications because of the following significant changes:

- An ever-evolving system landscape with more integration opportunities across other software vendors
- An increasingly complex suite of applications
- The portalization or web-ization of SAP ERP
- The need to implement SAP ERP solutions in an ever-shortening time frame

SAP has kept pace with all of this by evolving from a toolkit-based implementation solution approach (ASAP) to a benefits realization approach (ValueSAP) to an integrated project management and benefits tracking approach (Solution Manager). This evolution is shown in Figure 1.5.

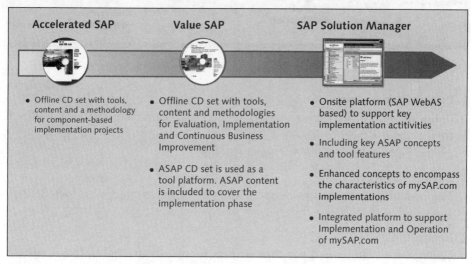

Figure 1.5 Evolution from ASAP to ValueSAP to Solution Manager

Let's now dive more deeply into each of these implementation methodologies.

1.4.2   ASAP Methodology

The ASAP methodology uses a toolkit of SAP ERP Accelerators that are based on the Best Practices of SAP ERP customer implementations from around the world and consist of a number of templates, questions, and scenarios. Most companies use this methodology, which has now been replaced by Solution Manager.

Different consulting companies add and subtract templates depending on their previous experiences, however, so think of ASAP as a general toolkit with modifications and enhancements made by different consulting companies, depending on their experience and learning.

ASAP Phases of an SAP Implementation:

The following sequential phases are part of ASAP methodology, which are also seen in Figure 1.6:

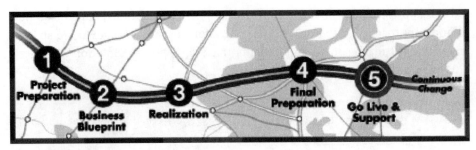

Figure 1.6 ASAP Project Lifecycle Phases

1. **Project Preparation**

   In this phase, a project framework is defined, and team members are mobilized to work on the specific project. This phase outlines the guiding principles of the project and establishes the operating rhythm.

2. **Business Blueprint**

   The business processes are defined, and the business blueprint document is signed off.

3. **Realization**

   The system is configured per the business requirements, and unit testing and integration testing are performed. Data mappings and data requirements are finalized for migration.

4. **Final Preparation**

   Integration and conversion testing are performed, and end users are trained.

5. **Go-Live & Support**

   Legacy data is migrated to SAP, and the new system is activated with post Go-Live support.

It is very important that you follow this methodology and perform gate checks at each stage so that the project scope is finalized and detailed at a more granular level as you go along. Sometimes organizations skip a stage to timebox an implementation, which can be extremely dangerous because you miss important steps that make an implementation successful. Also it gets more costly and harder to correct mistakes as you get deeper into the implementation.

Even though this approach has been around a long time, it still applies today.

Next you will learn about the variations of this approach, starting with ValueSAP.

1.4.3   ValueSAP Methodology

As SAP ERP evolved into one of the premier choices for companies looking to implement an ERP solution, many organizations started implementing the software on an organization-wide basis. This led to longer timeframes of project implementation, which led to higher implementation costs, which also led to concerns about how beneficial it was to implement the system.

SAP answered this question by developing the ValueSAP approach in which business drivers became the implementation focus. As a result, the toolkit available to implement an SAP system expanded to include an SAP implementation evaluation and a business benefits realization aspect.

In addition, the focus shifted to continuously improving the business benefits of using the SAP system as the tool to enable change management within the organization. SAP also tried to help track how organizations were evolving per the changing market conditions, thus providing a reality check for the implementations. The ValueSAP tool also provided more insights into benchmarking business processes of an organization against the best in the business (which were also going through a similar process of adapting to the continuously changing business environment and increasing globalization of the economy across the world).

1.4.4   Solution Manager

Solution Manager lets you manage SAP implementations and provides you with the integrated platform to manage your project. The key question is how Solution Manager is different from the ASAP and ValueSAP methodologies. Solution Manager provides the following added features and concepts:

► Multiple procedures for functional and technical aspects of an implementation are included. Previously, there was just one way of doing things (ASAP), but as SAP ERP evolved, variations needed to be accommodated to ensure the optimal implementation solution.

► More product-related information is available.

► An integrated approach is now used to manage the go-live analysis and platform for supporting the SAP ERP landscape.

► A business process repository is included that contains business process scenarios and business process definitions.

▶ Earlier business blueprinting was based on a Q&A database that was not tied to the implementation. Solution Manager provides additional tools for scoping and blueprinting, which can then be tied together to the testing process as well.

▶ The focus is shifted to a process oriented perspective. ASAP and ValueSAP were focused on implementing SAP ERP components such as Materials Management (MM), Sales and Distribution (SD), and so on. Now the focus is on processes, such as procure to pay, which starts with a purchase requisition and ends when payment to the vendor is disbursed.

Solution Manager is an integrated platform that runs centrally in a customer's solution landscape and ensures the technical capability of supporting a distributed system. It is the software tool to help implement SAP ERP, and then operate it and optimize it over a longer time span so that processes can be continuously improved and business benefits realized.

Solution Manager aims to satisfy not only the needs of the IT implementation but also the operation and optimization phases that you have to go through during the system's entire lifecycle. The scenarios supported by Solution Manager are shown in Figure 1.7.

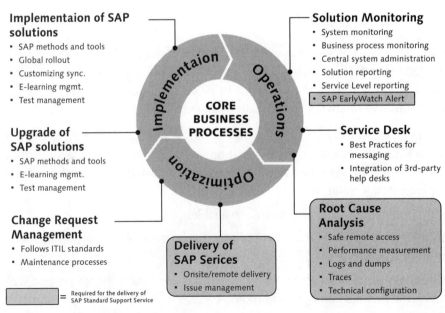

Figure 1.7   Solution Manager Processes

These scenarios are described by each phase as follows:

▶ **Implementation**

  ▶ **Implementation of SAP solutions**

  Solution Manager houses the SAP methods and tools to implement SAP ERP. You can develop templates for global rollout, identify and perform customizing synchronization, and manage the learning and knowledge management environments. In addition, you can use Solution Manager to manage test cases and then execute them automatically per a business scenario. Also, Solution Manager can be integrated with best-of-breed testing solutions (Mercury/HP Quality Center, Winrunner, etc.) to support testing requirements.

This component can also be used to enable the metrics related to configuration objects, training documentation, and other details.

  ▶ **Upgrade of SAP solutions**

  All of the tools identified in the implementation of SAP solutions can also be used when upgrading an SAP solution set to a new release or to a new enhancement package. In addition, specific templates and guidelines are available to facilitate the upgrade process.

▶ **Operations**

  ▶ **Solution monitoring**

  This component can be used to perform integrated system monitoring of disparate systems using one Solution Manager interface and is especially useful to the SAP ERP Basis team. You can perform business process monitoring, central system administration, solution reporting, and service-level reporting, as well as use the SAP EarlyWatch Alert tool.

  ▶ **Service desk**

  This component lets you manage the helpdesk ticketing process and assign tickets to relevant personnel per predefined rules, and allows you to integrate with any third-party consulting partner, and incorporates SAP's Best Practices for messaging.

  ▶ **Root Cause Analysis**

  In the past, SAP connected to your system using online support system (OSS) via Transaction OSS1. This has been replaced by Solution Manager, which allows SAP to perform safe remote access, performance measurement, log and dump analyses, and traces. It also lets SAP gather information about the technical configuration and settings to facilitate a more seamless interface with customers for problem solving and error analysis.

▶ **Optimization**

  ▶ **Delivery of SAP services**
    SAP Service delivery is available either remotely or on site. You can also perform issue management.

  ▶ **Change request management**
    This component lets you monitor the change controls to the project scope. In addition, it lets you enable change management activities by acting as one central repository for all documentation of an organization. It also allows you to follow ITIL standards and map your SAP ERP system maintenance processes.

Solution Manager and SAP Support Interaction

Let's look at some of the common Solution Manager functions in more detail. First, we will discuss how the interaction with SAP Support has been simplified and mapped in Solution Manager. Figure 1.8 shows the entire process of interacting with SAP Support to rectify any issues mapped into the following steps:

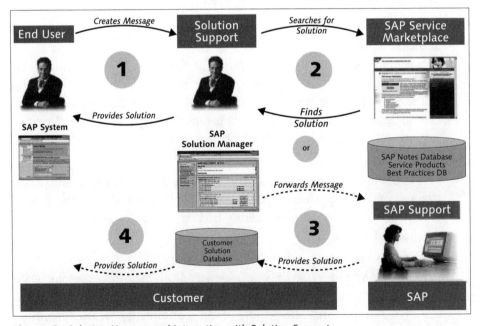

Figure 1.8 Solution Manager and Interaction with Solution Support

1. An **End User** creates a message that gets routed to **Solution Support** (internal IT helpdesk). **Solution Support** uses **SAP Solution Manager** to track all customer messages.

2. **Solution Support** can search for a solution from **SAP Service Marketplace**. Solution Support can directly search the **SAP Notes Database, Service Products,** and **Best Practices Database** to look for a possible solution. If the solution is found, it is communicated to the end user, and the message gets closed after validation by the end user.

3. If the solution is not available in **SAP Service Marketplace**, then **Solution Support** can forward the message to **SAP Support**. Depending on the priority of the message, the problem is worked on, and a suitable solution is provided back to **Solution Support**.

4. The solution is then communicated to the **End User**.

In a similar fashion, Solution Manager is also the standard vehicle of delivery for EarlyWatch Reports as shown in Figure 1.9. EarlyWatch is an SAP service that allows SAP to directly log into your system and perform a diagnostic analysis of the health of your SAP system, from both a database and application perspective.

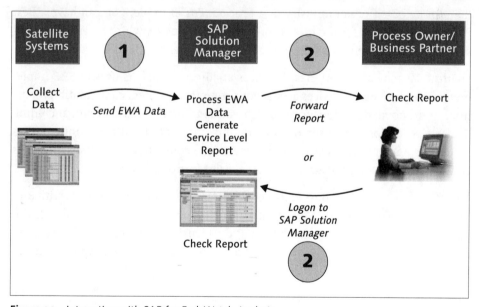

Figure 1.9 Interaction with SAP for EarlyWatch Analysis

The process is as follows:

1. Solution Manager collects the EarlyWatch Analysis (EWA) data from all satellite systems. SAP Solution Manager allows you to collate this data per your service level agreements defined with the hardware vendor.

2. The data is then processed in Solution Manger, and an appropriate service level report is generated, which can be forwarded to the process owner or business partner (Forward Report) who validates the report (Check Report) and takes action on the action items in red and yellow by logging on to the Solution Manager.

Now that you understand the various implementation methodologies, let's examine how you can use SAP Best Practices to accelerate your implementation and reduce the timeline to achieve your business benefits.

1.5   SAP Best Practices Solution Set

With the ever-increasing need to reduce the amount of time necessary to implement SAP solutions, SAP ERP comes prepackaged with a Best Practices solution set that can be based on an industry or a process. For example, you can have a Best Practice solution set for the professional services industry, which gives you a head start for your implementation if you are in that industry.

Figure 1.10 shows the SAP Best Practices architecture and its uses in SAP implementations. SAP Best Practices acts as your complete business configuration repository and knowledge repository, which contains predefined content, including detailed scenarios, end user documentation, installation guides, configuration guides, data migration sheets, training materials, configuration settings, business configuration sets, master data, test cases, print forms, and user roles.

You can also use the SAP Best Practices solution as a demo environment with SAP Best Practices content, and you can use it for the entire lifecycle management to develop new templates and documentation focusing on vertical industry solutions. Best Practices can also be used as a solution architecture support platform for development and presales support.

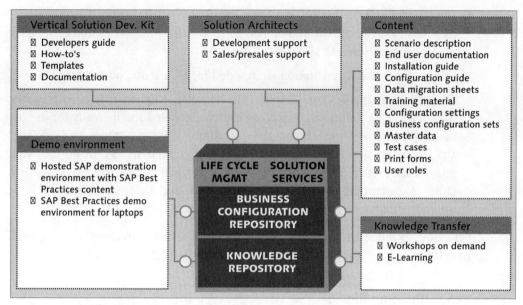

Figure 1.10 SAP Best Practices Architecture and Uses

According to SAP, the key benefits of using SAP Best Practices are as follows:

▶ SAP Best Practices provide the preconfigured business content, the tools, and the documentation that you need for a fast and smooth implementation.

▶ The installation time is reduced considerably by using automated configuration tools such as the Best Practices Installation Assistant, which uses other automation technologies, such as Business Configuration (BC) sets and extended CATT (eCATT) procedures (more on these later in the chapter), for rapid installation. This is a new tool in the ECC 6.0 release, which accelerates implementation time by automating system configuration steps. Instead of clicking through individual steps that allow you to customize your installation of Best Practices, you can activate a project that will perform the installation of a Best Practices solution in a fraction of the time it used to take. We will look at the Best Practices Installation Assistant in more detail a little later in the chapter.

▶ The transfer and generation of master data is also accelerated and facilitated by the use of eCATT. eCATT allows you to modify and import customer-specific master data into an SAP system.

▶ Comprehensive documentation is provided for all installation activities.

▶ Consulting companies can develop the Best Practices extensions as possible industry-specific solutions, which can then be installed and be ready for use by the customer. The hope is that in the near future, you can just insert a CD-ROM, and all of your Best Practice processes get configured based on the options you select during setup. This idea is similar to what you do when you buy Microsoft Office, for example, insert the Office CD-ROM, and are ready to use the software after making a few selections during setup.

Let's now examine the overall architecture and the steps involved in using SAP Best Practices.

1.5.1   Building Blocks

SAP Best Practices comes with *building blocks*, which are reusable preconfigured units that need to be assembled to design your own processes. So, instead of a consultant configuring individual settings, you can now configure a group of settings in one go. Building blocks allow you to work with different processes and still keep the overall design flexible. It also drastically reduces the time it takes to configure your SAP ERP solution, and the effort is focused on designing a solution that is specific to the customer.

Building blocks can vary in size as well as content. The goal is to reduce the overall redundancy in configuration. After you have decided which building blocks you want to use, you need to install them in a particular sequence per the installation guide using the tools and documentation provided by SAP.

1.5.2   Best Practices Installation Assistant

The Best Practices Installation Assistant is a new tool available from ECC 6.0 on that enables you to install the Best Practices very quickly. Figure 1.11 shows you the tool's interface. From a procedural perspective, you need to first install Layer 0 building blocks followed by Layer 1 building blocks. Layer 2 contains the list of scenarios that you want to activate.

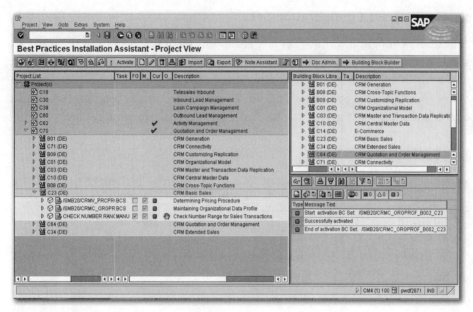

Figure 1.11 Best Practices Installation Assistant

Before the Best Practices Installation Assistant was available, you had to follow a script and run commands to perform Best Practices installations. Now, you can save time and reduce the likelihood of any errors, and the Best Practices Installation Assistant also provides you with tracking and logging functionality, enabling you to troubleshoot any installation errors that might occur.

The exact order in which you should activate these building blocks varies for each industry-specific Best Practices and is documented in more detail in the relevant Best Practices quick guide for installation. For example, to activate a particular scenario for consumer products Best Practices, you might need to activate different individual components in a particular sequence.

1.5.3 eCATT Procedures

SAP Best Practices comes prepackaged with eCATT procedures that allow you to quickly test end-to-end scenarios using automated functional test cases for all scenarios that come standard in the installation of the Best Practices solution. These procedures increase your ability to test early and catch any errors that might result from incorrect customization settings.

43

1.5.4 Business Configuration Set

A business configuration (BC) set is a group of Customizing settings. Figure 1.12 shows a schematic of what makes up a BC set. You pick the business processes that you want to configure, and the system automatically generates the configuration tables and views that constitute a BC set. These sets essentially represent snapshots of configuration settings that can be directly imported into your system.

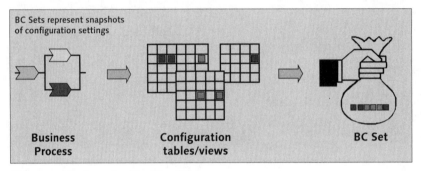

Figure 1.12 Business Configuration Sets

These BC sets let you accelerate the installation of building blocks and delivered scenarios by integrating with eCATTs that contain the parameters for configuration. Traditionally, eCATTs were used only for master data or transaction data loads, but these can now also be used to maintain configuration parameters. So, instead of going to a screen and entering configuration settings, you simply upload a text file that automatically updates the configuration of multiple values.

Now that you understand how you can accelerate your implementation efforts using SAP Best Practices, let's explore the role of SAP ERP Financials and Controlling consultants.

1.6 The Role of SAP ERP Financials and Controlling Consultants in SAP ERP Implementations

The main role of SAP ERP Financials and Controlling consultants is to help define and structure SAP ERP implementations by clearly defining the statutory and management reporting requirements. Because the legacy reporting typically resides in legacy financials, Controlling consultants have to fill in the gaps of most of the reporting needs of an organization by either identifying the reports in financials, or referring to the correct reports in logistics. Typically, the Controlling person is also the "reporting guru" for the project.

You will learn more about the Controlling aspects in later chapters in this book. However, note that the role of Financials and Controlling consultants extends beyond the configuration of individual components.

Broadly speaking, SAP ERP Financials and Controlling consultants also provide the following perspectives to other integrated processes:

▶ Management reporting perspective

▶ Integration perspective

▶ Accounting perspective

These perspectives are detailed in the next sections.

1.6.1 Management Reporting Perspective

The Controlling consultant is typically in charge of the overall reporting requirements and establishing the best way to fulfill them. This is the main role of the Controlling consultant. In short, the Controlling consultant is the management reporting guru.

Typically, in a non-ERP legacy system, management reports come from the financials component of the respective software. But in SAP ERP, management reporting is distributed across individual components. This requires a unique perspective from the Controlling consultant to communicate to other teams.

The Controlling team helps analyze the management reporting requirements and finalizes the individual reporting requirements across all components. For example, one of the most important aftereffects of an SAP ERP implementation is the integration of the inventory ledger to the GL. In a legacy environment, these were two ledgers; the inventory ledger was managed by MM and primarily tracked the quantities, whereas the valuation ledger/GL was maintained by Financials, which tracked the dollar values of the quantities. More often than not, these two never matched. With the implementation of SAP ERP, the valuation/GL and inventory ledgers are integrated. So any postings that are updated in the MM component also get posted in Financials. Therefore, inventory management reporting is owned by

MM in SAP ERP. In short, the source of inventory reporting is MM because the inventory ledger (quantity) is always reconciled with the GL (dollar).

1.6.2 Integration Perspective

SAP ERP Financials and Controlling consultants help analyze the integration touchpoints across components and help fill in the integration touchpoints in many situations. They also act as a common conduit of information transfer across teams. Furthermore, they keep the implementation team together and focused on the important issues.

For example, MM account determination and SD account determination help drive the integration of the purchasing and finance teams. While defining the account determination, a lot of cross team interaction happens, and the SAP ERP Financials and Controlling consultant acts as an integrator across the teams. Similarly, the Controlling person also needs to make sure that all account assignments across components are clearly defined and understood. Every component will need some sort of account assignment, so the role of the Controlling consultant is to work hand in hand with the Financial Accounting consultant and keep a tab on the overall integration of the project. This is especially true if you have production planning implemented, because that means a significantly larger role for the Controlling consultant as most of the advanced management reporting needed for production planning comes from product cost controlling.

1.6.3 Accounting and Audit Perspective

When defining a business process mapped to an SAP solution, often the way the process is configured depends on how the accounting should work. For example, when receiving goods, whether the material stock needs to be maintained in the system or can be expensed is decided per accounting guidelines. And, depending on which way you go, the configuration will be different for the material purchasing and inventory management. SAP ERP Financials and Controlling consultants help analyze the pros and cons of each process from an accounting perspective. This exercise is especially important in account determination for MM and SD. Correct and optimal account determination helps clearly outline the month-end process, which cuts down on the number of days to close the books.

In addition, sometimes the process needs to be redesigned to accommodate the accounting and audit perspective, which most of the other teams forget. So the

Controlling consultant helps to make sure that the delegation of authority and segregation of duties are adhered to per the corporate guidelines. A classic example involves the release strategies that need to be defined for purchase order approval. The Controlling department typically owns these strategies, but they need to be configured by a Logistics consultant. So the finance team acts as a keeper of accounting and audit perspective in the implementation.

Even though you certainly do incur a cost by buying licenses for SAP ERP, the most important cost factor in implementing SAP ERP is the labor and time involved in the implementation effort. Therefore, it is very important that you understand the role of SAP ERP Financials and Controlling consultants along with the SAP ERP implementation team structure.

1.7 Summary

In this chapter, you learned about the rationale of SAP ERP implementations and the broad solution set offered by SAP ERP implementations focusing on financials. You also learned about the various implementation methodologies, including ASAP, ValueSAP, and Solution Manager, which are available to manage your SAP implementations. Furthermore, you learned how you can accelerate your SAP implementation using SAP Best Practices. We also discussed the role of the SAP ERP Financials and Controlling consultant as the management reporting guru.

In Chapter 2, you will learn more about SAP ERP from a Controlling perspective. You will also learn about the approach you should take to implement Controlling components.

This chapter provides an overview of SAP ERP Financials and Controlling and outlines the typical implementation roadmap for implementing Controlling.

2 Controlling: An Introduction

In Chapter 1, you learned about the SAP ERP solution in general, with details about the suggested roadmap and implementation methodologies. This chapter focuses on the Controlling solution in more detail with an initial discussion of the overall SAP ERP Financials solution.

SAP ERP Financials is an extremely broad solution, covering the entire spectrum of business applications. As such, it is very important for you to understand what Financials or Controlling components make sense for your organization and what would work best for you. The focus should be on understanding the pain points of business and how you can implement a solution that addresses these points and meets not only the current requirements but also evolving future needs.

Specifically, in this chapter, you will first learn about the overall SAP ERP Financials solution and then learn about the details of each of the individual components. The overall perspective you will gain will help you make distinctions among the various solution sets available in SAP ERP for finance and controlling users.

In addition to learning about the solution map for the overall Controlling solution, you will also learn about the strategic direction of SAP ERP Financials for various components and how these are evolving. You will be introduced to the options that are available and what criteria you should use to pick one over the other.

The next section describes the key requirements for implementing an integrated financial business solution and the reasons for implementing a controlling system.

2.1 Key Requirements for the SAP ERP Financials Solution

The financial system must meet the business requirements both from a statutory perspective as well as from a management reporting perspective. The acid test for any implementation's success is to understand what matters most to the business and how you can use the system to meet those critical success factors. The following are the key challenges before evaluating an implementation of an SAP ERP solution:

▶ Understand the market realities, such as faster design to market and shorter attention span of consumers.

▶ Outline the nontraditional competitors.

▶ Understand the impact of the Internet, globalization, and disruptive technologies that change the way things work overnight.

Overall, you need to understand whether the current system supports the vision of your organization and the current and future business requirements.

So, if you are introducing a new product line, you must consider what that will do to your existing customer base. Will you gain new customers? How will you support your new customer base? The objective of this section is to understand what business users really want from an integrated financial and controlling solution. Let's first understand who are the key users of a financial and controlling system in an organization.

Finance and controlling stakeholders are not restricted to just the finance department. There are multiple stakeholders that need to be satisfied and managed. This becomes especially important considering that SAP ERP is a tightly integrated cohesive system and Financials bring all of the individual business components together. Following are some of the key stakeholders who are customers of financial and controlling information or need inputs from finance:

▶ **Senior management**
Executives need to know whether they are making the right strategic and tactical decisions to support value creation. Finance needs to warn them well in advance of any risks to the profit and loss and financial statements, so that they can initiate corrective action. This is especially important because the performance of any publicly traded company is judged every quarter by how well the company can meet or exceed its forecast numbers. Senior management includes CEOs, CIOs, CFOs, and so on. Senior management is one of the main customers for the Controlling component because a lot of reporting in Controlling can be tailored to answer specific business questions that are strategic in nature. Controlling provides you with the key data and facts on the basis of

which you can make critical decisions that affect the future course of the organization. One of the key tools to support senior management is the Executive Information System (EIS), which can be used to provide reports to executives in a format they like.

▶ **Auditors and regulators**
With the Enron and other accounting scandals, organizations are finding that auditors and regulators demand more transparency and the establishment of better controls and checks. Finance needs to ensure that appropriate security, internal controls, and compliance measures are established to meet their requirements. In addition to establishing internal financial controls such as segregation of duty and ensuring appropriate delegation of authority, internal auditors also need to ensure that the financial and controlling system has appropriate reporting abilities that trigger any deviations and exclusions. Enterprise Controlling allows you to generate specific reports from the Audit Information System (AIS), which can help you satisfy audit requirements along with regulator needs. AIS is extensively used by both internal and external auditors to make sure that controls are properly set up in the system per Best Practices.

▶ **Business managers**
Business managers need financial information to manage the costs and revenues of their business units. With the advent of the credit crunch, capital has become scarce, and business managers need to justify the investment and capital they seek from the board. Also, business managers need to make sure that only optimal business initiatives are financed. The most widely used components in Controlling are cost center accounting and profit center accounting, which allow business managers to manage overall cost expenditures and how they tie in with the revenue for their areas of responsibility. You can also use these Controlling components to generate managerial balance sheets, which help you to evaluate the overall performance of the location. Key business managers are cost center managers and division managers.

▶ **Shareholders**
Shareholders demand more visibility in company processes, and management is always under siege from activist investors if their expectations are not being met. Also shareholders have increased expectations about earnings per share, and their time horizon is extremely short so they need to see results quarter after quarter. This means that the information related to the breakout of the balance sheet by business units, segments, and other reporting criteria

should be included in the statutory reporting. Therefore, the information from Controlling components needs to be combined with the financials to publish addendums and additional information to the financial statements. Examples of shareholders include private equity groups, hedge fund activists, and financial institutional investors, as well as small investors who own shares of listed or unlisted companies.

► **Financial operations**
There is a growing shift toward shared services and streamlining financial operations to reduce costs and increase overall revenue per finance employee. The aim of this is to reduce the daily sales outstanding and reduce the administrative overhead associated with the collections efforts. This involves traditional users of financial information such as finance managers, controllers, and accountants, who help perform traditional number crunching and routine accounting transactions that happen for the business processes.

Now that you have an understanding of the different types of users who require and work with financial information, it is important to understand how the role of chief financial officer (CFO) has changed over time.

Traditionally, the CFO was only responsible for financial and statutory reporting. The key role of the CFO was to act as a controller who was responsible for publishing balance sheets, liaising with auditors, and setting up internal controls in the organization. However, with stricter regulatory controls and ever-evolving business dynamics, the role of the CFO is shifting toward risk management and strategy management. More and more CFOs are also taking over as CEOs, and this requires a thorough knowledge of not only the statutory financial reporting but also the management reporting capabilities of the system. The Controlling component allows you to tailor your management reporting needs to your business objectives.

Now that you understand the rationale for implementing SAP ERP, let's next explore the history of the SAP ERP Financials solution.

2.2 SAP ERP Financials Direction: A Historical Perspective

Let's start this history discussion with the SAP R/3 Financials system, which was designed to manage both financial accounting and management accounting. The financial accounting tool was known as FI (Financial Accounting), and Management Accounting was termed CO (Controlling). The overall solution was historically known as FI-CO, and there was a clear-cut distinction between the two subcomponents. However, as time went by, the distinction became less and less evident as organizations started doing more disclosures and as the Sarbanes-Oxley (SOX) Act came into being. As a result, conceptually, the financial solution became SAP ERP Financials, with both FI and CO becoming more integrated and harder to distinguish.

> **How Did Consultant Roles and SAP ERP Evolve?**
>
> Back in the stone age (five years ago), you were either an FI person (CPA, accountant type of person), or you were a CO person (MBA type of person). But this distinction disappeared as you became a Financials expert who would know both FI and CO. Furthermore, the importance of someone able to understand the business process grew significantly as the process did not and does not make a distinction between FI and CO. It is simply a procurement-to-payment business process that involves Financials, Controlling, Materials Management, Logistics, Invoice Verification, and a host of other subcomponents, depending on the complexity of the business scenario.
>
> Therefore, SAP implementers started thinking more in terms of processes rather than in terms of components. Also, overall, business related more to a process than to technical jargon.

SAP also added other tools such as Financial Supply Chain Management (FSCM), which takes a process-oriented view at managing the financials, and linked it to the supply chain of Accounts Receivable (AR) and Accounts Payable (AP).

Overall, as mentioned previously, the solutions became broader, more process-focused, and more attuned to the business realities of more transparent disclosure requirements.

The current direction of SAP ERP Financials, based on information and updates gleaned from recent SAPPHIRE conferences is as follows:

▶ More user friendly and easy to use

▶ More interoperable across disparate systems

▶ More focused on harnessing the data captured in transactional systems

▶ More about business intelligence-based solutions

▶ More central, with one system used for the entire organization

- More nimble and Web-based software design
- Less total cost of ownership (TCO) by combining all business applications under the SAP software umbrella
- More integration with Microsoft Outlook to drive adaptability using the Duet platform

The key change has been changing the reporting platform from one based out of individual SAP R/3 components to a common data warehouse platform where data can be collated, sliced, and diced per the requirements of the organization. With the recent acquisition of Business Objects by SAP, its solution set of reporting and on the fly analytics has been further expanded, allowing the delivery of reports in a way that is easy to use, modify, and operate. Previously, it was very difficult to change reports on the fly and required the assistance of the IT department. Now you can change, modify, and view reports while you try to understand a business problem.

In addition, SAP has introduced Duet in collaboration with Microsoft, which uses Microsoft Outlook to manage the interaction with the SAP system.

SAP is constantly looking for ways to bridge the gap between users and systems by providing new ways of assimilating and digesting the information from the system.

In the next section, you'll learn more about the SAP ERP Financials solution set available for financial business processes.

2.3 SAP ERP Financials: A Snapshot View

SAP ERP Financials is a complete solution to handle the myriad and continuously evolving financial needs as discussed in the previous section. This section describes the current SAP ERP Financials offering and how it is evolving to meet business needs.

2.3.1 SAP ERP Financials Solution Stack: The Big Picture

The SAP ERP Financials solution stack helps you reach these multiple goals of lowering the TCO by making SAP one system of record, by providing an integrated enterprisewide financial and controlling management platform. Let's take a look at the SAP ERP Financials component of the overall SAP ERP stack solution discussed in the previous chapter and shown in Figure 2.1.

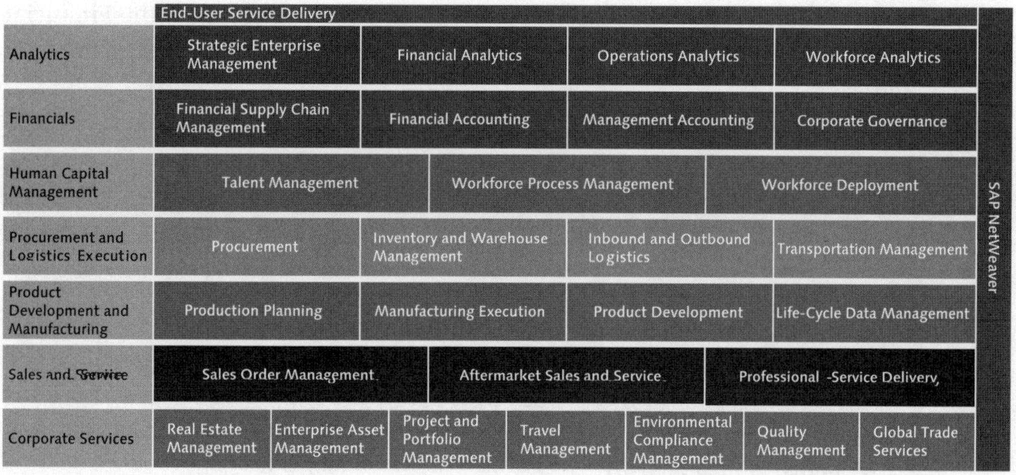

	End-User Service Delivery			
Analytics	Strategic Enterprise Management	Financial Analytics	Operations Analytics	Workforce Analytics
Financials	Financial Supply Chain Management	Financial Accounting	Management Accounting	Corporate Governance
Human Capital Management	Talent Management	Workforce Process Management		Workforce Deployment
Procurement and Logistics Execution	Procurement	Inventory and Warehouse Management	Inbound and Outbound Logistics	Transportation Management
Product Development and Manufacturing	Production Planning	Manufacturing Execution	Product Development	Life-Cycle Data Management
Sales and Service	Sales Order Management	Aftermarket Sales and Service		Professional -Service Delivery,
Corporate Services	Real Estate Management / Enterprise Asset Management	Project and Portfolio Management / Travel Management	Environmental Compliance Management	Quality Management / Global Trade Services

(SAP NetWeaver shown along right side)

Figure 2.1 SAP ERP Stack

The SAP ERP **Financials** component broadly comprises **Financials** (**Financial Supply Chain Management**, **Financial Accounting**, **Management Accounting**, **Corporate Governance**), and **Analytics** (**Strategic Enterprise Management** and **Financial Analytics**). These can then be further delineated into the detailed level footprint shown in Figure 2.2. Some of these components also touch other SAP ERP components. Review the figure to become familiar with the components.

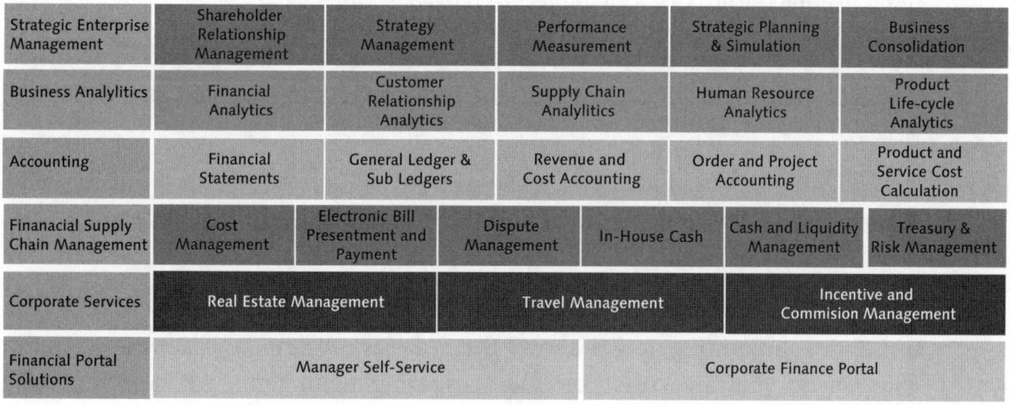

Strategic Enterprise Management	Shareholder Relationship Management	Strategy Management	Performance Measurement	Strategic Planning & Simulation	Business Consolidation
Business Analylitics	Financial Analytics	Customer Relationship Analytics	Supply Chain Analylitics	Human Resource Analytics	Product Life-cycle Analytics
Accounting	Financial Statements	General Ledger & Sub Ledgers	Revenue and Cost Accounting	Order and Project Accounting	Product and Service Cost Calculation
Finanacial Supply Chain Management	Cost Management	Electronic Bill Presentment and Payment	Dispute Management	In-House Cash / Cash and Liquidity Management	Treasury & Risk Management
Corporate Services	Real Estate Management		Travel Management	Incentive and Commision Management	
Financial Portal Solutions	Manager Self-Service		Corporate Finance Portal		

Figure 2.2 SAP ERP Financials Solution Components

Each subcomponent can also be represented in greater detail, with the **Financial Accounting** and **Management Accounting** components shown as an example in Figure 2.3.

Financial Accounting	Management Accounting
General Ledger (S2)	Profit Center Accounting (S2)
Accounts Receivable (S2)	Cost Center and Internal Order
Accounts Payable (S2)	Accounting (S2, S1)
Contract Accounting	Project Accounting (S2)
Fixed Assets Accounting (S2)	Investment Management (S2)
Bank Accounting (S2)	Product Cost Accounting (S2)
Cash Journal Accounting (S2)	Profitability Accounting (S2)
Inventory Accounting (S2)	Transfer Pricing (S2)
Tax Accounting (S2)	
Accrual Accounting (S2)	
Local Close (S2)	
Financial Statements (S2)	

Figure 2.3 Financial Accounting and Management Accounting Detailed Component Information

For more details about the Financial Accounting solution refer to my first SAP book: *Optimize your SAP ERP Financials Implementation*.

Now that you understand the overall structure of the SAP ERP Financials solution, you will learn how you can access the individual components using SAP Easy Access.

2.3.2 SAP Easy Access for SAP ERP Financials — Controlling Components

SAP Easy Access allows you to navigate through the individual components of the SAP ERP solution. Figure 2.4 shows the SAP Easy Access interface and the subcomponents you can access from the Accounting menu item. SAP Easy Access for SAP ERP Financials is structured according to groups (**Logistics** or **Accounting**), components (**Financial Accounting** or **Controlling**), and subcomponents (**Cost Element Accounting** or **Cost Center Accounting**).

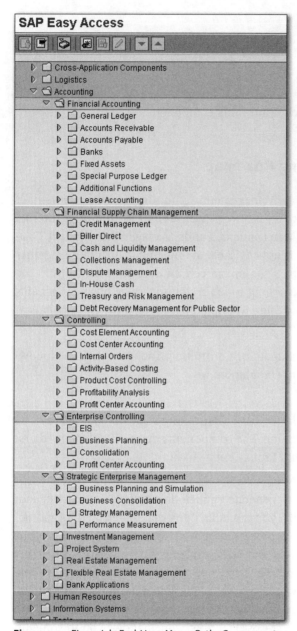

Figure 2.4 Financials End User Menu Path: Component

Of the components in the **Accounting** group, the remainder of this book will cover in depth the following components:

- **Controlling**
- **Enterprise Controlling**
- **Investment Management**

Now that you understand the components of Controlling, you will learn how and when you would implement each Controlling component.

2.4   SAP ERP Controlling Roadmap

As you learned earlier, Controlling/Management Accounting consists of a number of subcomponents: Cost Center Accounting, Profit Center Accounting, Internal Order Accounting, Investment Management, Funds Management, Product Costing, and Profitability Analysis. It is not advisable to implement all of these together because each of these components requires a certain degree of maturity in the business process, and it will take a long time for you to realize business benefits from your IT investment if you decide to implement all of these components at the same time.

Figure 2.5 shows a suggested roadmap for Controlling. You can define the following phases of the Controlling implementation:

- **Phase 1: Foundation**
  This phase allows you to build the basic Controlling structure and familiarizes your organization with Controlling. The components that are implemented first are Cost Center Accounting and Profit Center Accounting.

- **Phase 2: Stabilization**
  In this phase, the objective is to generate enough data and gain an understanding of the basic components that you can build upon that understanding and stabilize your Controlling business processes. You can start tracking mini projects using Internal Order Accounting and start implementing budgeting processes using Investment Management. Now you not only have the basic controlling processes implemented, but you also have established a more thorough capital budgeting process. In addition, you can also start gauging how your costs look overall by implementing Product Cost Planning, which allows you to come up with a standard cost estimate. All of these functionalities allow you to get ready for the next phase in which you further improve system capabilities and further optimize your business processes.

▶ **Phase 3: Enhance and Optimize**

This phase allows you to implement additional functionality such as Product Cost By Period or By Order, which allows you to implement additional complex functionality such as Actual Costing/Material Ledger later. At this point, you can also implement the additional functionality Budgeting Using Funds Management. Note, however, that Funds Management is typically implemented in public-sector companies as part of another SAP ERP PSM (Public Sector Management) solution set. You can also implement Profitability Analysis, which allows you to perform analysis of profitability by region, product, and a host of other key parameters.

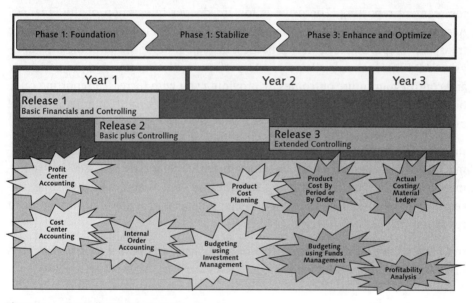

Figure 2.5 Controlling Implementation Roadmap

This overview covered the overall complexity of the Controlling solution and described how you can implement the business processes that make sense for your organization.

2.5 Summary

In this chapter, we discussed the SAP ERP Financials and, more specifically, the Controlling solution. You learned about the requirements of implementing SAP ERP Financials, Controlling's historical perspective, and the current SAP ERP Financials solution.

Overall, SAP ERP Financials can enable financial business process transformation by providing an integrated platform to manage all financial business processes. The integration of the new GL with Controlling allows you to generate allocation cycles in GL to perform controlling functions (such as assessment and distribution) for segment reporting. The drive is toward deeper integration of the Financial Accounting and Controlling components of SAP ERP Financials to enable more transparent reporting for external parties. Instead of doing an "after the fact" analysis, SAP ERP Financials allows you to perform analytical reporting to anticipate and control your future outcomes by providing you with increased reporting capabilities, including better financial audit and control checkpoints and better control of your financial processes.

In short, the power of SAP ERP Financials can be used to enable financial transformation by automating critical and labor-intensive financial processes and reducing the time for month-end closing activities, as well as automating routine processes, freeing up crucial time for strategic financial analytics and management reporting.

In Chapter 3, we'll discuss the process of configuring an optimal controlling enterprise structure in SAP ERP Financials.

The Controlling enterprise structure is not very complicated, but setting it up correctly can have far-reaching implications both in terms of management reporting and the overall timeline for the implementation.

3 Choosing the Optimal Controlling Enterprise Structure

The first step in implementing an SAP ERP solution is understanding the organizational structure and how it needs to be mapped in SAP ERP.

The SAP ERP enterprise structure is the fundamental data framework within the SAP ERP system. It sits above the master data and transactional data, as shown in Figure 3.1.

Typically, master data is created with reference to the SAP enterprise structure. Let's say you want to create a cost center. The cost center should be created with reference to a Controlling area. In this example, the cost center is the master data, and the Controlling area is the Controlling enterprise entity. Any Controlling transaction (assessment, distribution, or posting of expenses or revenue, etc.) is done for a particular cost center and Controlling area.

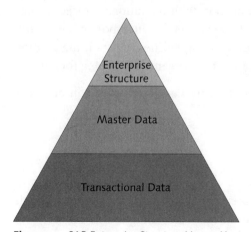

Figure 3.1 SAP Enterprise Structure Versus Master Data and Transactional Data

> **Tip**
>
> Changing the core organizational structure is not easy in SAP ERP, so it is very important to design a flexible organizational structure that will not only meet current needs but also future needs. A good practice is to listen to people who have done it before and follow best practices.

To understand how the Controlling component is structured, you also need to understand how Financial Accounting has been set up because it is the feeder component for most of the Controlling data. For details about the overall enterprise structure, including Financials, Logistics, Materials Management, Plant Maintenance, and Human Resources, refer to my first SAP PRESS book *Optimize Your SAP ERP Financials Implementation*. The focus of this chapter is understanding the Controlling enterprise structure.

In the next section, you will learn about the key Controlling organizational entities and how you can use them to set up your management reporting structure.

3.1 Controlling Organizational Entities

Controlling organizational entities are used to manage the management reporting structure of an organization. The owner of Controlling organizational entities is typically the cost controller who manages the entities in consultation with operational department heads. Unlike financial organization entities that can be solely defined by the finance department, Controlling organization entities (especially cost centers) need to be defined in conjunction with operational process teams. In addition, you need to involve your HR department to incorporate the organizational structure when defining your Controlling entities. Overall, the guiding principles should be the strategy and vision of the organization going forward.

Let's take a look at the Controlling organization entities — operating concern, controlling area, and cost centers — in detail.

3.1.1 Operating Concern

The operating concern is the organizational entity that tracks the profitability of an organization and structures the enterprise from a profitability perspective. This entity is the highest-level organizational unit in Controlling and is activated for

Controlling-Profitability Analysis (CO-PA). When you create an operating concern, only the operating concern object is created. All of the other details are created when you create the master data and characteristics for the operating concern. The menu path to create an operating concern is **IMG • Enterprise structure • Definition • Controlling• Create Operating Concern**.

The operating concern gets information from sales and distribution, cost accounting, finance, and non-SAP sources. It can be compared to a holistic report card of sales and distribution seen from a financial perspective. The structure of an operating concern is detailed in Figure 3.2.

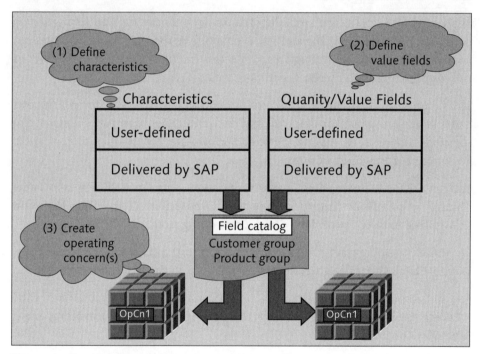

Figure 3.2 Operating Concern Structure

You need to define the following elements to structure your operating concern:

▶ **Characteristics**
These identify the parameters that define the sales market attributes and can contain attributes such as customer, sales region, and so on.

▸ **Value fields**
These identify how you will be measuring your sales, which can be in dollars, quantities, and so on.

Both the **Characteristics** and **Quantity/Value fields** can be either **User-defined** or **Delivered by SAP**, which can be chosen from a catalog that comes prepopulated.

You will learn more about the operating concern setup and details in Chapter 9, when we discuss Profitability Analysis in detail.

3.1.2 Controlling Area

The Controlling area is the umbrella organizational entity for Controlling that is used for managerial reporting and cost accounting purposes. All cost activities can happen in only one Controlling area, not across multiple Controlling areas. All of the costing activities require a Controlling area.

The Controlling area represents a common unit of cost structure for which costs and revenue are managed, allocated, and distributed. For example, if you want to transfer primary costs, allocate them, or perform any costing planning, all these activities happen within a Controlling area.

You can use the following menu path to copy an existing Controlling area to a new Controlling area: **IMG • Enterprise structure • Definition • Controlling• Maintain Controlling Area• Copy, Delete, Check Controlling Area**.

Or, you can use Transaction EC16 and select **Maintain Controlling area • Copy, Delete, Check Controlling Area**.

You can display an already existing Controlling area using the menu path **IMG • Enterprise structure • Definition • Controlling• Maintain Controlling Area• Maintain Controlling Area**.

You will learn more about the details of the Controlling area in Chapter 4.

3.1.3 Cost Center

The cost center is the smallest entity in Controlling that represents an area of responsibility at which costs are managed in your company. You can also implement budgeting at a cost center level. The important points for a cost center are listed here:

▸ Cost centers typically represent departments within an organization.

▸ Each cost center can be assigned to only one Controlling area, one profit center, and one company code.

▸ Each cost center must be assigned to a standard hierarchy structure.

▸ Cost centers are used to analyze planned and actual costs at the cost center level.

The menu path to create a cost center is **IMG • Enterprise Structure • Definition • Controlling • Define Cost Center,** or you can use Transaction KS01.

You will learn more about the cost center structure and setup in Chapter 5.

3.1.4   Profit Center

A profit center is an entity that resides in Controlling and represents an area of responsibility within your company; that is, it provides an internal view of your organization. A profit center is typically a unit that manages both *costs and revenues* and behaves as an independent operating unit for which a separate operating statement and balance sheet can be calculated. Following are some of the important points concerning profit centers:

▸ Each profit center must be assigned to a standard hierarchy.

▸ Profit centers can be created as regions, functions, products, or a combination of these attributes.

▸ Some of the organizations create a one-to-one assignment with a cost center.

▸ Each profit center can be assigned to one Controlling area.

▸ Profit centers are statistical cost objects and must be derived from a real cost object.

You can use the menu path **IMG • Enterprise structure • Definition • Controlling Accounting • Define Cost Center • EC-PCA: Create Profit Center** or Transaction KE51 to create a profit center. Profit centers were part of enterprise Controlling, but with the advent of the new GL, these have also been included in the Financial Accounting menu path.

You will learn more about the profit center structure and setup in Chapter 5.

> **Caveat**
>
> From a technical perspective, cost centers and profit centers are treated as master data in the system. However, it is important for you to treat these as enterprise structuring elements, so that you can optimally define your overall enterprise structure.

Next, you'll learn more how you can assign these organizational entities together to map your organizational structure to an SAP ERP enterprise structure.

3.2 Assignment of Organizational Entities

SAP ERP is an integrated system, which requires that all of its enterprise entities need to talk to each other. The only way to do this is by assigning organizational units to each other across components. In this section, you will learn about the various assignments that build the organizational hierarchy in the system.

Beyond this, you also need to understand the rules of assignment. Sometimes organizational structures do not meet the technical requirements of assignments. In that case, you have to find a feasible workaround or add organizational objects in other components to ensure that you achieve the optimal organizational structure for your organization.

We'll cover the assignments that can be made for Controlling organizational entities. You will learn how an assignment is actually performed along with the rules for assignment, caveats, and relationships (many to one, many to many, one to many, etc.) in each of the assignments. Let's begin with the assignment of company code to Controlling area.

3.2.1 Company Code to Controlling Area (N:1 or 1:1)

The company code and Controlling areas do not have to exist in a one-to-one relationship. Multiple company codes assigned to a Controlling area activate the cross-company code Controlling. Overall, you have the following options for this assignment:

▶ The company code can correspond to exactly one Controlling area.

▶ Several company codes can correspond to one Controlling area.

Remember the setting in the company code definition (Transaction OBY6), which automatically is populated with a value of 2 if you set up cross-company code accounting. If you have assigned only one company code to a Controlling area, then you will see 1 in the company code definition instead. The menu path to make company code to Controlling area assignments is **IMG • Enterprise Structure • Assignment • Controlling Area • Assign Company Code to Controlling Area,** or you can use Transaction OKKP. Figure 3.3 shows the assignment of multiple company codes (Co...) **DS01** and **US00** to the **Controlling Area US00**.

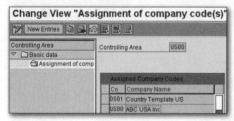

Figure 3.3 Assigning Company Codes to the Controlling Area

Multiple company codes can only be assigned to the same Controlling area if they have the same fiscal year variant and operating chart of accounts, as shown in Figure 3.4.

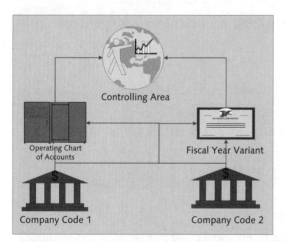

Figure 3.4 Relationship of Company Code and Controlling Area

Best Practice

Define one Controlling area for your entire organization because this simplifies group reporting and the drive toward one instance and one company. Also you do not have to deal with cross Controlling area issues.

3.2.2 Controlling Area to Operating Concern (N:1 or 1:1)

The operating concern is the highest level of Controlling entity at which profitability and contribution margins need to be analyzed within a client. The menu path to assign a Controlling area to an operating concern is **IMG • Enterprise Structure • Assignment • Controlling Area • Assign Controlling Area to Operating Concern**.

Figure 3.5 shows the assignment of Controlling area (COAr) **US00** and **US01** to operating concern **(OpCo) US00**.

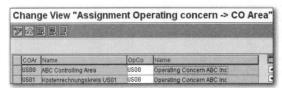

COAr	Name	OpCo	Name	
US00	ABC Controlling Area	US00	Operating Concern ABC Inc	
US01	Kostenrechnungskreis US01	US00	Operating Concern ABC Inc	

Figure 3.5 Assign Controlling Area to Operating Concern

Here are the rules for assignment, as illustrated in Figure 3.6:

▶ A Controlling area is assigned to only one operating concern.

▶ An operating concern can have multiple Controlling areas assigned to it.

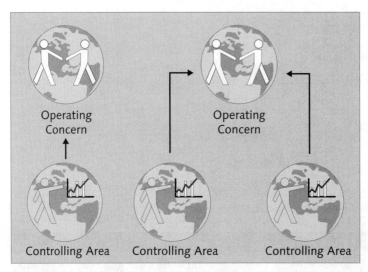

Figure 3.6 Controlling Area and Operating Concern (1:1/N:1)

3.2.3 Inheritance Principal

In addition to the normal assignments that are made one to one or many to one, SAP software also follows the inheritance principle whereby if you assign an enterprise object to a lower-level organizational entity, the system automatically assigns it to the higher entity one level above, which is then assigned to the next higher-level entity.

Figure 3.7 illustrates the inheritance principle in detail. In this case, you have assigned the **Cost Center 4210** and **Cost Center 4220** to **Company Code B**. However, even though you did not assign the **Cost Center 4210** or the **Cost Center 4220** to **Controlling Area 001**, the system automatically derives these assignments based on the assignment of **Controlling Area 001** to **Company Code B**.

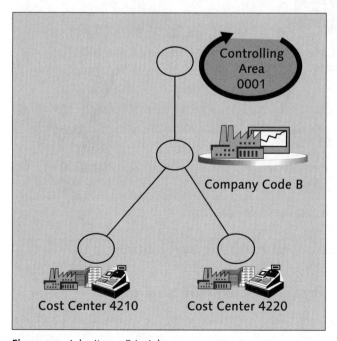

Figure 3.7 Inheritance Principle

Thus, even though you do not make most of the internal assignments, you can visualize your organizational hierarchy in a way that is similar to Figure 3.7 and build up your own enterprise structure.

The inheritance principle is not only applicable across Financials but also extends to Logistics organizational entities, which are assigned to financial entities. Let's illustrate this with an example. Figure 3.8 shows how you can derive the plant to controlling area assignment using the assignment of **Plant 0002 Munich** to **Company Code 0001 Europe** and **Company Code 0001 Europe** to **Controlling Area**.

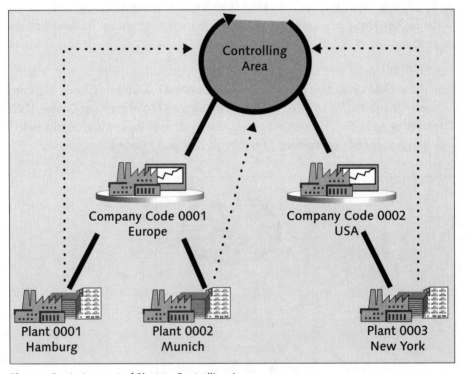

Figure 3.8 Assignment of Plant to Controlling Area

Next, you will learn about standard versus alternative hierarchy.

3.2.4 Standard Hierarchy Versus Alternative Hierarchy

The *standard hierarchy* in Controlling is derived from the assignments you have made across organizational entities. However, for reporting reasons, you might want to create an *alternative hierarchy* that might represent either past or future changes in the organizational structure. An alternative hierarchy can also be used to generate an additional layer of reporting.

An alternative hierarchy can also be used as a transient state that can later be incorporated into the standard hierarchy. So you can keep making initial changes in the alternative hierarchy, and after you have solidified the changes, you can generate a standard hierarchy from the alternative hierarchy.

3.2.5 Time Dependency of Enterprise Organizations

Controlling allows you to change and display your hierarchy for a specific date. This allows you to not only display the current organizational structure but also to understand the past and future structures and how these have changed over a period of time. You can set up and link your Controlling structure with HR, so that if an employee leaves or joins your organization, this is also reflected effective from the date the employee left or joined your organization.

Let's now look at some sample decision points in mapping your organization's Controlling entities.

3.3 Key Controlling Mapping Decisions and Best Practices

After you have outlined the organizational entities and how they are assigned to each other, you need to take a look at the key decisions to be made during the beginning of the *business blueprinting* of the project. We'll also highlight the *best practices* for mapping the organizational elements, but it is important that you consider the various local organizational level perspectives before finalizing your organizational structure.

3.3.1 One Operating Concern Versus Multiple Operating Concerns by Region

Most organizations implement one global operating concern across all Controlling areas, which allows one view of the profitability of the organization. However, if you need to differentiate the profitability view across diverse business divisions within a conglomerate, you can choose to implement multiple Controlling areas by division. You can also choose to differentiate operating concerns by region.

The following are the advantages of one global operating concern:

▶ Global profitability reporting capability using standard out-of-the-box reports

▶ One common yardstick for judging performance of the organization units across the enterprise

The following are the advantages of regional operating concerns:

▶ Provides specific regional subdivision of profitability analysis reporting

▶ Minimizes performance issues

▶ Meets local reporting requirements

3.3.2 Currencies in Controlling

Let's now take a detailed look at the currencies you can have in Controlling and the recommended ways of setting these up:

▶ **Controlling area currency**
This is the currency for cost accounting that needs to be set up while defining the Controlling area. As you know, the company code currency drives the legal reporting. You can choose to define the Controlling area currency to be the same as the management currency. Therefore, even if you have a holding company in the United Kingdom, if your market and the majority of management resides in the United States, it's best to define the Controlling area currency as USD, while the group currency (currency for consolidation and legal reporting) can be GBP.

> **Best Practice**
>
> The management currency should be the Controlling area currency because this is the most effective way to generate the reports in the currency that you want from the Controlling area.

The Controlling area currency is primarily based on the assignment control indicator and the currency type.

▶ **Object currency**
You can maintain the currency in the master data of each object in Controlling (an internal order, cost center, profit center, etc.). The system will default the company code to which the object is assigned as the object currency, but you

can change this per your requirements. You can specify separate currencies for sender and receiver objects.

You can only change the object currency to something other than the company code currency if the Controlling area currency is the same as the company code currency.

▶ **Transaction currency**

When documents are posted in Controlling, the system also records the transaction currency, which can be different from either the Controlling area currency or the object currency. Note that the system will always convert the transaction currency to the controlling area currency at the exchange rate specified using the exchange rate type "M: Average Rate" for actual values. In addition, if the object currency is different, then it is also converted using the Controlling area currency as the base. So, the system will first translate to the Controlling area currency and then convert to object currency.

All of these currencies are stored in the totals and line item tables in Controlling.

3.3.3 One Controlling Area Versus Multiple Controlling Areas by Region

Most organizations implement one Controlling area across all company codes. This allows one view of the costing across the organization because you don't need to run multiple reports to get an overall perspective. Also organizations implementing multiple Controlling areas have multiple currencies, which makes the comparison of costs much more difficult.

However, if you need to differentiate the costing across diverse business divisions within a conglomerate, then you can choose to implement multiple Controlling areas by division or by region. Another reason to implement multiple Controlling areas is if you have multiple global headquarters, based on different divisions, in different countries, and you need to track costs and revenue in different currencies.

The following are the advantages of one global Controlling area:

▶ Increases reporting capability for global reporting using standard out-of-the-box reports

▶ Allows global allocations

► Helps standardize the Controlling processes across the organization

The following are the advantages of regional Controlling areas:

► Provides flexibility to meet local managerial reporting requirements

► Minimizes system performance issues

► Allows you to define multiple standard and cost center hierarchies to support local reporting

---

Best Practice

Use one Controlling area per organization because this simplifies the technical and reporting architecture and accelerates the drive toward one organization.

3.3.4 Cost Centers Standard Hierarchy Definition: By Department or By Division

When defining a cost center standard hierarchy, it's important to understand the middle-level management reporting requirements as well as executive management reporting requirements. If the organization is decentralized, where middle-level management makes most of the decisions regarding cost management and control, it makes sense to implement a standard hierarchy by departments. On the other hand, if the organization is a top-driven, centrally managed corporation, then the cost center hierarchy needs to mirror the business unit structure.

Best Practices

► Implement the cost center standard hierarchy at the lowest level capturing both the departmental structure and the management reporting structure. Create the management reporting structure as the standard hierarchy and the departmental structure as an alternative hierarchy.

► Customize the cost center structure in multiple ways to meet business requirements.

3.3.5 Profit Center Hierarchy Definition

The profit center hierarchy definition should be created only when the managing person of the profit center is responsible for the revenue and costs combined together.

> **Best Practices**
>
> ▶ Keep the profit center structure extremely simple.
> ▶ Keep the number of profit centers to manageable levels, and you'll get a structure that is effective and simple.

Also remember the following:

▶ Typically, organizations map cost center and profit center in similar ways, which is not the correct approach because then you lose the distinction between the philosophy of cost center and profit center. You need to create only a limited number of profit centers, whereas cost centers can be more granular.

▶ A politically correct profit center structure is not the best organization structure for any of the organizational entities because this does not represent the true management reporting structure. If you use it, you have to create costly work-arounds to create the correct reporting structure.

In closing, it is very important to understand the reporting requirements of the organization before designing the enterprise structure. Also you should consider not only the current legacy reporting requirements but also future reporting requirements. After the enterprise structure has been put in place, it's very difficult to change it later. So be sure to outline the to-be state of the organization and then design the enterprise structure.

3.4   Summary

In this chapter, you learned about the key enterprise structure elements of Controlling. You also learned how these elements can be assigned to Financials and other Controlling organizational entities. In addition, we touched on the best practices of structuring an organization to meet current and future reporting needs.

Chapter 4 introduces the typical Controlling business processes and how these are integrated in SAP ERP. You'll also learn about the global settings you need to configure for Controlling processes.

PART II
Basic Controlling Processes

Gaining an integrated business process view of Controlling clarifies the way that Controlling works in your own organization and how it interacts with other parts of your SAP system. Clarity about the integrated view means you can really begin optimizing your implementation.

4 Controlling Business View

Historically, Controlling represented the management reporting aspect of Financials. With the arrival of SAP ERP 5.0 and the introduction of the new general ledger (GL), Financial Accounting and Controlling merged to provide a single unified functionality to users. So there is lot more convergence in the SAP ERP Financials solution than ever before. Controlling provides you with management decision-making reporting and acts as a glue to monitor, optimize and coordinate various functions and processes in an organization. The integrated business model of Controlling is shown in Figure 4.1. Gaining this integrated perspective will help you see how Controlling can and does work in your own enterprise and how you can optimize it further.

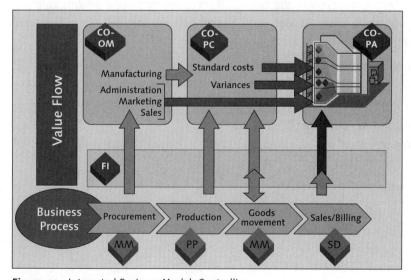

Figure 4.1 Integrated Business Model: Controlling

4.1 Layers of Controlling Reporting

As seen in Figure 4.1, there are three layers of Controlling reporting: *Cost element accounting* at the bottom integrates with *GL accounting*, which integrates with *non-financial SAP ERP applications*. The middle layer includes overhead cost Controlling, cost center accounting, and product costing, which can be used to manage the flow of costs in Controlling and help you when making a make or buy decision. The top layer of Controlling reporting comprises profitability analysis, which is used for analyzing the market profitability by segments.

As also seen in Figure 4.1, the actual values flow from business processes that happen in MM, PP, and SD to Financial Accounting, which then feeds it to Controlling. There are some processes that are internal to Controlling, which transfer costs from CO-OM (Controlling: Overhead Cost Controlling) to CO-PC (Controlling: Product Costing) and CO-PA (Controlling: Profitability Analysis). The data flow between Financial Accounting and Controlling happens on a regular basis. GL accounts are created as cost or revenue elements, enabling you to compare and reconcile Financial Accounting and Controlling. For illustrative purposes, we have covered only CO-OM, CO-PC, and CO-PA, but the sequence of activities in other Controlling components also mirrors the structure outlined. Let's quickly review the Controlling sub-components:

▶ **Cost Element Accounting (CO-OM-CEL)**
This provides an overview of the costs and revenues that occur within an organization. Reconciliation of costs and revenues that transfer from Financial Accounting occurs in this sub-component.

▶ **Cost Center Accounting (CO-OM-CCA)**
This provides an ability to assign costs to the actual source of the cost. Cost centers and cost center hierarchy is maintained in this sub-component.

▶ **Activity-Based-Accounting (CO-OM-ABC)**
The main purpose of this sub-component is to analyze the cross-departmental processes and optimize them.

▶ **Internal Orders (CO-OM-OPA)**
This sub-component monitors mini projects that need to be budgeted and planned for.

- ▶ **Product Cost Controlling (CO-PC)**
  This component helps in arriving at the per-unit cost of the product being manufactured. This gets the data from CO-OM and feeds into CO-PA to determine the overall profit margin of the product.

- ▶ **Profitability Analysis (CO-PA)**
  This provides the ability to analyze the profit or loss of an organization by market segments.

- ▶ **Profit Center Accounting (EC-PCA)**
  This helps in analyzing the profit or loss of an individual division or business unit and typically maps the organizational chart of responsibility and accountability.

It is important to explore the inter-linkages across Financial Accounting and Controlling components and the integration with non-financial components as well. This will help you understand the data flows in various business scenarios to Controlling, which will then help you build the foundation on which you can optimize your business processes.

> **Note**
>
> The only surefire way to improve your management reporting is to understand business processes and then tailor your reporting structure per your desired processes. Controlling typically takes the least amount of time to implement but is heavily dependent on the optimal implementation of the feeder components. The beauty of Controlling is that it allows you to pick up important nuggets of information and allows you to keep the focus on the bigger picture rather than getting lost at an operational level.

Figure 4.2 shows a sample screen for Controlling from an integrated business process perspective. First, you will learn the global settings of Controlling and understand the account assignment objects, commitment management, and settlement process in Controlling. Further you will be introduced to the integration of Controlling with procurement, PP, PS, PM, SD, and HR. Finally, you will learn the integration of SAP ERP Financials with Controlling, especially the new real-time integration of Financial Accounting with Controlling with the introduction of the new GL.

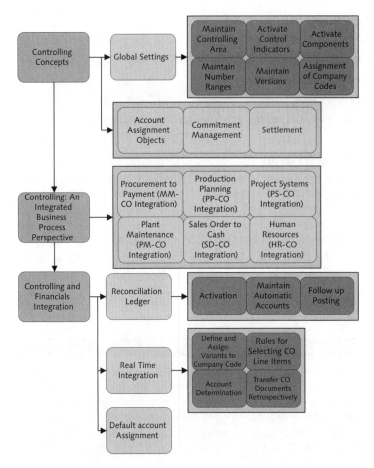

Figure 4.2 Controlling: Integrated Business Process Perspective

4.2 Basic Configuration Settings

Basic settings in Controlling allow you to set up Controlling in SAP ERP per your business requirements. Let's review the Controlling area, number ranges, and versions in this section.

4.2.1 Maintain Controlling Areas

You already know that the Controlling area is one of the most important organizational units, which needs to be set up in the enterprise structure of Controlling. In this subsection, you will learn the key attributes of the Controlling area. The menu path you can use for maintaining the Controlling area is **IMG • Controlling • General Controlling • Organization • Maintain Controlling area • Copy, Delete, Check Controlling Area• Maintain Controlling area• Delete SAP Delivery Data**. You can also use the Transaction codes EC16 (Copy, Delete, Check), OKKP (Maintain), and OKKP2 (Delete).

It is best to create a Controlling area by using Transaction EC16, which copies all the dependent objects. However, it makes the most sense to use Transaction OKKP to maintain and display a Controlling area. On executing OKKP, you will reach the screen shown in Figure 4.3.

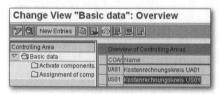

Figure 4.3 Maintaining a Controlling Area

By double-clicking in the **Controlling area US01**, you will reach the screen shown in Figure 4.4.

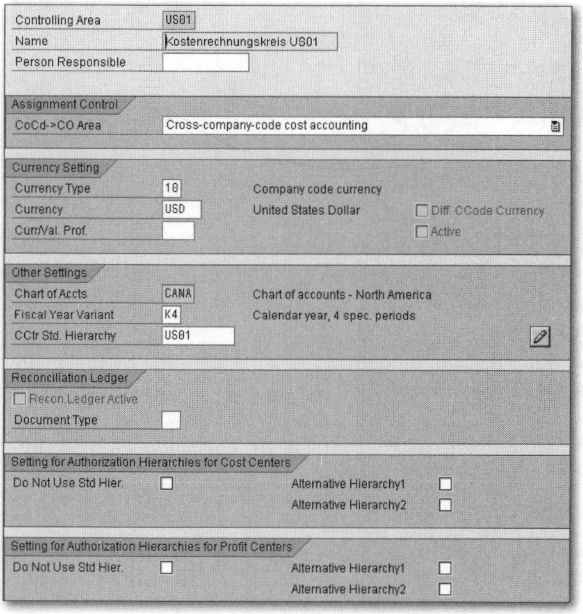

Figure 4.4 Maintain Controlling Area Parameters

By clicking on **Activate components/control indicators** shown in Figure 4.3, you can maintain the fiscal years valid for the Controlling area as shown in Figure 4.5.

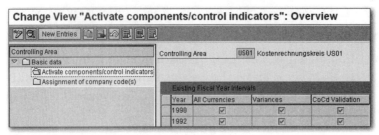

Figure 4.5 Activating Fiscal Years and Currencies

To see details of the components that are active for a fiscal year, double-click on the fiscal year. This will take you to the screen shown in Figure 4.6, in which we have chosen to activate **Cost Centers**, **Order Management**, **Commit. Management**, **Profit Analysis**, and **Profit Center Acctg**. You can also activate the following account assignment objects: **Projects, Sales Orders, Cost Objects**, or **Real Estate Mgmt**. In addition, you can maintain the indicators for capturing **All Currencies, Variances**, and **CoCd** (company code) **Validation**.

| Controlling Area | US01 Kostenrechnungskreis US01 |
| Fiscal Year | 1990 to 1991 |

Activate Components

Cost Centers	Component active
☐ AA: Activity Type	
Order Management	Component active
Commit. Management	Components active
ProfitAnalysis	Component not active
Acty-Based Costing	Component Not Active

☑ Profit Center Acctg
☑ Projects
☑ Sales Orders   ☐ W. Commit. Mgt
☑ Cost Objects
☑ Real Estate Mgmt

Other Indicators
☑ All Currencies
☑ Variances
☑ CoCd Validation

Alternative Authorization Hierarchies for Cost Centers
| Alternat. Hier.1 | |
| Alternat. Hier. 2 | |

Alternative Authorization Hierarchies for Profit Centers
| Alternat. Hier. 1 | |
| Alternat. Hier. 2 | |

Figure 4.6 Activating Components for Particular Cost Center

Two alternative authorization hierarchies for profit center and costs centers can also be maintained to help you control who accesses the profit center hierarchy by defining appropriate authorization groups.

If you have checked **CoCd Validation** in Figure 4.6, you can assign relevant company codes by clicking **Assignment of company code(s)** the left pane of Figure 4.5, shown earlier. This takes you to the Figure 4.7 where you can maintain the company codes by clicking on the **New Entries** button and then entering company code "US01".

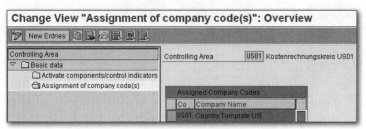

Figure 4.7 Assignment of Company Codes to Controlling Area

4.2.2 Maintain Number Ranges for Controlling Documents

Number ranges control the document number that gets generated when you post a Controlling document. The menu path is **IMG • Controlling • General Controlling • Organization • Maintain Controlling area• Maintain number ranges for Controlling documents** and the transaction code is KANK. Figure 4.8 shows how you can maintain the number ranges. First you need to enter your **CO Area** (Controlling area) as **US01** and then click on the change **Intervals** icon (represented by a pencil).

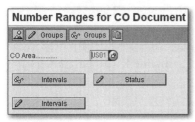

Figure 4.8 Maintain Number Ranges for Controlling Documents

This will take you to the next screen, shown in Figure 4.9, which shows the number ranges that have already been defined.

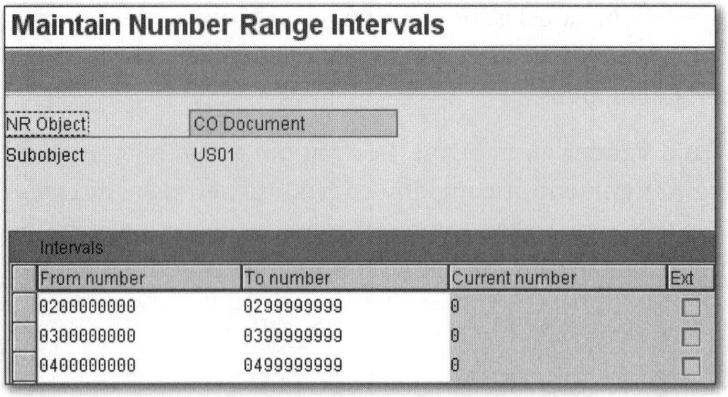

Figure 4.9 Maintaining Number Ranges for Controlling

To create a new number range, click on Change Groups (the pencil icon) and then select a group. You can assign multiple elements to the same group in the same screen. After you select the group, a new change interval icon will appear (plus sign). Clicking on that icon allows you to add a new number range.

4.2.3 Maintain versions

Versions in Controlling are used to distinguish working areas for planning and actual data. These allow you to create different scenarios based on market conditions or different planning assumptions. The most common version is *0* in which both the base plan and the actual values are recorded in Controlling. The menu path for maintaining versions is **IMG • Controlling • General Controlling • Organization • Maintain Controlling area• Maintain versions**. You can also use Transaction OKEQ.

Figure 4.10 shows the screen for maintaining the versions for a Controlling area. Here you can maintain these versions for **Settings in Operating Concern**, **Settings for Profit Center Accounting**, and general **Settings for Each Fiscal Year** by clicking on the left pane and maintaining the fiscal years that are relevant. The right pane displays the different versions that can be maintained. The parameters for each version are detailed as follows:

▶ **Plan**
This identifies that this version can post plan values.

▶ **Actual**
This indicator allows you to write actual values to the version.

▶ **WIP/RA**

This indicator allows the results analysis and work in progress (WIP) data to be written to the version.

▶ **Variance**

This indicator controls whether the variance calculation data is transferred to the version.

General Version Definition

Dialog Structure	General Version Overview					
▽ 🗀 General Version Definition	Version	Name	Plan	Actual	WIP/RA	Variance
🗀 Settings in Operating Concern	0	Plan/actual version	☑	☑	☑	☑
🗀 Settings for Profit Center Accounting	1	Plan Version: Change 1	☑	☐	☐	☑
▽ 🗀 Controlling Area Settings	2	Plan Version: Change 2	☑	☐	☐	☑
🗀 Settings for Each Fiscal Year	3	Actual Costs vs. Target Costs	☑	☐	☐	☑
🗀 Delta Version: Bus. Transactions from Ref. Version	100	PS: Progress Version	☑	☑	☐	☐
🗀 Settings for Progress Analysis (Project System)	110	PS: Forecast Version	☑	☑	☐	☐

Figure 4.10 Maintain Versions for Controlling

4.3   Basic Concepts in Controlling

In this section, you will learn the three basic concepts. These are:

▶ Account Assignment

▶ Commitments Management

▶ Settlement

These concepts can appear confusing but they form the foundation of your overall understanding of Controlling, so it is important to be clear about them. Once you understand these concepts, you can fully understand the core of Controlling. Let's begin by discussing the account assignment of Controlling objects and how you can define real and statistical Controlling objects.

4.3.1   Account Assignment of Controlling Objects

Account assignments form the core of Controlling reporting and analysis. For postings that use a cost element as the account, the SAP system uses the account assignment logic to make sure that the data is posted correctly in all the relevant components. These rules are always valid in Controlling. There can be two types of account assignment objects as seen here:

▶ **True CO Objects**

These can be cost centers, orders (true), projects (true), networks, make to order sales orders, cost objects, profitability segments, real estate objects, and business processes.

▶ **Statistical CO Objects**

These can be cost centers if used in revenue cost elements, cost centers if a true cost object already exists, statistical internal orders, statistical projects, and profit centers.

A couple of points regarding true and statistical Controlling objects include the following:

▶ True Controlling objects can be identified as senders and receivers and hence can be part of assessment cycles. However, statistical cost objects cannot be used to allocate costs.

▶ Statistical assignments are for information purposes only.

Here are the rules for account assignment of Controlling objects:

▶ For posting to Controlling, GL accounts should also be created as a cost element.

▶ At least one true account assignment must be defined for a posting in Controlling.

▶ Statistical objects can only be specified after you have assigned a true object.

▶ Only three additional statistical objects can be specified in addition to the true object.

▶ Only one true Controlling object can be posted in one line item except for the cost centers. If a cost center and another true object are posted, then the cost center is treated as statistical.

▶ Revenues are posted statistically to a cost center and a profit center.

▶ You cannot specify an object as true and statistical in the same posting. For example, a true project and a statistical project cannot be posted in the same posting.

▶ Profit centers are always statistical and should match the ones that are derived from the true cost center. For example, if you enter cost center ABCD that has profit center assigned to it as ABCD, then you cannot enter EFGH as the profit center in the same posting. You have to enter ABCD.

Table 4.1 lists the account assignment combinations and which of the account assignment objects will be treated as the real cost object.

Account Assignment Combinations	Real Cost Object
Cost center and internal order (statistical)	Cost center
Cost center and internal order	Internal order
Profitability segment and cost center	Profitability segment
Cost center and profit center	Cost center
Internal order and profitability segment	Not possible
Internal order and internal order (statistical)	Not possible
For Revenue accounts: Profit center and cost center	Not possible

Table 4.1 Account Assignment Combinations and Selected Real Cost Object

Now that you understand the account assignment concept in Controlling, let's move on to the concept of commitments.

4.3.2 Commitments Management in Controlling

Commitment is the recording of potential expenditures or revenue items before they actually happen. Commitment management allows you to make an early recording and analysis of such commitments for their cost and financial effects. Commitments can be entered for the following objects: Controlling production orders, production orders, internal orders, maintenance orders, sales orders, cost centers, networks, network activities, and projects.

On the account assignment side, commitment management represents the costs incurred, which are then assigned to the orders, cost centers, or projects. These are then known as orders commitment, cost centers commitment, or projects commitments, respectively. You need to activate commitment management before the SAP system can record the costs. Commitments management can be activated:

▶ For each Controlling area from a chosen fiscal year

▶ For orders per order type

▶ For cost centers per order center type

You will learn more about commitments management in Chapter 7 when we introduce Funds Management.

4.3.3 Settlement in Controlling

In Controlling, you can collect costs in transient cost objects. For example, if you are installing a turbine, initially you might not know the full value of the asset, so you will record it as part of the turbine installation project, which might be a WBS element. However, ultimately you need to settle the cost incurred to a fixed asset, which needs to be created in FI-AA. Sender objects receive the costs initially, but these are then transferred to receiver objects via a settlement rule. Receiver objects are then analyzed for management reporting. It is also possible to settle costs from one cost center to another cost center. For example, you record the costs incurred in the Finance department in the finance cost center, and then you need to allocate the costs to other departments by number of employees.

Settlement is the process of allocating the costs incurred on an object to one or more receivers. The system ensures that offsetting entries to credit the sender object are also made. Figure 4.11 shows the list of sender and receiver objects.

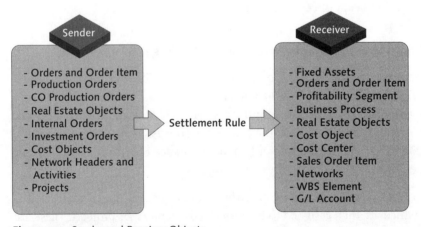

Figure 4.11 Sender and Receiver Objects

4.4 Procurement Process: Purchase Requisition to Check Writing

In this section, we will review the purchase requisition to check writing process and how they are integrated with Controlling in SAP ERP. Let's take a look at the procurement process for a consumable material charged to a cost center and consider the integration touch-points with Controlling.

The scenario is shown in Figure 4.12, which begins with a purchase requisition that gets converted to a request for quotation (RFQ) to multiple vendors. After multiple vendors submit their quotation, you choose one with the best terms and create a purchase order for it. When you receive the goods against the purchase order, the goods receipt is recorded in the system; when you receive the invoice from the vendor, invoice verification can be performed. Payment is made on the basis of the invoice created in the system.

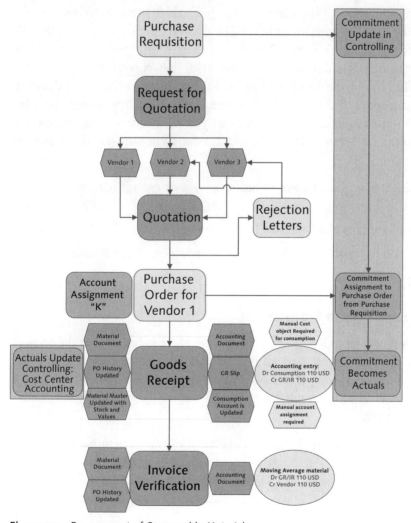

Figure 4.12 Procurement of Consumable Material

4.4.1 Commitment Management Flow in Procurement

As shown in Figure 4.12, the link to Controlling starts when the purchase requisition (PR) is created. The creation of PR creates a commitment item in Controlling. When the PR gets converted to a purchase order (PO), the commitment is reduced in proportion to the PR quantity reduced from the PO. If all the PR quantity gets converted, then the commitment gets transferred to the PO. Otherwise, you have commitments at both the PR and PO level.

When goods are received, the commitments get reduced and converted to actuals depending on the GR indicator in the PO. If the GR indicator is set in the PO, then commitments are reduced. However, if the GR indicator is not set, then commitments are not reduced. In the latter case, the actuals are only recorded when you have paid the vendor at the time of invoice verification. Commitments are also reduced at the time of invoice verification. It is entirely possible that a PO is not completely fulfilled and that you have received all you wanted to receive on the PO. For those situations, the following triggers the reduction of commitment:

▶ Setting the **Delivery Complete** indicator on goods receipt (GR) or in the PO item

▶ Setting the **Final invoice** indicator in the PO item

▶ Locking a PO item, only if no GR has happened against the PO item

▶ Deleting the PO item

4.4.2 Actuals Flow in Procurement

The actual costs get recorded in Controlling if the purchase order is of the account assignment category that is tied to a real Controlling object. For example, for account assignment category **K**, the system will post the expense line item actuals to cost center accounting. In this case, the real cost object will be the cost center assigned in the PO.

Now we can move on to the integration of PP and the manufacturing process.

4.5 Production Planning and Manufacturing Process Integration

SAP Supply Chain Management (SCM) allows you to perform planning using either SAP ERP PP (R/3) or SAP Advanced Planning and Optimization (APO). Figure 4.13 illustrates the typical supply chain planning processes with the segregation of planning processes in R/3 and in APO.

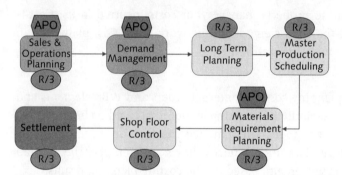

Figure 4.13 Supply Chain Planning and Integration with Controlling

The difference between planning processes in R/3 and APO is the amount of aggregation that is possible in each of these activities. In APO, the amount of aggregation is larger than the PP processes in R/3. As shown in Figure 4.13, the planning process originates with Sales and Operation Planning (SOP), which then leads to Demand Management, which feeds into Long term planning, which is an input to Master production scheduling, which feeds Materials Requirement Planning (MRP), which then feeds into operational level shop floor control. And all these processes ultimately are settled to Controlling. In addition, capacity requirements planning and stock control are also used as inputs to most of these SCM processes. The settlement process as described in Section 4.2.3 will be the integration point between supply chain planning and Controlling. Controlling is highly integrated with PP, especially while making a make or buy decision for a particular material using product costing.

4.6 Managing Projects and Capital Budgeting Integration

SAP Project Systems (PS) is the integrated framework used to manage projects in SAP ERP. PS is the receiver system for capturing the costs incurred as part of operating projects. It is heavily integrated with SAP ERP Financial Accounting, Controlling, MM, and PP. The integration aspects of PS-FI and a smattering of Controlling has been discussed in my other SAP PRESS book *Optimizing your SAP ERP Financials Implementation*. In this section, we will review the cost planning and settlement process in the context of project systems.

4.6.1 Integration of Cost Planning with Project Systems

Cost planning allows you to properly manage your costs incurred in PS. Cost is managed and tracked at the WBS element and network level. Cost planning can be done in the following ways in Controlling:

▶ **Easy cost planning**
This can be used for planning costs for internal orders and WBS elements and allows creation of separate individual costing models that can then be combined to create an overall costing model. These models can then be executed using a common *execution services*. Execution services allows you to trigger the creation of a PO, PR, or a goods movement, based on the costing planning results.

▶ **Manual cost planning in WBS elements**
Manual cost planning can be used to compare the plan to actuals and analyze variances. This allows you to enter the costs and activities. Manual cost planning sits right in between the budgeting process whereby the request comes for budget from the bottom up, and then after you have performed the cost planning, you decide how much budget you want to allocate for various activities. Planning is possible in multiple versions to allow for differences across the project timelines and use different baselines to compare against the actuals. The most common method of manual planning is the cost element planning method where you can plan at the cost element level.

▶ **Cost planning in networks**
As you saw earlier, cost planning in WBS elements is at an aggregated level. However, if you are interested in bottom up planning, then start at the network level using cost planning in networks. Networks can be used to estimate the internal and external processed work, services, and required resources in network activities. The system takes into account these lower granular level costs to come up with the plan costs. Costs get determined based on the planned activities and the price maintained in the system. Some of the key features

of network cost planning are calculation of plan costs based on activities and operating resources, unit costings, and invoicing plans. Unit costing is required earlier in the project lifecycle, whereas the invoicing plan allows you to reproduce when costs will occur over time for externally procured services and materials.

▶ **Copy functionality**
This allows you to copy your actuals to planning versions across periods to WBS elements and networks.

Three types of currencies can be managed in PS, which are:

▶ **Controlling area currency**
This is the currency of the Controlling area.

▶ **Object currency**
This is the currency of the WBS element, network, or project definition.

▶ **Transaction currency**
This is the currency in which the transaction actually occurs.

In addition to these currencies, for planning, you could define your own currency and translate the plan values into this user-definable currency. Periodic allocations allow you to map your planning understanding to changing realities by transferring costs from one account assignment object to another. Following are the typical period-end activities performed in PS to take stock of your cost planning:

▶ Periodic repostings in planning are corrective postings in projects based on shift in the dates.

▶ Planning overhead involves allocation of overhead in WBS element.

▶ Project planned interest calculation includes the cost of tied up capital in capital-intensive projects to make sure that you are planning appropriately.

▶ Planned results analysis is used in case of billing elements to settle the revenues to profitability segment.

▶ Planned settlement is used to settle the planned costs to cost centers, profitability segments, and so on.

You will learn more about cost planning in Chapter 5.

4.6.2 Cost Settlement in Project Systems

SAP PS has no organizational structure of its own. Rather, it builds on existing structures by making assignments to the organizational units in Financial Accounting and logistics. So PS can use various Controlling assignments to mirror the way costs are managed for a particular organization. The following types of orders can be assigned to PS objects:

- Internal orders
- Plant maintenance orders
- Sales orders
- Production orders

There are two ways in which you can transfer the costs from the order to the project:

- **Append**
  This increases the plan values in the project.

- **Apportion**
  This increase the assigned values for the project, which adds to the budget.

Costs and revenues collected in WBS elements or orders assigned to WBS elements ultimately need to be settled to one or more receivers. You can settle an order assigned to a WBS element to multiple objects:

- To the same WBS element to which it is assigned
- To a different WBS element or order
- To a different receiver such as cost center, asset, or profitability segment

If you settle from the order to a WBS element, then the actual costs are added to WBS element as usual, and the settlement is eliminated as internal business volume. Typically, WBS elements are finally settled to an asset or an asset under construction (AuC) at period end. A project can be settled either completely or partially. The settlement can be a single step (directly to the cost center, profitability segment, etc.) or multilevel (lower-level WBS elements are settled to the higher level WBS element, which is then settled to the cost center, profitability segment, etc.).

Now let's move on to learning about the integration of SAP Plant Maintenance (PM) with Controlling.

4.7 Plant Maintenance Integration

SAP Plant Maintenance (PM) is used to manage routine maintenance, preventive maintenance, and repair activities and is integrated with all the other components (MM, PS, Financial Accounting, and Controlling). The overall process view and integration of PM with SAP ERP Financial Accounting was discussed in my other SAP PRESS book *Optimizing your SAP ERP Financials Implementation*. In this section, you will learn the integration of PM master data and PM orders with Controlling.

4.7.1 Integration of Plant Maintenance Master Data to Controlling

Let's review some of the master data objects relevant for PM and how these are tied to Controlling objects.

Functional Location

All maintenance tasks are performed in the functional area. You need to categorize according to physical location or the overall manufacturing process. Functional location can be maintained in a hierarchical fashion. The functional data can be tied to the cost center in the Location and maintenance data tab. Other organization entities that can also be tied to the functional location are maintenance plant and partner data (supplier, purchaser, or responsible employee).

Equipment

This represents a physical entity that should be maintained independently. Typically, these are also maintained as assets. However, equipment is maintained more from a technical perspective to schedule and perform maintenance activities.

Equipment master data also contains time-dependent assignments to cost center, maintenance plant, and work center. In addition, serial numbers and partner data can also be maintained in equipment. Equipment can be installed to a functional location.

Bills of Materials

For PM, you can define bills of materials (BOM) that contain items relevant to PM. Additionally, the PM BOM has three important functions, as seen here:

▶ **Structuring of the object**
This details the structure of the object from the maintenance planning point of view.

▶ **Spare parts planning in the order**
This can be used to plan spare parts in the maintenance order.

▶ **Spare parts planning in task list**
This can be used to plan spare parts per the task list.

There are three types of PM BOMs: Material BOM, Equipment BOM, and Functional Location BOM.

4.7.2 Integrating Plant Maintenance Orders with Controlling

Plant notifications and maintenance order are the building blocks of transactions in plant maintenance order and customer service. Notifications can be created for a problem, maintenance request, and activity report. Bundled up notifications can then trigger the creation of maintenance orders. So let's take a look at the maintenance order and its salient points. PM orders form an integral part of detailing the tasks that occur in PM. In this section, we will be covering the integration perspective of PM with Controlling.

Figure 4.14 illustrates the PM order lifecycle that was detailed in "Optimizing your SAP ERP Financials Implementation" when we were discussing PM-FI integration. Plant Maintenance (PM) activities begin with a notification that can trigger a PM order.

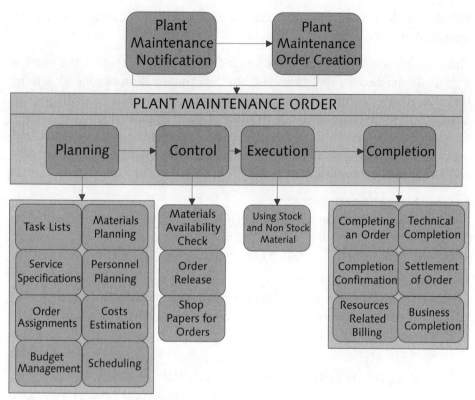

Figure 4.14 Plant Maintenance Order Lifecycle

The PM order goes through the phases of planning followed by control, execution, and completion. In the *planning phase,* cost estimation can be performed from either the Controlling perspective at the cost element level or from the PM view at the value category level. Cost elements track the type of expenses that you plan to incur, whereas value category denotes whether the cost will be incurred in house or will be paid externally for help with the maintenance activity. In customizing, cost elements are assigned to a value category so that you can track and manage your estimation costs from both the Controlling and PM perspective.

In the *control phase,* the system checks if the required materials are available in-house, and you can link the issue of the materials to the PM order. This is the integration of PM with MM. In the *execution phase,* you actually get the materials issued from your store and use them in the PM order. The *completion phase* starts off with a technical understanding, such as damage, cause of damage, and recording actual time required.

These are recorded in technical confirmation, which indicates that the order is technically finished for PM. However, business confirmation is done by settling the costs assigned to the PO to appropriate cost elements. The Controlling interlinkage with the maintenance order is the settlement of the maintenance order to an appropriate cost receiver. Now that you understand the Controlling view of PM lifecycle, let's take a look at the integration of PM orders with other Controlling and Financial Accounting applications:

▸ **Asset Accounting (FI-AA)**
From a Financial Accounting perspective, the PM orders can be settled to Asset Accounting directly, and the link from PM to assets is via the equipment master.

▸ **Funds Management (FI-FM)**
PM can be integrated with funds management for cash budget monitoring using funds and funds centers. In addition, commitment management can be more effectively managed in funds management for PM orders that require external services procurement.

▸ **Controlling Overhead Cost Management (CO-OM)**
Settlement rules to Controlling can be set for maintenance orders by linking PM with work centers. Maintenance orders are temporary collectors for costs and ultimately needed to be settled to an asset if the PM equipment is tied to an asset or to any other cost object, such as a cost center.

▸ **Controlling- Investment management (CO-IM)**
PM can also be integrated with investment management for detailed monitoring of accounts and managing the budgeting aspects of equipment. The order type is a classification characteristic of the maintenance planning order, and it influences the processing options of individual orders. Each order type can be used in all Controlling areas.

In the next section, we will cover the sales order to cash application process highlighting SD and Controlling (SD-CO) integration.

4.8   Sales Order to Cash Application Process Integration

Sales and Distribution (SD) helps you manage your sales processes from sales inquiry to cash application. In this section, you will learn about the integration of SD with Controlling. To perform margin analysis from an external market segment perspective, you need to implement profitability analysis in Controlling.

Figure 4.15 shows the integration of SD with Controlling-Profitability Analysis (CO-PA). Sales orders and billing documents transfer data directly to CO-PA using revenue elements. This then gets transferred to profitability segments of CO-PA. Profitability segments compile the data processed in Controlling and convert them in reporting formats for margin analysis. You can structure your profitability segments according to your requirements.

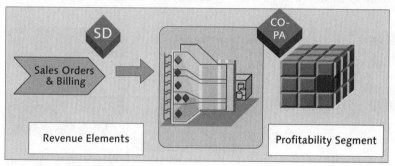

Figure 4.15   Integration Between SD and CO-PA

A lot of information gets recorded in CO-PA from multiple feeder components, such as Logistics and SAP ERP Financial Accounting; therefore, it can be used for sales planning and budgeting, which can then be forwarded to PP for sales and operations planning. This is where you fully leverage the potential of SAP ERP as an integrated application.

CO-PA allows you to manage deviations between plan and actual sales in dimensions that matter to you. For example, you can slice and dice your sales profitability by characteristics such as regions, product family, customer groups, and in myriad value fields such as quantities and order size. Figure 4.16 displays the details of how Controlling components interact with other Controlling components. You can calculate the margin by outlining the components of margin analysis shown in Table 4.2.

Margin Component	SAP ERP Application
Sales Revenue	SD Pricing
Less Sales Deduction and Sales Related Expenses	SD Pricing
Less Cost of Sales Material, Labor and Overhead	CO-Product Costing
Less Internal Order Costs related to R&D	CO-Internal Order
Less Costs pertaining to Sales and Marketing, Shared services and Administrative Non-operative Costs	CO-Cost Center Accounting
Sales Margin	CO- Profitability Analysis

Table 4.2 Calculating Sales Margin Using CO-PA

Profitability Analysis allows you to map in the system how you want to structure your margin analysis by defining your own characteristics and value fields.

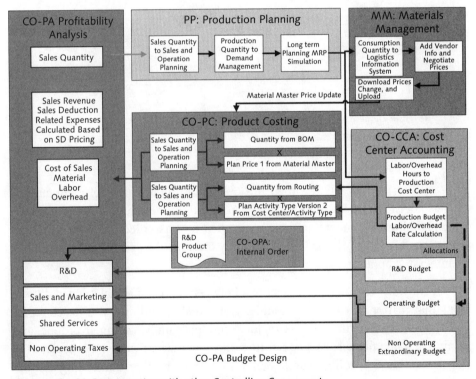

Figure 4.16 CO-PA Integration with other Controlling Components

Now that you understand how to calculate margin using CO-PA, let's look at an integrated budgetary perspective that you can implement using CO-PA. Review Figure 4.16 to see how the budget flows to and from CO-PA.

Based on the sales quantities you actually get in CO-PA, you can plan your sales quantity. The sales quantity then flows to PP's SOP. Based on this quantity, PP determines demand. After the demand is firmed up, you can perform long-term planning and structure your MRP simulation runs and long-term planning. The actual execution of PP is then managed in MM as actual goods movements are recorded and you perform procurement activities in line with the MRP runs.

With the integration of MM with the Financial Accounting GL, which is then subsequently integrated with Controlling, you record the cost information in cost center accounting. You need to perform cost center allocations to represent the costs accurately. These costs then directly flow as separate headings of operating budget and nonoperating budget to CO-PA.

The integration of SAP MM and cost center accounting allows you to calculate the per-unit product costs that then feed the cost of sales in CO-PA. This allows you to come up with a reasonable estimate of sales quantity that you should plan. This feedback loop ensures that the PP process is driven by sales that reflect the ground realities of the marketplace. It allows an organization to remain nimble and respond to any changes in the marketplace.

This completes the brief process perspective of integrating CO-PA with other Controlling components. You will learn more about CO-PA in Chapter 9. Next you will learn how your enterprise's human resources can be integrated with Controlling processes

4.9 Human Capital Management Integration

In this section, we will review the integration of HCM payroll with Controlling. Some key integration points of HR with Controlling are master data, personnel cost planning, and position budgeting and control. Each of these integration perspectives are detailed in this section.

> **Note**
>
> For details about integration of Human Capital Management with Financial accounting you can refer to my other SAP PRESS book *Optimizing your SAP ERP Financials Implementation*.

4.9.1 Master Data in Human Resources and Linkage to Controlling

Map your HR organizational structure to Controlling so that the costs can be tracked to the correct cost centers. These include the payroll costs as well as other administrative costs. If you have implemented payroll in HR, you need to assign the organization units in HR to Controlling so that the salary and administrative costs can be posted appropriately in Controlling. Before we go into the details of the integration of HR with Controlling, let's do a quick recap.

HR organizational structure in *personnel administration* is tied together broadly in the following sequence: *company code* is tied to *personnel area,* which houses *personnel sub area,* which houses *organization key*. On the other hand, HR organizational personnel structure consists of the position, job, and organizational unit.

In organization management, you can link the position data to the following fields: company code, cost center, controlling area, business area, employee group, employee subgroup, job, and organization unit. Cost centers are typically assigned to the organization units and, if required, to the position in the organizational plan.

This assignment ensures that you can generate reporting related to personnel cost planning, which is detailed next.

4.9.2 Personnel Cost Planning in Human Resources

The number of personnel needed for this fiscal year versus the previous year needs to be planned. This allows your organization to have the optimal mix of employees and contractors. Personnel cost planning feeds the overall cost planning process. Personnel cost planning feeds Controlling with the personnel-related costs, so that you can include them in the financial plans and forecasts. Personnel cost planning takes into account vacant positions and offers extremely precise planning capabilities for employee costs. The integration of personnel cost planning is across the following components:

▶ **Personnel Administration**

You can plan personnel administration data in personnel cost planning by including the following payment-related data:

- ▶ Employees
- ▶ Positions
- ▶ Jobs
- ▶ Organizational units

▶ **Payroll**

All payroll results can be included in the personnel cost plan.

▶ **Training and Event Management**

All personnel costs related to training and event management can also be recorded in personnel cost planning.

▶ **Compensation Management**

Planned compensation for jobs and actual disbursed compensation can be entered as well.

▶ **Position Budgeting and Control**

Budget data and commitment data can also be used in personnel cost planning.

▶ **Controlling**

Personnel cost planning data flows to Controlling so that the overall company costs can be managed.

▶ **Business Information Warehouse (BW)**

Detailed plan versus actual reports can be executed in BW.

Personnel cost planning allows you to simulate how employee-related costs will appear six months hence, based on the projected headcount numbers. The process flow for personnel cost planning is outlined here:

1. **Planning preparation**

   In this phase of personnel cost planning, as a personnel cost planner, you get general guidance from management about the future employee headcounts. You define the overarching rules and regulations that form the basis of future planning activities.

2. **Data collection**
Based on the overall direction from management, you need to collect data for employees, jobs, and positions, and then project how these will look in the future. You also consider the projected salary hike and market conditions to come up with broad numbers that form the basis of personnel cost planning.

3. **Create personnel cost plans**
In this phase, you first create a personnel cost plan for each planning scenario you want to simulate and each planning period. After this personnel cost plan is created, you can then execute each personnel cost plan. This allows you to make the plan data available to line managers. Line managers can then detail out the personnel cost plan and make modifications as required. This allows the personnel cost planner to finalize the personnel cost plan.

4. **Approve and release the cost plan**
The detailed personnel cost plan is then send to management for approval and finalization. After the manager reviews and approves the cost plan, you can release the cost plan in the system.

5. **Transfer cost plan to Controlling and other components**
From now on, someone in accounting takes over and transfers the approved and finalized cost plan to Controlling, training and event management, and compensation management. This completes the personnel cost planning cycle, and this plan forms an input mechanism to the overall cost plan. In training and event management and compensation management, you use this plan as an input to the budgeting process.

4.9.3 Position Budgeting and Control

Position budgeting and control allows you to budget for specific open positions and to manage your overall HR efficiently. Position budgeting is typically used as part of funds management, which is implemented in public sectors where the personnel costs are one of the major components of the total costs.

It allows you to populate the costs that you have been incurring over the fiscal years and provides you a starting point to plan and prepare budgets for your organization. Position budgeting and control allows you to finance employees efficiently within the budgetary limits. This is primarily used to integrate the budget available in funds management along with the HR organizational structure and persons. The tools described next can be used to budget the position:

▶ **Commitment processor**
This is tied to funds management and is used to monitor the funds usage. It allows you to automatically generate personnel commitments that help in monitoring the personnel expenses commitment. The account assignments are automatically determined from funds management wherever possible. Using personnel cost savings, it is possible to assign a budget that is not required, instead of releasing it.

▶ **Personnel budget plan management**
This provides the tools to map the personnel budget plan and assign the persons and positions to the same. Personnel budget planning allows you to have a realistic understanding of the overall budgetary allocation required in the coming months based on the new positions identified as well as the renewal of the existing positions. This simplifies the budgetary process by providing all the available HR data to be used in the base calculation.

4.10 Controlling and Finance Integration

In the past, Controlling was intended for management reporting purposes only. There was limited integration between Controlling and Financial Accounting. However, all financial documents required a Controlling component in case there was a relevant cost element assigned to the GL account. So Controlling was primarily a receiver component of SAP ERP Financial Accounting. If you changed anything in Controlling, nothing flowed back to Financial Accounting unless you activated some extra ledgers.

In this section, you will learn how you can integrate Controlling and Financial Accounting so that both can talk to each other. Default account assignments in Controlling will also be covered in this section. Prior to the introduction of the new GL, you needed to implement a reconciliation ledger. However, with the new GL, you can implement real-time integration of Controlling and SAP ERP Financial Accounting, which removes any reconciliation activity at month end. You will first learn about the reconciliation ledger.

4.10.1   Reconciliation Ledger

The reconciliation ledger tracks all the activities and transactions within the Controlling component at a summarized level of object type and object class. The reconciliation ledger helps primarily in reconciling Controlling with Financial Accounting. The reconciliation ledger, however, provides a good starting point for analyzing costs on an overall basis because it contains the data in a summarized form. The reconciliation ledger structure contains the following information about the data flows:

▸ Which business transaction caused the data flow?

▸ Between which object types (cost center, network, order, reconciliation object, business process, WBS element, sales document item) and object classes (overhead, production, investment, profitability analysis)?

▸ Between which company codes, business areas, and functional areas?

▸ To which cost element or account was the posting recorded?

Some common configuration transactions associated with the reconciliation ledger are detailed next. Let's start with the activation of the reconciliation ledger.

Reconciliation Ledger Activation

By using Transaction KALA, you can activate the reconciliation ledger by specifying the Controlling area and the document type for the reconciliation posting. Figure 4.17 shows that you have maintained the **Document Type AB** for **Controlling Area US01**. Now you just need to click **Execute** (clock icon) to activate the reconciliation ledger for the Controlling area.

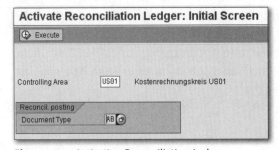

Figure 4.17   Activating Reconciliation Ledger

Maintain Automatic Accounts for CO-FI Reconciliation

By using Transaction OBYB, you can maintain the GL account that will be used for the reconciliation postings between Controlling and SAP ERP Financial Accounting. This is especially important from the perspective of secondary cost elements as these exist only in Controlling and do not have a corresponding equivalent in SAP ERP Financial Accounting. Therefore, you have to assign a corresponding GL account for the postings which occur only in Controlling so that these can then be posted back to Financials. Figure 4.18 shows how you can maintain the GL **Account 690000** in the **Account assignment** tab. The setting needs to be maintained for a particular **Chart of Accounts CANA**. Transaction CO1 automatically comes when you run Transaction OBYB.

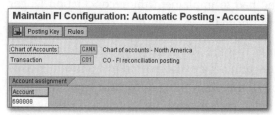

Figure 4.18 Define account for CO-FI reconciliation posting

Follow-up Posting to Reconciliation Ledger

Transaction KAL1 is used if postings were made before the reconciliation ledger was active. The transaction should be run in the background for performance reasons. You need to enter the **Fiscal Year** and **Period** for which you want to run the follow up posting to reconciliation ledger (see Figure 4.19).

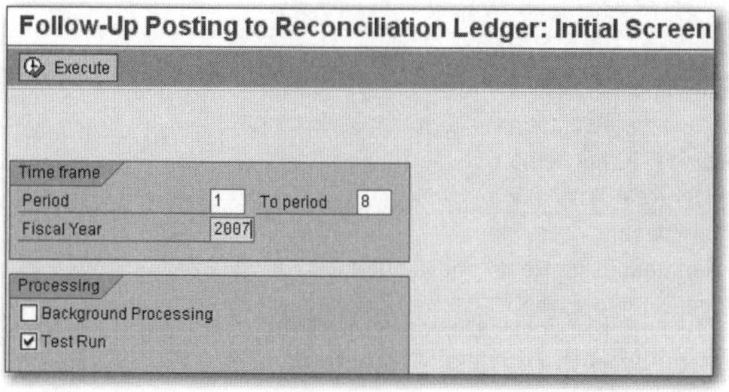

Figure 4.19 Follow-Up Posting to Reconciliation Ledger

> **Note**
>
> If you implement the new GL and activate real-time integration, then the reconciliation ledger is not needed because the GL is always reconciled with Controlling. It is recommended that you use real-time integration in place of the reconciliation ledger because the reconciliation ledger will not be supported in the long term. Also you will not see the old menu paths, which is why these were not shown in the earlier transaction codes.

4.10.2 Real-time Integration of Controlling with Financial Accounting

With the introduction of the new GL, you can integrate Controlling with the GL in real time. This is especially important because you can now perform allocation functions in the GL. Previously, you had to implement the reconciliation ledger that needed to be maintained and reconciled every month.

With real-time integration, the values that are relevant for GL accounting immediately get posted. All the finance documents are also posted to Controlling. This real-time integration allows you to call the Controlling document from the financial document and vice versa. The menu path for real-time integration along with the configuration options is shown in Figure 4.20, and is **Financial Accounting (New) • Financial Accounting Global Settings (New) • Ledger • Real Time Integration of Controlling with Financial Accounting**.

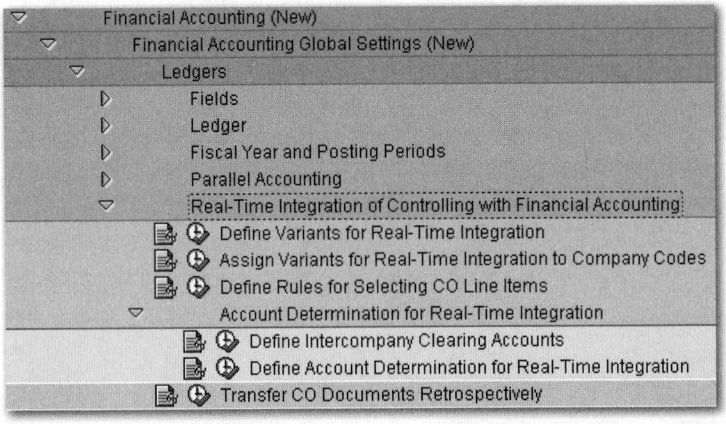

Figure 4.20 Real-Time Integration of Controlling with Financial Accounting

As you can see from Figure 4.20, you first need to define the variants for real-time integration, which then needs to be assigned to company codes. You can also define rules for selecting Controlling line items. In addition, you can define accounts for integrating Controlling with SAP ERP Financial Accounting. You can also bring in documents from Controlling retrospectively if you have implemented in between a fiscal year. First you will learn about defining variants.

Define Variants for Real-Time Integration

Variants help you define the attributes of the real-time integration of Controlling with Financial Accounting. In this step, you will learn to define the variants for real-time integration. You can follow **IMG· Financial Accounting (new) · Financial Accounting Global Settings (new) · Real-Time Integration of Controlling with Financial Accounting· Define Variants for Real-Time Integration**. Figure 4.21 shows the properties of a real-time variant (**Var. for R-T Integ.) 0001**.

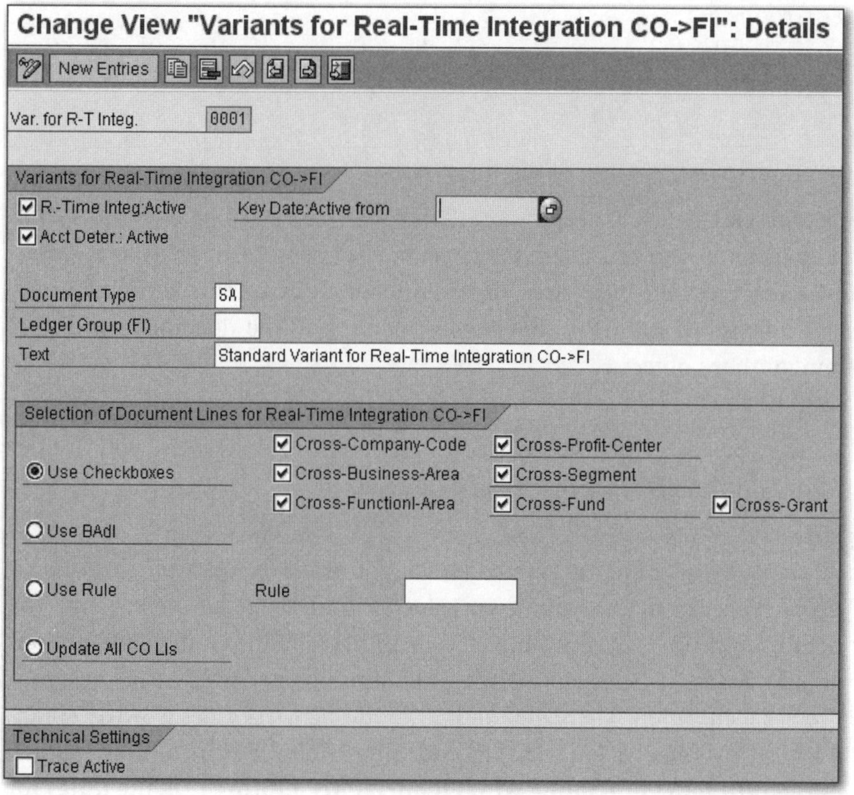

Figure 4.21 Define Variants for Real-Time Integration

The fields shown in Figure 4.21 are listed and explained here:

▶ **R-Time Integ: Active**
This flag ensures that you have activated the real-time integration.

▶ **Key Date**
Active from: If you implement real-time integration after you have gone live and have production, then you should enter an effective date from which the integration is active.

▶ **Acct Deter**
Active: This flag activates account determination.

▶ **Document Type**
This identifies the document type that will be used for reconciliation document postings for CO-FI.

▶ **Ledger Group (FI)**
You can enter the ledger group for which you want to activate the real-time integration.

▶ **Text**
Here you can enter text describing the variant.

▶ **Use Checkboxes**
If you check this, you can select the checkboxes **Cross-Company-Code**, **Cross-Profit-Center**, **Cross-Business-Area**, **Cross-Functional-Area**, **Cross-Segment**, **Cross-Fund**, and **Cross-Grant**. This allows you to select all the document lines that have any of these objects.

▶ **Use BAdI**
This allows you to enter a business add in that can be defined by you to filter the list of Controlling items that should be selected.

▶ **Use Rule**
This allows you to define the rule by which you want to select the Controlling line items. You can define your own rules by following the menu path. The rule definition process is very similar to defining validations and substitutions and should typically be performed by someone in the ABAP team per your functional specification. The menu path for defining these rules is **IMG· Financial Accounting (new) · Financial Accounting Global Settings (new) · Real-Time Integration of Controlling with Financial Accounting · Define Rules for Selecting CO Line Items.**

► **Update All CO LIs**

This selects all the Controlling line items that get posted. So every time a document posts only in Controlling, the system will post a corresponding document in Financial Accounting.

► **Trace Active**

This activates the trace.

Assign Real-Time Variants to Company Code

After defining the variant in the previous step, you need to assign the same to company codes so that the integration can be activated for the company code. You can follow this path: **IMG· Financial Accounting (new) · Financial Accounting Global Settings (new) · Real-Time Integration of Controlling with Financial Accounting · Assign Variants for Real-Time Integration to Company Codes**. Figure 4.22 shows that you have assigned the **Variant for Real-Time Integration 0001** to **Company code US01**.

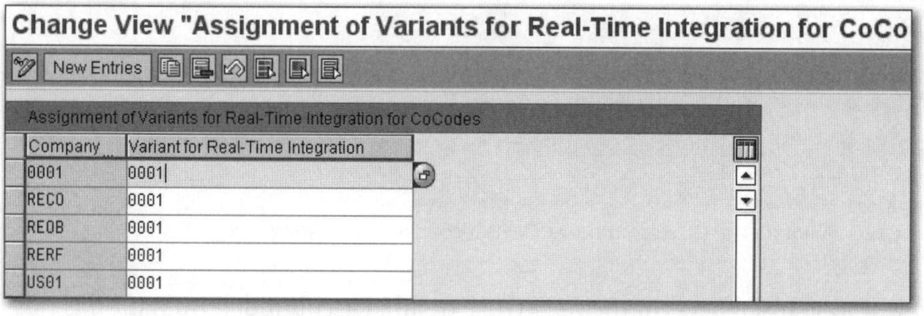

Figure 4.22   Assign Variants to Company Code

Define Account Determination for Real-Time Integration

In this step, you will learn how to define the accounts that will be hit when a CO-FI reconciliation document is posted. In the reconciliation ledger, you can only define one GL account for reconciliation. However, using extended account determination, you can define multiple accounts depending on your business scenario. The menu path is **IMG · Financial Accounting (new) · Financial Accounting Global Settings (new) · Real-Time Integration of Controlling with Financial Accounting · Account Determination for Real-Time Integration · Define Account Determination for Real-Time Integration** and the transaction code is OK17. Figure 4.23 shows the screen where you can maintain **Extended Account Determination**.

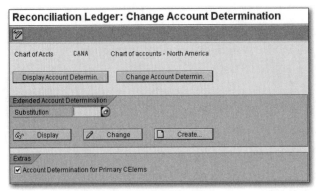

Figure 4.23 Define Account Determination

When you click on **Display Account Determin.**, the screen shown in Figure 4.24 appears, which is similar to the previous screen for CO-FI reconciliation shown earlier in Figure 4.18.

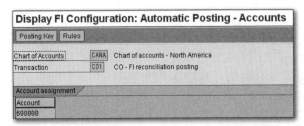

Figure 4.24 Maintain the GL Account for CO-FI Reconciliation Posting

However, as you see here, in the new GL, extended account determination is possible by using substitution rules for the CO-FI reconciliation posting. Substitution can be used to override the previous account determinations, which are determined by standard account determinations defined earlier.

A typical example might be to define different GL accounts for different company codes by using extended account determination. However, this was not possible earlier because the definition of the GL account was via chart of accounts.

> **Note**
>
> Extended account determination is dependent on the Controlling area, whereas standard account determination needs to be configured by the chart of accounts.

4.10.3 Transfer Controlling Documents Retrospectively

If you implemented Controlling without real-time integration for a particular company code and now want to transition to real-time integration, you can transfer Controlling documents retrospectively until a particular date. This will be especially useful if you migrated to the new GL in the middle of your fiscal year. This transaction can also be used to correct any errors if documents are not posting to financial accounting from Controlling. Remember, this is your backup transaction code if things go wrong. The menu path for transferring the documents is **IMG•Financial Accounting (new) • Financial Accounting Global Settings (new) • Real-Time Integration of Controlling with Financial Accounting • Transfer CO Documents Retrospectively**. You can also use Transaction FAGLCOFITRNSFRCODOCS. Figure 4.25 shows the selection parameters for transferring Controlling documents retroactively to SAP ERP Financial Accounting.

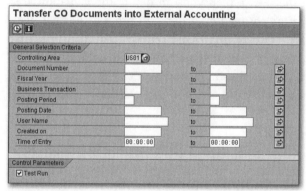

Figure 4.25 Transfer Controlling Documents Retrospectively

You can run this transaction code by **Controlling Area**, **Document Number** range, **Fiscal Year** range, **Business Transaction** range, **Posting Period(s)**, **Posting Date(s)**, **User Name(s)**, and **Created on** range. You can always run this in **Test Run** before executing this for real.

> **Note**
>
> This transaction replaces the previous Transaction KAL1, which was used in the normal CO-FI reconciliation ledger to transfer documents that were posted in the ledger before online integration was activated.

4.10.4 Default Account Assignments for Controlling

Automatic postings require that you default Controlling account assignments, Otherwise, many times the transaction will not post. This is especially true for postings that happen in the background, based on the movement types, such as MM inventory-related transactions. The same is also true for SD post goods issue transactions. In all these cases, you need to define which cost object the transaction should hit, or there will be an error. In other cases, you want to default the account assignments so that you can ensure consistency of entry and avoid user errors, when you allow users to choose the account assignment at the time of data entry.

In this section, default account assignments are defined in cost center accounting, which allows you to default the cost center and profit center. The first step is defining the cost element and then identifying whether business area or cost center is mandatory. Then in the next screen you can define the valuation area and the business area to which the cost center, order, and profit center has been assigned. The menu path is **IMG• Controlling • Cost center accounting • Actual Postings• Manual Actual Postings • Edit automatic account assignment**. The Transaction code is OKB9. Figure 4.26 illustrates how you can define the default account assignment.

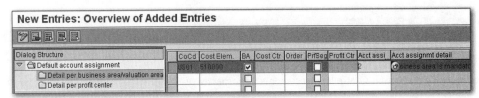

Figure 4.26 Defining Default Account Assignment

The following parameters now need to be defined:

▸ **CoCd**
Enter the relevant company code "US01".

▸ **Cost Elem.**
This identifies the cost element for which you are defining the default cost object.

▸ **BA**
This allows you to specify that business area account assignment takes priority.

► **Cost Ctr**

You can choose to define the default cost center by cost element if the same cost center needs to be maintained for all the valuation areas.

► **Order**

This identifies the internal order that should be defaulted.

► **PrfSeg**

This indicator should be checked if you want the system to find the profitability segment using the substitution rule.

► **Profit Ctr**

This is where you can maintain the profit center if you have chosen **Detail per profit center** in the left pane.

► **Acct assi**

Here you can choose one of the three options:

  ► **1**: Valuation area is mandatory.

  ► **2**: Business area is mandatory.

  ► **3**: Profit center is mandatory.

► **Acct assignmt detail**

This displays the detail for account assignment. Thereofore, if you chose **2**, then **Business Area is mandatory** is displayed.

If you choose **2**, that is **Business area is mandatory**, you need to maintain the account assignments in the next screen (see Figure 4.27) by clicking on **Detail per business area/valuation area**. Here you can maintain the business area by valuation area, which is typically at plant level.

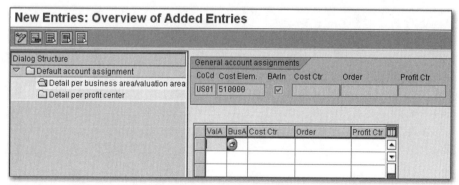

Figure 4.27 Defining the Cost Center by Business Area

4.11 Summary

This chapter introduced you to the integrated business model of Controlling and demonstrated how it allows you to optimize your management reporting structure and setup. First you were introduced to the global enterprise structure settings in Controlling, where you learned about the Controlling area, versions, number ranges, and assignment of company codes to Controlling areas. Next you learned about the basic Controlling concepts related to account assignments, commitments management, and settlement process. This laid the foundation of the chapter, which allowed us to discuss the business-oriented perspective of Controlling. You learned about the integration of Controlling with procurement to the payment process, PP process, PS, PM processes, sales order to cash process, and HR process.

Lastly you learned about the integration of the Controlling with SAP ERP Financial Accounting by understanding the reconciliation ledger, real-time integration between Controlling and SAP ERP Financial Accounting, along with the default account assignments that need to be defined for Controlling objects. This chapter lays the foundation of your overall optimization endeavor of Controlling processes. You should come back to it to revise your basic conceptual understanding of Controlling.

Now let's go on to Chapter 5, in which you will learn about cost center accounting, cost element accounting, profit center accounting, and internal orders.

This introduction to the various tools and techniques will simplify and allow you to design optimal processes for your organization from a Controlling perspective. Another important thing to consider while reading this chapter is that most of these processes follow the same architectural structure.

5   Optimizing Cost Element Accounting, Cost Center Accounting, Profit Center Accounting, and Internal Order Accounting

In this chapter, you will learn how to configure and implement *cost element accounting, cost center accounting, profit center accounting*, and *internal order accounting*. We will clarify some of the key features of each of these components so that you can standardize and optimize your existing Controlling processes. It is extremely important for you to think through and map the overall structure of your organization into these four components. This allows you to launch yourself into a learning cycle where you can get increased benefits from implementing additional components.

You will proceed from defining your cost center and profit center hierarchies along with the cost element and internal order definition, to performing planning in cost center accounting that can be replicated across other components because the overall architecture of planning remains the same. You will also learn how to implement budgeting in cost center accounting and internal order accounting with availability control setup. The concept of funds commitment is also highlighted, which allows you to map out your future commitments. This helps tremendously in analyzing the overall risk that your organization has in terms of future liabilities.

Internal order lifecycle from creation to settlement is discussed from a functional and configuration perspective. The tools discussed allow you to optimally design your internal order lifecycle per your organization's requirements. In addition, you will learn about the period-end and fiscal year-end activities that need to be performed to support the closing processes in Controlling. Figure 5.1 covers the cost element accounting, cost center accounting, and profit center accounting structures. Let's dive into cost element accounting now.

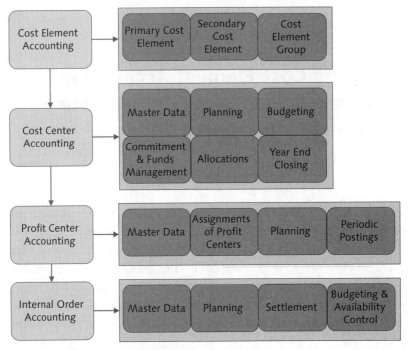

Figure 5.1 Basic Controlling Processes

5.1 Cost Element Accounting

The basic question that cost element accounting answers is the detailed understanding of what costs have been incurred. Cost element accounting is not a typical accounting system but a mechanism to record data from Financial Accounting that forms the basis of cost accounting. In this component, no routine transactions are recorded. So the most important aspect in cost element accounting is the master data that should be created when the relevant GL account is created. Let's tackle cost element master data first.

5.1.1 Types of Cost Elements

Let's learn about the key attributes of cost elements and the process of creating cost elements:

► **Primary cost elements**
Tied to a P&L GL account these elements can either be directly created at the time the GL account was created or by clicking on **Edit cost element** or via the menu path in cost element accounting. You need to have a GL account created before creating a primary cost element. The costs for a primary cost element originate outside of Controlling.

► **Secondary cost elements**
These are primarily used for allocation cycles and can be created solely in Controlling. Secondary cost elements are used either as intermediary receivers or senders that must not have real costs. The menu path is **SAP Menu • Accounting • Controlling • Cost element accounting • Master Data • Cost Element • Individual Processing • Create Primary/Create Secondary/Change/Display/Delete/Display changes**. The Transactions are KA01/KA06/KA02/KA03/KA04/KA05.

Figure 5.2 illustrates how a primary cost element can be changed. Let's review these steps:

1. Enter the **Cost Element** "610100", the **Controlling Area**, which is seen as **US01**, and a **Valid From** and **to** date.

2. On the **Basic Data** tab, to enter a **Name** and **Description**.

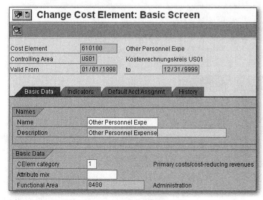

Figure 5.2 Changing a Cost Element

The other options seen on this screen are described here:

- **CElem category** identifies the cost element category and can be selected as follows:
  - **1**: Primary Costs/Costs reducing revenue
  - **3**: Accrual/deferral per surcharge
  - **4**: Accrual/deferral per debit=actual
  - **11**: Revenues
  - **12**: Sales deduction
  - **22**: External settlement

The cost element category allows you to distinguish between primary and secondary cost elements. These can be used to distinguish within the primary cost elements whether it is a cost element (expense account) or revenue element (revenue account):

- **Attribute mix**
  This can be used to further distinguish the cost elements per your requirements.

- **Functional Area**
  This allows you to represent your departments as functional areas such as production, sales, marketing, administration and so on. This allows you to create P&L accounting per cost of sales accounting. The functional area entered in the corresponding GL master flows to the cost element master data as well and cannot be entered from this screen.

In Figure 5.3, you can see the indicators for recording quantity, where the unit of measure can also be entered.

Figure 5.3 Defining Indicators

- **Record qty**
  This flag allows you to record quantities against the cost element.

- **Unit of Measure**
  This identifies the unit of measure for posted activities.

- Selecting the **Default Acct Assgnmt** tab brings you to the screen shown in Figure 5.4.

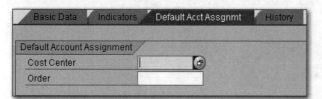

Figure 5.4 Defining Default Account Assignment for Cost Element

This is where you can define the default cost center or order for a particular cost element. This setting is useful only if cost elements map to the same cost center across all company codes. Remember, you learned about defaulting cost centers and orders by valuation area and cost element earlier in Chapter 4. The **History** tab records all the changes made on the cost element.

5.1.2 Cost Element Group

The cost element group is a grouping of similar cost elements for reporting purposes. By using cost element groups, you can build a hierarchical cost element structure that can be extremely useful for reporting purposes. You can use cost element groups in all the Controlling transactions such as cost center planning and allocation cycles. This allows you to process all the cost elements in one transaction. The menu path is **SAP Menu • Accounting • Controlling • Cost element accounting • Master Data • Cost Element Group • Create/Change/Display**. The Transactions are KAH1/KAH2/KAH3. Figure 5.5 shows the screen for changing an existing cost element group, **CANA**.

The cost element groups are broken into these headings: **Manufacturing, Operating Expenses, Other Expenses,** and **Secondary Cost Elements. Manufacturing** is then broken up into **SAP Manufacturing Clearing Accounts, Inventory Reserves, and Manufacturing Variances**. Primary cost elements (**510000** to **510099**) are then assigned to **SAP Manufacturing Clearing Accounts.**

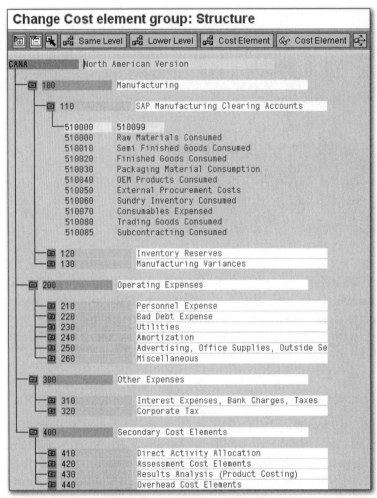

Figure 5.5 Changing an Existing Cost Element Group

To change an existing cost element group, assign new cost elements or change the assignment of cost elements to a different level. The **Same Level** and **Lower Level** buttons help create a cost element group at the same level or creates a new lower level below the same level, respectively. The other two buttons for **Cost Element** allow you to insert a cost element or to display a cost element attached to a cost element group.

Now let's move on to cost center accounting.

5.2 Cost Center Accounting

Cost center accounting (CO-OM-CCA) is used for internal Controlling purposes and to make the costs more transparent in an organization. The overall objective of CO-OM-CCA is to trace the source of a cost. If you have overhead costs, they need to be allocated to the actual department that owns that cost. Table 5.1 shows you the three types of decision-making responsibilities that a manager can have.

Responsibility Areas	Responsibility of Manager	Performance Metrics	Examples
Cost Center	Managing costs per plan	Plan versus Actual Costs	HR department, IT department
Profit Center	Manages costs and responsible for generating revenues. Owns the overall profit of the group.	Operating Results of the Profit Center	Manufacturing units
Investment Center	Manages costs and revenues and can make investment decisions.	Return on Investment	Business unit

Table 5.1 Types of Responsibility Areas

Cost center accounting focuses only on costs allowing you to detail out the costs and makes the managers responsible for the costs incurred by their departments.

Note
Cost center accounting is typically one of the earliest components that an organization implements.

Figure 5.6 shows you the process involved. Let's examine master data first.

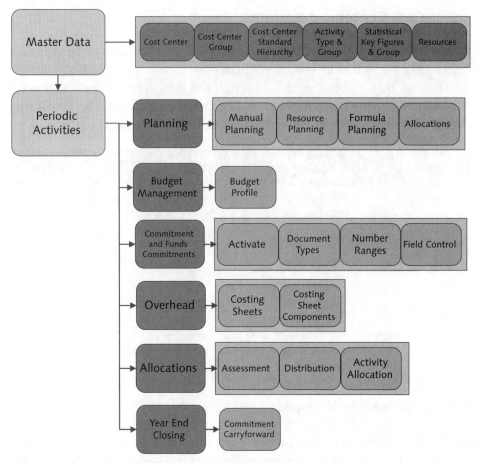

Figure 5.6 Cost Center Accounting

5.2.1 Cost Center Accounting Master Data

First you will learn about the various master data elements of cost center accounting such as cost center, cost center group, cost center standard hierarchy, activity type and activity type group, statistical key figures, and resources. Then you will learn about the following cost center accounting business transaction. The most important aspect in cost element accounting is the master data.

Cost Center

Cost centers are the organizational units where costs are incurred. These can be created from a variety of perspectives such as responsibility, physical location, and functional area. The structure of the cost center is heavily dependent on each organization and mimics the organization structure.

Before creating a cost center, you should outline the standard hierarchy to guide the overall structure and set of the cost centers. Each cost center needs to be assigned to the standard hierarchy. Standard hierarchy needs represent a grouping of all the cost centers for a particular Controlling area. This allows you to visualize your organization from the Controlling perspective. The menu path to follow for creating, changing, displaying change is **SAP Menu • Accounting • Controlling • Cost center accounting • Master data • Cost Center • Individual Processing • Create/Change/Display/Delete/Display Change**. The Transactions are KS01/KS02/KS03/KS04/KS05.

To understand more about a cost center, let's take a look at how a cost center looks in cost center accounting. Figure 5.7 shows you the **Basic data** tab of the cost center screen where you can change the Cost Center **10100**. All the cost centers are created for a **Controlling Area US01** with **Valid From** and **to** dates.

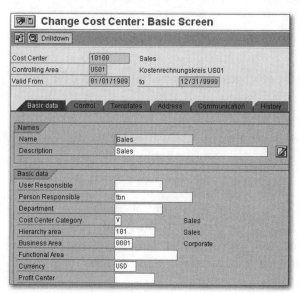

Figure 5.7 Entering Basic Data in Cost Center Master Data

You need to maintain the following parameters identifying the cost center:

▶ **Name and Description**
This identifies the name and description of the cost center.

▶ **User Responsible**
This is the SAP user ID of the responsible person.

▶ **Person Responsible**
This is free form text with which you can maintain the responsible person even if you have not created a SAP user ID.

▶ **Department**
This can be used to capture the department of your organization and is used for reporting purposes.

▶ **Cost Center Category**
This identifies the category of the cost center and can be used to build additional logic for activity types. Typical examples for a cost center category are production, sales, and administration.

▶ **Hierarchy area**
This can be used to map the cost center to the standard hierarchy components. You have to choose a predefined hierarchy area for your cost center.

▶ **Business Area**
This can be used to link the business area to the cost center.

▶ **Functional Area**
This can be used to establish the link between the cost center and the functional area.

▶ **Currency**
This identifies the currency of the cost center.

▶ **Profit Center**
This can be used to assign profit centers to the cost center.

Figure 5.8 displays the screen for maintaining the control parameters. You can choose to record quantity by flagging the **Record Quantity.** You can choose to lock the parameters for data entry for the cost center. For example, in this case, we have chosen to not record any **Actual revenues** or **Plan revenues** for the identified cost center.

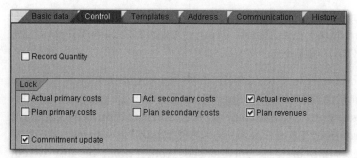

Figure 5.8 Control Parameters for Cost Center Master Data

Figure 5.9 shows you a view of the Templates tab and the information you will need to populate it with.

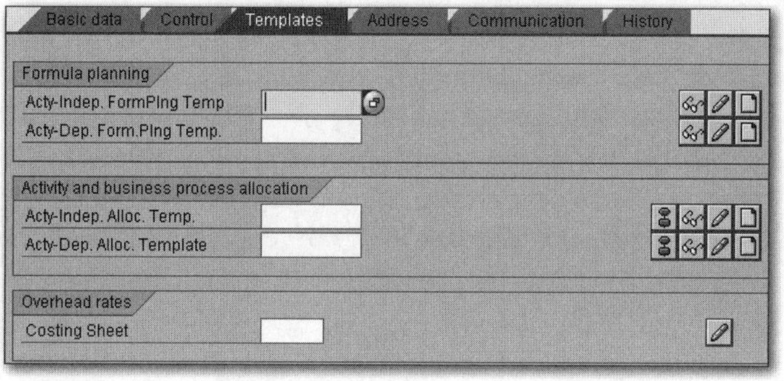

Figure 5.9 Cost Center Templates

This is where you can maintain the various cost models that are relevant for the formula planning, activity and business process allocation, and overhead rates. You will learn more about these in the planning Section 5.2.2. On the **Address** tab, you need to maintain the correspondence address details. The **Communication** tab has the data related to telephone numbers, fax number, and printer destination. The **History** tab has the details pertaining to any changes that were made in the cost center. Now that you understand the cost center, let's take a look at the cost center group.

Cost Center Group

Cost center groups allow you to depict your organizational structure by grouping similar types of cost centers in a group. The menu path to create, change or display the cost center group is **SAP Menu • Accounting • Controlling • Cost center accounting • Master data • Cost Center Group • Create/Change/Display**. The Transactions are KSH1/KSH2/KSH3.

Figure 5.10 shows you the cost center group **US01** that has been set up. You have the broad classification of **Sales, Marketing, Manufacturing, General & Administration, and Assessments**. Within **General & Administration,** you can have further cost center groups of **G & A Finance, G & A- Human Resources,** and **G & A- Legal**. The cost center is ultimately assigned to a cost center group because **10100**, defined in the previous step, is assigned to **Sales** cost center group **101**.

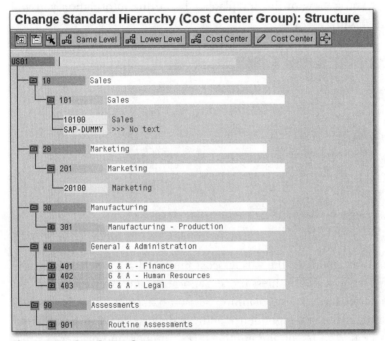

Figure 5.10 Cost Center Group

Cost Center Standard Hierarchy

By combining all the cost center groups together for an organization, you essentially build up your standard hierarchy. This includes all the cost centers for a given period that are active, which allows you to look at your organization from an overall Controlling perspective. The menu path is **SAP Menu • Accounting • Controlling • Cost center accounting • Master data • Standard hierarchy •**

Change/Display, and the Transactions are OKEON/OKENN. Figure 5.11 shows you the screen depicting your standard hierarchy **US01**. The maintenance screen is divided into four broad areas:

▶ The top-left pane is the search area where you can find a cost center or cost center group by search criteria.

▶ The bottom-left pane shows the results of your search.

▶ The top-right pane shows the overview area.

▶ The bottom-right shows the details for cost center sales that you have selected in the overview area.

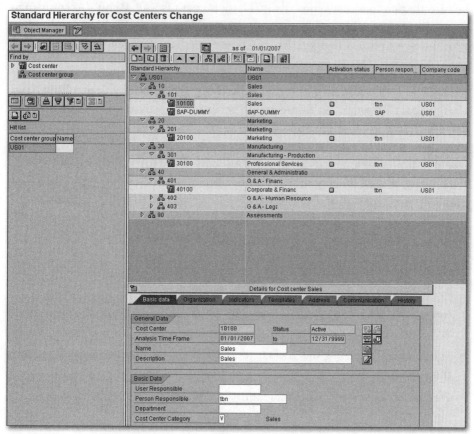

Figure 5.11 Maintaining the Standard Hierarchy of Cost Center

You can drag and drop the cost centers that you find in your search list into the overview pane. As you can see, this is similar to the cost center group structure that you saw in the previous step. However, the distinction is that every cost center should be part of the standard hierarchy, which is not the case with the cost center group.

Activity Type

This allows you to enter the different activities in cost center accounting for your Controlling area. You can also record quantities that are measured in activities. You can then use activities to set up your rules for allocation cycles. Activity types can be directly tied to a cost center also. The menu path is **SAP Menu • Accounting • Controlling • Cost center accounting • Master data • Activity Type • Individual Processing • Create/Change/Display/Delete/Display changes**. The Transactions are KL01/KL02/KL03/KL04/KL05.

Figure 5.12 shows you how to create an **Activity Type KWH** by **Controlling Area**. On the **Basic Data** tab, the **Name** and **Description** of activity type **KWH** is **Power KwH** and **Power Units consumed per month**, respectively. The activity unit is identified as **KWH**, whereas the cost center category is marked as **W**, which represents administration. You can also set **Allocation default values** for the activity type, which is used when you are running your allocation cycles. Let's take a look at the various types now:

- **ATyp category** identifies the method of activity quantity planning and activity allocation.
- **Allocation cost elem** is the secondary cost element that is used to allocate the activity type.
- **Actual qty set** allows you to manually enter the quantity that you want to receive in the receiver.
- **The Average price** flag means that the activity process for the activity remains the same throughout the year.
- **Plan quantity set** sets the plan quantity and prevents you from changing it during planning.

Create Activity Type: Basic Screen

Activity Type	KWH	Power KwH
Controlling Area	0001	Kostenrechnungskreis 0001
Valid From	01/01/1997	to 12/31/9999

Basic data | Indicators | Output | History

Names
Name	Power KwH
Description	Power Units consumed per month

Basic data
Activity Unit	KWH	Kilowatt hours
CCtr categories	W	

Allocation default values
ATyp category	1	Manual entry, manual allocation
Allocation cost elem	640100	IAA Production hours
Price indicator		
☐ Actual qty set	☐ Average price	
☐ Plan quantity set	☐ PreDistribFixedCosts	

Variance Values for Actual Allocation
Actl Acty Type Cat.		As in planning
Act. price indicator		

Figure 5.12 Create Activity type

You can lock this activity by marking the **Lock** indicator in the **Indicators** tab. **Output unit** and **Output factor** can be maintained in the **Output** tab. The **History** tab records any changes that happen for the activity type.

Activity Type Group

This allows you to group similar activity types together so that you can use these when executing transactions in cost center accounting. The menu path is **SAP Menu • Accounting • Controlling • Cost center accounting • Master data • Activity Type Group• Create/Change/Display**, and the Transaction is KLH1/KLH2/KLH3. Figure 5.13 shows that **KWH** and **FST** are grouped in the **POWER** activity group. You can use **Same Level** to add more activity types to this group. You can create subgroups and attach them to this main activity group by using **Lower Level**.

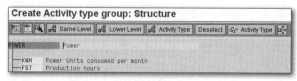

Create Activity type group: Structure

Same Level | Lower Level | Activity Type | Deselect | Activity Type

POWER	Power
—KWH	Power Units consumed per month
—FST	Production hours

Figure 5.13 Defining the Activity Type Group

Statistical Key Figures

Statistical key figures can be used to represent cost centers, activity types, orders, business processes, profit centers, or real estate objects. These are primarily used as parameters for running allocations such as distribution or assessment. The menu path is **SAP Menu • Accounting • Controlling • Cost center accounting • Master data • Statistical Key Figures• Individual Processing • Create/Change/ Display/Delete**. The Transactions are KK01/KK02/KK03. Figure 5.14 shows you the statistical key figure **MITARB** that represents **Employees**. You need to define a unit of measure for your statistical key figure. For units with no dimensions, **ST** can be used.

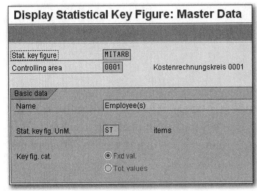

Figure 5.14 Display Statistical Key Figure

The statistical key figure can be defined as either **Fxd val.** (fixed value) or **Tot. values** (totals values). Fixed values are constant and are applied through the rest of the fiscal year. On the other hand, totals values are applied only for the fiscal period in which the allocation cycle is run.

Statistical Key Figure Group

Statistical key figures allows you to group statistical figures together so that they can then be used in cost center accounting transactions. Statistical key figures used as tracing factors can then be collected in groups during allocation processing. Follow **SAP Menu • Accounting • Controlling • Cost center accounting • Master data • Statistical Key Figure group• Create/Change/Display**. You can also use Transactions KBH1/KBH2/KBH3. Figure 5.15 shows you the statistical figure **EMPLOYEE** that has been created for statistical figure **MITARB**.

Create Statistical Key Figure Group: Structure

⊞ ⊟ ⊠ | 🔲 Same Level | 🔲 Lower Level | 🔲 Statistical Key Figure | Deselect | ⚡ Statistical Key Figure

EMPLOYEE | Employees

└─ MITARB Employee(s)

Figure 5.15 Create Statistical Key Figure Group

Resources

Resources are goods and services that are used in various business processes. Resources can be used to generate detailed planning activities for cost center planning, orders, and WBS elements. These provide you with one more layer of reporting other than cost elements. The menu path is **SAP Menu • Accounting • Controlling • Cost center accounting • Master data • Resources group • Create/Change/ Display**, and the Transactions are KPR2/KPR2/KPR3.

Figure 5.16 shows how to add a resource by **CO Area** (Controlling area). You need an identifier for **Resource Machine1** with **Valid From** and **Valid To** dates. The unit of measure also needs to be maintained. In the **Name** field, you can enter a general description of the resource. **Cost ele..** refers to the cost element for which the resource can be planned. If nothing is entered then the resource can be used across all the primary and secondary cost elements. **Plnt** specifies the logistics plant for which the resource can be planned.

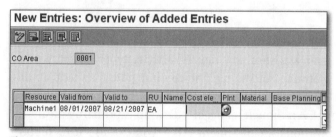

Figure 5.16 Create Resources

> **Note**
>
> Resource cannot be used for actual costs. It can only be used for planning. All other objects can be used for planning and actuals

5.2.2 Cost Center Planning

Cost center planning forms the part of short-term planning that typically has the time span of a fiscal year. In cost center planning, you enter the plan values for costs, activities, and statistical key figures for a particular cost center and planning period. This is done prior to you recording the actuals and allows you to compare the variances between actuals and plan values. Any large variances act as a signal to take corrective action and fix any business processes. Typically, organizations implement cost center planning initially, get in the rhythm of using the information, and then move on to complex Controlling initiatives. But this forms the building block of all your Controlling activities and is a strong prerequisite before you implement standard costing.

Cost center planning allows you to monitor, control, and plan the Controlling business structure by clearly outlining the goals and targets and then measuring them against it. Here you will learn to define the parameters for manual planning, resource planning, and formula planning and to recognize when you will use each type of planning.

> **Note**
>
> It is very important that the planning done in cost center planning lead to actionable items. If it is just a report spat out by the system and nobody does anything about it, then it is merely an academic exercise, carried out as a chore every month by accountants. Take action based on what you see.

In this section, you will learn about the key settings of manual cost center planning that can be used to plan statistical key figures, activity types, primary costs, secondary costs, budget planning, and so on. You can integrate manual planning with internal orders and PS as well. It is also possible to interface manual planning via the manager's desktop. Even though manager's desktop is primarily meant for administrative and organizational management tasks, you can use it to support manual planning functions in Controlling. You can customize the planning profiles and planning layouts per the manager's requirements, which allows them to perform routine manual planning tasks directly from the manager's desktop.

Let's see how we can perform manual planning using primary costs as a simple example.

Costing Variants

Defining costing variants is the first step towards enabling you to plan at a level below the cost element. For example, if you want to track the cost at each cost center by material rather than by the cost element, you need to define a costing variant. You can follow the menu path **IMG • Controlling • Cost center accounting • Planning • Manual Planning • Detailed Planning of Primary Cost Elements• Define Costing Variants**, or use Transaction OKY4.

Figure 5.17 shows a costing variant comprised of **Costing Type** and **Valuation Variant**. In our example, **Costing Type** has been chosen as Primary Cost Element, whereas the **Valuation Variant** is also chosen as Vltn-Primary Cost Element. These get defaulted and cannot be changed for Costing Variant PP. You can define a new costing variant to choose a different combination.

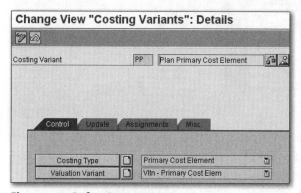

Figure 5.17 Define Costing Variant

Valuation Variant

This contains a strategy sequence for selecting prices from the material master. The menu path is **IMG • Controlling • Cost center accounting • Planning • Manual Planning • Detailed Planning of Primary Cost Elements• Define Valuation Variants**, and the Transaction is OKY8. Figure 5.18 shows you the valuation variants that can be selected for a costing variant. For our example, **013: Vltn-Primary Cost Elem** has been selected.

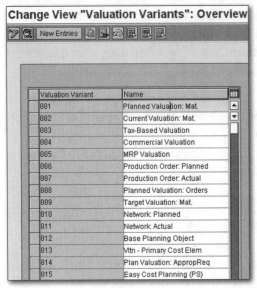

Figure 5.18   Define Valuation Variant

By double-clicking on this, you will reach the screen shown in Figure 5.19 where you can maintain the **Strategy Sequence** in which the material price will be determined. The identified sequence is shown under **Strategy Sequence**, which is the sequence in which the system searches for prices in the accounting view of the material master.

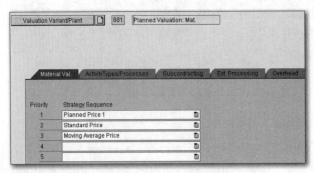

Figure 5.19   Define Valuation Variant Details

Now that you understand how you can set up an additional layer of reporting for cost center planning, let's take a look at resource planning, which can be used to support the cost center planning.

5.2.3 Resource Planning

Resource planning helps you carry out detailed planning by resources. This allows you to plan the cost elements from a resource perspective by identifying the quantity of resources consumed. You can maintain the price of the resources separately, which allows you to calculate the consumption value of the resources. Resource planning allows you to capture an activity whose origin is external rather than internal, which is used when you perform activity input planning. The posting in resource planning happens on the primary cost element.

Price Table definition

In this step, you need to either select the pricing table (that you want to use) or copy an existing table and modify it to define your own price table for resource planning. You can follow **IMG • Controlling • Cost center accounting • Planning • Resource Planning • Define Price Tables**, or use Transaction KPRI. The following standard tables are available:

- **132:** Price per Cost Center
- **136:** Price per Controlling Area
- **137:** Price per Country/Region
- **138:** Price per Company Code/Business Area
- **139:** Price per Profit Center

After defining your table, you need to configure your access sequence (AS) for resource planning.

Access Sequence Definition

This allows you to search valid prices for each condition type. The menu path to follow is **IMG • Controlling • Cost center accounting • Planning • Resource Planning • Define Access Sequence**. Figure 5.20 shows you the standard access sequence (AS) **K001: Cost Center Resources** that can be used for resource planning.

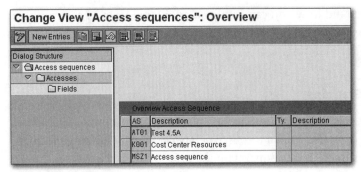

Figure 5.20 Define Access Sequence

If you select K001 and click on **Accesses**, you reach the next screen shown in Figure 5.21. Let's look at the tables that can be used for entering the resources by cost centers:

▶ **132:** Price per Cost Center

▶ **137:** Price per Country/Region

▶ **136:** Price per Controlling Area

As you can see, the AS moves from more specific prices (**By Cost Center**) to general prices (**By Controlling Area**). The **Exclusive** indicator stops any further searching if the correct combination of resource per prices has been found.

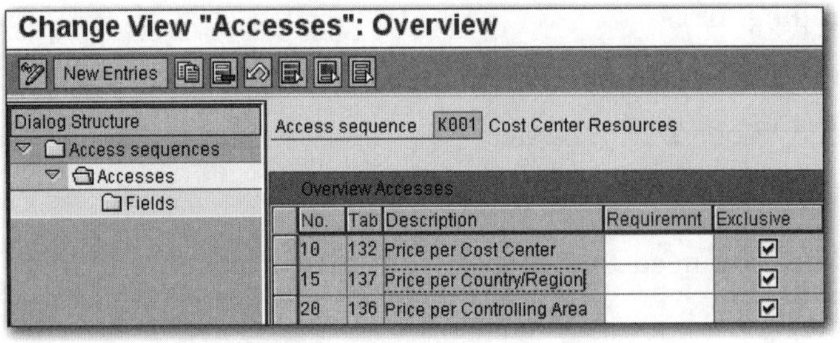

Figure 5.21 Define Access and the Table Sequence

By selecting **Table 132** and clicking on **Fields** you reach the screen shown in Figure 5.22. This identifies the parameters by which you can enter the resource prices. For our example, you can enter the resource prices by Controlling area, version, resource, and cost center.

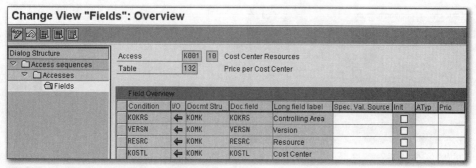

Figure 5.22 Identify the Fields and Tables

Condition Types

Condition types control how you enter the prices of resources: an absolute amount, percentage, manually specified price, or derived from the material master. Each condition type requires you to maintain the AS that allows you to search the system per your requirements. The menu path is **IMG • Controlling • Cost center accounting • Planning • Resource Planning • Define Condition Types** and the Transaction is KPR4. Figure 5.23 shows how to maintain the condition type for maintaining the resource prices. It ties the condition type (**CEl..**) **CQ01** with access sequence (**AcSq**) **K001**.

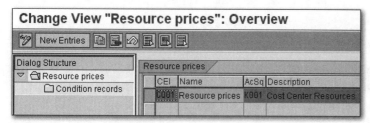

Figure 5.23 Define Condition Types for Resource Prices

By selecting the condition type **CQ01** and selecting **Condition records**, the popup shown in Figure 5.24 appears. Here you can need to choose an appropriate access from the AS. In our example, we chose **Price per Cost Center**.

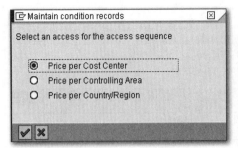

Figure 5.24 Choose the Access Sequence

On pressing Enter, you reach the next screen shown in Figure 5.25, where you will choose the **Controlling Area** "US01". If you want, you can further narrow it down with **Version** and **Fiscal Year**. **Application** and **Usage** get defaulted as **CQ** and **A**, respectively, and cannot be changed.

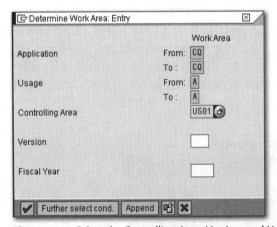

Figure 5.25 Select the Controlling Area, Version, and Year

Upon pressing Enter, you can maintain the resource prices in the next screen as shown in Figure 5.26. Here you need to maintain the **Resource**, **FrP** (Fiscal Period from which the Price is effective), **Cost Ctr** (Relevant Cost Center), **Amount**, **Curr.** (Currency of resource price), and **PrUn.** (Price unit).

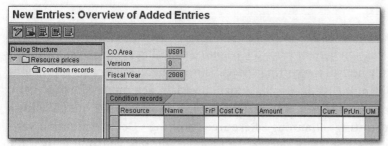

Figure 5.26 Enter the Resource Name and Prices

Costing Sheets

Costing sheets is the equivalent of the pricing procedure in purchasing and SD in cost center accounting. You specify the selected condition types you will be using and identify the sequence in which the condition types will be used for resource planning. The menu path is **IMG • Controlling • Cost center accounting • Planning • Resource Planning • Define Costing Sheets**. The Transaction is KPRC. Figure 5.27 shows you the **RES1: CO Resource Prices** costing sheet.

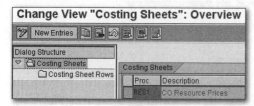

Figure 5.27 Define Costing Sheets

By selecting **RES1: CO Resource Prices** and clicking on **Costing Sheet Rows** you will reach the next screen as shown in Figure 5.28 where you can choose the steps of **Costing sheet Rows.** Here the condition type **Resource prices** is maintained as shown earlier in the condition type definition.

Change View "Costing Sheet Rows": Overview

	Step	Description
	10	Resource prices

Costing sheet RES1 CO Resource Prices

Figure 5.28 Define Costing Sheet Rows

Valuation Variant:

You learned earlier about valuation variant in 5.2.2. In this step, you will learn to define the valuation variant from the resource planning perspective. Valuation variant essentially houses the costing sheets. This is where it all comes together as far as resource planning is concerned. Valuation variant determines the processing sequence of the costing sheets. You can follow this menu path **IMG • Controlling • Cost center accounting • Planning • Resource Planning • Define Valuation variants**. The Transaction is KPR8. Figure 5.29 shows you the valuation variant for resource planning. The valuation variant needs to be defined by Controlling area. **C.Analysis** allows you to test whether your condition types are working properly. These should not be flagged in normal operations.

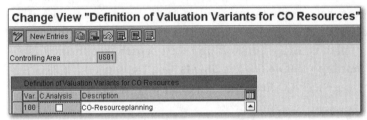

Figure 5.29 Define Valuation Variants

Assign Costing Sheets to Valuation Variants

In this step, costing sheets are assigned to the valuation variant. The menu path is **IMG • Controlling • Cost center accounting • Planning • Resource Planning • Assign Costing Sheets To Valuation Variants**. The Transaction is KPR8. Figure 5.30 shows how you can assign the costing sheet (**Proc.**) **RES1** to the valuation variant (**Var**) **100**.

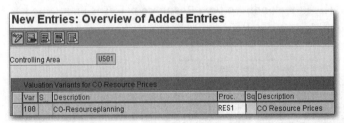

Figure 5.30 Assign Costing Sheets to Valuation Variants

5.2.4 Cost Center Budget Planning

Cost center accounting also allows you to set up your monthly budget by cost center. It allows you one more tool to plan in addition to primary cost planning and secondary cost planning. You can compare the actual values against the budgeted values and establish timely availability checks in case the budget is exceeded. This is where you will learn the process of budgeting from cost center accounting and the relevant settings that you will need to make to enable the budgeting process. The prerequisite to implementing budget planning is to create a budget profile.

Budget Profile

The budget profile allows you to establish the structure of budgeting in cost center accounting. The menu path to follow: **IMG • Controlling • Cost center accounting • Budget Management • Define Budget Planning Profiles**. The Transaction is OKF1. Figure 5.31 shows you the standard cost center budget profiles that are available. You can copy these to create your own profile that meets your unique requirements.

Figure 5.31 Define a Cost Center Budget Profile

Let's take a look at the **COST00** by double-clicking on the profile. This takes you to the Figure 5.32 where you can maintain the properties for the budget profile.

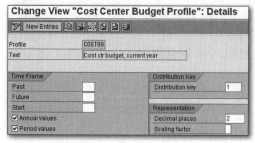

Figure 5.32 Detailing a Cost Center Budget Profile

Let's review these now:

▶ **Time Frame**
Here you can maintain the budgeting analysis period in the **Past** and in the **Future**. You can also maintain the start period for the budgeting process. In addition, by flagging **Annual Values** and **Period Value**, you can indicate that you want to perform budgeting for the whole fiscal year and for the individual fiscal periods, respectively.

▶ **Distribution Key**
This identifies how the values are distributed across the fiscal periods. The various options follow:

   ▶ **0:** Manual distribution.

   ▶ **1:** Equal distribution.

   ▶ **2:** Distribution as before.

   ▶ **3:** Distribution by percentage.

   ▶ **4:** Distribute according value to following no-value periods.

   ▶ **5:** Copy values to following no-value periods.

   ▶ **6:** Carry forward single value.

   ▶ **7:** Distribute according to number of days in period.

Decimal factors and **Scaling factors** control how the data will be shown when you output the data. After setting the budget profile, you can enter the cost center budgets using the transaction described next.

Entering Cost Center Budgets

Here you can enter the budgets against the cost centers. The menu path **SAP Menu • Controlling • Cost center accounting • Planning • Cost center budgets • Change/Display**. The Transaction is KPZ2/KPZ3. Figure 5.33 shows you the screen for entering the budget. You need to enter the **Profile** and **Cost Center** or **Cost center group** to enter your budget.

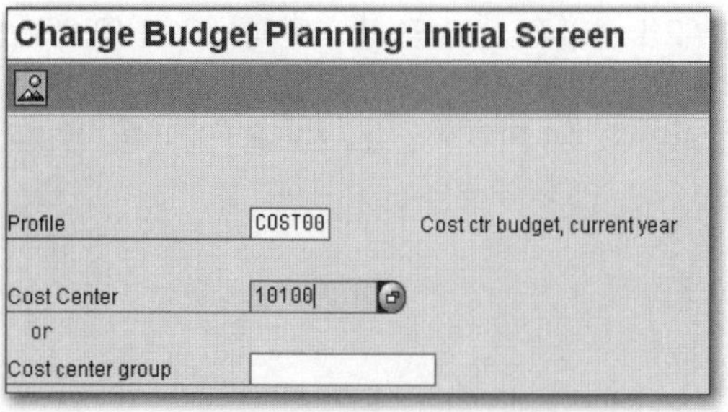

Figure 5.33 Change Budget Planning

Figure 5.34 shows how you can enter the budget for **Cost Center 10100, Control-ling Area US01**, and current year **2007 Period 1** as **10,000.00 USD**.

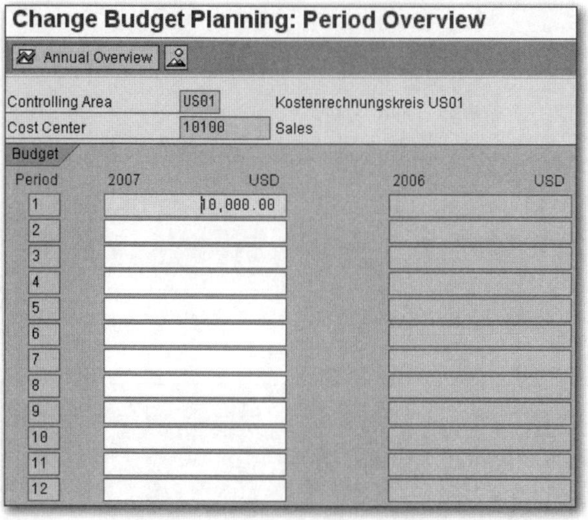

Figure 5.34 Enter the Budget by Period and Cost Center

This can then be compared against the actual values, and you can monitor if the budget is within the limits.

5.2.5   Commitment and Funds Commitment

This allows you to enter commitments in Controlling that happen only via Finan-cial Accounting. Funds commitment is used to reserve the budget in case you do not know how the actual transactions will happen and when, but you want to keep the budget as a reserve for forecasted revenues and expenses. Funds commitment can be used to reserve the budget for cost centers, internal orders, and projects. In this subsection, you will learn about the configuration setting of commitments and funds commitments. Figure 5.35 shows the process by which commitments and funds commitments are configured.

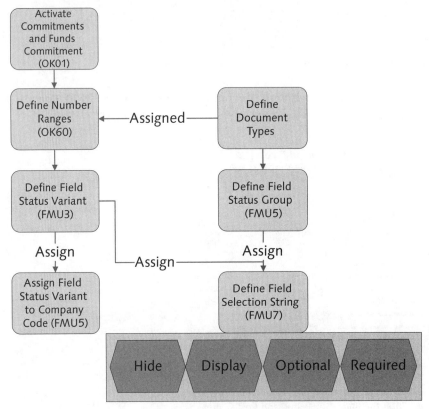

Figure 5.35 Configuring Funds Commitment in Cost Center Accounting

Let's examine this process now.

Activate Commitments Management

In this step, you activate the commitments management in the Controlling area. You already learned how to activate components in Chapter 4, so we will not go into the details. The menu path **IMG · Controlling · Cost center accounting ·**

Commitments and Funds Management • Activate Commitments Management • **Activate Commitments Management in Controlling Area**. The Transaction is OK01.

Define Number Ranges for Funds Commitment

In this step, you define the number range for document types to be posted in funds commitment. The menu path is **IMG • Controlling • Cost center account-ing • Commitments and Funds Management • Define Number Ranges for Funds Commitment**. The Transaction is OK60. Figure 5.36 shows you the screen for maintaining the number ranges for funds commitments documents. You need to click on **Interval** and then define the number ranges with the range of documents. The figure shows the number range (**No.**) **01** with the document numbers **From number 0000000001 To number 0099999999**.

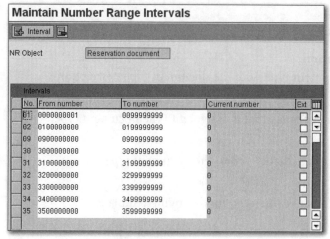

Figure 5.36   Define Number Ranges for Funds Commitment

Document Types for Funds Commitment

Now you need to define the attributes of document types. The menu path is **IMG • Controlling • Cost center accounting • Commitments and Funds Management • Define Document Types for Funds Commitment**. Figure 5.37 shows you the screen for maintaining the document types for funds commitment. This shows the broad heading of **Document Types for Earmarked Funds**.

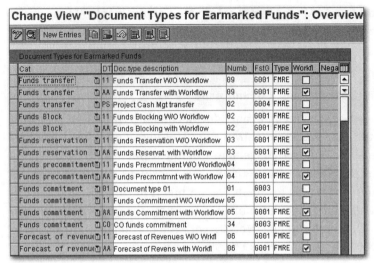

Figure 5.37 Define Document Types for Funds Commitment

The parameters for document types are:

▶ **DT/ Doc. type description**
This identifies the document type with the document type description.

▶ **Numb..**
This identifies the number range that is assigned to the document type.

▶ **FstG**
This is the field status group that is tied to the document type.

▶ **Type**
This is the group key for the earmarked fund copying template.

▶ **Workfl..**
This will indicate what the posting time will be when you request it via workflow.

▶ **Nega**
This indicates that only negative amounts are allowed in this document type.

Field Status Variant

In this step, you will define the field status variant. The field status variant, the field status group, and the field selection string allow you to control which fields are required, displayed, optional, or suppressed. You can follow this menu path for defining the field status variant: **IMG • Controlling • Cost center accounting • Commitments and Funds Management • Field Control for Funds Commitment • Define field status variant**. You can also use Transaction FMU3. Figure 5.38 shows the field status variant **FMRE** that has been defined for funds reservations.

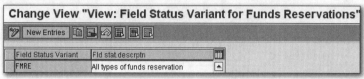

Figure 5.38 Define Field Status Variant

Assign Field Status Variant to Company Code

Now you need to assign this to your company code. To do this you will need to follow this menu path: **IMG • Controlling • Cost center accounting • Commitments and Funds Management • Field Control for Funds Commitment • Assign field status variant to company code**.

Define Field Status Group

This is the point at which you define the field status group. You will need to follow the menu path **IMG • Controlling • Cost center accounting • Commitments and Funds Management • Field Control for Funds Commitment • Define field status group**, or use Transaction FMU5. Figure 5.39 shows the **Field status group G001**.

Figure 5.39 Define Field Status Group

Define Field Selection String

Field selection string allows you to outline which fields will be hidden, display only, optional entry, or will be required entry. The menu path to follow is **IMG • Controlling • Cost center accounting • Commitments and Funds Management •**

Field Control for Funds Commitment • Define field selection string. The Transaction to be used is FMU7. Figure 5.40 shows you the screen for maintaining the **Field sel.** (field selection string) **MITTELRESER: Funds Reservations**.

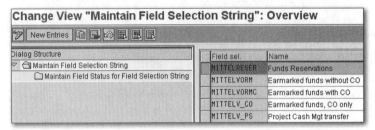

Change View "Maintain Field Selection String": Overview

New Entries

Dialog Structure
▽ 🗀 Maintain Field Selection String
　　🗀 Maintain Field Status for Field Selection String

Field sel.	Name
MITTELRESER	Funds Reservations
MITTELVORM	Earmarked funds without CO
MITTELVORMC	Earmarked funds with CO
MITTELV_CO	Earmarked funds, CO only
MITTELV_PS	Project Cash Mgt transfer

Figure 5.40　Define Field Status String

By selecting **MITTELRESER** and then clicking on **Maintain Field Status for Field Selection String**, you will see the screen shown in Figure 5.41. In this screen, you can maintain the individual fields such as **Fund** as **Opt. entry**; whereas **Funds Center** is a **Req. Entry**.

Change View "Maintain Field Status for Field Selection String": Overvi

Dialog Structure
▽ 🗀 Maintain Field Selection String
　　🗀 Maintain Field Status for Field Selection String

Field selctn string　MITTELRESER

Description	Hide	Display	Opt. entry	Req. entry
Reduction in local currency only	○	○	●	○
FM account assignment can be changed in follow-or	○	○	●	○
Item amount	○	○	●	○
Document approval status	○	●		
Order Number	●	○	○	○
Document date in earmarked funds document	○	●	○	○
Blocking indicator (header)	○	●		
Blocking indicator (Item)	○	○	●	
Value adjustment docmument: Description	○	○	●	○
Do not carry forward open documents in the fiscal ye	●	○	○	○
Usage may exceed reserved amount without limit	○	○	●	○
Funds precommitment document block	○	●		
Grouping Number for Earmarked Funds	○	○	●	
Completion indicator for earmarked funds documen	○	○	●	
Costs due on	●	○	○	○
Indicator: final completion (paid)	○	○	●	
Commitment Item	○	○	●	○
Funds Center	○	○	○	●
Functional Area	○	○	●	○
Reason for decision for workflow	○	●		
Fund	○	○	●	○
Grant	○	○	●	○
Business Area	○	○	●	○
Date of Last Change	○	●		
Last changed by	○	●		
Entry date	○	●		
Created by	○	●		

Figure 5.41　Define the Field Status Selection String

Assign Field Status String

In this step, you assign the field status string to the field status variant and the field status group. The menu path is **IMG · Controlling · Cost center accounting · Commitments and Funds Management · Field Control for Funds Commitment · Assign field status string**, and the Transaction is FMUN. Figure 5.42 shows you the screen where you can assign **Field selctn string** (field selection string) **MITTEL-RESER** to the **Field Status Variant FMRE** and **Field Status group G001**.

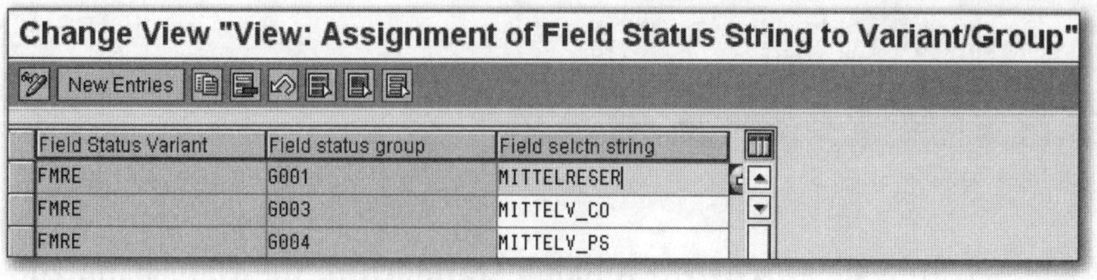

Field Status Variant	Field status group	Field selctn string	
FMRE	G001	MITTELRESER	
FMRE	G003	MITTELV_CO	
FMRE	G004	MITTELV_PS	

Figure 5.42 Assign Field Status String

5.2.6 Overhead Costing Sheets

Labor and material costs form one component of the overhead costs. Overhead costing is used to allocate the overhead. The basis of the overhead calculation is based on the primary cost elements that are classified as overhead costs. These costs can then be allocated by either percentage or quantity. Overhead costing can be allocated both on the plan data and actual values. Before you begin configuring the costing sheet, you need to define secondary overhead costing elements with the cost element type of 41.

Define Costing Sheet

As you learned earlier, the costing sheet pulls all the things together in one neat package. It integrates all the components of overhead costing. You can follow this menu path: **IMG · Controlling · Cost center accounting · Actual Costing · Period End Closing · Overhead · Define Costing Sheets**. Figure 5.43 shows how you can define a costing sheet for overhead costing. As you can see, **Costing Sheets** are identified in the right pane. You can, however, define the **Costing sheet rows** that have the all the details, including the base rate, overhead rate, and credit details by rows.

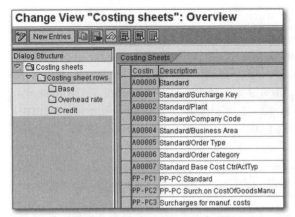

Figure 5.43 Define Costing Sheets

If you select the costing sheet (**Costin**) **A00000:Standard** in the right pane and click on **Costing sheet rows** on the left pane, then you will reach the next screen shown in Figure 5.44. As you can see, basic **Material** cost and **Material OH** (material overhead) have been maintained. These options are then added to **Wages and Salaries** along with the **Manufacturing OH** (manufacturing overhead) to give you the **Cost of goods manufactured**. This when added with **Administration OH** and **Sales OH** gives you the **Cost of goods sold.**

Row	Base	Overhea	Description	From To Row		Credit	
10	B000		Material				
20		C000	Material OH	10		E01	
30			Material usage......				
40	B001		Wages				
45	B002		Salaries				
50		C001	Manufacturing OH	40	45	E02	
60			Manufacturing costs...	40	50		
70			Cost of goods manufactured...				
80		C002	Administration OH			E03	
90		C003	Sales OH	70		E04	
100			Cost of goods sold...				

Figure 5.44 Define Costing Sheet Rows

You can maintain each of these components separately by identifying which cost elements pertain to which type of calculation **Base.** You have to click on **Base** to maintain these, which will take you to next screen as shown Figure 5.45. This screen shows you the **Calculation base** of **B000: Material**. Here the range of **Cost Elements 510000** and **510040** are maintained as pertaining to material costs.

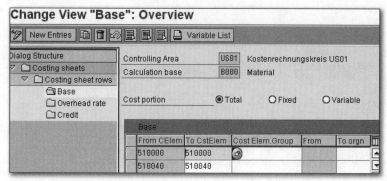

Figure 5.45 Define Base

Clicking on **Overhead rate** (Figure 5.45) brings up the screen seen in Figure 5.46, which is where the overhead rates can be maintained.

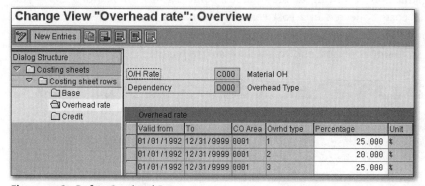

Figure 5.46 Define Overhead Rate

The **O/H rate C000: Material OH** has been maintained as 25% for **Ovrhd type 1**. You can maintain the following overhead types:

- **1:** Actual overhead rate.
- **2:** Planned overhead rate.
- **3:** Commitment overhead rate.

If you click on *Credit*, you can maintain the **Cost Element** and **Cost Center** for the credit element in the costing sheet as shown in Figure 5.47. Here the **Cost Elem. 840000** and **Cost Center** 30100 have been maintained for the **Credit E01: Credit Material**.

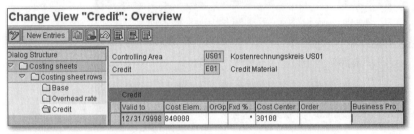

Figure 5.47 Define Credit in the Costing Sheet

5.2.7 Allocations

The allocation process in cost center accounting allows you to transfer costs across your organization according to predefined business rules. Allocations allow you to transfer costs collected in a cost center to receivers per a predefined rule and allow you to record costs as they occur. Then on the basis of business rules you can allocate them at period end to get an accurate picture.

> **Example**
>
> If you treat finance as administrative overhead, then you will want to record the employee wages and salaries initially in the finance cost centers because it would be highly inefficient to record this transaction when it actually occurs. However, at month end, you need to allocate the costs to business units per predefined rule such as number of employees in each department or number of financial transactions recorded for each department.

Allocation methods simplify data entry and are easy to use because these rules are defined only once and then the allocations are run at month end. There are two types of allocations:

▶ Assessment, which is used in allocating primary and secondary costs in cost center accounting and activity-based costing

▶ Distribution, which is used in allocating primary costs in cost center accounting

Table 5.2 highlights the difference between distribution and assessment allocation processes per important parameters. This will allow you to distinguish between these two processes.

Parameters	Assessment	Distribution
Original Sender Cost Element	Sender cost elements are assigned cumulatively and are not recorded in receivers.	Primary cost element is retained in the receiver.
Sender and Receiver Information	Controlling document contains the sender and receiver information.	Controlling document's line item has the sender and receiver information.
Utility	When you do not want to know the composition of costs. For example, you just want to know the overall administrative overhead applied and not the details such as the cost of writing paper, cost of cafeteria, and so on.	This is important if you want the details pertaining to individual costs that make up the composition of the overhead. For example, when you are trying to understand what percentage was sales administration versus sales marketing, which added as an overhead to the sales.

Table 5.2 Difference Between Assessment and Distribution

5.2.8 Year-End Closing

Now you will learn how to carry forward commitments to the next fiscal year. During year end, you can carry forward commitment values from purchase requisitions, open purchase orders and contracts, and fund commitments. You can follow **SAP Menu • Accounting • Controlling • Cost center accounting • Year End Closing • Commitment Carryforward**, or use Transaction KSCF. Figure 5.48 shows the selection parameters (**Cost center** range) for carrying forward commitments to the new fiscal year.

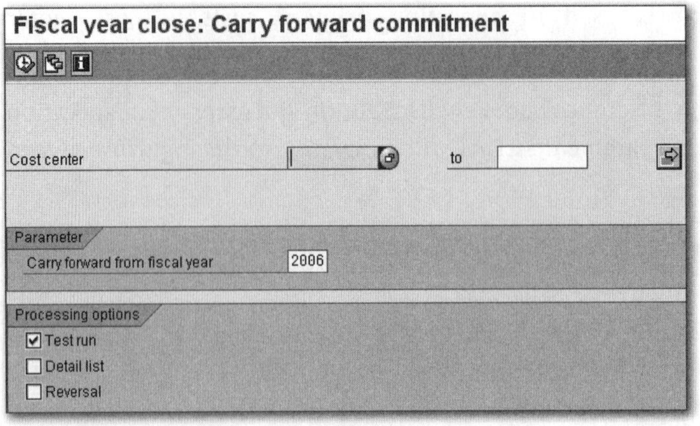

Figure 5.48 Fiscal Year Carryforward of Commitment

After you execute this transaction, the commitment will show up in the period 1 of the new fiscal year. You can execute this in **Test run** before you run it for real. If you want to reverse the commitment carryforward, you can check the **Reversal** flag and execute the transaction.

Let's move to profit center accounting now.

5.3 Profit Center Accounting

Profit center accounting (PCA) is primarily used for management-related reporting for internal purposes. It is primarily used for profit center reporting by either the cost of sales method or the period accounting method. Defining an organizational unit as a profit center entails that the unit is managed independently by a person who is responsible for the profit (revenue and costs) of the unit. There is always some confusion about the role of PCA and how it is different from other components such as profitability analysis and special purpose ledger. All these can be used to support profitability reporting, but they have different perspectives. The key differences are highlighted in Table 5.3.

Parameters	Profit Center Accounting	Profitability Analysis	Special Purpose Ledger
Focus	Internal	External	Can be both
Functional viewpoint	Responsibility and person focused	Market oriented	Primarily for accounting; not for reporting
Technology viewpoint	Special case of special purpose ledger	Based on a different concept altogether of characteristics and value fields	Very custom solution that can be used to enhance profit center accounting
Integration with operative accounting	Separate and independent of account assignment objects	Highly integrated. profitability segment is a key account assignment object	Can have its own account assignment objects

Table 5.3 Distinctions Among CO-PCA, CO-PA, and FI-SL

Figure 5.49 shows you the process for profit center accounting.

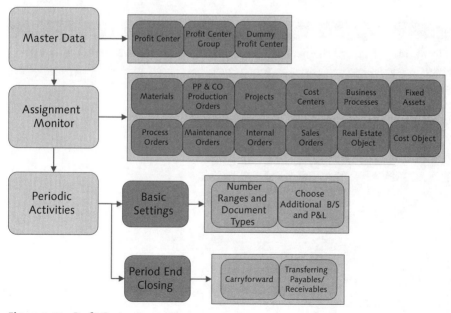

Figure 5.49 Profit Center Accounting

Let's start by learning about the profit center master data.

5.3.1 Profit Center Master Data

In this subsection, you will learn the key attributes of profit center and the process of creating a profit center.

Create Profit Center

Profit center represents the management-oriented organization unit that allows you to understand how costs and revenues are being managed within a responsibility area. The menu path is **SAP Menu• Accounting• Enterprise Controlling • Profit center accounting • Master data • Profit Center • Individual Processing • Create**, and the Transaction is KE51.

Figure 5.50 shows you the **Basic** data for profit center maintenance. Profit center is always created for a **Controlling Area US01**. You need to maintain the **Name**, **Long Text**, and **Analysis Period**. Initially, the **Status** will be **Inactive: Create** when you are first creating your profit center. You need to maintain the **User Responsible**, **Person Respons.**, **Department**, and **Profit Ctr Group.** Profit center group should be the part that conceptually is similar to the standard cost center hierarchy.

> **Note**
>
> With the introduction of the new GL, you can also maintain the **Segment** for a profit center.

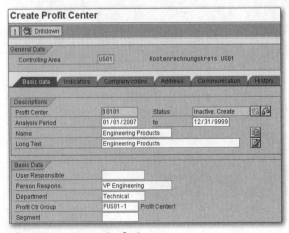

Figure 5.50 Create Profit Center

Clicking on the Indicators tab brings you to the screen shown in Figure 5.51.

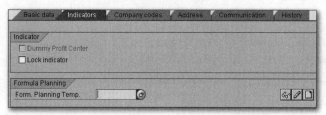

Figure 5.51 Indicators within the Profit Center Master

Here you can check **Lock Indicator** if you do not want any postings to happen to this profit center. You can also maintain the Formula Planning Template (**Form. Planning Temp.**). If you click on the **Company codes** tab, you will see all the **CoCd** (company codes) assigned automatically to the profit center, which belong to the Controlling area as shown in Figure 5.52 You can choose to dis-associate some company codes from the profit center if desired.

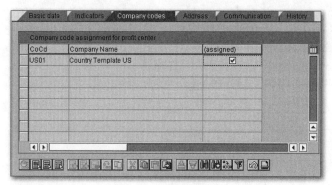

Figure 5.52 Company Code Assignment

Address and **Communication** details can be maintained in their respective tabs. The **History** tab displays all the changes that you make in the profit center.

Create Profit Center Group

You can create profit center groups to group similar profit centers that can then be used in various reporting tools. This allows you to create a hierarchical structure of profit centers. The process of creation is similar to the cost center group creation. The standard hierarchy of profit centers is a special case of profit center groups that contain all the profit centers of your organizations for a Controlling area. The menu path to follow is **SAP Menu • Accounting • Enterprise Controlling • Profit center accounting • Master data • Profit Center Group • Create**. You can also use Transaction KCH1.

Create Dummy Profit Center

You need to create a dummy profit center in profit center accounting so that if the system does not find any assigned profit centers for some objects, it posts the dummy profit center. This allows you to post the financial data and keep that in sync. The menu path is **IMG • Enterprise Controlling • Profit center accounting • Master data • Profit Center • Create Dummy Profit Center**, and the Transaction is KE59.

Tips

▶ Do not use the dummy profit center as a dumping ground for your postings to be allocated later. It can create a major month-end close headache, and it is never advisable to run allocation cycles from the dummy profit center.

▶ Dummy profit centers need to be thoroughly analyzed at month end and should be cleaned up every month. Otherwise, you will not get a true picture of your profitability by responsibility area.

Figure 5.53 shows how you can create a **DUMMY** profit center.

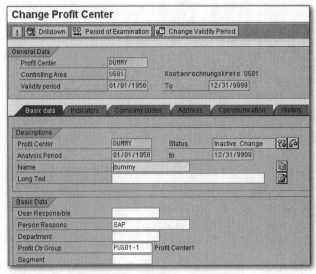

Figure 5.53 Define Dummy Profit Center

This covers all of the crucial aspects of master data in profit center accounting.

5.3.2 Profit Center Master Data Assignment Monitor and Assignments

Because profit center is a statistical cost object, you need to assign it to a real cost object so that the posting flows to a profit center. Other than assignment, you do not need anything else to post data to profit center accounting. The moment you assign the profit center, the data will come from all over the place.

> **Note**
>
> This assignment is an important event of discovery that allows you to understand how your organization is split up. It allows you to visualize your organization from the responsibility perspective at a granular level.

Assignment Monitor allows you to track and manage your assignments of profit center to other cost objects. The menu path is **SAP Menu • Accounting • Enterprise Controlling • Profit center accounting • Master data • Current Settings • Assignment Monitor**. The Transaction is 1KE4. Figure 5.54 shows you the Assignment Monitor. You can use this to find the cost centers that are not assigned to any profit center, cost centers that are assigned to profit centers, and profit centers that are not assigned to a cost center. You can do a similar exercise for all other cost objects.

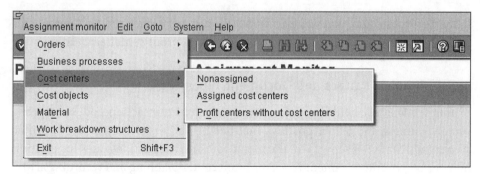

Figure 5.54 Assignment Monitor (1KE4)

Table 5.4 shows the transaction codes that allow you to assign profit centers to different cost objects.

Assignment of Profit Center to:	Transaction Code
Materials/Fast Assignment	S_ALR_87003972
Materials/Master	S_ALR_87004117
Sales Order/Substitution	S_ALR_87004101
Sales Orders	S_ALR_87004092
PP Production Orders	S_ALR_87004086
Process Orders	S_ALR_87004078
Controlling Production Orders	S_ALR_87004070
Cost Objects	S_ALR_87004060
Projects	S_ALR_87004296
Cost Center	S_ALR_87004478
Internal Orders	S_ALR_87004473
Maintenance Order	S_ALR_87004460
Business Processes	S_ALR_87004465
Real Estate Objects	S_ALR_87004447
Fixed Assets	S_ALR_87004454

Table 5.4 Transaction Codes for Profit Center Assignments

In the next subsection, you will learn about the number ranges and document types for local documents that need to be created only in profit center accounting.

5.3.3 Number Ranges and Document Types

In this section, you will learn the menu paths and transaction codes for profit center planning and actual postings that need to be made only in profit center accounting. Table 5.5 shows you the menu path and transaction codes for creating number ranges and document types for profit center planning and recording actual profit center postings that occur only in profit center accounting.

Area	Basic Setting	Menu Path	Trans.Code
Profit Center Planning	Maintain document types for local documents	IMG • Enterprise Controlling • Profit center accounting • Planning • Basic Settings for Planning • Maintain Document Types • Maintain Document Types for Local Documents	GCBA
Profit Center Planning	Maintain document types for rollup	IMG • Enterprise Controlling • Profit center accounting • Planning • Basic Settings for Planning • Maintain Document Types • Maintain Document Types for Rollup	GCBR
Profit Center Planning	Define number ranges for local documents	IMG • Enterprise Controlling • Profit center accounting • Planning • Basic Settings for Planning • Maintain Document Types • Define number ranges for Local Documents	GB02
Profit Center Planning	Maintain number ranges for rollup	IMG • Enterprise Controlling • Profit center accounting • Planning • Basic Settings for Planning • Maintain Document Types • Maintain number ranges for Rollup	GL20
Profit Center Actual	Maintain document types for actual postings	IMG • Enterprise Controlling • Profit center accounting • Actual Posting • Basic Settings: Actual • Maintain Document Types • Maintain Document Types for Local Documents	GCBX
Profit Center Actual	Maintain number ranges for local documents	IMG • Enterprise Controlling • Profit center accounting • Actual Posting • Basic Settings: Actual • Maintain Document Types • Maintain number ranges for Local Documents	GB02

Table 5.5 Defining Document Types and Number Ranges for Local Postings in Profit Center Accounting

In the next subsection, we will cover how you can map additional balance sheet and P&L accounts that cannot be mapped via a cost object to profit center accounting.

5.3.4 Choose Additional Balance Sheets and P&L Accounts

The goal for profit center accounting is to map each and every account to a profit center to be able to generate balance sheets by profit centers. This requires that balance sheet accounts that do not have a cost object assigned to them, such as AP, AR, inventory, work in progress, and so on, also require a profit center to be defaulted to these. Using the configuration settings detailed here, you can maintain the default profit centers for a range of balance sheet accounts. You can follow the menu path **IMG· Enterprise Controlling · Profit center accounting · Actual Posting · Choose Additional Balance Sheet and P&L account · Choose Accounts**. You can also use Transaction 3KEH.

Figure 5.55 shows you the screen where you can maintain the range of accounts (**Account from**) **100000** and (**Account to**) **20000** and the default profit center (**Def. PrCtr**) **10101**, which will get populated after you make this entry. This setting needs to be made for **CO Area US01**.

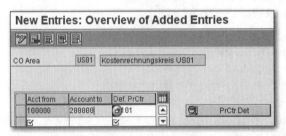

Figure 5.55 Choose Accounts

However, as you can see, that this is a very simplistic setting that might not be useful to organizations that have more complex rules for determining the profit center than just a direct GL assignment. You can use the derivation rules functionality to map the profit center in much more flexible fashion. The menu path **IMG· Enterprise Controlling · Profit center accounting · Actual Posting · Choose Additional Balance Sheet and P&L account · Derivation Rules for Finding the Profit Center**, or use Transaction 3KEI.

Figure 5.56 shows how you can set up default determination for the profit center. Based on your requirement, you need to identify the **Source Fields** as "RACCT: Account Number" and the **Target Fields** as "PRCTR: profit Center". If you want, you can add more source fields to this to make the determination more specific such as company code, plant, and so on.

Default assignment to a profit center: Change Structure of Rule Defini

Maintain Rule Values

Derivation rule

Step Description | Step Determination for Profit Center

Definition | Condition | Attributes

Source Fields

Name	Det	Name
RACCT		Account Number

Target Fields

Name	Det	Name
PRCTR		Profit Center

Figure 5.56 Define a Derivation Rule for Profit Center Determination

After you define the source fields, you can maintain the conditions that must be fulfilled for the system to determine the profit center on the **Condition** tab as shown in Figure 5.57.

Definition | Condition | Attributes

Only Execute If All Conditions Listed Below Are Met

Name	Det	Description	O	Value	Description

Figure 5.57 Define Condition for Derivation Rule

After defining the conditions, you can maintain the **Attributes** as shown in Figure 5.58 where you can **Issue error message if no value found.** You can also branch to additional steps if required.

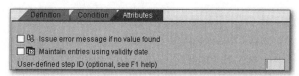

Definition | Condition | Attributes

☐ Issue error message if no value found
☐ Maintain entries using validity date
User-defined step ID (optional, see F1 help)

Figure 5.58 Define Attributes for the Derivation Rule

After you have set up the derivation rule, you can maintain the rule values by clicking on **Maintain Rule Values** button shown in Figure 5.56. This will allow you to enter the values for the profit center by the source fields as shown in Figure 5.59.

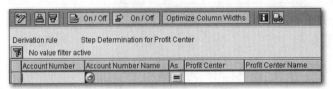

Figure 5.59 Maintain Rule Values for the Derivation Rule

5.3.5 Period-End Closing

If you have posted actual transactions in profit center accounting or have used additional accounts defined in Section 5.3.4, you need to carry forward the balances to the new fiscal year or new period within the same fiscal year. The menu path is **SAP Menu • Accounting• Enterprise Controlling • Profit center accounting • Actual Posting • Period End Closing • Balance carryforward**. The Transaction is 2KES.

Figure 5.60 shows you the parameters for carrying forward actual balances in profit center accounting to the new fiscal year. You need to enter the **Company Code** and **Carry Forward to Fiscal Year** and then execute the transaction. This will carry forward all of the balances to the new fiscal year for the company code.

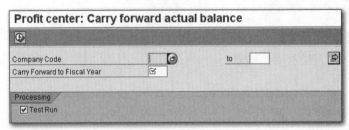

Figure 5.60 Balance Carryforward

The menu path is **SAP Menu • Accounting • Enterprise Controlling • Profit center accounting • Actual Posting • Period End Closing • Transfer Payables/receivables**, and the Transaction is 1KEK. Except for receivables and payables, all the transactions in profit center accounting are transferred in real time. However, you need to transfer payables and receivables periodically at the end of each period. This allows you to generate balance sheet on a profit center basis. Figure 5.61 shows you the screen that you can use to carryforward the payables and receivables to the profit center accounting for a fiscal period. You need to enter the **Period** and **Fiscal year**. The system automatically picks up all the company codes assigned to the Controlling area. You can choose to transfer all the **Line items** or just the balances.

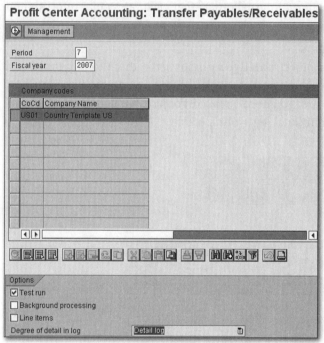

Figure 5.61 Transfer Payables/Receivables

5.4 Internal Order Accounting

Figure 5.62 shows you the process that underpins the discussion in this section. Internal order accounting is primarily used for managing small projects that need to be budgeted and managed independently, for example, setting up a marketing kiosk in a cultural event. "Internal orders" is a general term that can be used for overhead cost orders, capital investment orders, internal orders with revenues, accrual orders, and so on. Internal order accounting allows you to plan, collect, and settle the costs associated with a mini project in a process-oriented fashion, so it mimics exactly the way business operates. You can, however, use internal orders for multiple Controlling-oriented activities as listed here:

▶ **Orders for transient activities**
These are one-off mini projects that are not regular and occur for a limited time-frame, for example, sales kiosks at a SAP Financials conference.

▶ **Long-term cost monitoring activities**
You can also set up long-term internal orders that occur at regular intervals and allow you to establish a pattern, such as quarterly maintenance activities.

▶ **Statistical internal orders**
These are not true cost objects, and you cannot settle these to any other cost object. However, these allow you to track and report specific parameters of costs recorded. In this case, you need a real cost object, but you can use internal orders to provide an additional layer of reporting.

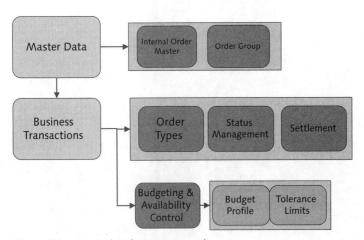

Figure 5.62 Internal Order Learning path

5.4.1 Internal Order Master Data

Internal order master data is used to monitor the costs. Following are the types of internal orders with their business significance:

▶ Overhead cost orders used for monitoring overhead costs that are recorded during internal order execution

▶ Investment orders that you know will be later converted to fixed assets

- Accrual orders used to track the costs incurred on a periodic basis
- Orders with revenues used to record revenues in internal orders

Internal Order

In this step, you will learn the key attributes of internal orders and the process of creating an internal order. The menu path to follow is **SAP Menu • Accounting • Controlling • Internal Orders • Master data • Order manager • Special Functions • Order • Create/Change/Display**, and the Transactions are KO04/KO01/KO02/KO03. An internal order needs to be created by Controlling area. Figure 5.63 shows you the screen for maintaining internal orders by using an order manager transaction. To define an internal order, you have to define an **Order type**. The figure shows how you can maintain the **Assignments** along with the **Description General Marketing Campaign**.

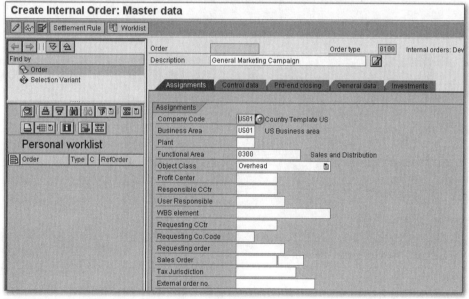

Figure 5.63 Internal Order: Assignments

In the order manager transaction, you can find your internal orders by maintaining the **Selection Variant** in the left pane and maintaining your **Personal worklist** that allows you to maintain your own range of internal orders. The various assignments that can be maintained are **Company Code, Business Area, Plant, Functional**

Area, Object Class, Profit Center, WBS Element, Sales Order, Tax Jurisdiction, and **External Order no.** Other fields that are not so obvious are explained here:

- **Responsible CCtr** (cost center) and **Requesting Co. Code**
  This is integrated with investment management, and the cost center and company code that you enter here will get transferred to the AuC.

- **Requesting Order**
  This is the order to which other orders can be assigned.

Figure 5.64 shows you the screen for maintaining the **Control data** for an internal order. While you are creating, the internal order, system will automatically set the **System status** as **CRTD**. The system status essentially controls which transactions are allowed for the internal order.

> **Note**
>
> From SAP ERP 5.0 onward, you can also define your **User status,** which you can change as desired.

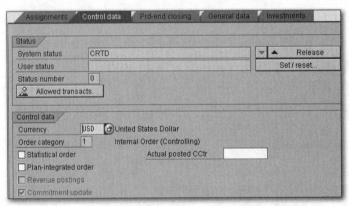

Figure 5.64 Internal Order: Control Data

In addition, you can maintain the following **Control data** parameters:

- **Currency**
  Here you can maintain the currency for the internal order.

- **Order category**
  This helps you define the technical properties of an order type. You need to pick an order category that pertains to internal order accounting.

▶ **Statistical order**
This flag marks the internal order as statistical.

▶ **Actual posted CCtr**
If you mark the cost center as statistical, then you can also specify which cost center will receive the real postings.

▶ **Plan-integrated order**
This flag is only checked if you are using integrated planning for internal orders.

▶ **Revenue postings**
This flag controls whether the internal order will allow revenue postings.

Figure 5.65 shows you the screen for maintaining the period-end closing activities. The following parameters can be maintained in this screen:

▶ **Results Analysis Key**
This is used to define the valuation of the internal order. For sales orders, you can use results analysis to valuate nonvaluated stock at month end and the stock that has been delivered but not invoiced yet. For projects, you can use the results analysis key to valuate work in progress.

▶ **Costing Sheet and Overhead Key**
These can be maintained for calculating the overhead, and the **Interest Profile** allows you to define the rules for calculating interest.

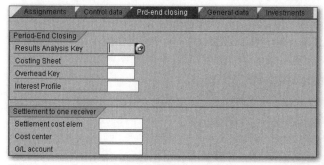

Figure 5.65 Internal Order: Period-End Closing

You can also define one receiver for the internal order by identifying the settlement cost element, cost center, and GL account. Figure 5.66 shows you the screen of general data related to administrative details pertaining to internal orders, such as estimated costs, processing group, work start, end of work, and so on.

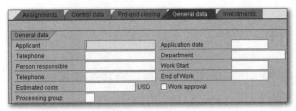

Figure 5.66 Internal Order: General Data

Figure 5.67 shows you the **Investments** tab for maintaining the investment-related data for an investment order.

Using this screen, you can tie the internal order to investment management, which will be discussed in more detail in Chapter 6. Here you can maintain the following parameters:

▶ **Investment profile**
This allows you to automatically create an AuC when creating an internal order and can help you default the asset class for the AuC and the depreciation simulation.

▶ **Scale**
This can be used to categorize your investments from the amount of capital required.

▶ **Investment program/Position ID**
This allows you to define the investment program and position ID within the investment program to which the internal order should be assigned.

You can define the **Asset class** and **Capitalization date** for assets that will be created from the settlement of this internal order.

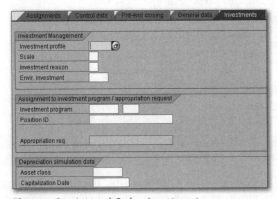

Figure 5.67 Internal Order: Investments

Now that you have learned to define an internal order, you will next learn about creating an order group.

Create Order Group

Order groups group together similar internal orders that allows you to perform reporting, settlement, and overhead calculation. The menu path is **SAP Menu • Accounting • Controlling • Internal Orders • Master data • Order Group • Create/Change/Display**. The Transactions are KOH1/KOH2/KOH3. Figure 5.68 shows how you can maintain an order group (**SALES_MKTG**) that has the orders pertaining to **SALES** and **MARKETING**. In the **Marketing** order group, the internal order **100000: General Marketing** has been assigned.

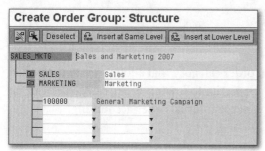

Figure 5.68 Create Order Group

5.4.2 Create Order Type

Order types allow you to classify internal orders. This is one of the main configuration activities that you need to make for defining the types of internal orders, and it ties all the other components of internal order customizing settings together. Order types define the order category, number range assignments, and control indicators that allow you to control the partner update, order classification, settlement profile, planning profile, budgeting profile, and status management. You can follow **IMG • Controlling • Internal Orders • Order Master data • Define Order Types**, or use Transaction KOT2_OPA. An alternate menu path is **SAP Menu • Accounting • Controlling • Internal Orders • Master data • Current Settings • Order Types**, or Transaction S_ALR_87005266.

Figure 5.69 shows you the different order types that come predefined in the system. You can copy these to create your own order type. The ones that we are more interested in for internal order accounting range from 0100 to 0400.

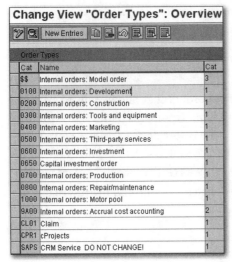

Figure 5.69 Define Order Types

Order types need to be assigned to an order category that allows you to define the multitude of attributes for an order type. The following order categories can be defined for an order type that is relevant for internal order accounting:

▶ **01** Internal Order (Controlling)

▶ **02** Accrual Calculation Order (Controlling)

▶ **03** Model Order (Controlling)

If you double-click on order type **0100: Internal orders: Development** in Figure 5.69, you can maintain the characteristics of the order type as shown in Figure 5.70. You can maintain the following parameters:

▶ **Number range interval**
Here you can choose the number range by clicking on the pencil icon.

▶ **Settlement profile**
This allows you to define the parameters that can be used for controlling the settlement process of internal orders. You will learn more about the settlement process in subsequent sections.

▶ **Planning profile/Execution profile/Budget profile**
This can be used to default the internal order planning, execution services, and budgeting parameters.

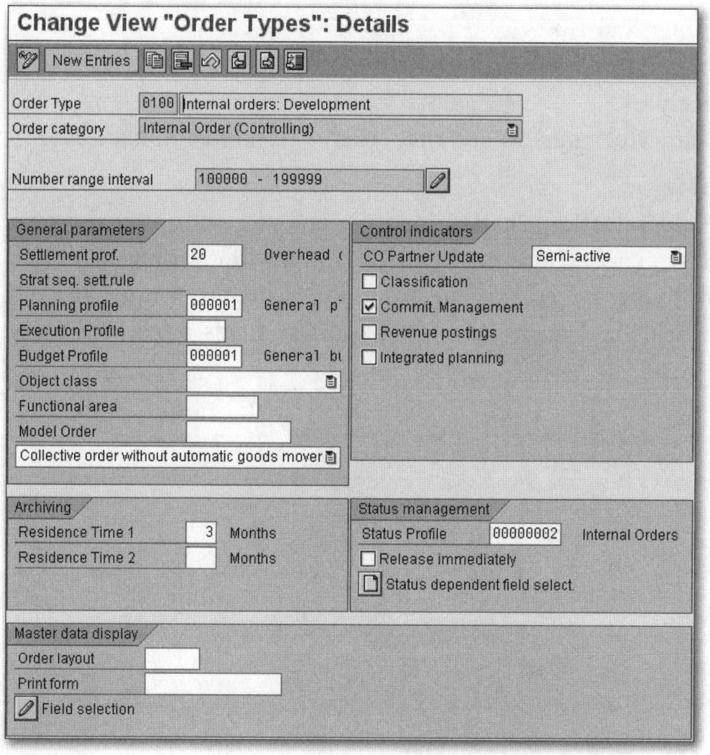

Figure 5.70 Order Type Configuration Details

▶ **Object Class**
This allows you to classify the cost objects as overhead, production, production, or profitability.

▶ **CO Partner Update**
This allows you to reduce the number of totals records by setting the indicator as **Semi-active** or **Not Active**.

▶ **Commit. Management**
This flag activates commitment management in Controlling for the internal order type.

▶ **Revenue postings**
This allows you to post revenues.

▶ **Integrated planning**
This flag activates integrated planning for the order type.

▶ **Status Profile**

This allows you to choose an appropriate status profile for an order type.

▶ **Release immediately**

If you check this indicator, then the internal order is released automatically.

▶ **Master data display**

If you click on **Field selection Change** (pencil icon) you will reach the next screen shown in Figure 5.71. Here you can maintain how the various fields will look when you are trying to create an internal order. Using this setting, you can get rid of useless fields and make the most important fields a required entry (**Req. entry**).

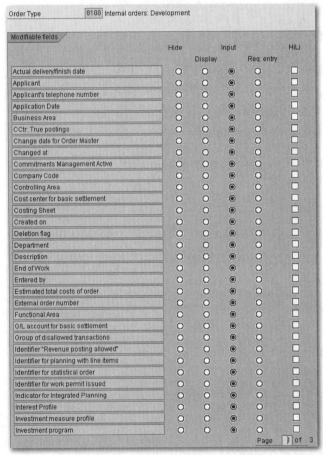

Figure 5.71 Field Selection by Order Type

5.4.3   Status Management

An internal order goes through its lifecycle starting from CRTD, which you saw when you created the internal order. Status management allows you to control how the status will move from CRTD to other statuses. This allows you to control the business transactions that are allowed for an internal order at any given moment.

After the order is created, you need to release the internal order for it to start receiving actual postings. This is done by setting the status as REL. When the order is in REL status, then most of the business transactions are allowed. After the internal order is done, you can mark it technically complete (TECO), which means that now you cannot perform actual postings on the internal order because the order has been completed. After you have settled the order, then you can mark it as settled and closed (SETC). This prohibits any further postings to the internal order.

You can achieve all this by maintaining the status profile, which allows you to define a status profile, assign it to a user status, and then control the transactions based on the user status. As you learned earlier in Section 5.4.2, status profile is assigned to the order type, which is maintained in the internal order master.

So let's discuss how to create a status profile. The menu path you can follow is **IMG • Controlling • Internal Orders • Order Master data • Status Management • Define Status Profiles**. The Transaction is OK02. Figure 5.72 shows you the screen where you can maintain the status profiles. It is best to create your own status profile by copying an existing status profile.

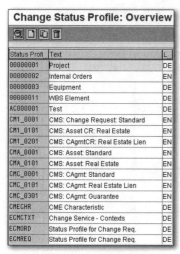

Figure 5.72   Define Status Profile

If you double-click on **Status Profi.. 00000002: Internal Orders**, then you will reach the next screen as shown in Figure 5.73. This has two statuses **LKD: Locked** and **PLIM: Write Plan Line Items**. The following parameters can be maintained:

▶ **Status**
This is the status number that determines the sequence in which user statuses are determined. The lower the number, the earlier the status gets activated. The status numbers need to be arranged in an ascending order.

▶ **Status/Short Text**
This is the identifier with the details for the status of the internal order as it completes its lifecycle.

▶ **Init. St**
If you set this indicator, then the internal order will get created with this status initially.

▶ **Lowest**
This lowest status number determines the status number that the next status should have.

▶ **Highest**
This helps you in checking whether the old statuses can be deactivated after you have moved to a new status number. The system compares the new status number against the number in the field, and if it is less than that, then it deactivates the previous status.

▶ **Posit**
This identifies the line in which the allowed status will get displayed.

▶ **Priority**
This identifies the status display priority at a particular position.

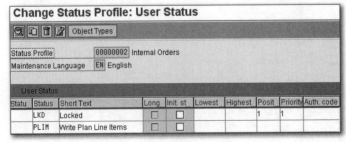

Figure 5.73 Define Status and Properties of Status

If you double-click on **LKD**, you will reach the next screen shown in Figure 5.74.

Change Status Profile: Transaction Control

| Status Profile | 00000002 Internal Orders |
| Status | LKD Locked |

Transaction Control

| Business Transaction | Influence | | | | Next action | | |
	No influ	Allowed	Warning	Forbidd.	No acti	Set	Delete
Planning stat. key figures	O	O	O	⦿			
Release	O	O	O	⦿	⦿	O	O
Remove deletion flag	O	O	O	⦿	⦿	O	O
Repost costs	O	O	O	⦿			
Repost revenue	O	O	O	⦿			
Revoke technical completion	O	O	O	⦿	⦿	O	O
Settlement account assignment	O	O	O	⦿			
Technically complete	O	O	O	⦿	⦿	O	O
Total cost planning	O	O	O	⦿			
Unit costing (planning)	O	O	O	⦿			
Unlock	O	O	O	⦿	⦿	O	O
Variance calculation	O	O	O	⦿	⦿	O	O

Figure 5.74 Define Status Profile: Status= Locked

Here you can maintain which **Business Transactions** do not have any influence (**No influ..**), which are **Allowed**, which will give you a **Warning**, and which are Forbidden (**Forbidd**). So this is essentially the field status group for statuses. However, you can maintain the following subsequent actions for each business transaction:

▶ **No acti …**
This ensures that the transaction does not have any impact on the status.

▶ **Set**
This ensures that if this transaction is executed on an internal order, then the corresponding status (LKD, PLIM, etc.) will be set up.

▶ **Delete**
If you indicate this indicator for any business transaction, then the corresponding status to which the business transaction is tied is deleted.

Figure 5.75 shows you the details of the PLIM.

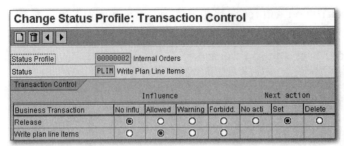

Figure 5.75 Define Status Profile: Status = Write Plan Line Items

This allows you to configure that if the **Release** business transaction occurs, then you can write plan line items because PLIM will become active.

> **Note**
>
> Business transactions are tied to user status, which is tied to status profile, which is tied to order type, which needs to be maintained in the internal order master.

Now that you understand the integrated master data and business transaction mapping of internal orders, you will learn about the internal order settlement process.

5.4.4 Internal Order Settlement Process

The basic purpose of an internal order is to receive the costs during its life and then pass on these costs to one or more receivers as part of the settlement process. Fixed assets, cost centers, and profitability segments can be valid receivers for an internal order settlement. There are two types of settlements that are possible in an internal order:

▸ **Settlement to one receiver**
This can be a straightforward settlement process based on the master data that is maintained in the internal order. Note that this functionality was not available prior to SAP ECC 5.0.

▸ **Comprehensive settlement**
This follows the standard settlement process in which you can settle costs to multiple receivers with different distribution rules.

In this section, you will also learn to maintain the settlement profiles that are again assigned to the order type, which is then assigned to the internal order master.

The menu path is **IMG • Accounting • Controlling • Internal Orders • Planning • Manual Planning • Maintain Settlement • Maintain Settlement Profiles**. Figure 5.76 shows you the screen for maintaining the **Settlement profile: 50: Investment measure**.

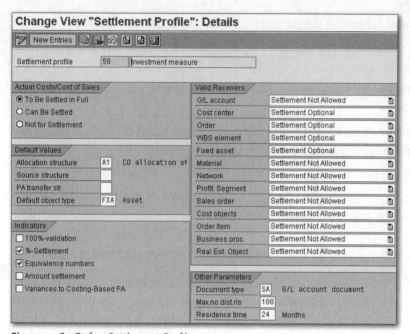

Figure 5.76 Define Settlement Profile

The settlement profile essentially controls the following aspects:

▶ **Actual Costs/Cost of Sales**
You can choose to define whether the settlement needs to be done in full (**To be Settled in Full**), or whether the settlement is even allowed (**Not for Settlement**). Choosing **Can Be Settled** allows you to settle partially.

▶ **Default values**
You can maintain the default values of the allocation structure, source structure, profitability transfer structure, and default object type.

▶ **Valid Receivers**
Here you can specify the valid receiving objects that are not allowed and that are optional.

▶ **Other Parameters**

Here you can specify the document type, the maximum number of distribution rules, and the archiving time before you archive the posted settlement documents.

▶ **Indicators**

This lets you define the various indicators for the settlement profile.

▶ **100%-validation**: The system checks whether the cumulative percentage against all the receivers total to 100%.

▶ **% Settlement**: This allows you to use percentages in the settlement distribution rules.

▶ **Equivalence numbers**: You can use equivalence numbers (e.g., 2:3:3) to distribute the settlement amount to receivers.

▶ **Amount settlement**: This allows you to directly enter amounts to receivers.

▶ **Variances to Costing-Based PA**: This indicator allows you to transfer the variances to costing-based profitability analysis during the settlement process.

5.4.5 Budgeting and Availability Control in Internal Order Accounting

You learned about the budgeting process in Chapter 4 where we discussed setting up an original budget and then updating the budget using budget supplements and returns. This makes up the current budget against which the system will check whether the actual postings have exceeded the budget. Let's now move on to learning about maintaining budget profiles and availability controls.

Maintain Budget Profile

A budget profile allows you to control whether availability control needs to be active and which budget values need to checked. For internal order accounting, the budget check happens against the current budget, whereas for PS, the check can be either against the current or released budget. You can follow **IMG • Accounting • Controlling • Internal Orders • Budgeting and Availability control • Maintain Budget profiles • Maintain Budget Profile**, or use Transaction OKOB.

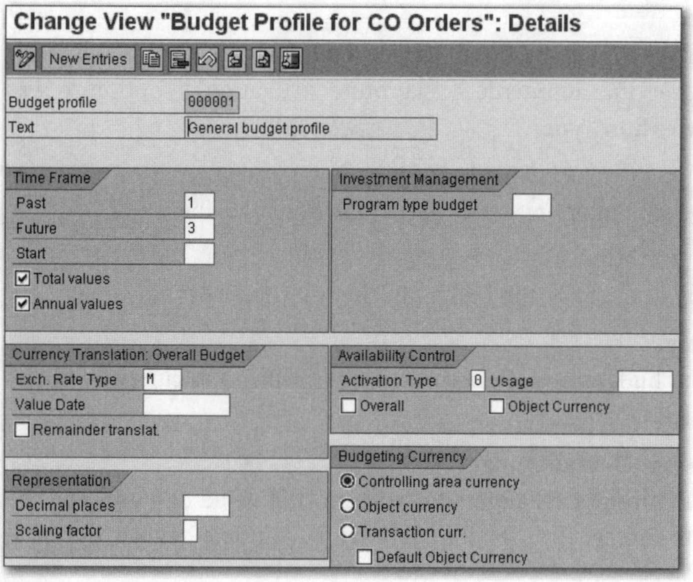

Figure 5.77 Maintain Budget Profile for Internal Order

Figure 5.77 shows you the screen for maintaining a budget profile. The following parameters can be maintained in a budget profile:

▶ **Time Frame**

Here you can maintain the number of years you can go back in the **Past** and forward in the **Future**. The field **Start** allows you to specify how many years from the current year the budgeting process should start. **Total values** and **Annual values** allow you to plan/budget total and annual values, respectively.

▶ **Program type budget**

This allows you to specify the program position. If you enter a program position here, then the internal order need to be assigned to one of the program positions for it to be relevant for budgeting.

▶ **Activation Type**

This setting forms the core of the availability control by specifying the following activation types:

  ▶ **0:** Cannot be activated.

  ▶ **1:** Automatic activation with budget allocation.

  ▶ **2:** Background activation.

185

▶ **Usage**
Here you can enter tolerance in **% of Assigned to Budgeted value**, which if exceeded will trigger the automatic background activation if option **1** was selected as the **Activation Type**.

▶ **Overall**
This counts the overall budget rather than just the annual values.

▶ **Object currency**
This forces the system to check the budget in the internal order currency.

▶ **Budgeting currency**
You can specify your budgeting currency as the Controlling area currency, object currency, or transaction currency.

▶ **Currency Translation: Overall Budget**
Here you can maintain the exchange rate type and the value date that will be used to translate the internal order transactions to compare against the budgeted value.

After you have defined the availability control, you need to define the tolerance limits, which will tell the system what to do in case the budget is exceeded.

Define Tolerance Levels for Availability Control

Tolerance levels allow you to define the system checks that happen when the budget reaches a certain percentage. The menu path is **IMG • Accounting • Controlling • Internal Orders • Budgeting and Availability control • Define Tolerance Levels for Availability control**. Figure 5.78 shows you the screen for maintaining the tolerance limits for availability control, which allows you to define the following parameters:

▶ **COAr**
This identifies the Controlling area.

▶ **Prof**
This represents the budget profile that was defined in the previous step.

▶ **Tr. Grp**
The **++** signs indicate that all the transaction types are selected for defining the tolerance limits.

▶ **Act**

This identifies the action that needs to be taken on the basis of the three parameters:

   ▶ **1:** Warning.

   ▶ **2:** Warning with mail to responsible person.

   ▶ **3:** Error message.

▶ **Usag.**

Here you can specify the tolerance levels, which if crossed, trigger the action identified in the previous step.

▶ **Abs. Variance**

This allows you to specify the maximum permissible absolute variance beyond which the action will be triggered regardless of the usage percentage defined in **Usag....**

COAr	Prof.	Text	Tr.Grp	Act.	Usag	Abs.variance
0001	000001	General budget profile	++	1	30.00	
RECO	000001	General budget profile	++	1	90.00	
REOB	000001	General budget profile	++	1	90.00	
SG01	000001	General budget profile	++	1	90.00	

Figure 5.78 Define Tolerance Limits for Availability Control

5.5   Summary

In this chapter, you were introduced to the basic methods of budgeting, such as cost center budgeting and internal order budgeting. Cost element accounting, cost center accounting, profit center accounting, and internal order accounting are typically the Controlling components that are easiest to implement and which also give you the maximum value out of implementing SAP ERP. This is because you can tailor your Controlling processes in more detail as you build on these to determine your optimal Controlling structure.

In this chapter you also learned about setting up primary and secondary cost elements and cost element groups in cost element accounting. Then you were introduced to cost centers, cost center groups, cost center standard hierarchies, activity types and groups, statistical key figures, and groups and resources definition. These form the basis of performing cost center planning manually, and were followed by a detailed explanation of the resource planning concept in cost center accounting. These planning tools will get you rolling quickly to get your planning process ironed out. The various features and functionalities that make your planning exercise faster and more customized to your needs were also discussed.

From learning about budgeting in cost center accounting to learning about cost center planning and implementing funds commitment, you gained an understanding of capturing future funds being locked up, providing you with an overall commitment exposure for your organization.

You also learned about the overhead costing sheets that can be set up in cost center accounting to calculate the cost of goods manufactured. Cost center accounting was followed by profit center accounting where you learned about profit center, profit center group, and the assignment of profit centers to other cost objects. You also learned about some of the key settings that allow you to create a balance sheet by profit centers. We then proceeded to key period-end and fiscal year-end closing activities for profit center accounting.

Internal order accounting allows you to track short-term projects that need to be capitalized or transferred to other cost objects. You learned about the internal order master and internal order group. This was followed by an explanation of order types and how this relates to status management and the settlement process in internal order accounting. Finally you learned about activating budgeting and availability control.

In Chapter 6, you will learn about budgeting using investment management.

PART III
Budgeting

Outline your capital budgeting process, learn about various types of budgeting and make full use of your budgeting process to positively impact your business.

6 Optimizing Capital Budgeting Using Investment Management

In this chapter, we will dive into the Investment Management process highlighting the integration points inherent in the capital budgeting process. The capital budgeting process is one of the most important but least understood functions for an organization as far as Controlling is concerned. Often, capital budgeting is confused with planning. The focus of this chapter is to help you clearly outline your capital budgeting process in the system and then use the same to drive change in your organization. Organizations have multiple types of budgeting that need to be performed. Broadly these can be classified as follows:

▶ **Capital budgeting**
This typically involves a longer time frame for the budgeting process. The rule of thumb is that it spans multiple budgeting years. And you have to perform a discounted cash flow analysis before embarking on a project like this. You need to understand your return on investment and then track the actuals against these over a period of time. For example, if you have a business transformation SAP ERP implementation project that spans multiple years and aims to completely replace your entire legacy system, it should be tracked like a capital project.

▶ **Revenue budgeting**
This typically involves budgeting for operating expenses by fiscal year. So you need to budget for activities that need to be accomplished in one fiscal year. A typical example for revenue budgeting is budgeting for payroll over a fiscal year, which feeds into the operating budget, which then feeds into the overall revenue budget for the year.

Both capital and revenue budgeting can be implemented in SAP in multiple ways. However, the best practice to implement capital budgeting is *Controlling-Investment Management* (CO-IM), whereas revenue budgeting can be implemented using *Funds Management* (FI-PS-FM).

> **Note**
>
> SAP Funds Management is typically implemented by public sector organizations, which have clearly define budget outlays for one fiscal year because they have to match the taxes collected with the expenditures made during the year. Most other organizations choose to budget and track big expenditures in Investment Management and use cost center accounting to plan and budget revenue expenditures.

You will learn how to implement Investment Management to optimize your budgeting process. It is also important to understand that in some of organizations, the budgeting process is not ingrained and is more of an after the fact reporting. So you can use SAP ERP budgeting tools to drive the proactive understanding of the budgeting process and emphasize the importance of sticking to the budget.

6.1 Investment Management

The Investment Management component provides you with functions related to planning, investment, and financial processes for capital investments and projects. In this chapter, we will be covering the Investment Management functionality highlighting the integration with other components and a typical business scenario for Investment Management. The broad Investment Management lifecycle is shown in Figure 6.1, which begins by creating the appropriation requests to plan your capital budgeting process and ends at the capitalization to a fixed asset.

You first need to perform **Planning** to understand the detailed aspects of the investment idea. At this point, you are not sure whether you want to implement this, so it is idea generation and brainstorming where you identify the areas of improvements and incorporate suggestions that will allow you to improve your organizational capabilities. All of these suggestions for improvements can be captured as an **Appropriation Request**. The appropriations requests identified are then sent for approval. Note that all the appropriation requests are part of an overall **Invest-**

ment Program for your organization, which allows you to prioritize the appropriation requests that are received. If the appropriation requests are approved, then these are included in the formal **Budgeting** process. At this point, you will be creating the associated **Investment Measures,** which can be an internal order or a WBS element. And you will be budgeting the amount that will be needed to complete the investment measure.

After the **Execution** for the investment measure starts, you will start recording the **Actuals** in the **Investment Program.** This allows you to track your actuals against the budget. On successful execution of the investment measure, you need to perform the **Settlement** of costs to either a specific cost center and then subsequently capitalize the same to **Fixed Assets** if applicable.

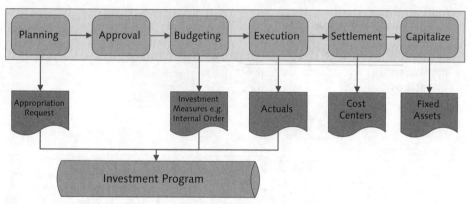

Figure 6.1 Investment Management Lifecycle

Now that we are clear about the Investment Management lifecycle, let's take a look at the learning path for understanding Investment Management and how it can be used to map your organization's budgeting process in the system (see Figure 6.2).

First, you will learn how to define the **investment program,** which includes master data, planning, and budgeting attributes. This represents the overall organizational structure under which you will be executing Investment Management planning and budgeting in SAP ERP. Next, you will learn about the process of creating an **Appropriation request,** which also needs to be planned and approved. Finally, you will learn about **investment measures,** which need to be planned and budgeted for. You will also learn the process of investment measure settlement and capitalization.

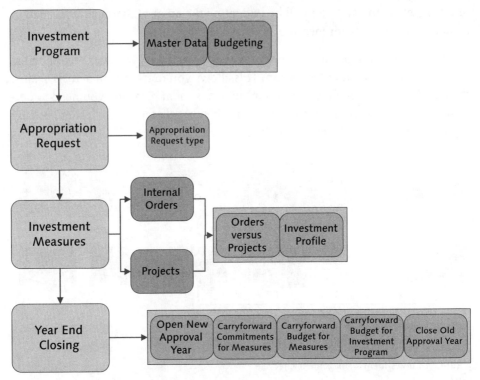

Figure 6.2 Investment Management: Structure

6.1.1 Investment Program: An Introduction

The investment program provides you the framework for capital budgeting processes. Using the investment program, you can map your organization in a hierarchical structure to track and manage your investment measures. This structure is completely independent of your enterprise structure (company code, plants, etc.) and allows you to flexibly design a structure that meets your capital budgeting requirements. You can plan and assign your investment measures to the investment program structure allowing you to perform integrated investment planning. Investment program allows you to track, monitor, and oversee the complete Investment Management process.

As long as you keep the fiscal year and the currency of the investment program the same, you can also map the same investment program node to investment measures from multiple company codes and controlling areas. However, for investment programs that span multiple controlling areas, you need to create at least one top-level program position for each controlling area to enable mapping of lower-level program positions.

The investment program definition allows you to do both top down budgeting and bottom up planning processes in tandem. The investment measures such as WBS elements, maintenance orders, and orders can only be assigned to the lowest investment program node. This allows you to plan at the lowest level and then allocate the budget top down based on the plan numbers.

This is most useful to the CFO of the organization to track the capital allocation in your organization and optimally assign the capital to varying business needs. The reporting functionality available in Investment Management allows you to track the use of the capital investment programs and assess whether you are getting the required benefit from your investments.

In this section, you will learn how to define your investment program master data and perform planning and budgeting functions for your investment program. First, you will learn how you can define your organization's investment program.

6.1.2 Investment Program: Master Data

Investment program master data represents the hierarchical structure that is used to map your organizational hierarchy as far as capital budgeting is concerned. In this subsection, you will first learn how to define a program type and then to create an investment program position for a particular program type. The program type allows you to classify your investment programs and can be used to control various aspects of an investment program. The menu path to follow is **IMG • Investment management • Investment Programs • Master Data • Define Program Type**.

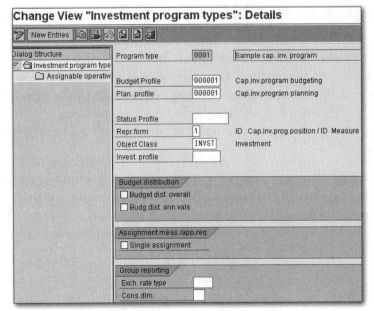

Figure 6.3 Define Program Type

Figure 6.3 shows how you can create a **Program type 0001: Sample cap. inv. program** along with the various parameters, which allow you to control various aspects of capital budgeting process. The following parameters need to be maintained for a program type:

▶ **Budget Profile**
You learned about the budget profile in Chapter 5. This can be used to control the various parameters of budgeting if you are using budget control system.

▶ **Plan. profile**
This can be used to control the various parameters for cost planning.

▶ **Status Profile**
This can be used to control how the status of investment measures flow from created to released to technically complete, and so on.

▶ **Repr.form**
Representative form can be used to indicate whether the investment program position is represented by text or by a position ID, which is the posi-

tion ID for program positions, WBS element ID for WBS elements, and internal order number for internal orders.

▶ **Object Class**
The object class for Investment Management is investment. Other options are overhead, profit analysis, and production.

▶ **Invest. profile**
This controls the automatic creation of assets under construction (AuC) when you create an internal order or WBS element. You can also control the asset class for AuC and depreciation simulation.

▶ **Budget dist. overall**
Flagging this indicator ensures that the assigned measures can never receive more overall budget than available on program position to which they are assigned. This is a consistency check and allows you to make the budget structure more binding.

▶ **Budg. dist. ann. vals**.
This is another control which ensures that the system will check whether the assigned measure's budget got exceeded in comparison with the particular fiscal year's distributable budget.

▶ **Single assignment**
If you check this flag, then investment measures and appropriation requests could only be assigned to one program position.

▶ **Exch. rate type**
This allows you to specify the exchange rate type that should be used for currency translation in Investment Management.

▶ **Cons. dim**.
There you can maintain the consolidation dimensions (companies, profit center, business area, etc.) if you are transferring group shares from EC-CS to investment program reporting.

You can choose to assign appropriate objects by clicking on **Assignable operative** in the left pane. This will take you to the next screen as shown in Figure 6.4. Here you can maintain the **ObTyp** (Object types) that will be applicable for the **Program type**. In this case, the **Appropriation requests, Orders, and WBS elements** are maintained as relevant for the **Program type 0001: Sample cap. inv. program**.

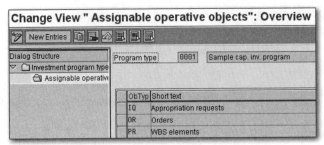

Figure 6.4 Assign Operative Objects to Program Types

Now that you know how to define a program type, let's take a look at an investment program that gets created in the system based on the preceding settings.

The investment program definition contains general specifications for the entire investment program such as program type, approval year, and so on. The menu path for the investment program definition is **SAP Menu • Accounting • Investment Management • Programs • Investment Program Definition • Create**. The Transaction is IM01.

Figure 6.5 shows how you can create an investment program definition (**Inv. program**) **ABC_Inc: ABC Inc Capital Budgeting 2007**. Here you need to maintain the following parameters:

▶ **Approval year**
This is the year in which the investment program has been approved. You can approve investment measures that span multiple years, but the approval year for them will be this year.

▶ **Program type**
This identifies the program type that was defined in the previous step.

▶ **Budg.dist annl**
This indicator was discussed earlier when defining program type and gets defaulted here. Otherwise, you can maintain this only for a particular investment program.

▶ **Budg.catg**.
This allows you to categorize your budgets and is only needed if you need to capitalize partial components of the investment program.

▶ **Assignment Lock**

After you have identified the relevant measures for the investment program, you can lock any new assignments of investment measures.

▶ **Person respons**.

Here you can identify the persons responsible for the investment program.

▶ **Fi. Year Variant**

This allows you to define the fiscal year variant that identifies the start and finish of your budgeting cycle. Typically this is kept as same to the controlling area.

▶ **Default lang.**

This field allows you to define the default language.

▶ **Currency**

Here you can maintain the currency that is relevant for the investment program

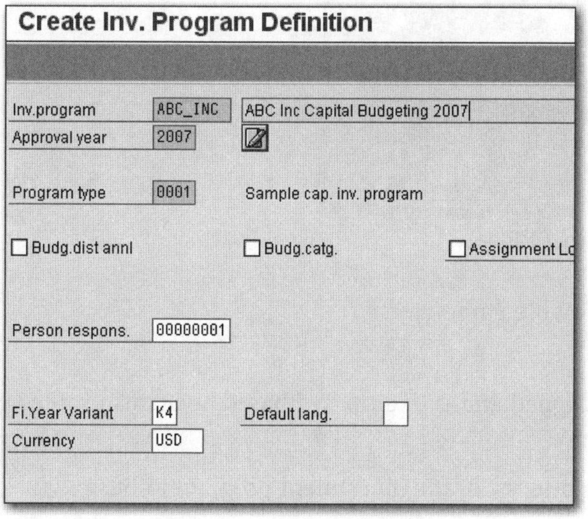

Figure 6.5 Creating Investment Program Definition

After you have created the investment program, you should create the investment program position. The investment position allows you to generate the hierarchical structure that is applicable for the investment program defined earlier. The menu path is **SAP Menu • Accounting • Investment Management • Programs • Investment Program Position • Create**, and the Transaction is IM11. Figure 6.6

shows the screen for creating a top level **Position ID (ABC: ABC Inc Position)**, which is tied to an **Inv. program (ABC_INC: ABC Inc Capital Budgeting 2007)** and **Approval year 2007**.

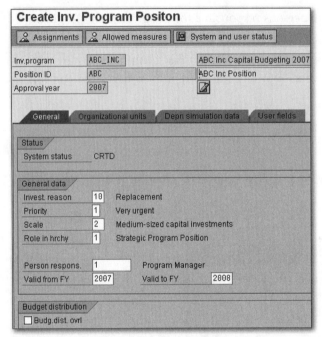

Figure 6.6 Create Investment Program Position

Here you can maintain the following parameters:

- **System status**
  This automatically gets assigned and is determined based on status profile.

- **Priority**
  Here you can identify the priority of the investment program to business.

- **Scale**
  This helps you categorize the types of investments according to size and scope and is used primarily for reporting purpose.

- **Role in hrchy**
  This allows you to identify whether the investment position is restricted to local ERP planning or can be extended to SEM: Integrated Investment planning. The following indicators can be maintained: empty, for when the

investment position is restricted in the local ERP system; **1**, which allows you to maintain budget and plan values in local system; However, the plan values can be overwritten by integrated investment planning; and **2**, which identifies that the program position is a totals position only. This means that the plan and budget values occur at lower levels and are rolled up to the program position.

▶ **Person respons.**
Here you can maintain the person responsible for the investment position.

▶ **Valid from FY/Valid to FY**
These specify the validity periods of the fiscal year for which the position ID is relevant.

▶ **Budg. dist. ovrl**
This is the consistency check that ensures the budget available to assigned measures is never more than the position budget.

You can maintain the allowed values of some of these fields using the configuration menu path shown in Table 6.1.

Allowed Value Definition	Menu Path/Transaction Code
Define Person Responsible	IMG • Investment management • Investment Programs • Master Data • Allowed Values for Certain Master Data Fields • Define Person Responsible/OPS6
Define Reasons for Investment	IMG • Investment management • Investment Programs • Master Data • Allowed Values for Certain Master Data Fields • Define Reasons for Investment
Define Priorities for Investment	IMG • Investment management • Investment Programs • Master Data • Allowed Values for Certain Master Data Fields • Define Priorities
Define Scale for Investment	IMG • Investment management •Investment Programs • Master Data • Allowed Values for Certain Master Data Fields • Define Scale
Define User Fields	IMG • Investment management • Investment Programs • Master Data • User Fields • Enter Short Descriptions for User Fields/ OITM1

Table 6.1 Allowed Values for Certain Master Data Fields

If you click on the **Organizational units** tab, you will reach the next screen shown in Figure 6.7. Here you can make the assignments to enterprise structure units such as **Controlling area, Profit Center, Cost Center, Company, Company Code, Business Area, Bal. sheet item, Plant, Plant section**, and **Functional Loc..** In addition, you can maintain the **Currency** of the investment position along with the country where the investment (**Ctry of invest.**) is being made. These assignments allow you to build an Investment Management budget in line with your organizational requirements.

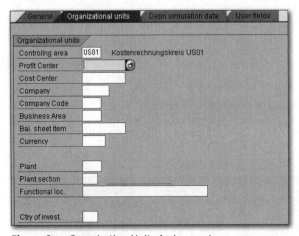

Figure 6.7 Organization Units Assignment

If you click on the **Depn simulation data** tab, you will reach the next screen shown in Figure 6.8. Here you can maintain the default **Asset Class** and **Capitaliz. date** for the AuCs that automatically get created from the investment measures.

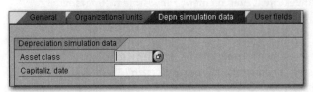

Figure 6.8 Depreciation Simulation Data

Now in Investment Management, you might want to create your own fields that can be used for various reporting tasks. These can be maintained by using the menu path shown in Table 6.1. And if you click on the **User fields** tab, then you can maintain these values as well. System allows you to maintain up to 12 user fields with 4 text fields, 2 quantity fields, 2 amount fields, 2 date fields, and 2 flags that can be named as per your requirements (see Figure 6.9).

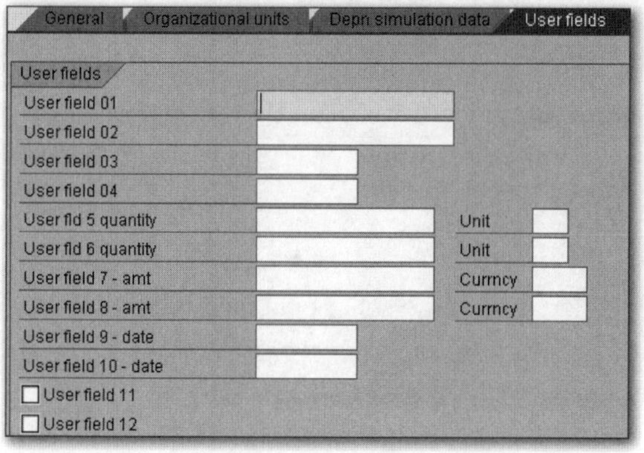

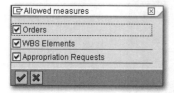

Figure 6.9 Define User Fields

If you click on the **Allowed measures** button in Figure 6.6, you can select the investment measures that are relevant for the investment program assignments. You will see the screen shown in Figure 6.10 where you can select **Orders, WBS Elements,** and **Appropriation Requests** as relevant for investment program.

Figure 6.10 Identify Allowed Measures

If you click on the **System and user status** button in Figure 6.6, you can display the relevant status for the investment program position as shown in Figure 6.11. When you are creating the investment position, the status will be **CRTD: Created**.

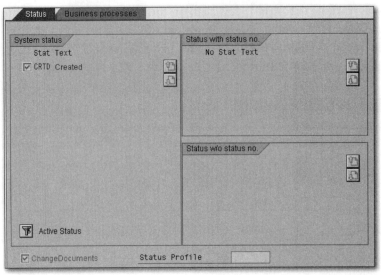

Figure 6.11 System and User Status

If you select **Business processes**, you can see the list of processes that can be done on the program position for the status CRTD, as shown in Figure 6.12. Here you can perform all the transactions except Revoke status **Released** and **Unlock** because these appear in red. Anything that is in green can be processed.

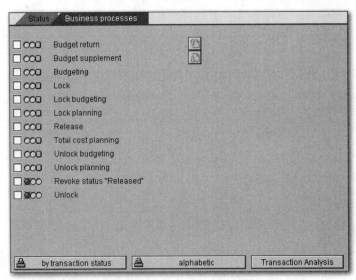

Figure 6.12 Business Processes Allowed

If you click on the **Assignments** button shown in Figure 6.6, you can maintain the assignments of the investment measures by choosing the relevant investment measure as shown in Figure 6.13.

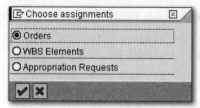

Figure 6.13 Choose Orders to be Assigned to the Position

If you click on **Orders** in Figure 6.13, you can select the orders that should be assigned to the investment position as shown in Figure 6.14. Here you can also maintain the **Perc.assn** (percentage assignment) that is applicable for the investment program position. This allows you to split one investment measure to multiple positions. The **Old** indicator automatically checks itself off, if the investment measures have been carried forward from a previous approval year during fiscal year change.

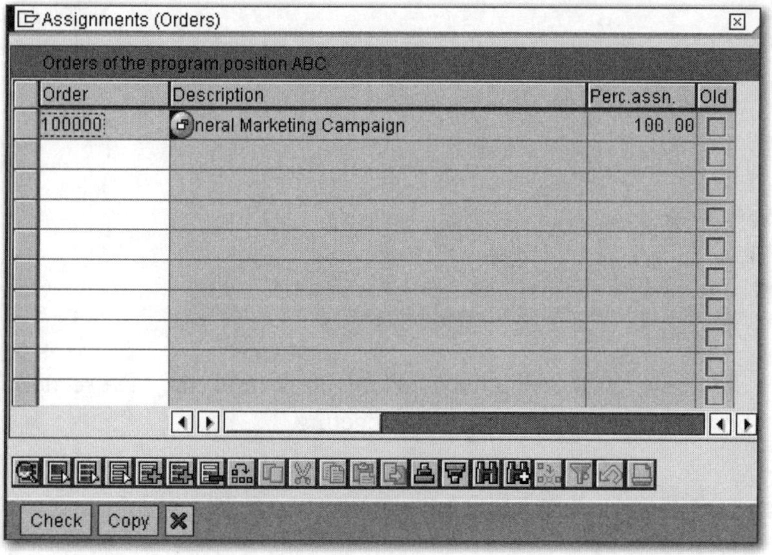

Figure 6.14 Assign Orders to Positions

> **Note**
>
> Orders, WBS elements, and appropriation requests can only be assigned to the lowest node.

As we discussed earlier, you can maintain the investment program structure in a hierarchical fashion. The menu path is **SAP Menu • Accounting • Investment Management • Programs • Master Data • Investment Program Structure • Change**, and the Transaction is IM22. Figure 6.15 shows how you can create your investment program structure by geography. In this example, a **Top** position of **ABC** and then subpositions of **EUR, ASIA, NA and SA** were created. They were then mapped to the individual countries within the region.

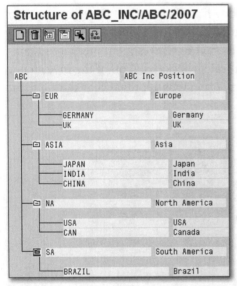

Figure 6.15 Creating Positions Within the Investment Program

This completes the master data set up for your organization. In the next section, you will learn about the investment program budgeting.

6.1.3 Investment Program: Budgeting

Budgeting is typically done after you have completed the planning phase and obtained an approval of appropriation measures. The key distinction between budgeting and planning is that budgeting is more binding than planning. During budgeting, the rolled up plan values are corrected and then distributed top down as the budget based on your organizational realities.

To speed up the budgeting process, you can adopt the planned values and then increase or decrease them by a percentage using the revaluate function. This allows you to quickly come at the baseline budgeting process and then you can tailor these numbers to what you want by increasing or decreasing individual budgetary allocations.

This overall budget is then assigned to the investment measure so that you can control how closely the budget is tied to the actual postings and make the comparison between budgeted and actual values on an ongoing basis.

In this subsection, you will learn how to integrate the budget profile with Investment Management for all the investment measures and for specific investment measure of projects:

▸ **Assign Budget Profile to Program Type**
Since the budget profile controls the parameters for budget and program type controls the parameters for Investment Management, they need to be married together, so that Investment Management can talk to budgeting process.

Menu Path
IMG • Investment management • Investment Programs • Budgeting in Program • Assign Budget Profile to Program Type

Figure 6.16 shows how you can assign the budget profile (**Profile**) "000001" to investment program type (**Pro...**) "0001". This establishes the link between budgeting and investment measures that belong to the program type.

Change View "Assign planning profile to inv. prog. type"

	PTyp	Name	Profile	Text
	0001	Sample cap. inv. program	000001	Cap.inv.program planning

Figure 6.16 Assign Budget profile to Investment program type

▸ **Specify program type in budget profile for projects**
You can also assign the program type to a budget profile by individual invest-

ment measure. This is especially useful if you want to define different budget profiles for projects and internal orders. In this step, you will learn how to assign the project program type to budget profile. The menu path is **IMG • Investment management • Investment Programs • Budgeting in Program • Budget Distribution to Investment Measures • Control of Project Budget via Budget Profile/Program Type • Specify Program Type in Budget Profile**. The Transaction is OIB3. Figure 6.17 shows how you can specify the **Budget program type 0001** in budget profile (**Prof.) 000001**.

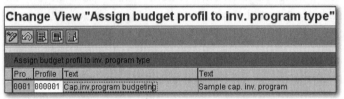

Figure 6.17   Specify Program Type in Budget Profile

▶ **Store budget profile in project profile**
In this step, you can assign the project profile to the budget profile. This defaults the budget profile whenever you create a project with the project profile. You can change this while creating your projects. Follow **IMG • Investment management • Investment Programs • Budgeting in Program • Budget Distribution to Investment Measures • Control of Project Budget via Budget Profile/ Program Type • Store Budget Profile in Project Profile**. Figure 6.18 shows how you can store the budget profile in project profile.

Change View "Assign Budget Profile to Project Profile"

Prj.Prf	Description	Profile	Text
0000001	Standard project profile	000001	General budget profile
0000002	Investment projects	000001	General budget profile
CPR0001	cProjects-PS Integration (Automat. Case)	000001	General budget profile

Figure 6.18   Store Budget Profile in Project Profile

6.1.4   Appropriation Requests

An appropriation request is the initial request that helps in the bottom up planning of the investment program, which is the overall investment plan of your organization. By using appropriation requests, you can indicate the wish list of capital projects or orders that need to be initiated. Appropriation requests identify the return on investment, documents pertaining to the request, and any additional details that need to be attached to the same. It is possible to achieve the business goal by multitudes of options that can be indicated in the appropriation request as well. You cannot record the actual postings in appropriation requests. After the appropriation request is approved, it can then be transferred to one of the investment measures: orders or projects. And then you can record the actuals against the internal order. So appropriation requests cannot be used for budgeting, but they form an important input to the budgeting process. Let's discuss the appropriation request first.

6.1.5 Appropriation Request Types

The appropriation request type controls most of the functionality that is achieved using appropriation requests. It allows you to classify the appropriation request and houses all the control parameters for master data maintenance and planning of appropriation requests. The menu path is **IMG • Investment management • Appropriation Requests • Master Data • Control Data • Maintain Appropriation Request Types**.

SAP ERP comes preconfigured with two appropriation types: "1" for orders and "2" for projects. Figure 6.19 shows the screen that details the attributes of the **1: Orders as investment measures** appropriation request. The following parameters can be maintained:

▶ **App. Reqst type**
This is the identifier of the appropriation request type.

▶ **Number range**
Here you can maintain the number range according to which appropriation requests will be generated.

▶ **Control**
Using this you can control how the appropriation requests will be created. You can tie it to an internal order, a WBS element, or as an independent number assignment using number ranges defined in the previous bullet.

▶ **Cost/Rev. planning prof.**
Here you can maintain the cost and revenue planning profiles that need to be used for the appropriation request type.

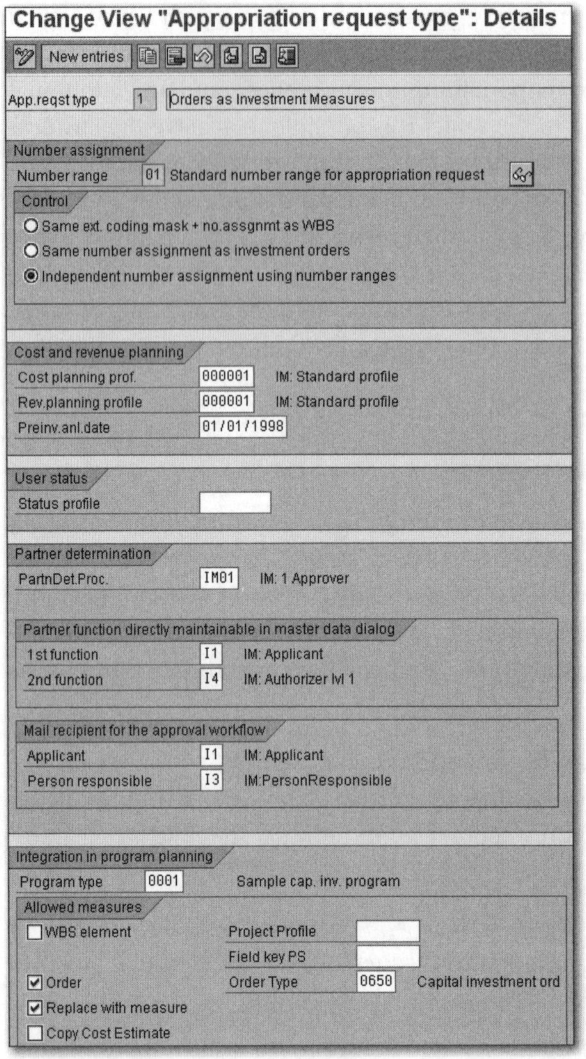

Figure 6.19 Details of Orders as Investment Measures

▶ **Preinv. anl. Date**
This is the date that will get used to calculate the pre-investment analysis such as net present value or internal rate of return. This is the default and can be changed by appropriation request.

▶ **Status profile**
This field allows you to maintain the status profile that controls the various statuses of the appropriation request.

▶ **PartnDet.Proc**

Here you can maintain the partner determination procedure that controls which partner functions are allowed for which business transactions.

▶ **1st Function**

Here you can maintain the partner function that will get shown first when someone creates an appropriation request.

▶ **2nd Function**

This is the second partner function that will get shown. Here you can maintain the approver of the appropriation request.

▶ **Applicant**

This identifies the person who created the appropriation request. If you have activated workflow, then an email will come to the applicant that the appropriation request has been approved.

▶ **Person responsible**

Here you can maintain the partner function that determines the person responsible for executing the appropriation request. After the appropriation request is approved, the system will send an email to this partner function.

▶ **Program type**

Here you can maintain the program type that will integrate the appropriation request to the investment program.

▶ **WBS element/Order**

Here you need to choose the investment measure to that the appropriation request will get converted.

▶ **Replace with measure**

If you set this flag, then after the appropriation request is converted to an order or WBS element, the request is released. This also means that you can no longer see the appropriation request in the reports for appropriation requests.

▶ **Copy Cost Estimate**

Setting this flag carries over the cost estimates done at the time of creating the appropriation request to the investment measure.

▶ **Project Profile**

This identifies the key pertaining to project profile.

▶ **Field key PS**

This is the key indicating the user-defined fields in project systems.

▶ **Order Type**
Here you can assign the order type that will get created when the appropriation request gets converted to the investment measure.

Table 6.2 shows the various settings that can be maintained for configuring appropriation requests. Because the focus of this chapter is on budgeting, we will not go into the details of each of these settings.

Layout for Appropriation Request	Menu Path	Transaction Code
Define Screen Layout for Appropriation Requests	IMG • Investment management • Appropriation Requests • Master Data • Control data • Define Screen Layout for Appropriation Requests	OITL
Specify Tab Layout for Appropriation Requests	IMG • Investment management • Appropriation Requests • Master Data • Specify Tab Layout for Appropriation Requests	OITO
Maintain Number Ranges for Appropriation Requests	IMG • Investment management • Appropriation Requests • Master Data • Control Data • Define Number Assignment	IMAN
Process Costing Variants	IMG • Investment management • Appropriation Requests • Planning • Cost Planning • Process Costing Variants	OKYZ
Define Planning Profiles for Cost Planning	IMG • Investment management • Appropriation requests • Planning • Cost Planning • Define Planning Profiles for Cost Planning	OIF2
Assign Appropriation Request Type to Planning Profile	IMG • Investment management • Appropriation Request • Planning • Cost Planning • Assign Appropriation Request Type to Planning Profile	
Appropriation Requests: Approvals Levels	IMG • Investment management • Appropriation Requests • Approval • Define Approval Levels for Appropriation Requests	
Activate Event-Linkage for Workflow Task	IMG • Investment management • Appropriation Requests • Approval • Activate Event-Linkage for Workflow Task	OITN

Table 6.2 Configuration Settings for Appropriation Requests

6.1.6 Investment Measures: Integration with Asset Accounting

Investment measures allow you to manage the accounting and controlling aspects of AuCs and for other measures to monitor the costs. These are used primarily when the assets are not capitalized directly, and you need to track the costs in the interim while they are in the process of becoming assets. Another important contributor might be large in-house involvement that necessitates segregating the components which should be capitalized and which should be expensed.

If you create an investment measure and tie it to an AuC, it allows you to have a subledger of the AuC GL account and to classify in the asset history sheet correctly.

> **Note**
>
> Networks currently do not classify as investment measure because you cannot settle these to an AuC. So for networks, you will have to establish a link with WBS elements that is then linked to an AuC.

6.1.7 Orders Versus Projects as Investment Measures

Orders allow you to track relatively less complex internal activities in the process of collecting data about the costs at various stages of planning and execution. You can ultimately settle these costs to other cost objects or to an AuC. *Projects* on the other hand are relatively complex one-time activities that have clearly identified goals and a definite start and finish date outlined. Table 6.3 highlights the key differences between projects and orders to allow you to choose appropriate investment measure for tracking your costs.

Parameters	Orders (CO-OM-PA)	Projects (PS)
Hierarchical structure for cost objects	No	Yes
Dimensions	Single dimension	Multidimensional
Integration	Primary integration with other controlling functions	Primary integration is with other logistics functions
Complexity	Low to medium	High
Repetitive	Can be repetitive	Single-time activity with start and end dates
Level of Importance	Operational	Tactical or strategic

Table 6.3 Comparison of Orders and Projects

Measures are represented as either internal orders or WBS elements and allow you to augment the existing Overhead Orders (CO-OM-OPA) and Project Systems (PS) by extending the integration with Asset Accounting (FI-AA). Investment measures are not just orders and WBS elements. These have special functions that allow them to become relevant for asset accounting at month end.

From an investment lifecycle management perspective, investment measures are used when the appropriation requests are approved for execution.

In this section, you will learn how to configure the investment profile that controls various parameters for investment measures.

6.1.8   Investment Profile

The most important configuration from Investment Management is the investment profile. By assigning the investment profile to an internal order or WBS element, you mark these as relevant for Investment Management.

In this step, you will learn how to configure an in investment profile and then assign it to a model order. You can follow th menu path **IMG • Investment management • Internal Orders as Investment measures • Master Data • Define investment profile • Define Investment Profile**, or use Transaction OITA.

Figure 6.20 shows the parameters for the Investment profile **000001: Model with AuC, summary settlement**. You can define your own investment profiles by copying this and changing the parameters if required. The various parameters that need to be maintained for an investment profile are as follows:

▸ **Manage AuC**
  Flagging this indicator automatically creates an AuC for all the assigned investment measures.

▸ **AuC per source structure/assignmt**
  This creates separate AuCs per source structure for each source assignment. This allows you to post the debits posted separately by cost elements to various assets. The source structure is maintained in the settlement profile.

▸ **Inv. Meas. Ast. Class**
  This allows you to default the asset class for the AuC to be created, which is linked to the investment measure.

▸ **Fixed default class**
Flagging this will make the default asset class defined in the previous bullet unchangeable.

▸ **Summary Settlement**
This ensures that the settlement of debit items is executed in a summary form.

▸ **Line item settlement and list of origins**
This will perform the settlement by line item and keep track of the origins of the settlement by line item.

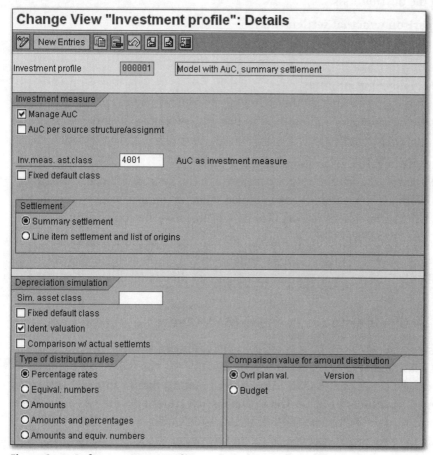

Figure 6.20 Define Investment Profile

▶ **Sim. asset class**
Here you can maintain the asset class whose depreciation terms will be used for depreciation simulation. You can change this manually in the investment measure if the investment measure is not released automatically on creation.

▶ **Fixed asset class**
This forces the default in the previous bullet to be unchangeable.

▶ **Ident. valuation**
This ensures that the same depreciation terms and depreciation start are carried to all the distributions.

▶ **Comparison w/actual settlements**
This allows you to display the actual capitalizations in depreciation simulation data.

▶ **Types of distribution roles**
This allows you to specify the following distribution rules: percentage rates, equivalence numbers, amounts, amounts and percentages, and amounts and equivalence numbers.

▶ **Comparison value for amount distribution**
Here you can specify the value against which the system will check the depreciation simulation amounts: overall plan value or budget value. You can also maintain the version of the depreciation against that the comparison is done.

Now that you understand the functionality of investment profile, let's take a look at how you can assign this to a model order. You can either assign it directly in the internal order master data, or you can assign it to the model order.

6.1.9   Assign Investment Profile to Model Order

In this step, you will learn how to assign the investment profile to the model order. System will automatically search for the model order by the order type of the internal order. The menu path is **IMG • Investment management • Internal Orders as Investment measures • Master Data • Define investment profile • Assign investment profile to model order**. The Transaction is OITA. Figure 6.21 shows how you can assign the **InvProfile 000001** to the model **Order $**.

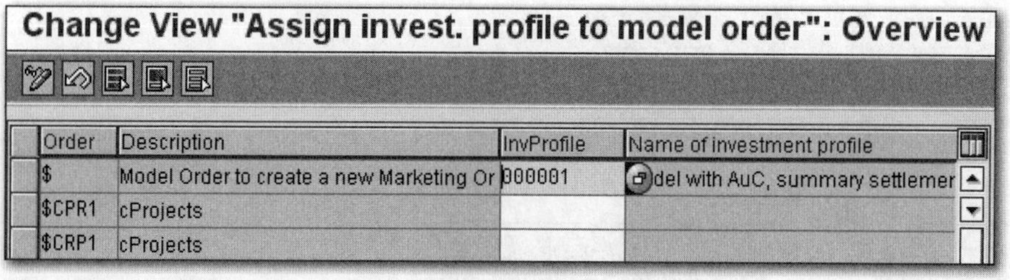

Change View "Assign invest. profile to model order": Overview

Order	Description	InvProfile	Name of investment profile	
$	Model Order to create a new Marketing Or	000001	del with AuC, summary settlemer	
$CPR1	cProjects			
$CRP1	cProjects			

Figure 6.21 Assign Investment Profile to Model Order

Similarly, you can establish the link between the WBS element and Investment Management by assigning it directly in the WBS element, or you can assign the investment profile to the project profile that is used when you create the WBS element.

6.2 Investment Management Year End Closing

Investment Management in most organizations is an annual process. So SAP ERP also treats Investment Management as a cyclical process based on an organization's planning schedule. As you learned while defining the investment program, you need to define this by approval year. However, this does not mean that you completely start fresh. You will probably start from the structure that was defined the previous year and then modify it to take into account the new realities for the fiscal year.

In this section, you will learn the key processes that need to be performed at year end to help you launch your new Investment Management cycle. The sequence of the activities that need to be performed are shown in Figure 6.22.

First, you need to open a new approval year for the investment program. Also the budget and commitments of investments measures of the previous year can be carried forward to the new fiscal year. The budget of the previous investment program is also carried forward if required. After all of these activities are completed, the previous year is closed. You will learn each of these steps in subsequent subsections. First, you will learn how to open a new approval year for the investment program.

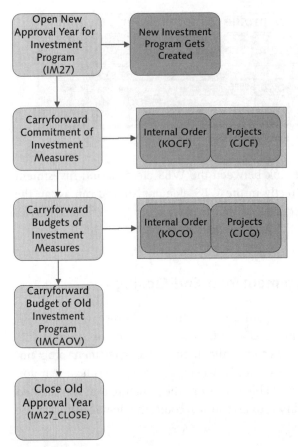

Figure 6.22 Fiscal Year Change for Investment Management

6.2.1 Open a New Approval Year for the Investment Program

This activity allows you to start a new approval year for Investment Management. This will then allow you to budget and post values in the new approval year. The menu path is **SAP Menu • Accounting • Investment management • Programs • Periodic Processing • Fiscal Year Change • Open new approval year**, and the Transaction is IM27. Figure 6.23 shows how you can open a new approval year. You need to maintain the **Investment Program ABC_INC** and current **Approval year 2007**. If you click on **Copy program structure**, then the complete structure gets copied to the new approval year.

Open New Approval Year

Investment Program   ABC_INC

Position ID

Approval year   2007

Target investment program

     Investment program

     Position ID

     Approval year

Settings

     ☑ Copy program structure

     ☐ Carry fwd. meas./app.req.

     ☐ Carry forward budget values

     ☐ Carry forward plan values ...

         ... to version(s)   0   to

Selection of measures/approp.requests for carryforward

     Status selection profile

Figure 6.23   Open New Approval Year

On executing this transaction (the clock icon) you will be able to reach the next screen shown in Figure 6.24. This will show you that the new ABC_INC 2008 has been created.

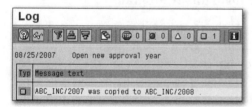

Log

08/25/2007   Open new approval year

Typ	Message text
☐	ABC_INC/2007 was copied to ABC_INC/2008 .

Figure 6.24   Results of the Opening of the New Fiscal Year

6.2.2   Commitments and Budget Carryforward of Investment Measures

You can also carry forward commitments and budgets to the new approval year. This is especially important for budgets because it allows you to carry forward any budget that is not used in the previous fiscal year. Table 6.4 shows the transaction codes and the menu path for carrying forward budget and commitments to the new fiscal year. The parameters for carryforward are the old fiscal year and a range of orders or projects as applicable.

Investment Measure	Carryforward	Menu path	Transaction Code
Projects	Commitments	**SAP Menu • Accounting • Investment management • Investment Projects • Year End Closing • Budget Commitments**	CJCF
	Budget	**SAP Menu • Accounting • Investment management • Investment Projects • Year End Closing • Budget Carryforward**	CJCO
Orders	Commitments	**SAP Menu • Accounting • Investment management • Internal Orders • Year End Closing • Budget Commitments**	KOCF
	Budget	**SAP Menu • Accounting • Investment management • Internal Orders • Year End Closing • Budget Carryforward**	KOCO

Table 6.4 Carryforward Budget and Commitments for Orders and Projects

6.2.3 Carryforward Budget of Old Investment Program

If you have carried forward the budget for the investment measures and did not carry forward the budget for the investment program, you might have a situation where the budget at the investment program level is lesser than the budget that was allocated at the investment measure level. This necessitates that you carry forward the budget at the program level. In this step, you will learn how to carry forward the budget of the old investment program as well. The menu path is **SAP Menu • Accounting • Investment management • Programs • Periodic Processing • Fiscal Year Change • Budget carryforward**, and the Transaction is IMCAOV.

Figure 6.25 shows the screen where you can maintain the parameters for carrying forward the budget to the new approval year. Note that this transfer happens still within the same approval year and investment program. You cannot carry forward the budget to a new approval year. If you check the **Budget as supplmt/return** box, then the budget is not treated as an original budget. It is treated as an addition or subtraction to the original budget.

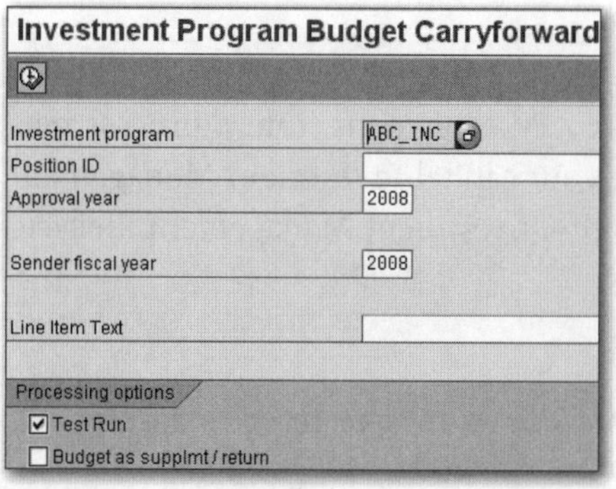

Figure 6.25 Investment Program Budget Carryforward

6.2.4 Close Old Approval Year

After you have done the carryforward for commitment and budget, you need to close the old approval year. This will prevent any postings in the previous approval year. The menu path is **SAP Menu • Accounting • Investment management • Programs • Periodic Processing • Fiscal Year Change • Close Old Approval Year**. The Transaction is IM27_CLOSE. Figure 6.26 shows the screen where you can maintain the parameters for closing the old approval year. Closing the old approval year will allow you to carry forward any budget values and plan values to the new approval year.

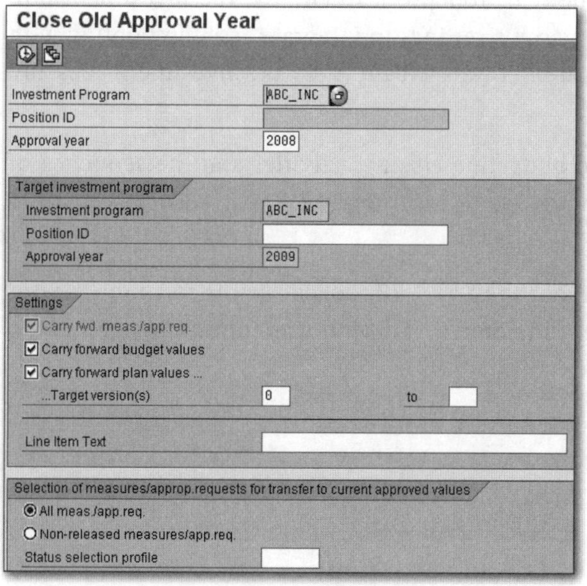

Figure 6.26 Close Old Approval Year

6.3   Summary

In this chapter, you learned about Investment Management from a process perspective and learned how you can optimize your capital Investment Management using SAP ERP. You were first introduced to the Investment Management lifecycle sequence:

1. Creation of appropriation request
2. Approval and conversion of appropriation request to investment measures
3. Budgeting of investment measures
4. Execution of investment measures
5. Settlement of investment measures
6. Capitalization to fixed assets

Then you learned how you can map your organization's investment program using a combination of investment program and investment position in a hierarchical form. You also learned how you can integrate the budgeting process with the investment program and investment measures.

Having cleared the overall structure, you learned about appropriation requests and how they can be configured and integrated with the investment program. Next you were introduced to the internal orders and projects as investment measures and the distinction between the two. You also learned how the investment profile can be used to control the various settings to integrate asset accounting with Investment Management to automatically create AuCs on investment measure creation.

Finally, you learned about the budgeting closing activities and the sequence of steps that you need to follow to open a new approval year and close the old approval year.

In Chapter 7, you will learn about the SAP ERP tools available for public sector management and how you can implement and optimize Funds Management to optimize your budgeting process.

Funds Management allows you to manage your budgeting processes within the governmental and public sector framework and supports both centralized and decentralized budgeting structures.

7   Using Funds Management to Optimize Public Sector Budgeting

Funds Management allows you to manage the budgeting process for revenue and expenditure items and helps you establish the common processes and framework for the budgeting cycle on a year-to-year basis. In the previous chapter, we covered capital budgeting using Investment Management. Next, you will learn more about public sector management (PSM). The SAP ERP ECC components that support public sector management include the following:

- Funds Management
- Grants Management
- Tools for budgeting, specific to the U.S. federal government
- Tools for U.S. fund accounting
- Position Budgeting and Control
- Expenditure Certification

In this chapter, you will learn more about the Funds Management (PSM-FM) component, which will help you understand the budgeting process in public sector companies.

Prior to SAP ERP ECC 5.0, Funds Management was part of the Financial Accounting menu path. However, because SAP added a lot more functionality and features specific to the public sector accounting and budgeting rules, Funds Management now has been included in the Public Sector Funds Management path. In this chapter, we will explore the basic Funds Management functionality and how it can be used to manage revenues and expenditures for individual areas of responsibility.

Funds Management allows you to control expenditures and revenues by monitoring the source of funds and the use of funds. Another unique perspective of Funds Management is that it can be tied to the organizational responsibility areas to effectively manage the budgeting process for revenue items within or across years.

7.1   Funds Management: An Introduction

Funds Management is an elaborate budgeting tool that is typically implemented in and meets the requirements of public sector organizations. In this section, you will be introduced to the basic structure of the **Funds Management Process** that is shown in Figure 7.1.

Funds Management allows you to create a **Budget Structure** using the Funds Management master data elements of funds center, fund, funded program, commitment item, and functional area. You can create a hierarchy of funds center and commitment item to map your organizational structure (*funds center hierarchy*) and the structure of the type of expenditure or revenue (*commitment item hierarchy*). This allows you to create multidimensional budget reporting.

After you have outlined your budget structure, you need to perform **Budget Planning** using various templates available for budget planning, entry, and release. This allows you to manage your budget on an ongoing basis.

Next, you will activate **Availability Control,** which is one of the strong points of Funds Management and allows you to customize your budgeting rules per activity groups, tolerance profiles, and the availability control ledger that resides in the special purpose ledger (FI-SL) and can be further customized to suit your requirements. Finally, you record your actual values and commitments as you go through the budget execution process. This allows you to use the excellent reporting tools available in Funds Management.

Finally you need to perform the **Closing Operations** that allow you to carry forward the commitment and the budget, if required, to the new fiscal year.

Overall, all of these processes can be supported by multiple solution sets that are available in SAP ERP ranging from the **Former Budgeting** process to the new improved functionality of the **Budget Control System (BCS)**, which has far more features to manage your budgeting process. SAP ERP also has specific budgetary ledgers that are customized for Germany and Spain.

Furthermore, you can use **Grants Management** to manage federal grants. The two components of Grants Management — grantee and grantor management — allow you to allocate funds to grantees and manage the allocation from grantors. In addition, SAP ERP has specific components that are designed only for the U.S. Federal government and the German government.

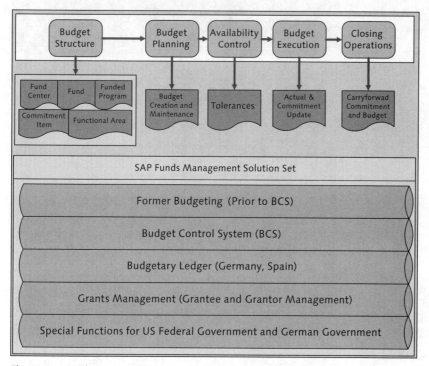

Figure 7.1 Funds Management Process

In this chapter, we will primarily discuss BCS with a broad introduction to the other components, as shown in Figure 7.2. First, you will learn about the **Basic Settings for Funds Management**, followed by an introduction to the **Master data** elements of Funds Management. This will be followed by a detailed explanation of the configuration settings for **Budgeting, Availability Control** and an introduction to the **Closing Operations.**

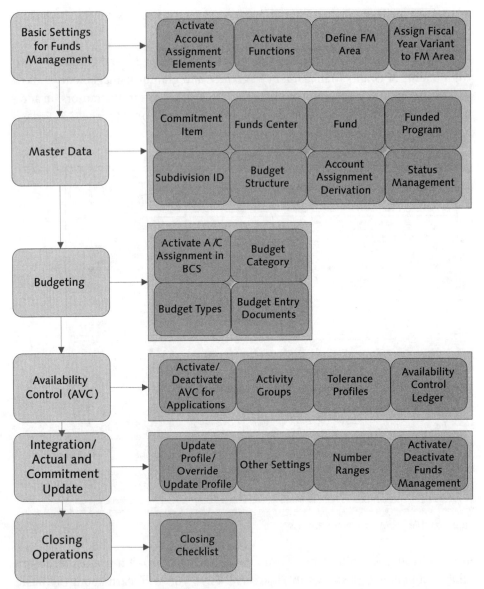

Figure 7.2 Funds Management Structure

7.2 Basic Settings

The steps you need to perform to configure basic Funds Management settings are as follows:

▶ Activate account assignment elements.

▶ Activate functions.

▶ Define a Funds Management area.

▶ Assign a fiscal year variant to a Funds Management area.

All of these steps are basic pre-requisites that are needed to set up and implement Funds Management.

7.2.1 Activate Account Assignment Elements

Account assignment elements are the building blocks of the Funds Management configuration. The key account assignment elements are listed here:

▶ Fund

▶ Functional area

▶ Grant

▶ Funded Program

If you activate these account assignment elements (also known as sets), Funds Management can communicate with other components of SAP ERP Financials.

To activate account assignments in Funds Management, use menu path **IMG • Public Sector Management • General Settings for Public Sector Management • Basic Settings: Account Assignment Elements • Activate Account Assignment Elements**. You will be taken to the screen shown in Figure 7.3.

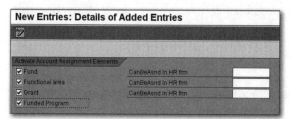

Figure 7.3 Activate Account Assignment Elements

You can select **Fund**, **Functional area**, **Grant**, and **Funded Program** and then save the entries to be activated in Funds Management.

CanBeAsnd in HR frm lets you specify the date from which you want the account assignment element to be active in Human Resources infotypes.

After you activate account assignment elements, you need to configure the appropriate assignments in the following components:

▶ **Controlling**
Assign cost objects or cost elements to the account assignment elements.

▶ **Asset Accounting**
Assign asset accounting elements in the asset master record or when you are posting a transaction for the asset (these elements become available in asset accounting after you assign cost objects or cost elements to account assignment elements).

▶ **Payroll**
For all relevant infotypes, enter the account assignments in the Human Resources master data after the date when you activate them.

Note

For more details about when to activate account assignment objects, refer to SAP Note 518610. It is very important to have fulfilled all of the requirements before you activate an account assignment object. Also, when production is live, it is not advisable to change these assignments. However, if the situation warrants a change, then make sure that you thoroughly test it.

7.2.2 Allow BLANK as the Value for Account Assignment Elements

After you activate account assignment elements, the system requires that they contain a value when posting an entry. However, there are situations when the derivation of account assignment is not possible because an appropriate derivation rule was not set up or because the system comes up with a conflicting account assignment determination. To ensure that the system does not produce an error message, you can allow "blank" as a value for account assignment elements.

This is also useful if you have implemented Funds Management after other SAP ERP components have gone live; configuring this setting allows you to not worry about the old data in previous fiscal years. For example, if you activated Funds

Management on 01.01.2008 and there was a goods receipt for a cost center that was created on 12.30.2007, the system would not produce an error message when you open that goods receipt because now it should also have a funds center and commitment item because you activated Funds Management. In addition, there would not be any problems when you invoice the goods receipt.

The menu path to configure this setting is **IMG • Public Sector Management • General Settings for Public Sector Management • Basic Settings: Account Assignment Elements • Allow BLANK as Value for Account Assignment Elements**.

Figure 7.4 shows the screen that displays, which contains the following configuration items:

▶ **FM...**
This identifies the Funds Management area for which you are allowing blank values.

▶ **Grant/Fund/Func. Area/Funded Prg**
These indicators, if checked, denote that the grant, fund, functional area, or funded program can have blank values.

▶ **ToYr**
This specifies the year up to which these settings are valid.

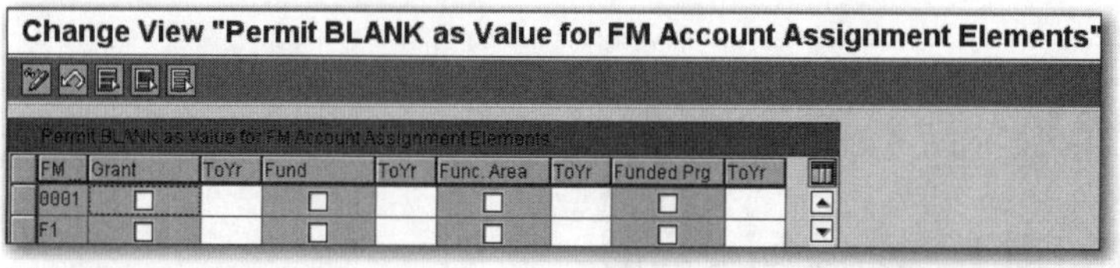

Figure 7.4 Allow BLANK as the Value for Account Assignment Elements

In the next subsection, you will learn how to activate additional functions pertaining to Funds Management.

7.2.3   Activate Functions

Before activating Funds Management, you need to make sure that the following organization entities have been defined in the enterprise structure:

▶ Create company code
▶ Maintain Funds Management area

▸ Maintain Controlling area

After defining these, you need to assign a company code and Controlling area to the Funds Management area.

Then you need to perform the following additional steps, which allow you to activate functions in Funds Management:

▸ Activate global Funds Management functions (PSM-FM)

▸ Activate global functions for BCS

▸ Activate global functions for German government

▸ Activate multiyear budget execution

Activate Global Funds Management Functions (PSM-FM)

This lets you activate or deactivate specific functions for Funds Management. The menu path is **IMG • Public Sector Management • Funds Management Government • Basic Settings • Activate Global Funds Management Functions (PSM-FM)**.

Figure 7.5 shows how you can activate **Funds Management (PSM-FM)** by selecting the checkbox.

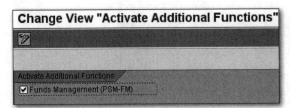

Figure 7.5   Activate Global Funds Management Functions (PSM-FM)

Activate Global Functions for Budget Control System

While using Funds Management, you can either using **Former Budgeting** or **the Budget Control System (BCS) for your budget processes.** In older versions of SAP, Former Budgeting was used, but from ECC 5.0 on, it is recommended that you use BCS. In this step, you will learn how you can activate global functions for BCS.

To activate BCS as the budgeting tool for use with the Funds Management public sector solution, use the menu path **IMG • Public Sector Management • Funds Management Government • Basic Settings • Activate Global Functions for Budget Control System (BCS).**

Figure 7.6 shows the screen to which you are taken, where you can configure the following parameters to activate BCS:

▶ **FM**
This identifies the Funds Management area for which you are activating BCS.

▶ **From year**
This identifies the year from which point on the BCS component will be active for the Funds Management area.

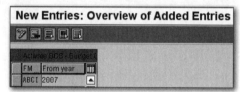

Figure 7.6   Activate Global Functions for Budget Control System (BCS)

Activate Global Functions for German Government

This step allows you to activate specific functions that are pertinent to German government companies. The menu path is **IMG • Public Sector Management • Funds Management Government • Basic Settings • Activate Global Functions for German Government.** In the screen shown in Figure 7.7, select **Authorities Germany** to allow you to use additional functionality available in Funds Management for German government users.

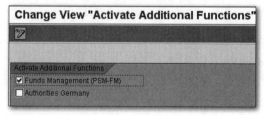

Figure 7.7   Activate Global Functions for German Government

Activate Multiyear Budget Execution

Most of the revenue budgetary outlays are for a single fiscal year. However, there might be situations (e.g., a five-year plan to build a major highway, a multi-year IT implementation across multiple geographic locations, etc.) when you want to use budgetary outlays for multiple years, which allows you to process business transactions without reference to a fiscal year. You can activate multi-year budget execution by using the menu path IMG • Public Sector Management • Funds Management Government • Basic Settings • Activate Multi-Year Budget Execution.

Figure 7.8 shows how you can **Activate** the multi-year budget functionality for Funds Management Area (FM) **ABCI**.

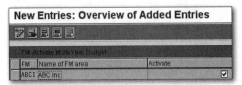

Figure 7.8 Activate Multiyear Budget Execution

Let's now take a look at some other important basic settings for Funds Management, such as defining a Funds Management area and assigning a fiscal year variant to a Funds Management area.

7.2.4 Define a Funds Management Area and Its Global Parameters

While defining the enterprise structure for Funds Management, the first step is to define a Funds Management area and then define the global parameters for it.

The menu path to define the Funds Management area and its global parameters is **IMG • Public Sector Management • Funds Management Government • Basic Settings • Define Global Parameters**, or you can use Transaction OF15.

Figure 7.9 shows the initial screen where you can enter the FM Area, for example, **"ABCI"**, along with the FM area text, for example, "ABC Inc".

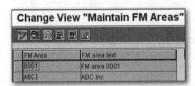

Figure 7.9 Define FM Area

Then, click on the **ABCI** line, and you will reach the next screen as shown in Figure 7.10, where you can configure the parameters for the Funds Management area:

► **Budget Profile**

This needs to be configured if you are using BCS. It brings together the control parameters for budgeting by outlining the parameters for availability control, currency translation, time horizon, and format.

► **Fund profile**

If you are using BCS, then this field is not relevant. If you are not using BCS, then you can use a fund profile to control budgeting parameters.

► **Fi. Year Variant**

This identifies the fiscal year variant for budgeting and can be different from the fiscal year variant for the company code.

► **No. range no.**

This denotes the number range interval within a Funds Management object.

► **Status Profile**

This key is used to control the user statuses that control which transactions are allowed and which are not.

► **Ranking order**

This is the order in which the system will search entries. The default entry is **Funds center, commitment item, fund**.

► **AuthorizGroup**

This can be used to control access to different Funds Management areas.

Change View "Maintain FM Areas": Details

FM Area	ABCI

Maintain FM Areas

FM area text	ABC Inc
Budget Profile	000001
Fund profile	000001
Fi.Year Variant	K4
No. range no.	
Status Profile	FM000001
Ranking order	Funds center, commitment item, fund
AuthorizGroup	

Figure 7.10 Define Global Parameters for FM Area

233

In addition to maintaining the fiscal year variant in the global parameters, you can assign a fiscal year variant to a Funds Management area for a group of Funds Management areas, as shown in Section 7.2.5.

7.2.5 Assign Fiscal Year Variant to Funds Management Area

In this step, you will learn the process of assigning a fiscal year variant across Funds Management areas. The *fiscal year variant* controls the budgeting cycle start and end months. This allows you to have a budgeting cycle different from your fiscal reporting cycle. The menu path is **IMG • Public Sector Management • Funds Management Government • Basic Settings • Fiscal Year Variant • Assign Fiscal Year Variant to FM Area**, or you can use Transaction **OF32**.

Figure 7.11 shows the screen where you can assign an **FM Area**, such as **0001** or **ABCI**, to the appropriate **Fiscal Year Variant K4**. K4 signifies a January to December fiscal year for budgeting.

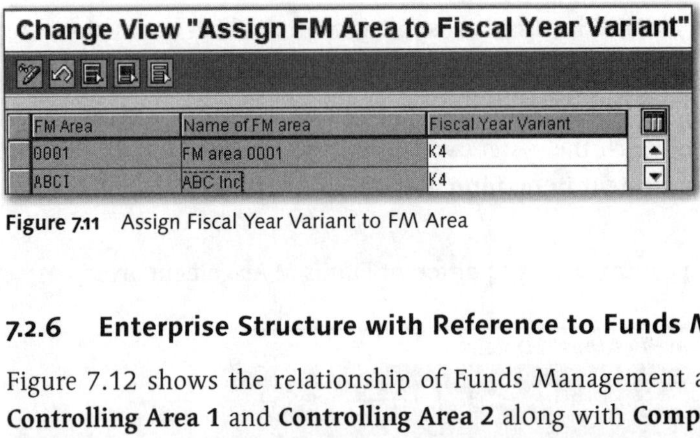

Change View "Assign FM Area to Fiscal Year Variant"

FM Area	Name of FM area	Fiscal Year Variant	
0001	FM area 0001	K4	
ABCI	ABC Inc	K4	

Figure 7.11 Assign Fiscal Year Variant to FM Area

7.2.6 Enterprise Structure with Reference to Funds Management

Figure 7.12 shows the relationship of Funds Management area (**FM area**) with **Controlling Area 1** and **Controlling Area 2** along with **Company Code 1 to Company Code 4**. The Funds Management area is the highest level below the **Client**.

You can have multiple Funds Management areas in the system, but they need to be assigned to the appropriate Financial Accounting and Controlling enterprise entities.

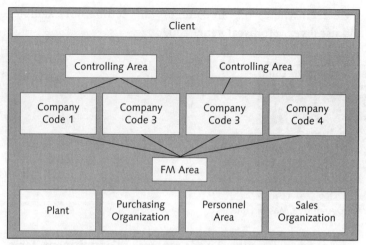

Figure 7.12 Enterprise Structure Setup of Funds Management

> **Key Point**
>
> A Funds Management area needs to be assigned to both a company code and a Controlling area. This forms the overall budgeting structure of your organization by inheriting the Controlling and Financial Accounting architecture.

Let's now take a look at the Funds Management master data elements.

7.3 Master Data

This section covers the configuration settings for Funds Management master data, along with a detailed description of the individual master data elements: funds center, commitment item, fund, funded program, subdivision ID, and budget structure.

7.3.1 Activate Year-Dependent Master Data

You can use this functionality to limit the master data created for one particular fiscal year to only a particular Funds Management area. The menu path is **IMG • Public Sector Management • General Settings for Public Sector Management • Master Data • Account Assignment Elements • Year-Dependent Master Data • Activate Year-Dependent Master Data**, or you can use Transaction OFM_ACT_MD_YEAR.

Figure 7.13 shows the screen where you can configure this setting, for example, for **FM Area ABCI** and fiscal year (**To fiscal year**) **2007**.

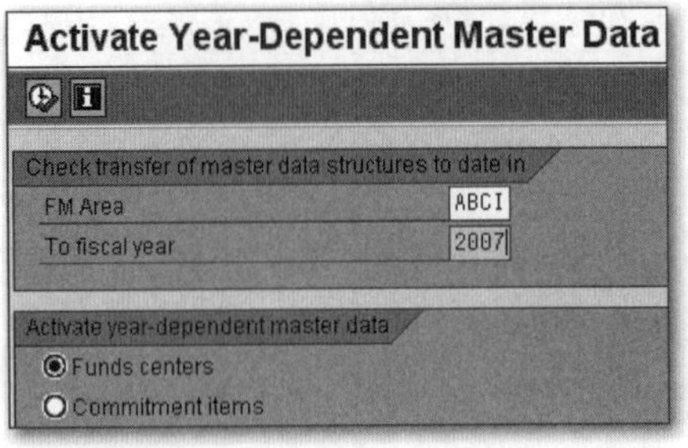

Activate Year-Dependent Master Data

Check transfer of master data structures to date in
FM Area   ABCI
To fiscal year   2007

Activate year-dependent master data
⦿ Funds centers
○ Commitment items

Figure 7.13 Activate Year-Dependent Master Data

You can activate year dependency for either **Funds centers** or **Commitment items** by selecting the appropriate radio button. After you click on the Execute icon, you will see the screen shown in Figure 7.14. You need to click on the **Activate** button to **Activate Year-Dependent Master Data**.

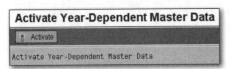

Activate Year-Dependent Master Data

⌀ Activate

Activate Year-Dependent Master Data

Figure 7.14 Activating Year-Dependent Master Data

In the next subsection, you will learn about the commitment items master data, which is also one of the account assignment elements for Funds Management. Commitment items can be arranged in hierarchies, so you will first learn about the master data structure for commitment items and then how you can create a hierarchy of the commitment items.

7.3.2 Commitment Items

Commitment items allow you to set up and structure your functional units (expenditure and revenue structures) in a hierarchy. They divide the content of the budget and business transactions into revenue items and expenditure items.

Figure 7.15 shows the menu path for creating a commitment item and also shows the subitems used to create, change, or display the **Hierarchy** and **Commitment Item Groups**.

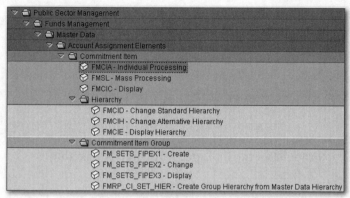

Figure 7.15 Menu Path and Transactions to Create a Commitment Item

To create a commitment item, use the menu path **SAP Menu• Accounting • Public Sector Management • Funds Management • Master Data • Account Assignment Elements • Commitment Item • Individual Processing**, or use Transaction FMCIA.

When you execute the transaction, you have to enter the Funds Management area, for example, "ABCI", and then the screen shown in Figure 7.16 appears.

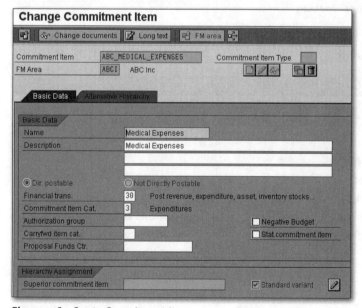

Figure 7.16 Create Commitment Item

Here, you need to enter the **Commitment Item**'s identifier, such as "ABC_MEDI-CAL_EXPENSES". In addition, you can maintain the following parameters on the **Basic Data** tab:

▶ **Name and Description**
These identify the name and description of the commitment item.

▶ **Dir. postable**
This allows you to post actual revenues and expenditures. For summarization commitment items, you should set the indicator **Not Directly Postable**.

▶ **Financial trans**.
You can configure the control parameters that let you indicate what type of feeder systems (Financial Accounting, Materials Management) can post to this commitment item. The following are the options that are available in financial transactions:

   ▶ **30**: Post revenue, expenditure, asset, inventory stocks

   ▶ **40**: Post goods receipt, goods issue

   ▶ **50**: Clearing

   ▶ **60**: Post rcvbls and pybls from goods and services

   ▶ **70**: Post customer clearing

   ▶ **80**: Post bank clearing, bill of exchange

   ▶ **90**: Post cash holdings

> **Note**
>
> You cannot change this setting if you have actuals and budget values populated for the commitment item.

▶ **Commitment Item Cat.**
This identifies the commitment item category and is used to categorize and structure the reporting requirements you need to set up in the Funds Management information system. The following are the options that are available for a commitment item:

   ▶ **1**: Balance

   ▶ **2**: Revenues

   ▶ **3**: Expenditures

- ▶ **4**: Balances
- ▶ **5**: Clarification Worklist

▶ **Authorization group**
This allows you to restrict the use of commitment items.

▶ **Carryfwd item cat.**
Carryforward item category is used to distinguish how you want to carry forward commitment item balances to the next fiscal year.

▶ **Proposal Funds Ctr**
This is the default value that should be used if no funds center is entered in the document.

▶ **Negative Budget**
If selected, this will allow negative budgets for the commitment item.

▶ **Stat. commitment item**
Flagging a commitment item as statistical removes it from availability control checks. You cannot directly budget for a statistical commitment item.

▶ **Superior commitment item**
You need to enter the commitment item that is immediately above this item in the hierarchy.

If you select the Alternative Hierarchy tab, you can configure the variant and the superior commitment item for the alternative hierarchy. This allows you to build separate hierarchies that can be used to build additional reporting logic.

Now let's take a look at some of the configuration settings that are used for configuring a commitment item.

Enhancements for Commitment Items
FMMD0015: Checks the name of a commitment item when you create or change the commitment item, provides control of fields as display variants, and enters default values in fields.
FMMD0016: Performs a consistency check of values you enter when you press Enter.
FMMD0017: Additional tab for user-defined fields in the master record.
FMMD0016: Changes data records exported with the RFFMDBI81 program.

Create Variant in FM Area/Fiscal Year

You will now learn how to create an alternative hierarchy variant for a Funds Management area and fiscal year. Alternative hierarchies allow you to generate a new way of organizing commitment items. Using menu path **IMG • Public Sector Management • Funds Management Government • Master Data • Account Assignment Elements • Commitment Item• Create Variant in FM Area/Fiscal Year,** you will reach the screen shown in Figure 7.17. Variant **000** is automatically created, and you can choose to create another variant by clicking on the **New Entries** button.

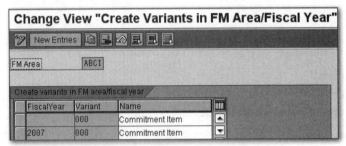

Figure 7.17   Create Variants in FM Area/Fiscal Year

Maintain Commitment Item Type

Commitment item types are used to set up validation rules that check whether a particular commitment item type is allowed for posting the request. You can also use these to generate additional reporting capabilities. Use menu path **IMG • Public Sector Management • Funds Management Government • Master Data • Account Assignment Elements • Commitment Item • Maintain Commitment Item,** or Transaction OFM_HSART.

Figure 7.18 **shows the screen where you maintain the Commitment item types (CI Ty.) 1, 2, 3,** and **4** with **Name Operating Budget**, **Capital Budget**, **Custody**, and **Advance**, respectively. The commitment items shown are predefined; however, you can add more and customize these to suit your requirements.

If you click on the Check checkbox, then the acceptance request validates that the appropriate commitment item is being charged for the expenditure item. If not, the system will issue an error message.

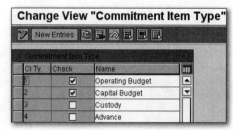

Figure 7.18 Define Commitment Item Type

In addition to the configuration items we've discussed in this section, you can set up masks for commitment item naming conventions, reproduce a budget structure, and copy commitment items.

7.3.3 Funds Center

You use a funds center to represent the organizational units (responsibility areas, departments, and projects) of your organization. Typically, these correspond one to one with your cost center structure. Let's take a look at the properties of a funds center and how to create it.

To create a funds center, use the menu path **SAP Menu • Accounting • Public Sector Management • Funds Management • Master Data • Account Assignment Elements • Funds Center • Individual Processing** or Transaction FMSA.

You will reach the screen shown in Figure 7.19, where you need to enter the **Funds Center** "10100", the validity of the funds center **From fiscal year** "1900" To fiscal year "9999", and the FM Area "ABCI". You can also enter a reference **Funds Center** and **FM Area**, which will allow you to copy the data from a reference object and make appropriate changes.

Create Funds Center in FM Area

FM area	

Funds Center	10100		
From fiscal year	1900	To fiscal year	9999
FM Area	ABCI		

Reference	
Funds Center	
FM Area	

Figure 7.19 Create a Funds Center in FM Area

241

After entering the details, press Enter. This will take you to the next screen, as shown in Figure 7.20.

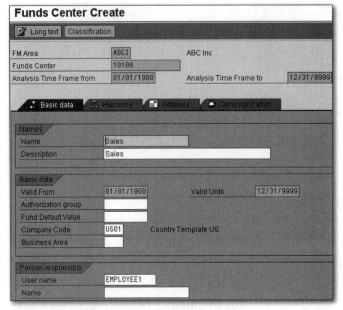

Figure 7.20 Funds Center Create: Basic Data

On the Basic data tab, you need to maintain the following additional details about the **Funds Center 10100**:

▶ **Name/Description**
Enter the name and description for the funds center "Sales".

▶ **Authorization group**
Control who has access to the funds center for budgeting and posting.

▶ **Fund Default Value**
Enter the default fund value in case the actual posting does not have the fund information.

▶ **Company Code**
Enter the company code "US01", to which the funds center is assigned.

▶ **Business Area**
Maintain an assignment to a business area for the funds center.

▶ **User name/Name**
Identify the funds center manager's SAP user ID and name.

If you select the **Hierarchy** tab, you can see the fiscal year assignment and maintain the hierarchy variant and the corresponding superior funds center.

The address and other communication details can be entered on the **Address** and **Communication** tabs, respectively.

Now that we have looked at the various screens of a funds center master, let's look at the funds center Customizing options:

▶ Create/Change Hierarchy variant.

▶ Assign Hierarchy variant to FM area.

▶ Define Top Funds Center for Collective Expenditure.

▶ Define Funds Center for Budget.

Create/Change Hierarchy Variant

This configuration setting is used to generate the standard and alternate hierarchies while defining funds centers. Variants allow you to maintain the assignment of one funds center across multiple hierarchies. Figure 7.21 shows how you can create a Hierarchy Variant 0001 by combining various departments (**Main Department A,** which is made up of **Department A 1** and **Department A 2,** and **Main Department B**, which is made up of **Department B 1** and **Department B 2**) to form the overall **Organization**. Using a different variant, you can set up an entirely new organization structure.

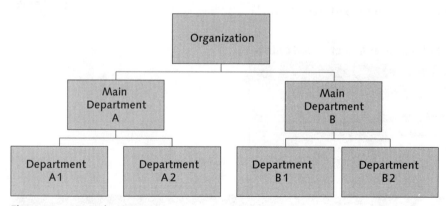

Figure 7.21 Hierarchy Variant

Using menu path **IMG • Public Sector Management • Funds Management Government • Master Data • Account Assignment Elements • Funds Center • Hierarchy Variant • Create/Change Hierarchy Variant** or Transaction FMSF, you will reach the screen shown in Figure 7.22. You need to maintain the Hierarchy Variant "ABC" with a Name of "ABC Funds Management" for the FM Area "ABCI".

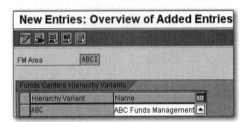

Figure 7.22   Create Hierarchy Variant

Assign Hierarchy Variant to FM Area

In this step, you will assign the hierarchy variant created in the previous step to the Funds Management area and the fiscal year. This identifies the current funds center hierarchy. You use menu path **IMG • Public Sector Management • Funds Management Government • Master Data • Account Assignment Elements • Funds Center • Hierarchy Variant • Assign Hierarchy Variant to FM Area, or** Transaction FMSG.

Figure 7.23 shows how you have assigned the **Fiscal Year** "2007" and **Hierarchy Variant** "ABC" to the **FM Area** "ABCI".

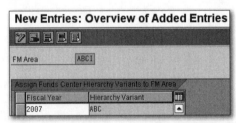

Figure 7.23   Assign Funds Center Hierarchy Variants to FM Area

---

Note

If your funds center structure is year independent, then enter "0000" in the **Fiscal Year** column.

Define Top Funds Center for Collective Expenditure

In this step, you define the top funds center for collective expenditure, which allows you to delineate to local authorities the funds center hierarchy that is used for collective expenditures.

The menu path is **IMG • Public Sector Management • Funds Management Government • Master Data • Account Assignment Elements • Funds Center • Hierarchy Variant • Define Top Funds Center for Collective Expenditure**.

Assign a **Top funds center** of "10000" to **FM Area** "ABCI" and **Year** "2007", as shown in Figure 7.24.

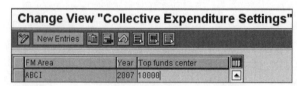

Figure 7.24 Define Top Funds Center for Collective Expenditure

Define Funds Center for Budget

The funds center for budget is used as a default entry whenever a commitment item master record is created. It then flows through to all of the transaction records that require a funds center. The menu path is **IMG • Public Sector Management • Funds Management Government • Master Data • Account Assignment Elements • Funds Center • Hierarchy Variant • Define Funds Center for Budget**.

Assign **Funds center** "100" to **FM Area** "ABCI" and **Year** "2007", as shown in Figure 7.25.

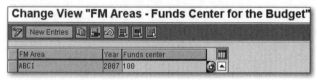

Figure 7.25 Define Funds Center for Budget

In addition to these Customizing options, you can also create additional text types, and copy funds centers by importing from and exporting to an external file.

7.3.4 Fund

You can use *funds* to further subdivide budgets and use budgets in more detail. Typically, the breakout is based on the application of funds and financing period, and whether these have been allocated for a specific purpose. However, you can use a fund to facilitate further breakout into administration and accounting units for additional reporting and analysis.

Figure 7.26 shows how you can use the fund (**Fund 1, Fund 2, and Fund 3**) to add a layer of reporting for tracking expenditures and revenues in addition to **commitment items** and **funds centers**. The addition of fund allows you to use the same organization structure across multiple use and application of funds.

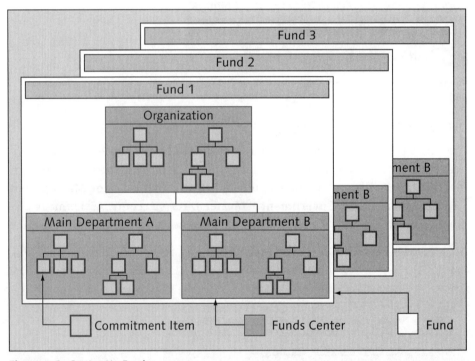

Figure 7.26 Setting Up Funds

> **Note**
>
> A fund is active as long as BCS is not active. If BCS is active, then you will have to activate funds using Customizing settings.

After it has been activated in public sector management, the fund can be used as an additional account assignment in other components, as follows:

▶ **Asset accounting**
Maintaining a fund in an asset master record allows you to post asset acquisitions and depreciation postings to the correct fund. This ensures that you can also get a breakout by fund in the asset history sheet.

▶ **Controlling**
Adding a fund allows you to post expenses and revenue by fund, which can be used in all of the sender and receiver transactions that happen in Controlling.

▶ **Human Resources**
You can record the correct fund for personnel expenses, time sheets, and travel expenses.

Create Fund

Now that you understand the rationale for funds, let's take a look at how they are created. You use menu path **SAP Menu• Accounting • Public Sector Management • Funds Management • Master Data • Account Assignment Elements • Fund• Create**, or Transaction FM5I.

You need to maintain the following details for a fund as shown in Figure 7.27:

▶ **Fund**
This is the identifier of the fund, for example, 1010001.

▶ **Name/Description**
This identifies the description of the fund, for example, "Sales Ad Campaigns".

▶ **Valid from/To**
These dates identify the valid from and valid to dates for the fund.

▶ **Fund Type**
This can be used to classify the fund. You will learn more about configuring fund types later.

▶ **Authorization group**
This allows you to restrict access to funds.

▶ **Bdgt profile fund**
This is the budget profile for the fund.

▶ **Customer for fund**

If you know the source of the fund, you can maintain the customer number in this field.

▶ **Fund application**

If you know how the fund will be used, you can maintain that information here. This is used as a grouping criterion.

▶ **Balance update**

If you check this, the totals record of the fund is carried forward into the next year at fiscal year end.

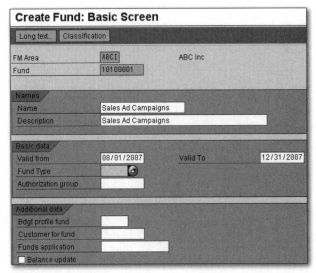

Figure 7.27   Create Fund

Create Fund Group

A fund group allows you to categorize similar funds using the menu path **SAP Menu· Accounting • Public Sector Management • Funds Management • Master Data • Account Assignment Elements • Fund • Fund Group • Create/ Change/ Display**. The corresponding Transactions are **FM_SETS_FUND1/FM_SETS_FUND2**, and **FM_SETS_FUND3**.

Figure 7.28 shows a sample **Fund group 10100: Sales**, which was created by assigning the fund **10100001: Sales Ad Campaigns**.

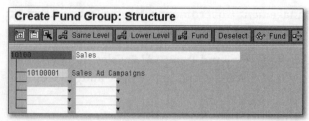

Figure 7.28 Create Fund Group

Application of Funds

Application of funds lets you categorize how you want the application or use of funds to be denoted in the system. The menu path is **SAP Menu • Accounting • Public Sector Management • Funds Management • Master Data • Account Assignment Elements • Fund • Application of Funds • Create, and** the Transaction is FM5I.

Figure 7.29 shows how you can create **Funds application** "CAPITALIT" for **FM Area** "ABCI" with a **Description** of "Capital IT projects for Sales and Distri". When you enter a transaction, you can always enter the appropriate application of funds to specify the use of funds, which can then be used for analysis and reporting.

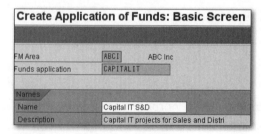

Figure 7.29 Application of Funds

The only additional Customizing that you can perform at this point for a fund is to define the type of fund.

Define Funds Management Fund Type

You can classify and group funds by defining fund types that can then be entered for a fund during the fund master data entry. The menu path is **IMG • Public Sec-**

249

tor Management • Funds Management Government • Master Data • Account Assignment Elements • Fund • Create FM Fund Types.

Figure 7.30 shows how you can configure **Fund Type** "SALE: Sales and Marketing related", "FIN: Finance", and "ADMN: Administration," with a **Budget Scope** of "Annual Budget" for **FM... ABCI**.

New Entries: Overview of Added Entries

Create FM Fund Types

FM	Fund Type	Fund type text	Budget Scope
ABCI	SALE	Sales and Marketing related	Annual Budget
ABCI	FIN	Finance	Annual Budget
ABCI	ADMN	Administration	Annual Budget

Figure 7.30 Define Fund Types

FM Master Data Recap

To summarize:

▶ Commitment items represent revenues and expenditures in Funds Management.

▶ Funds are used to track sources and application of funding.

▶ Funds centers represent organizational entities responsible for managing funds.

7.3.5   Funded Program

Funded programs are projects with an operational purpose and a defined time frame. For example, "SAP ERP Implementation," "United Way program," and so on, are funded programs. Setting up a funded program allows you to record budget control postings and monitor the performance of the programs over a period of time.

A funded program is based on the functionality of the business data toolset (BDT) and is used to create another layer of reporting to track transient programs that do not go on forever.

A funded program is automatically integrated into a sales order, a plant maintenance order, networks, and network activities.

Create Funded Program

In this step, you will learn how to create a funded program using the menu path **SAP Menu • Accounting • Public Sector Management • Funds Management • Master Data • Account Assignment Elements • Fund • Funded Program • Edit** or Transaction FMMEASURE.

Figure 7.31shows the screen for entering the details for a funded program:

▶ **Funded Program**
This is the identifier for the funded program.

▶ **FM Area**
In our example, **ABCI** is the Funds Management area.

▶ **Name/Description**
Enter the name and description of the funded program.

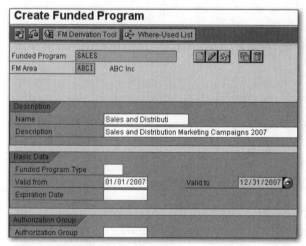

Figure 7.31 Create Funded Program

▶ **Funded program type**
Enter the funded program type, which is used to further classify the funded program for reporting and analytics.

▶ **Valid from/Valid to**
Define the validity dates of the funded program.

▶ **Expiration date**
Denotes the date after which you cannot process any new commitment items

for this funded program. You can still clear the existing open commitment items for the program.

▶ **Authorization group**
Restrict access to the funded program to specific personnel.

Create Funded Program Group

For additional reporting and classification, you can group funded programs together using the menu path **SAP Menu** • **Accounting** • **Public Sector Management** • **Funds Management** • **Master Data** • **Account Assignment Elements** • **Fund** • **Funded Program** • **Funded Program Group** • **Create** or Transaction FM_SETS_FUNDPRG1.

Figure 7.32 shows the initial screen for maintaining a **Funded Program Group** called "SALES_MKTG" for **FM Area** "ABCI".

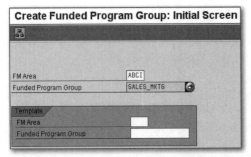

Figure 7.32 Sales and Marketing Funded Program Group Creation

If you click on the hierarchy icon (with the symbol that looks like an organizational structure diagram), you will reach the screen shown in Figure 7.33. Maintain the funded programs "SALES: SALES & Distribution" as part of "SALES_MKTG: Sales and Marketing".

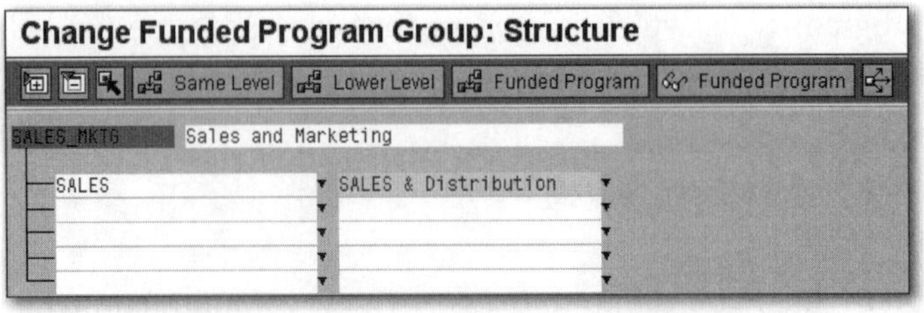

Figure 7.33 Assign a Funded Program to a Funded Program Group

Create and Maintain Funded Program Type

Funded program types are used primarily for reporting and classification purposes. You can maintain funded program types by using the menu path **IMG • Public Sector Management • Funds Management Government • Master Data • Account Assignment Elements • Funded Program • Create and Maintain Funded Program Type.**

Figure 7.34 shows **Funded Program Types (FPT)** "SALE: Sales and Distribution" and "MKTG: Marketing".

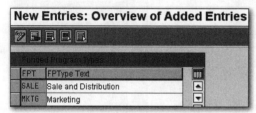

Figure 7.34 Create Funded Program Type

7.3.6 Functional Area

A *functional area* mirrors the departmental view of the organization. For example, marketing, research and development, operations, manufacturing, and so on are functional areas.

Functional areas describe how funds are being used. You can use functional areas if organizational groupings (funds centers), functional groupings (commitment items), and sources (funds) are insufficient to meet your requirements. This is especially useful if you have to meet cost of sales accounting requirements and legal requirements.

Figure 7.35 shows how another layer of reporting has been added to the combination of **Fund, Commitment item, and Funds center** by adding Functional Area. Now for the same **Fund (Fund 1 or Fund 2),** you can get the breakout of both expenditure and revenue by **Functional Area A** and **Functional Area B.**

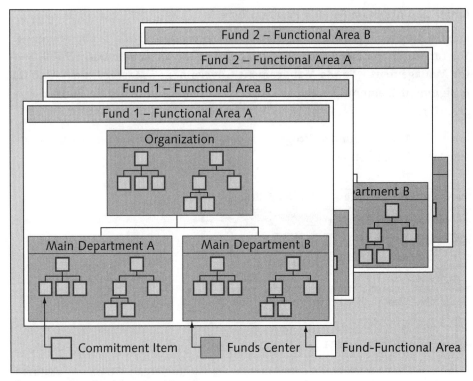

Figure 7.35 Fund and Functional Area

Functional area activation does the following:

▶ Lets you input functional areas in all budgeting transactions.

▶ Makes sure that the updates in Funds Management occur with the functional area.

▶ Lets you assign a functional area to an account in the new general ledger (GL), and hence the actual posted values automatically flow from the feeder systems (GL, Accounts Receivable, Accounts Payable, etc.) to Funds Management.

7.3.7 Subdivision ID

The *subdivision ID* can be applied to all of the master data (commitment item, funds center, fund, and functional area) in Funds Management. The subdivision

ID allows you to save and make sense of complex master data. For example, for master data Fund, an organization might use the first digit of the subdivision ID pertaining to Fund to denote the type of maintenance, the second digit to denote the maintenance department, and so on. Thus, the subdivision ID allows you to split the complex master data into a number of substrings that can also be used for reporting.

This, in turn, allows user-defined information to be included in the account assignment data. Furthermore, below the subdivision ID, you have to define the corresponding subdivision structure, which is made up of individual substrings of an account assignment element for each subdivision ID.

To create and define a subdivision ID, use the menu path **IMG • Public Sector Management • Funds Management Government • Master Data • Account Assignment Elements • Subdivision of Master Data • Create and Define Subdivision ID,** which will take you to the screen shown in Figure 7.36.

In this screen, you need to first select an **Assignment Element Commitment Item** and then create a **Subdivision ID** for the **COMMITMENT.**

You can then maintain the parameters for the substrings:

▶ **Substring**
Choose the Substring 1 to Substring N (limited to whatever is allowed in the system).

▶ **Description**
Enter a description for the substring 1, for example, "Department".

▶ **Total Length**
Identifies the total length of the substring 1.

▶ **Position**
Identifies the place or position of the substring 1.

Similarly, you can maintain the other substrings for the commitment item to denote the business unit, operating group, company, or other characteristics that make sense from a classifying and reporting perspective.

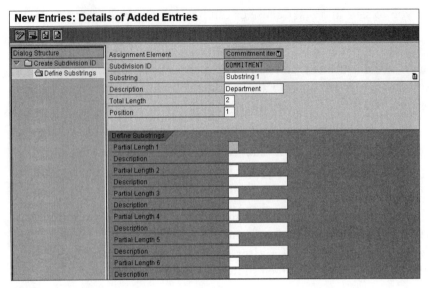

Figure 7.36 Define Subdivision ID

You have now configured all of the master data required to be set up in Funds Management and learned how you can optimize it to suit your requirements.

7.3.8 Budget Structure in Budget Control System (BCS)

A *budget structure* allows you to specify the combination of funds centers, funds, and commitment items for which you can budget or make postings. If you do not set up a budget structure, the system considers all of the combinations of commitment items and funds centers as relevant for budgeting.

The key functions of a budget structure are listed here:

- Create clarity in budgeting by defining the budget structure, which allows you to visualize the kind of expenditures you will be incurring across your organization and the subsequent rationale for budgeting.

- Distinguish central versus local budget allocation needs.

- Provide better system performance because the system only processes the relevant budget objects and not the whole hierarchy.

Figure 7.37 shows the distinction between setting up the budget structure and not setting up the budget structure. With the budget structure, the system automatically derives the budget addresses, and you do not have to use a Funds Management account assignment in a 1:1 fashion from the posting address. So **1** can derive the **budget address** directly from **1.1.1** and **1.1.2**, the **posting address**, instead of via **1.1**.

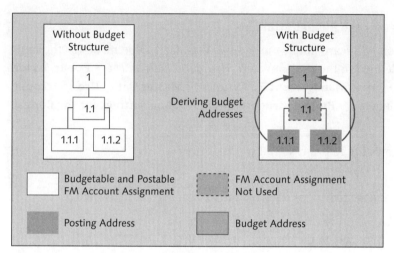

Figure 7.37 Budgeting With and Without Budget Structure

You can either use Former Budgeting or BCS to set up your budgeting structure. In this section, we will cover the key Customizing settings for the budget structure in BCS.

Create Budget Structure

In this step, you will create a key for the budget structure definition that can be used across several fiscal years. The menu path is **IMG • Public Sector Management • Funds Management Government • Master Data • Use of Account Assignment Elements • Budget Structure (BCS) • Create Budget Structure.**

Figure 7.38 shows how you can create the budgeting structure (**BudStruc**) "SAP0000000: ABC Budget Structure" for FM Area (**FMA**) "ABCI".

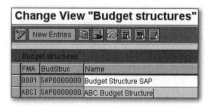

Figure 7.38 Create Budget Structure

Configuring this budgeting structure allows you to configure further settings that can then be used to restrict the budgeting process to specific account assignment elements.

Define Settings for the Budget Structure

In this step, you will learn about the settings that need to be made for the budget structure defined in the previous step. The menu path is **IMG • Public Sector Management • Funds Management Government • Master Data • Use of Account Assignment Elements • Budget Structure (BCS) • Define Settings for the Budget Structure**.

Figure 7.39 shows the relevant settings:

▶ **FM Area**
The Funds Management area for which the budget structure is being set up.

▶ **Fiscal Year**
The fiscal year for which the settings are relevant.

▶ **Chk Posting Address**
If you select this indicator, postings are only allowed for the budget addresses defined in the Funds Management area and fiscal year.

▶ **Budget Structure**
The budgeting structure that was defined in the previous step.

▶ **Drv Strgy f. BA**
The strategy for deriving the budget address from a posting address.

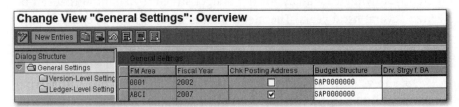

Figure 7.39 General Settings for Budget Structure

After you select the **ABCI FM Area** and click on the **Version-Level Setting** node in the left pane, you will reach the screen shown in Figure 7.40. You can maintain the versions for which you will be using the budget structure on this screen.

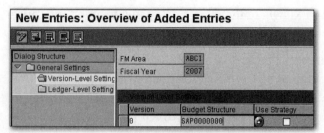

Figure 7.40 Version Level Settings for Budget Structure

If you select the **Ledger-Level Setting** node in the left pane, you will reach the screen shown in Figure 7.41.

New Entries: Overview of Added Entries

Dialog Structure	FM Area	ABCI
▽ ☐ General Settings	Fiscal Year	2007
☐ Version-Level Setting		
☐ Ledger-Level Setting		

	Posting Ledger	No Chk Posting Address	No Index Update
	9A	◉ ☐	☐

Figure 7.41 Ledger Level Settings for Budget Structure

You can maintain the following settings:

▸ **Posting Ledger**
Select either 9A:Payment budget or 9B: Commitment Budget.

▸ **No Chk Posting Address**
Deactivates the separate check for posting addresses for each posting ledger. This is only useful if you activated **Chk Posting Ledger**, shown previously in Figure 7.39.

▸ **No Index Update**
Turns off the automatic update of the index of the budget structures separately for each ledger.

7.3.9   Account Assignment Derivation

The link between posting address and corresponding budget address is not automatically determined by the addresses' hierarchical master data assignments, unlike in other cases in SAP ERP where the master data assignment or enterprise structure assignment establishes the link.

Account assignment derivation can be used to establish the link between the posting address and its corresponding budgeting address, allowing you to assign the budget for budget addresses for all hierarchies. Instead of the standard 1:1 assignment, you can also define N:1 assignment rules between posting addresses and budgeting addresses.

7.3.10 Status Management

Status management allows you to subdivide your budgeting process into phases. You can define the budgeting phases as planning, budgeting entry, budget update, and closing. After you have defined these different phases, you can control what transactions you want to perform in each phase using status management. Each phase is mapped in the system as a status. Defining the statuses allows you to control which budgeting transactions are allowed for a particular budgeting phase. You can adapt the standard SAP ERP status management to your specific requirements by creating your own status profiles.

The following are the steps to customize status management:

1. Create a status profile.
2. Assign the status profile to an object type.
3. Define user statuses.
4. Assign business transactions to the user statuses.

The standard setup contains the status profile FM000001, which houses the predefined user status BUSP (GL account posting blocked) and MRSP (funds reservation blocked).

Define Status Profiles

Let's now review how you can define your own status profile by using the menu path **IMG • Public Sector Management • Funds Management Government • Master Data • Status Management • Define Status Profiles** or Transaction BS02.

Figure 7.42 shows **Status Profile FM000001: Funds Management** and **GM01: Grants Management Example1**.

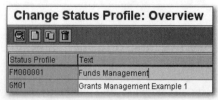

Figure 7.42 Define Status Profiles

If you double-click on **FM000001: Funds Management**, you will reach the screen shown in Figure 7.43. You can maintain the **User Status** with the corresponding **Short Text**, and the **Lowest** and **Highest** indicators, along with their positions (**Posit**) and **Priority**.

Change Status Profile: User Status

Object Types

| Status Profile | FM000001 | Funds Management |
| Maintenance Language | DE | German |

User Status

Statu	Status	Short Text	Long	Init. st	Lowest	Highest	Posit	Priority	Auth. code
	ACNA	Keine Verfügbarkeitskontro	☐	☐					
	BUSP	Sachkontenbuchung gesp	☐	☐					
	MRSP	Mittelreservierung gesperr	☐	☐					

Figure 7.43 Details of the Status Profile

You can then assign the status profile to a Funds Management area using the menu path **IMG • Public Sector Management • Funds Management Government• Master Data • Status Management• Assign Status profile to FM Area** or Transaction OF35.

This completes the master data and basic settings you need to configure to set up your Funds Management system. In the next section, you will learn more about the budgeting process and how you can configure different types of budgeting activities within your budgetary framework. First, you will learn about the types of budgeting transactions that can be set up in the system.

7.4   Budgeting

The following budgeting processes are supported in Funds Management:

▶ **Enter**

Lets you enter new budget data at the beginning of the budgetary cycle. The system will post the planning data as budgetary values using the Enter process.

▶ **Supplement**

Lets you increase the overall budget for the fiscal year for specific account assignment elements.

▶ **Return**

Lets you reduce the available budget in a Funds Management account assignment. The overall budget is reduced.

▶ **Transfer**

Lets you transfer the budget from one Funds Management account assignment to another without impacting the overall budget for the fiscal year.

▶ **Distribution**

Lets you transfer the budget from a higher node to a lower node. This process is only possible if there is a budget available for distribution. The sender and receiver have to be in the same hierarchical path of the structure.

▶ **Revenues Increasing the Budget**

Lets you post revenues that increase your expenditure budget.

▶ **Balanced Entry**

Lets you enter only the source data for revenue commitment items and target data for expenditure commitment items. The system will automatically ensure that the source and target are identical per fiscal year and per year of cash effectivity.

▶ **Carryover**

Lets you carry forward the residual (unconsumed) budget to another fiscal year at the end of the current year.

▶ **Transfer Using Cover groups**

Lets you make the budget accessible to other account assignments by transfer CE posting. This also requires both sender and receiver account assignments.

▶ Figure 7.44 shows the progression from entering budget data to a budget decrease, to the redistribution of the budget using transfers to the budget carryforward at the end of the fiscal year (to move over the budget to the new fiscal year). That is, you start off with an original budget of 100 (Transaction 1), which was reduced by 20 (Transaction 2). Then, you redistributed the budget from **A** to **B** (**Transaction 3**). Finally, you carry forward **5** from fiscal year **2003** to **2004** (**Transaction 4**).

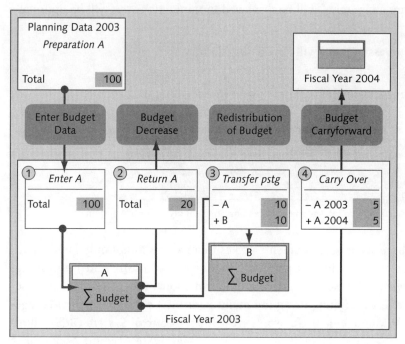

Figure 7.44 Budgeting processes

In this section, we will cover the configuration settings for budgeting, planning, and executing Funds Management.

7.4.1 Activate the Account Assignment in the Budget Control System

In this step, you will learn how to activate account assignments in Funds Management in BCS. The menu path is **IMG • Public Sector Management • Funds Management Government • Budget Control System (BCS) • Budgeting • Basic Settings • Use of Master Data • Activate Account Assignment Elements in Budget Control System.**

Figure 7.45 shows how you can activate the account assignment elements: **Fund**, funds center (**F.center**), commitment item (**C.Item**), functional area (**Func. Area**), **Grant, and Funded Program** for the Funds Management (**FM...**) **ABCI**.

You have the following options:

▶ **Optional**
The account assignment will be displayed in transactions but will be optional.

▶ **Mandatory**
The account assignment will be a required entry.

▶ **Not Used**
The account assignment will not appear in budgeting transactions.

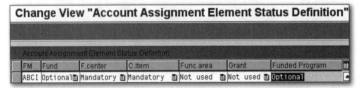

Figure 7.45   Activate Account Assignment Elements in the Budget Control System

Activating these account assignments makes them active in not only Funds Management but also requires assignments in Asset Accounting and Controlling. You can however choose to deactivate fund, functional area, and grant in Asset Accounting and Controlling using the menu path **IMG • Public Sector Management • Funds Management Government • Budget Control System (BCS) • Budgeting • Basic Settings • Use of Master Data • Deactivate Account Assignment Elements in Controlling**.

7.4.2   Define Budget Category

In this step, you will learn how to define a budget category by Funds Management area by using the menu path **IMG • Public Sector Management • Funds Management Government • Budget Control System (BCS) • Budgeting • Basic Settings • Definition of Budget Data • Define Budget Category**.

Figure 7.46 shows the parameters to be set up for budget category activation, as follows:

▶ **FM Area**
ABCI identifies the Funds Management area for which the budget category needs to be set up.

▶ **Budget Category**
You can choose **Payment budget (Ledger 9F)**, **Commitment budget (Ledger 9G)**, or **Financial budget (Ledger 9J)**.

▶ **Time Horizon**
This identifies the number of years that should be used for budgeting for each budget category.

▶ **Start Next Year**
This indicates that the time horizon starts with the next year.

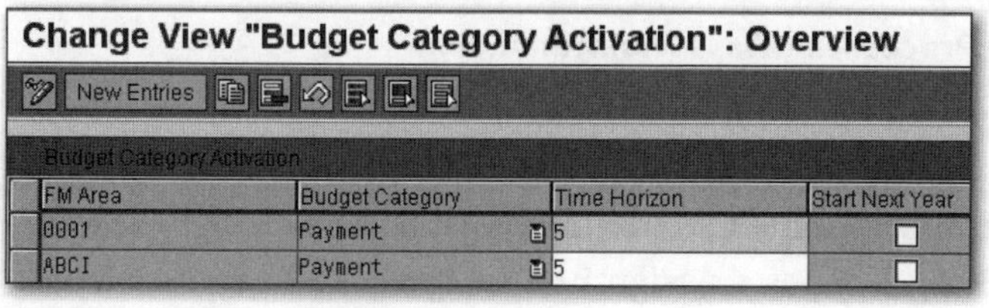

FM Area	Budget Category	Time Horizon	Start Next Year
0001	Payment	5	☐
ABCI	Payment	5	☐

Figure 7.46 Define Budget Category

7.4.3 Budget Types

In this step, you will learn how to define budget types by Funds Management area. You can also assign budget types to process areas in the same step. In addition, you can define statistical budget types and assign those to process areas as well.

Define Budget Types

Budget types allow you to distinguish the various budgeting activities. Several budget types come standard with SAP ERP, but you can also set up your own budget types by using the menu path **IMG • Public Sector Management • Funds Management Government • Budget Control System (BCS) • Budgeting • Basic Settings • Definition of Budget Data • Budget Types • Define Budget Types**.

Figure 7.47 shows the standard SAP ERP budget types, including **INIT** (Initial), **REVI** (Revised), and **CONT** (Contingency).

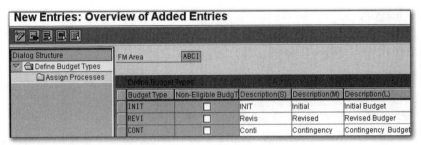

Figure 7.47 Define Budget Types

Assign Budget Types to Processes (Mass Maintenance)

After you have defined your budget types, you need to assign them to processes using menu path **IMG • Public Sector Management • Funds Management Government • Budget Control System (BCS) • Budgeting • Basic Settings • Definition of Budget Data • Budget Types • Assign Budget Types to Processes (Mass Maintenance)**.

Figure 7.48 shows the **Mass Maintenance** screen after assigning **Enter** and **Prepare** Process to the **INIT** Budget Type. This screen allows you to maintain the assignments of processes and budget type in one go rather than setting these up individually.

Change View "Assign Budget Type To Process (Mass Maintenance)"		

FM Area	Process	Budget Type
0001	Carry For. Recv	BT01
0001	Carry For. Send	BT01
0001	Enter	BT01
0001	Prepare	BT01
0001	Receive	TR01
0001	Receive	TR02
0001	Return	BT01
0001	Send	TR01
0001	Send	TR02
0001	Supplement	SU01
0001	Supplement	SU02
ABCI	Enter	INIT
ABCI	Prepare	INIT
ABCI	Supplement	REVI
ABCI	Receive Cov.El.	CONT

Figure 7.48 Assign Budget Types to Processes (Mass Maintenance)

7.4.4 Budget Entry Documents

Budget entry documents are created whenever you post a document in budgeting. In this section, you will learn how to define the configuration settings for budget entry documents. Figure 7.49 shows the typical settings you need to maintain for the document definition in budgeting:

▶ **Define Document Types**

▶ **Maintain Number Range Interval for Entry Documents**

▶ **Maintain Number Range interval for Budget Change Documents**

▶ **Define Number Range Interval for Document Family**

▶ **Define Layout for Budgeting Workbench**

▶ **Define Layout for Multiple Budget Entry**

▶ **Assignment of Forms for Printing Budget Documents**

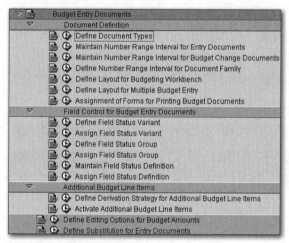

Figure 7.49 Budget Entry Documents Configuration Settings

These will be discussed in more detail in the following subsections.

Define Document Types

Document types let you classify budget entry documents in terms that make sense in your organization. You can create your own document types by using the menu path **IMG • Public Sector Management • Funds Management Government •**

Budget Control System (BCS) • Budgeting • Budget Entry • Budget Entry Documents • Document Definition • Define Document Types.

Figure 7.50 shows the document types with the following parameters:

- ▶ **Document Type**
  This is the identifier of the document, for example, **0001**, **0002**, and **WF01**.

- ▶ **Number range**
  This is the associated number range for the document type.

- ▶ **Workflow**
  This flag lets you trigger a workflow for the document type.

- ▶ **Scenario for Value Type**
  This lets you specify the appropriate scenario supported by the document type:

  - ▶ **Budget**: Only the budgeting amounts are contained in the entry documents.

  - ▶ **Release**: Only the released amounts are contained in the document.

  - ▶ **Budget with automatic release**: You can restrict the document to a specific budgeting process such as enter, return, supplement, transfer, and so on.

  - ▶ **Statistical**: Only statistical values are contained in the budgeting document.

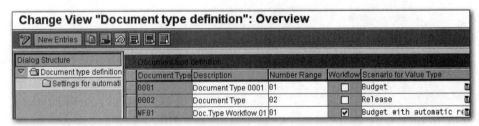

Figure 7.50 Define Document Types for Budget Entry

If you select **WF01** and then select the **Settings for automatic release** node in the left pane, you can maintain the **Processes** associated with the document type, as shown in Figure 7.51. You can maintain the Process "Enter" for the **Document type WF01** in this screen.

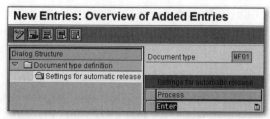

Figure 7.51 Define Settings for Automatic Release

Maintain Number Range Interval for Entry Documents

When you post any budget values, the system automatically generates a document number to capture the transaction. In this step, you will learn how to define the number ranges for entry document types defined in the previous step. The menu path is **IMG • Public Sector Management • Funds Management Government • Budget Control System (BCS) • Budgeting • Budget Entry • Budget Entry Documents • Document Definition• Maintain Number Range Interval for Entry Documents**, and the Transaction is FMEDNR.

Figure 7.52 shows you the screen for maintaining the number range object (**NR Object**) "FM entry doc. nr." for the **Funds Management area (Subobject) ABCI**. Number ranges (**No**) **01** and **02** have been maintained for **Year 2007**. You can maintain additional intervals by clicking on the **Interval** button.

Maintain Number Range Intervals

	Interval				
NR Object		FM entry doc. nr.			
Subobject		ABCI			

Intervals

No	Year	From number	To number	Current number	Ext
01	2007	0000000001	0999999999	0	☐
02	2007	1000000001	1999999999	0	☐

Figure 7.52 Define Number Range by Financial Management Area

Maintain Number Range Interval for Budget Change Documents

Similar to the number range for entry documents, you can maintain the number range for budget change documents using the menu path **IMG • Public Sector Management • Funds Management Government • Budget Control System (BCS)**

• **Budgeting** • **Budget Entry** • **Budget Entry Documents** • **Document Definition** • **Maintain Number Range Interval for Budget Change Documents** and Transaction FMLINR.

Figure 7.53 shows you the screen for maintaining the number range object (**NR Object**) **FM line item number** for the Funds Management area (**Subobject**) **ABCI**. Number ranges (**No**) **01** and **02** have been maintained for **Year 2007**. You can maintain additional intervals by clicking on the **Interval** button.

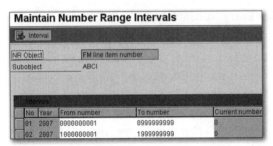

Figure 7.53 Maintain Number Range Interval for Budget Change Documents

Define Number Range Interval for Document Family

Number ranges for a document family can also be maintained by using the menu path **IMG** • **Public Sector Management** • **Funds Management Government** • **Budget Control System (BCS)** • **Budgeting** • **Budget Entry** • **Budget Entry Documents** • **Document Definition** • **Define Number Range Interval for Document Family** and Transaction FMEDFAFMNR.

Figure 7.54 shows the screen for maintaining the number range object (**NR Object**) **Nber range for DOCFAM** for the Funds Management area (**Subobject**) **ABCI**. Number ranges (**No**) **01** and **02** have been maintained for **Year 2007**.

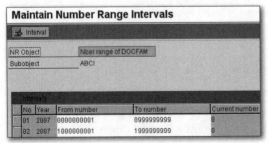

Figure 7.54 Define Number Range Interval for Document Family

You can maintain any additional intervals by clicking on the **Interval** button.

Define Layout for Budgeting Workbench

You can also define how you want to structure your budgeting workbench by using the menu path **IMG • Public Sector Management • Funds Management Government • Budget Control System (BCS) • Budgeting • Budget Entry • Budget Entry Documents • Document Definition • Define Layout for Budgeting Workbench.**

Figure 7.55 shows the standard layouts (**SAP001** to **SAP005**) that are available for you to modify or to copy.

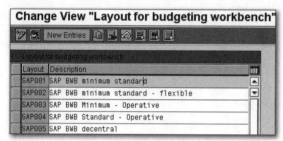

Figure 7.55   Define Layout for Budgeting Workbench

If you double-click on **SAP004: SAP BWB Standard - Operative**, you will be able to configure the layout variant as shown in Figure 7.56. The following fields need to be maintained:

- ► **Description**
  Denotes the description of the line layout.
- ► **Year of Cash Effectivity/Budget Type**
  Defines an input field as either **Header** or **Column**. Both **Year of Cash Effectivity** and **Budget Type** have been marked as **Header**. That means that the value entered is valid for all of the rows of the entries.
- ► **Fund/Fund Center/Commitment Item/Funded Program**
  These are marked as **Column,** and you will have to enter the individual line item values for each of these.
- ► **Column Position**
  Contains the position of the item that has been marked as **Column**.

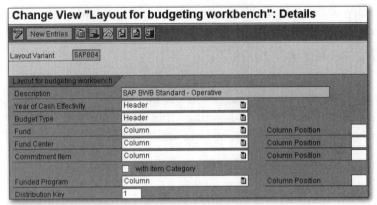

Figure 7.56 Define Layout for Budgeting Workbench - Details

▶ **with Item Category**
Displays the commitment item category in addition to the commitment item.

▶ **Distribution Key**
Maintains the relevant distribution key:

  ▶ **0**: Manual distribution

  ▶ **1**: Equal distribution

  ▶ **2**: Distribution as before

  ▶ **3**: Distribution by percentage

  ▶ **4**: Distribute values to following no-value periods

  ▶ **5**: Copy values to following no-value periods

  ▶ **6**: Carry forward single value

  ▶ **7**: Distribute according to number of days in period

Similarly, you can define a layout for the multiple budget entry transaction FMPEP using the menu path **IMG • Public Sector Management • Funds Management Government • Budget Control System (BCS) • Budgeting • Budget Entry • Budget Entry Documents • Document Definition • Define Layout for Multiple Budget Entry.**

Assignment of Forms for Printing Budget Documents

In this step, you will learn how to assign the forms that will be used for printing budget documents in the budgeting workbench (Transaction FMBB) or in the entry document display transaction (Transaction FMEDD). The menu path is **IMG • Public Sector Management • Funds Management Government • Budget Control System (BCS) • Budgeting • Budget Entry • Budget Entry Documents • Document Definition • Assignment of Forms for Printing Budget Documents.**

Figure 7.57 shows the assignment of **Name of Form Object Z_BUDGET_FORM** for **Doc Type 0002, Process BALA.**

Figure 7.57 Assignment of Forms for Printing Budget Documents

The following processes can be maintained with different forms:

▶ **BALA**: Balanced Entry

▶ **COVR**: Carry Over

▶ **DIST**: Distribution

▶ **ENTR**: Enter

▶ **RBBP**: Revenues increasing budget

▶ **RETN**: Return

▶ **SUPL**: Supplement

▶ **TRAN**: Transfer

▶ **TRCE**: Transfer using cover groups

Additional Budget Line Items

You can define in which areas you want to work with additional budget line items using the menu path **IMG • Public Sector Management • Funds Management Government • Budget Control System (BCS) • Budgeting • Budget Entry • Budget Entry Documents • Additional Budget Line Items • Activate Additional Budget Line Items.**

Figure 7.58 shows the **Original Ap..** (application) with **Description,** and the indicator (**Additional L...**), which lets you enable the creation of additional budget line items.

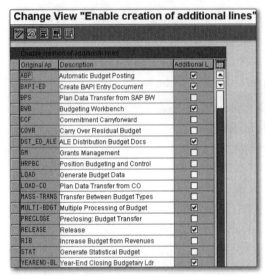

Figure 7.58 Activate Additional Budget Line Items

> **Note**
>
> Do not deactivate the **BAP-ED: Create BAPI Entry Document** and **BWB: Budgeting Workbench**, which come as pre-activated in the SAP system.

Now that you understand the budgeting process, we will take a look at the availability control checks available in SAP Public Sector Management (PSM).

7.5 Availability Control

The availability control (AVC) component allows you to monitor the availability of funds in Funds Management. Figure 7.59 shows the overall structure of AVC and how it works.

It allows you to check the **Consumed amounts** against the **Consumable budget** within the budgeting process. Before any posting can happen, it has to go through the **Posting control,** which checks whether AVC is active for the **Control object** and then compares the **Consumption level in %** using the **Tolerance profile.** If due to the new posting, the consumption level becomes higher than the one specified in the **Tolerance profile**, **Posting control** will give a RED light, stopping the posting and displaying an error message.

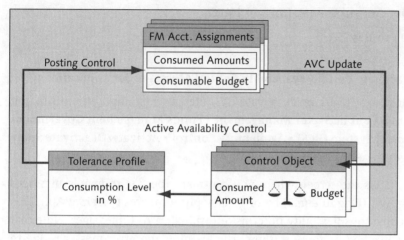

Figure 7.59 Check Standard Customizing of Availability Control

In this section, we will cover the configuration settings you need to set up for AVC.

7.5.1 Activate/Deactivate Availability Control for Applications

In this step, you will learn the process of activating AVC for Funds Management. The following settings are covered:

- Check standard AVC Customizing.
- Activate/deactivate certain AVC messages for applications.

Check Standard Availability Control Customizing

You can check the standard AVC Customizing using the menu path **IMG • Public Sector Management • Funds Management Government • Budget Control System (BCS) • Availability Control • Check Standard Customizing of Availability Control** or Transaction FMAVCCUSTDEF.

This essentially checks whether the following AVC components have been already defined in the system:

- ▶ **Data Sources**: FMBC, FMBP, FMBF, FMUC and FMUP

- ▶ **Availability Control Ledgers**: 9H or 9I.

- ▶ **Activity Groups**: From 10 to 95.

- ▶ **Availability Control Events:** IMLE or IMLO

- ▶ **Tolerance Profiles**: 1000

Activate/Deactivate Certain Availability Control Messages for Applications

You can choose to activate or deactivate AVC messages by application using the menu path **IMG • Public Sector Management • Funds Management Government • Budget Control System (BCS) • Availability Control • Activate/Deactivate Some AVC Messages for Applications.**

Figure 7.60 shows the screen where you can mark the flag to enable messages when calling AVC (**Flag to ena...**) by original application area (**Original Ap.**). This gives you tremendous flexibility in terms of turning on AVC messages. Note that AVC is not controlled by these settings. The warning and error messages due to non-availability of sufficient budgets can be controlled using these settings.

Change View "Enable Availability Control Checks"

Original Ap	Description	Flag to ena
BAPI-ED	Create BAPI Entry Document	☑
BAPI-UPD	Update BAPI Totals Records	☐
BWB	Budgeting Workbench	☑
COPY	Copy/Reset Data	☐
COVR	Carry Over Residual Budget	☑
DST_ED_ALE	ALE Distribution Budget Docs	☑
LOAD	Generate Budget Data	☑
LOAD-CO	Plan Data Transfer from CO	☑
MASS-RVSAL	Entry Document Reversal	☑
MASS-TRANS	Transfer Between Budget Types	☑
MULTI-BDGT	Multiple Processing of Budget	☑
PP	Planning Processor	☑
PRECLOSE	Preclosing: Budget Transfer	☑
RELEASE	Release	☑
RIB	Increase Budget from Revenues	☐
YEAREND-BL	Year-End Closing Budgetary Ldr	☐

Figure 7.60 Enable Availability Control Checks by Applications

> **Note**
>
> Do not deactivate the settings that have already been activated in standard SAP PSM.

7.5.2 Activity Groups

Activity groups allow you to break out postings so that you can then define separate AVC rules for each activity group (in the tolerance profile definition).

In this step, you will learn the process of defining new activity groups and defining separate derivation strategies for these activity groups.

Edit Activity Groups

You can define your own activity groups by using the menu path **IMG • Public Sector Management • Funds Management Government • Budget Control System (BCS) • Availability Control • Activity Groups • Edit Activity Groups** or Transaction FMAVCCUSTDEF.

Figure 7.61 shows the different activity groups that come pre-configured. To define your own activity groups, click on **New Entries.**

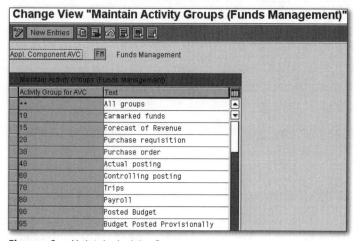

Figure 7.61 Maintain Activity Groups

Edit Derivation Strategy for Activity Groups

You can also define your own derivation strategy for the custom activity groups defined in the previous step by using the menu path **IMG • Public Sector Management • Funds Management Government • Budget Control System (BCS) • Availability Control • Activity Groups • Edit Derivation Strategy for Activity Groups** or Transaction FMAVCDERIACTG.

Figure 7.62 shows the three derivation types (**Assignment** and two types of **Derivation Rule**) that allow you to customize how these activity groups are derived from the value types and controlling assignments.

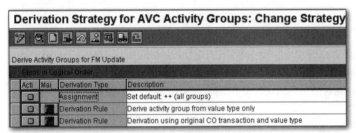

Figure 7.62 Derivation Strategy for Availability Control Groups

The derivation strategy can use one of the following methods:

► **Move**
A value is assigned to an activity group.

► **Derivation Rule**
Values are assigned as input parameters/source fields to an activity group as a target field.

Now that you understand activity groups, let's explore the details of tolerance profiles.

7.5.3 Tolerance Profiles

Tolerance profiles are used to group together tolerance limits for activity groups. You can define either usage rates (e.g., 80% of the budget) or absolute values (e.g., less than $1,000 USD as compared to the budget value) as parameters that will constitute your tolerance profile. If you define 80% and 100% as the parameters, then you can configure the system to display a warning message when the budget is 80% exhausted and an error message if the budget is completely exhausted. Or, you can specify that if the actual values have reached the budget minus $1,000 USD then the system will display a warning message.

In this step, you will learn how to define tolerance profiles and their tolerance limits, using the menu path **IMG • Public Sector Management • Funds Management Government • Budget Control System (BCS) • Availability Control • Edit Tolerance Profiles**.

Figure 7.63 shows the standard **Tolerance profile 1000: SAP Standard profile**. You can maintain the **Currency** of the availability control if all of your budgetary decisions are in one currency. Otherwise, leave this value blank.

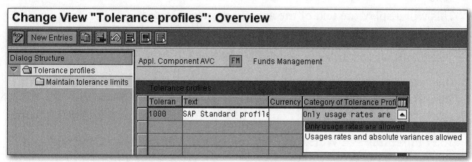

Figure 7.63 Define Tolerance Profiles

Category of Tolerance Profile has two options: **Only usage rates are allowed** or **Usage rates and Absolute variance are allowed**. You select the appropriate tolerance profile category depending on your requirements.

Now, if you select the tolerance profile **1000: SAP Standard profile** and select the **Maintain tolerance limits** node in the left pane, you will see the screen shown in Figure 7.64.

Change View "Maintain tolerance limits": Overview

New Entries

Dialog Structure								
▽ ☐ Tolerance profiles	Tolerance Profile	1000	SAP Standard profile					
☐ Maintain tolerance lir								

Maintain tolerance limits

Ceiling Type	Activity	Text	Order	Inactive	Message Type of	Usag	Availability Control Event
Expenditures (outgoing ☐	++	All groups		☐	Warning ☐	90.00	
Expenditures (outgoing ☐	++	All groups	1	☐	Error message ☐	100.00	

Figure 7.64 Maintain Tolerance Limits

You can maintain the following parameters:

▶ **Ceiling Type**
Lets you specify how AVC checks expenditures or revenues. Ceiling types come preconfigured in the system. You have two options: **Expenditure (outgoing amount)** or **Revenue (incoming amount)**. Typically, settings are configured for expenditures.

▶ **Activity group for AVC**
Lets you specify the activity group, or you can use **++** as a wildcard to denote all of the activity groups.

▶ **Text**
This will display the text of the activity groups selected.

▶ **Order**
This identifies the order in which the tolerance limit is checked.

▶ **Inactive**
Setting this flag deactivates the entry.

▶ **Message type of Availability Control**
You can set this as a **Warning, Error message,** or **Information message**.

▶ **Usage rate in %**
This identifies the usage rate that will trigger the AVC check. In this example, when 90% usage is reached, the system will issue a warning message. At 100%, an error message is issued.

▶ **Availability control event**
This can be configured to send an internal mail either once or repeatedly when an AVC event occurs.

7.5.4 Availability Control Ledger

The *availability control ledger* (AVC ledger) is part of a special purpose ledger and contains the BCS budget data and actual/commitment data of Funds Management. In the standard system, two ledgers are supported: 9H for payment budget, and 9I for commitment budget. However, you can choose to define additional ledgers if the standard ledgers do not meet your requirements. You can also set up your own derivation strategy for user-defined ledgers. In a standard delivered system without a derivation strategy or with an empty derivation strategy, the SAP system will assign the budget addresses in FI-PSM to FI-SL and the appropriate ledger 1:1.

If you need to change this, you can define your own strategy for account assignment derivation.

In this step, you will learn the process of customizing the AVC ledger. The following settings will be discussed:

- Maintain a customer-specific ledger for availability check.
- Define the consumable budget.
- Define filter settings for commitment/actual values.
- Assign tolerance profiles and strategy for control objects.

Maintain Customer-Specific Ledger for Availability Check

You can define your own AVC ledger using the menu path **IMG • Public Sector Management • Funds Management Government • Budget Control System (BCS) • Availability Control • Settings for Availability Control Ledger • Maintain Customer-Specific Ledger for Availability Check.**

Figure 7.65 shows the standard AVC ledgers **9H: FM Payment Budget Availability Control** and **9I: FM Commitment Budget Availability Control**.

You can maintain the following parameters for these ledgers:

- **Data Source for Consumed Amount**
  The following options are available for this:

  - **FM Commitment budget (CB)**
  - **FM Financial budget**
  - **FM Payment budget (PB)**
  - **FM PB Commitment/Actual Data**
  - **FM CB Commitment/Actual Data**

Figure 7.65 Maintain Customer-Specific Ledger for Availability Check

▸ **Data Source for Consumable Budget**
The following options can be configured for this:

- ▸ **FM Commitment budget (CB)**
- ▸ **FM Financial budget**
- ▸ **FM Payment budget (PB)**

Thus, the system provides you with a tremendous amount of flexibility in terms of how you can configure the AVC ledgers.

Define the Consumable Budget

As you learned in the previous step, you need to pick one of the options — commitment budget, payment budget, or financial budget — as the consumable budget. However, what makes up the consumable budget can also be customized to suit your requirements.

Therefore, you need to define which budget values should be part of the active availability control. The menu path to do this is **IMG • Public Sector Management • Funds Management Government • Budget Control System (BCS) • Availability Control • Settings for Availability Control Ledger • Define Filter Settings for Budget Values • Define the Consumable Budget.**

Figure 7.66 shows how you can define the consumable budget for the **Control Ledger 9H: FM PB Availability Control From Fiscal Year 2007**.

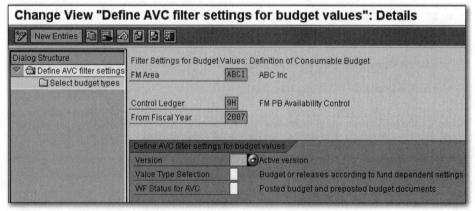

Figure 7.66 Define Availability Control Settings for the Consumable Budget

You can configure the following settings:

▶ **Version**

Enter the version for which the budget will be considered. If you leave this blank, then Active version is automatically chosen.

▶ **Value Type Selection**

Specify the value type. If you leave this field **BLANK**, then the system-defined settings for value type are automatically selected. If you select **B**, you can enter the budget types by selecting the **Select budget types** node in the left pane.

▶ **WF Status for AVC**

This lets you indicate whether a posted budget only is considered for AVC or if a pre-posted budget is also considered for AVC. If you leave this **BLANK**, then both posted and pre-posted are selected. If you choose **P**, then only posted values are selected.

▶ If you select the **Select budget types** node in the left pane, you will be taken to the next screen (provided you have chosen **B** in the **Value Type Selection** field in the previous step), as shown in Figure 7.67. You can enter the budget types you want to be relevant for the consumable budget. In this case, we have selected **CONT: Contingency Budget**, **INIT: Initial Budget**, and **REVI: Revised Budget**, as applicable for the consumable budget.

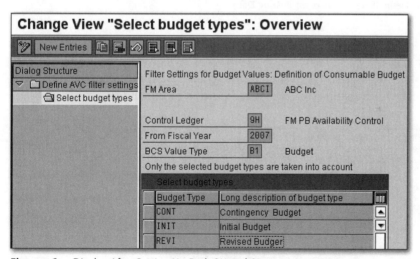

Figure 7.67 Display After Setting Up Both 9H and 9I

Define Filter Settings for Commitment/Actual Values

Earlier, you learned how you can customize particular budget types (contingency budget, initial budget, and revised budget) to constitute the consumable budget for AVC.

You can also customize your commitment and actual values that make up the consumed budget using the menu path **IMG • Public Sector Management • Funds Management Government • Budget Control System (BCS) • Availability Control • Settings for Availability Control Ledger • Define Filter Settings for Commitment/Actual Values**.

Figure 7.68 shows the initial screen you see after following this menu path. You need to select the ledger and then select the **Exclude value types node in the left pane**.

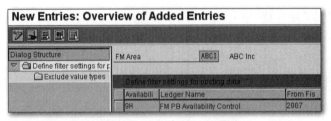

Figure 7.68 Define Filter Settings for Posting Data

This will take you to the next screen (see Figure 7.69) where you can maintain the **Value types** (for our example, **58: Down Payment Requests** and **60: Parked Documents**). These value types should be excluded from the actual/commitment items, which will constitute the consumed portion of the budget.

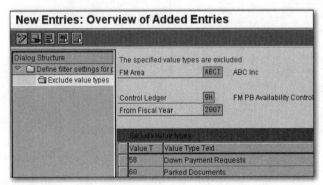

Figure 7.69 Exclude Value Types

The following are the value types that can be maintained here:

- **50**: Purchase Requisitions
- **51**: Purchase Orders
- **52**: Business Trip Commitments
- **54**: Invoices
- **57**: Payments
- **58**: Down Payment Requests
- **60**: Parked Documents
- **6B**: Clarification Worklist FI-CA
- **61**: Down Payments
- **64**: Funds Transfers
- **65**: Funds Commitment
- **66**: Transfer Postings
- **80**: Funds Block
- **81**: Funds Reservation
- **82**: Funds Precommitment
- **83**: Forecast of Revenue
- **84**: Payment Reservation (Not for General Use)
- **95**: Secondary Cost Postings (CO)

You can also maintain the excluded value types for **Control Ledger 9I: FM Commitment Budget Availability Control**, as shown in Figure 7.70.

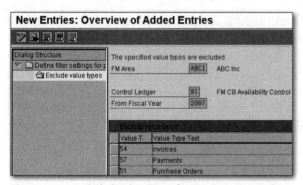

Figure 7.70 Excluded Value Types for Commitment Budget

Assign Tolerance Profiles and Strategy for Control Objects

Earlier, you learned how to define tolerance profiles and also how you can configure AVC ledgers. In this step, you combine the two by assigning the tolerance profile and derivation strategy to the AVC ledger using the menu path **IMG • Public Sector Management • Funds Management Government • Budget Control System (BCS) • Availability Control • Settings for Availability Control Ledger • Assign Tolerance Profiles and Strategy for Control Objects**.

Figure 7.71 shows Availability ledger **9H: FM PB Availability Control** From Fiscal year **2007** with the following assignments:

▶ **Tolerance Profile:** 1000

▶ **Strategy for Deriving Tolerance Profile:** 9HSAP000

▶ **Strategy for Deriving Control Objects:** 9HSAP000

▶ **Determination of Grant in Controlling Objects:** Grant Identical in Budget Address and Derived Control Object

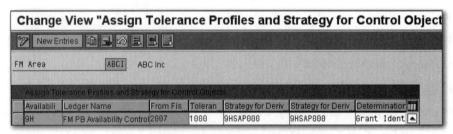

Figure 7.71 Assign Tolerance Profiles and Strategy for Control Objects

7.5.5 Define Activation of Availability Control

After you have completely defined the AVC Ledger, there is a last step that needs to be completed to activate the AVC. The menu path is **IMG • Public Sector Management • Funds Management Government • Budget Control System (BCS) • Availability Control • Define Activation of Availability Control.**

Figure 7.72 shows how you can set up the Activation status of availability ledger as **Active with strict check logic** from a particular fiscal year, in this case **2007**.

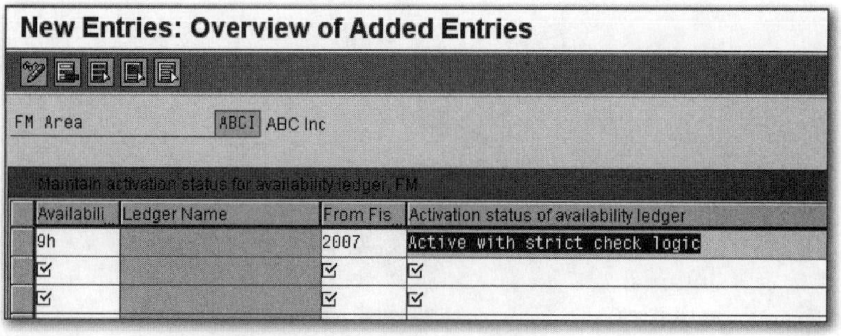

Figure 7.72 Define Activation of Availability Control

Other options include the following:

- **Ledger not active**
- **Active without availability checks**
- **Active with usual check logic**
- **Active with soft check logic**
- **Active with strict check logic for document chains**

Now that you understand the process of setting up AVC using activity groups, tolerance profiles, the AVC ledger, and Customizing settings to include specific budget types for a consumable budget, let's take a look at the settings you need to configure for integrating actual and commitment value flows from feeder components (AR, AP, GL, etc.) to Funds Management.

7.6   Integration/Actual and Commitment Update

In this section, you will learn how you can set up the integration of Funds Management with other components per your requirements. You will also learn how to configure specific settings required for updating actual and commitment data.

Figure 7.73 shows you the integrated architecture of how Funds Management is related to other SAP ERP components. All of the other components (**HR - Human Resources, HR - Travel Management, FI/SD - Revenues, FI/CO - Internal Activities, FI-PS - Procurement without purchasing, MM - Procurement with purchasing**) are tightly integrated with reference to the **Commitments** and the **Actual** values that flow from these feeder components to SAP-PSM Funds Management.

287

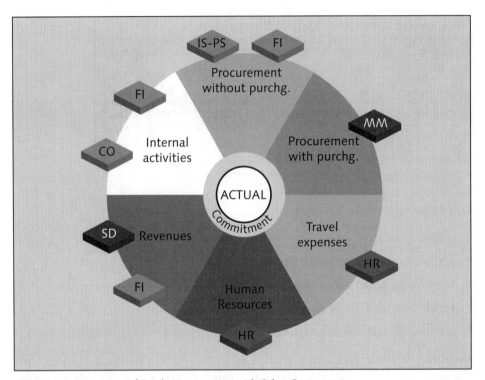

Figure 7.73 Integration of Funds Management with Other Components

In this section, you will learn how these components are integrated with FI-PSM-FM and the key settings that allow you to configure the integration per your requirements. We will cover the following Customizing items:

- **Assign Update Profile to FM Area**
- **Override Update Profile**
- **Make Other Settings**
- **Define Number Ranges for Actual Transactions**
- **Assign Number Range to Funds Management Area**
- **Activate/Deactivate Funds Management**

7.6.1 Assign Update Profile to Funds Management Area

An *update profile* is the link between Funds Management and the feeder components. In an update profile, parameters are grouped together to control commitment and actual data updates in Funds Management.

In this step, you will learn how to assign an update profile to a Funds Management area using the menu path **IMG • Public Sector Management • Funds Management Government • Actual and Commitment Update/Integration • General Settings • Assign Update Profile to FM Area**. Figure 7.74 shows the assignment of the **Update profile 000500** to the **FM Area ABCI**.

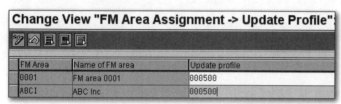

Figure 7.74 Assign Update Profile to Funds Management Area

Some of the available update profiles are listed here:

- **000100**: Payment budget; Payment basis; Due date
- **000101**: Payment budget; Payment basis; Posting date
- **000102**: Payment budget; Invoice basis; Posting date
- **000109**: Payment Budget; Payment Basis; Posting Date; GNJAHR
- **000200**: PB more than 1 yr: CB 1 yr Ex. Dutch justice
- **000201**: PB more than 1 yr: CB 1 yr Ex. Netherlands
- **000300**: Separate PB/CB budget lines; EU
- **000350**: Separate PB/CB budget lines; standard
- **000351**: BL active for cmmt and payment budget (Colombia)
- **000359**: Separate FM Acct Assgnmt PB/CB; Approved Amounts CB
- **000400**: CB with target fiscal years Ex.German local auths
- **000500**: Payment prog.avlblty control Ex. Canadian govt
- **000600**: Former Budgetary Ledger - US Government
- **000601**: Budgetary Ledger - US Government

You have to consider the following when choosing an update profile:

▶ **Invoice Basis**
Invoices and goods receipts are updated in FI-PSM-FM. The primary costs and asset acquisition costs are also updated. Additionally, the commitments are carried forward to the next fiscal year.

▶ **Payment Basis**
Payments are also updated after you run the payment transfer program RFFMS200.

The other key parameter of an update profile is the date that is used to update PSM-FM:

▶ **Due date**
This is the date that is picked up in update profile 000100.

▶ **Posting date**
This is the most common date used in other update profiles and affects how the system updates the actual and commitment values in PSM-FM using the posting date of the transaction.

7.6.2 Override Update Profile

As you can see, the update profile itself might not suit all requirements. To address this, you can override the update profile using the menu path **IMG • Public Sector Management • Funds Management Government • Actual and Commitment Update/Integration • General Settings • Override Update Profile.**

Figure 7.75 shows the initial screen for making changes to the update profile. You have two options: you can make changes either by value type or by update profile.

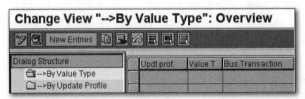

Figure 7.75 Override Update Profile

After you select the **–>By Value Type** node in the left pane, you will see the screen shown in Figure 7.76. You can maintain the **Update profile, Value Type,** and **Bus. (Business) Transaction** combination, and change the relevant parameters depending on your requirements, as follows:

▶ **Statistical Update**
If you deselect this flag, statistical updates will not have an impact on the budget.

▶ **Payment/Commitment Budget**
You can select from the following dates: **Posting Date, Due Date,** or **Dlv.** (Delivery) **Date.**

▶ **PB-Encumbrance Tracking for Payment/Commitment Budget**
This can be either **Period-Based** or **FY-Based** (fiscal year-based).

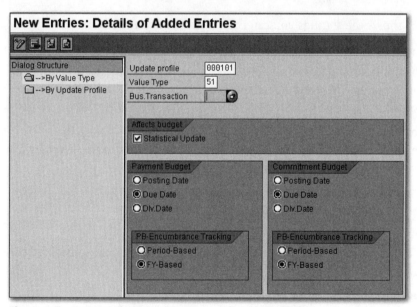

Figure 7.76 Maintain the Value Type Settings for Update Profile

7.6.3   Make Other Settings

In addition to the changes you can make by profile, value type, and business transaction, you can also make generic changes by using the menu path **IMG • Public Sector Management • Funds Management Government • Actual and Commitment Update/Integration • General Settings • Make Other Settings.**

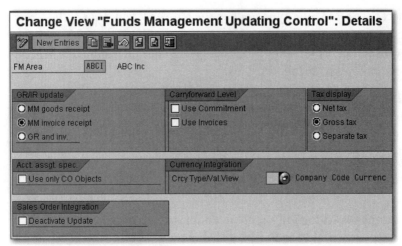

Figure 7.77 Make Other Settings

Figure 7.77 shows the settings you can configure for **FM Area ABCI**:

▶ **GR/IR Update**
You can specify to update the GR/IR-related impact to budgeting at the time of **MM goods receipt, MM invoice receipt,** or when both **GR and inv.** (invoice) are recorded.

▶ **Carryforward level**
You can specify whether to use commitments, and whether to use invoices for the carryforward of the residual budget to the next fiscal year.

▶ **Tax Display**
Tax can be displayed as **Net tax**, **Gross tax**, or **Separate tax**.

▶ **Use only CO objects**
Setting this flag makes sure that only real Controlling objects are considered for deriving account assignments.

▶ **Currency Integration/Valuation View**
You can specify one of the following:

  ▶ **10**: Company code currency

  ▶ **30**: Group currency

  ▶ **40**: Hard currency

  ▶ **50**: Index-based currency

  ▶ **60**: Global company currency

▶ **Deactivate Update**

Setting this flag will deactivate Funds Management commitment updating for sales orders.

7.6.4 Number Ranges for Actual Data Documents

In this section, you will learn how to define the number ranges for Funds Management actual documents and then assign those to a Funds Management area.

Define Number Ranges for Actual Transactions

The number ranges for actual transactions can be defined using the menu path **IMG • Public Sector Management • Funds Management Government • Actual and Commitment Update/Integration • Basic Settings • FM Line Items • Define Number Ranges for Actual Transactions**.

Figure 7.78 shows how you can create a number range **(No.) 01** for the Funds Management area **(Subobject) ABCI** and Number range object **(NR Object) FM-document**.

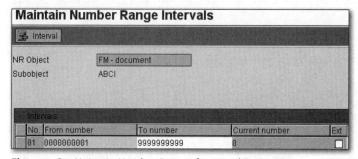

Figure 7.78 Maintain Number Ranges for Actual Transactions

Assign Number Range to FM Area

The number range created in the previous step now needs to be assigned to the Funds Management area using the menu path **IMG • Public Sector Management • Funds Management Government • Actual and Commitment Update/Integration • Basic Settings • FM Line Items • Assign Number Range to FM Area**.

Figure 7.79 shows an assignment of the **FM Area ABCI** to **Number range no. 01**.

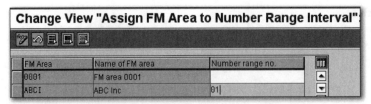

Figure 7.79 Assign Funds Management Area to Number range

7.6.5 Activate/Deactivate Funds Management

Activating Funds Management is the culmination of all of the configuration steps you have performed so far. In this step, you activate Funds Management by using the menu path **IMG • Public Sector Management • Funds Management Government • Actual and Commitment Update/Integration • Activate/Deactivate Funds Management**.

Figure 7.80 shows the screen for activating Funds Management with the following parameters:

▶ **Co...**
US01 identifies the company code for which you want to activate Funds Management.

▶ **FM.../FMA text**
ABCI is the Funds Management area for "ABC Inc".

▶ **AA Derivtn**
If this flag is set, it activates the account assignment derivation, and documents will start having the Funds Management account assignments.

▶ **Update**
If this flag is set, documents will start posting to Funds Management from the feeder systems (AR, AP, GL, etc.) for the company code and Funds Management area.

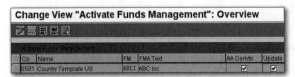

Figure 7.80 Activate Funds Management

To set the flag **AA Derivtn**, you must have assigned the Funds Management area to the company code, and account assignment derivation must have been defined.

Before you can set the **Update** flag for a company code, the following conditions must be fulfilled:

- The Funds Management area must be assigned to the company code.
- The currency key must exist for the Funds Management area.
- A fiscal year variant must be assigned to the Funds Management area.
- A budget profile must be assigned to the Funds Management area, if you use Former Budgeting.
- A budget profile for the fund should only be assigned to the Funds Management area if you use Former Budgeting and use funds.
- A status profile must have been assigned to the Funds Management area if you are working with status management.
- A number range interval (for Funds Management line items) must have been assigned to the Funds Management area.
- An update profile must have been assigned to the Funds Management area.
- An account assignment derivation must have been defined.

You learned in this section how you can customize the integration of Funds Management with other SAP ERP components by using an update profile and then changing some of the parameters of the update profile by value type. This provides you with sufficient flexibility to design the integration framework per your requirements. In the next section, you will learn some of the key closing operations that need to be performed for Funds Management.

7.7   Closing Operations

Closing operations enable you to execute year-end closing activities pertaining to Funds Management.

As shown in Figure 7.81, the residual budget and the open commitments of the **Old Fiscal Year** are carried forward to the **New Fiscal Year** as part of closing operations.

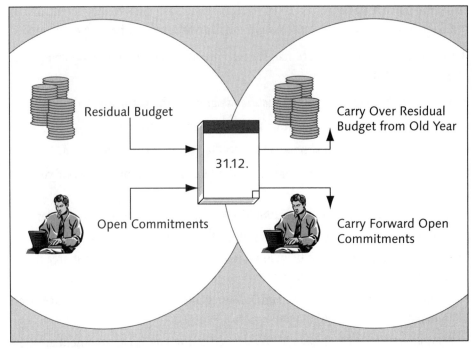

Figure 7.81 Closing Operations

You do not need to perform the closing operations if you do not want the budget of the previous fiscal year to get carried forward to the new fiscal year. The majority of the settings that control the closing operations are part of the update profile, where you can specify whether you want to carry forward balances and, if yes, for which value types.

Caveat

Commitment carryforward in Funds Management always reflects the current state of affairs. So if you ran the closing operations, and then there was a change in the feeder components, that change would not automatically get transferred to Funds Management. So you should close Funds Management only after all other components' closes have been completed.

The following are the preparation activities that need to be completed for commitment carryforward and budget carryforward:

▶ **Closing open items**
Try to close open items that use up commitment budget, such as purchase requisitions, purchase orders, or earmarked funds. This will return the budget back, which can then be carried forward to the new fiscal year.

▶ **Commitment carryforward**
The general rule is to carry forward only those documents that can be reduced in the next fiscal year. This can be configured by setting up selection rules and excluding some value types.

▶ **Budget carryforward**
If a commitment has been carried forward to the new fiscal year, you can carry forward the corresponding budget as well. In addition, you can set up rules for carrying forward residual budget, which can then be distributed as well to specific receivers.

▶ **Fund balance carryforward**
Balance carryforward in funds allows you to see how funds are distributed across years.

7.8 Summary

In this chapter, you learned about the Funds Management of public sector management (PSM-FM), which is used primarily for budgeting public sector outlays.

You were first introduced to the basic settings and master data setup of Funds Management, which includes commitment item, funds center, fund, funded program, subdivision ID, functional area, and budget structure. You also learned how to set up account assignment derivation rules and to configure status management in Funds Management.

Next, you were introduced to the budgeting process where you learned about the various types of budgets, budget categories, and budget entry documents.

We also explored availability control in Funds Management and how you can customize it using activity groups, tolerance profiles, and the availability control ledger.

You next learned about the integration of Funds Management with other feeder systems using update profiles and setting up number ranges and assignment of number ranges to Funds Management areas for actual documents from feeder systems.

Finally, you learned about the typical closing operations such as commitment carry-forward and budget carryforward, which are performed at year end, if required.

In Chapter 8 you will learn about product cost controlling with a detailed exploration of product cost planning, product costing by period, and actual costing and the material ledger.

PART IV
Product Costing

Learn how to plan, manage, and optimize the costing activities of your product.

8 Optimizing Product Costing Decisions using Product Cost Controlling

Now that you understand the overall concepts of Controlling and cost element accounting, cost center accounting, profit center accounting, internal order accounting, internal order integration, and Investment Management, let's proceed to learning about product cost controlling. Our focus in this chapter is on the product costing component of Controlling that allows you to plan, manage, and optimize your costing activities.

First you will be introduced to product cost planning, which allows you to plan the costs of materials without any reference to orders. Next you will learn about cost object controlling that helps you in reaching make or buy decisions by understanding in detail the cost breakdown. Cost object controlling can be performed by period, by order, or by sales order. Finally you will learn about actual costing that allows you to carry material prices in multiple currencies and perform actual costing.

Now let's understand what product cost controlling is before we tackle its optimization.

8.1 Product Cost Controlling: An Introduction

The basic question that product costing aims to answer is this: What are the material costs of a product? This is the main goal of product costing. So product costing allows you to analyze the cost structure of a company's products. Analyzing costs helps in understanding the value added by each process step and each organization unit. It also gives you a clear understanding of the overhead costs, production, and material costs that can be used to improve production efficiency. Taking it one step further, it can be used to support make or buy decisions, determine true inventory values, and come up with price floors for a unit product. We also need the ability to calculate the plan costs and the actual costs. Also sometimes it becomes imperative that you calculate the cost in multiple currencies to understand the impact of currency translation on inventory. Product cost controlling functionality allows you to delineate the following aspects of costing:

▶ Standard cost of finished and semi-finished products

▶ Detailed cost analysis with cost variances in production and planning

▶ Plan and monitor costs on cost objects

▶ Calculation of work in progress

▶ Costing settlement to financial accounting and profitability analysis

The SAP ERP solution for product cost controlling consists of the following three components to support the preceding requirements:

▶ Product cost planning

▶ Cost object controlling, that is, costing by period, by order, and by sales order

▶ Actual costing/material ledger

These are also shown in Figure 8.1, which highlights the key components and the structure of product cost controlling.

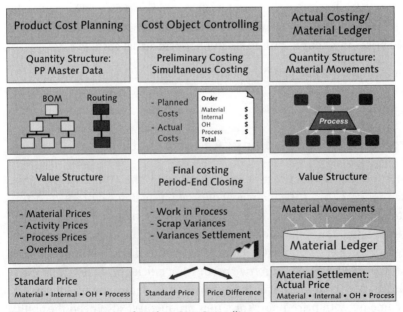

Figure 8.1 Components of Product Cost Controlling

In product cost planning, the focus is on determining the standard price based on an understanding of material costs, internal costs, OH (overhead) costs, and process costs. The input to product cost planning comes from quantity structure of Production Planning (PP) master data, whereas the values are updated from material prices, activity prices, process prices, and overhead.

On the other hand, cost object controlling goes one step further and tries to use the standard price estimate calculated from *product cost planning* and comes up with the price difference. This can be achieved by multiple types of costing, which can be preliminary costing and simultaneous costing, where you get an input of planned and actual costs. Finally at period end, you execute various processes, such as WIP (work in process) and variance calculation, which allow you to understand the overall price difference along with the actual standard price.

Actual costing/material ledger, on the other hand, allows you to keep track of your actual costs as they occur by tracking all the material movements along with their quantity structure. These then update the material ledger where you can determine the actual price of the material with a break up of material cost, internal cost, overhead cost, and process cost. All three components are dependent on each other's inputs and are heavily integrated. And the sequence in which you implement this is from left to right (in Figure 8.1) to use the maximum benefit and integrated perspective from the implementation.

First let's learn more about product cost planning

8.2 Product Cost Planning

Product cost planning (CO-PC-PCP or PCP) is an area where you can plan costs for materials without reference to orders, and set prices for materials and other cost accounting objects. You can analyze costs to help provide answers to questions such as the following:

▶ What is the value added of a particular step in the production process?

▶ What proportion of the value added can be attributed to a particular organizational unit?

▶ What is the cost breakdown including primary costs or transfer prices?

▶ How high are the material, production, and overhead costs?

▶ How can production efficiency be improved?

▶ Can the product be supplied at a competitive price?

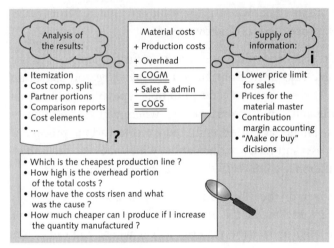

Figure 8.2 Purpose of Product Cost Planning

Based on these questions, the purpose of CO-PC-PCP is as seen in Figure 8.2 and explained here:

▶ Calculate the Cost of Goods Manufactured (COGM), which comprises material costs, production costs, overhead costs, and COGS (Cost of Goods Sold) for each unit produced. This is COGM plus sales and administration costs.

▶ Find out the cost breakdown by each step in the production process.

▶ Comparison cost to optimize the COGM.

Now that you understand the rationale for implementing product cost planning, you will learn the implementation details for product cost planning in subsequent subsections. Let's begin with learning about the integration of product cost planning with other modules.

8.2.1 Integration

CO-PC-PCP is heavily integrated with PP and is effective only in conjunction with PP. All of the master data of CO-PC-PCP is heavily dependent on PP for BOMs, routing, and work center, and relies on overhead cost controlling (CO-OM) for cost centers, activity types, and business transactions.

8.2.2 Components and Costing Sequence

CO-PC-PCP can be categorized into the following broad business process components:

▶ Cost estimate with quantity structure for costing materials with quantity structure in PP.

▶ Cost estimate without quantity structure for costing materials without quantity structure in PP.

▶ Price update of material master based on material cost estimates.

▶ Reference and simulation costing for new products and services.

▶ Easy cost planning and execution for ad hoc costing.

▶ Production cost Controlling information system to analyze the costing results for decision-making purposes.

However, all of these components follow a particular costing sequence, which is dependent on the product lifecyle. Figure 8.3 shows a typical product lifecycle and shows how a product moves from being a new product when it is just a product idea to its first prototype. Then it becomes ready to market and goes through saturation and decline.

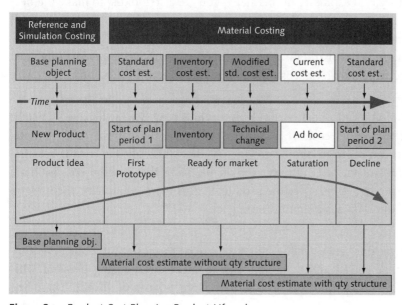

Figure 8.3 Product Cost Planning Product Lifecycle

The product cost planning components are listed here (follow along with Figure 8.3), as well as the phase of which each is a part:

▸ **Product idea**

At this stage, you do not have enough information about the individual parts and components, so costing is primarily a guess. You can use the base planning object to create a reference costing. The costing type that you can use at this stage is reference and simulation costing.

▸ **First prototype**

Now you have an idea about the technical specifications because they have been refined and finalized. This allows you to create a material cost estimate without quantity structure because you still do not know the PP details. This is the first planning cycle that you will establish for the product, which allows you to arrive at a standard cost estimate for the product.

▸ **Ready for market**

As you start marketing and selling the product, you now understand the demand requirements in more detail and can identify the *inventory requirements* for the product based on the production cycle and the demand. At this stage, you need to integrate your costing with the logistics components. This allows you to make a material cost estimate with quantity structure and allows you to finalize the inventory cost estimate. At this stage, you are also looking to make the necessary technical changes so that you can improve the product. This is where all the re-launches come in. Due to the technical changes, you might need a modified cost estimate. This might mean that you might have to perform the cost estimation using a material cost estimate without quantity structure.

▸ **Saturation**

Once the product has been around for a while now, you will have sufficient data for the product cost. This allows you to use the current cost estimate, where you can perform ad hoc costing. At this stage, all the quantity-costing components are known, and you should be using the material cost estimate with quantity structure. After the product attains market maturity, the integration of master data has a significant impact.

▸ **Decline**

When the product is in decline mode, you need to reestablish your inventory levels so that you produce only enough to meet the reducing demand. This allows you to initiate the next plan period where you can perform the base line again.

As you saw, material costing or product cost planning is an iterative understanding of your costs based on the information available at that point of time. Constant modification of product costing parameters allows you to optimally find out the cost to the nearest degree.

8.2.3 Cost Component Structure

The cost component structure allows you to group cost elements into cost components. These cost components allow you to break down the cost of material, process, or activity type. The grouping of costs into groups such as material and labor allows you to understand the reason for the increase in cost. The cost component structure can also be used to pass over the material costs to material valuation as standard price and COGM to profitability analysis. The menu path you need to follow is **IMG • Controlling• Product Cost Controlling • Basic settings for material costing • Define cost component structure**, and the Transaction is OKTZ.

Figure 8.4 shows a **Cost Comp. Str.** (cost component structure) **01** that has been marked as **Active.** Marking the indicator as active allows you to use cost component structure in costing with or without quantity structure. Setting **Prim. Cost Comp Split** indicates that the cost component split is pertaining to a primary cost component split. If you do not set this indicator, then the cost component split is for COGM.

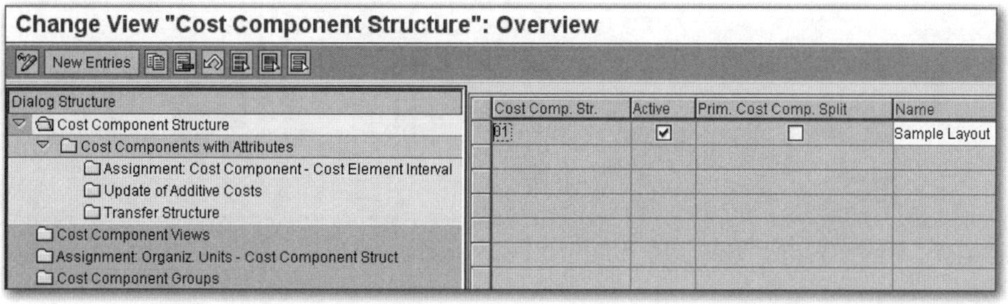

Figure 8.4 Define Cost Component Structure

If you select the **Cost Component Structure 01** in the right pane, and then click on **Cost Components with Attributes,** you reach a screen in which you can maintain up to 40 cost components within one cost components structure. If you double-click on the cost components (**Cost Com..**) **Raw Materials**, which is assigned to the cost component structure (**Cost Comp. Str.**) **01**, you will reach the next screen shown in Figure 8.5, which allows you to control the attributes of cost components. The following attributes can be controlled:

▶ **Cost Share**
Variable Costs or **Fixed and Variable Costs**.

▶ **Cost Rollup**
If this is flagged, then you can perform cost rollups.

▶ **Cost Summarization**
Here you can assign two cost component groups (**Cost Comp. Grp1** or **2**) that allow you to summarize the costing data. Note that you can define the cost component groups by double-clicking on **Cost Component Groups** in the left pane.

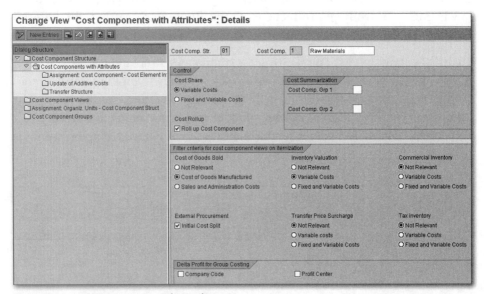

Figure 8.5 Cost Components with Attributes

These are the filter criteria for cost component views on itemization:

▶ **Cost of Goods Sold**
Here you can mark the cost component as either **Not Relevant** or part of either **Cost of Goods Manufactured** or **Sales and Administration Costs**.

- **Inventory Valuation/ Commercial Inventory/Transfer Price Surcharge/ Tax inventory**
  These can be classified as **Not Relevant**, **Variable costs**, or **Fixed and Variable Costs**.

- **External Procurement**
  Here you can flag this as part of initial cost split.

- **Delta profit for Group Costing**
  This can be marked as relevant for **Company Code** or **Profit Center** or both.

If you click on **Assignment Cost Component-Cost Elements**, you will reach the screen shown in Figure 8.6. Here you can maintain the range of Cost Elements (**From cost el.** and **To cost ele.**) that are assigned to the cost component **1: Raw Materials** and cost component structure **01**. For defining the cost element range, you also need to maintain the **Chart of Accts CANA**.

Change View "Assignment: Cost Component - Cost Element Interval": Over

New Entries

Dialog Structure	Cost Comp. S	Chart of Accts	From cost el.	Origin group	To cost ele.	Cost Com	Name of Cost Com
▽ Cost Component Structure	01	CANA	510000		510000	1	Raw Materials
▽ Cost Components with Attributes	01	CANA	510030		510040	1	Raw Materials
Assignment: Cost Component - Cos	01	CANA	510060		510070	1	Raw Materials
Update of Additive Costs	01	CANA	520050		520050	1	Raw Materials
Transfer Structure	01	CANO	409000		409999	1	Raw Materials
Cost Component Views	01	CAPE	6010000000		6010000000	1	Raw Materials
Assignment: Organiz. Units - Cost Compone	01	CAPE	7010000000		7010000000	1	Raw Materials
Cost Component Groups	01	CAPL	411000		411000	1	Raw Materials

Figure 8.6 Assignment of Cost Component to Cost Element Interval

You can also define the update of additive costs and the transfer structure to transfer the costs to CO-PA by clicking on **Update of Additive Costs** and **Transfer Structure**, respectively. If you click on **Cost Component Views** in the left pane, then you will reach the next screen shown in Figure 8.7. Here you can maintain the cost component views that are used to transfer the cost to other components. For example, if you want to transfer your material costs, inventory valuation view controls that transfer, and you should make the changes there.

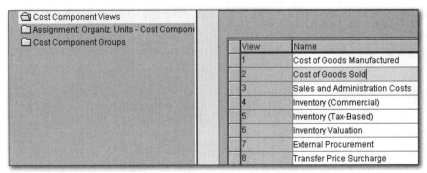

Figure 8.7 Cost Component Views

If you double-click on the **View 2: Cost of Goods Sold**, you will reach the next screen shown in Figure 8.8.

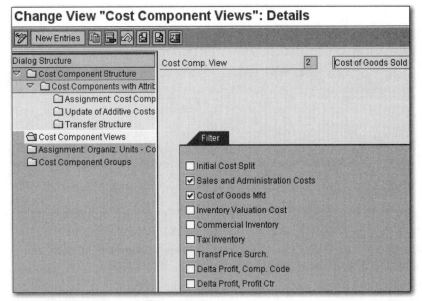

Figure 8.8 Detailing Cost of Goods Sold

This allows you to **Filter** the costs by **Sales and Administration Costs** and **Cost of Goods Mfd.** So all these costs will flow if you choose this view. If you click on **Assignment: Organiz. Units- Cost Component Struct**, you will reach the next screen shown in Figure 8.9.

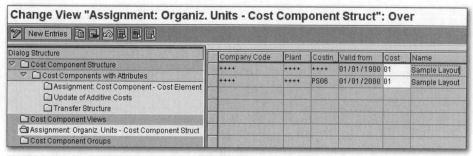

Figure 8.9 Assignment of Organizational Units to Cost Component Structure

Here you maintain the assignment of organization units to component structure that were defined in the previous steps:

- ▶ **Company Code**
  ++++ indicates that all of the company codes are selected.

- ▶ **Plant**
  ++++ indicates that all of the plants are selected.

- ▶ **Costing**
  This identifies the costing variant and ++++ indicates all of the relevant costing variants.

- ▶ **Valid from**
  This identifies the validity date from which the assignment is valid.

- ▶ **Cost...**
  This is the cost component structure that you were defining in previous steps.

8.2.4 Costing Variant

Costing variant is the basis of all the costing estimates. This is the lynchpin to which all of the costing activities are tied. A costing variant houses the controls parameters for costing, helping you determine the type of costing that you need to perform. You can control whether you are going to perform the material cost estimate or base object cost estimate depending on the costing variant. Figure 8.10 shows the customizing parameters for material costing.

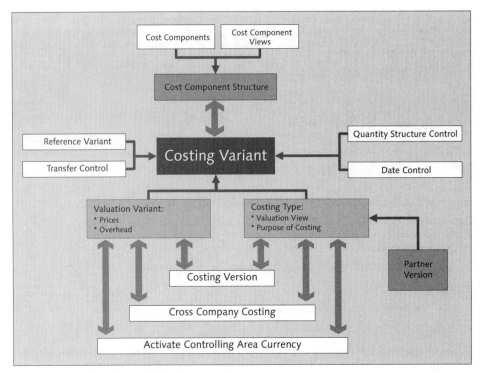

Figure 8.10 Define Costing Variant

As you can see, the costing variant sits in the center. You need to maintain the following parameters to fully define a costing variant:

▶ **Costing Type**
This defines the valuation view to be costed, purpose of costing, and price update along with a partner version to capture the partner cost component split.

▶ **Valuation Variant**
This identifies the prices that are used to valuate the materials, activities, and processes along with the assignment of costing sheet and price factors for inventory costing.

▶ **Reference Variant**
This allows you to specify how an already costed quantity structure is used in the cost estimate.

▶ **Transfer Control**

This allows you to specify how you will transfer the cost estimates to other financial components such as CO-PA.

▶ **Cost Component Structure**

The cost component is also integrated with the costing variant.

▶ **Quantity structure control**

This allows you to integrate with logistics master data such as BOM and routings. Of course, this is only used if you are using material costing with quantity update.

▶ **Date control**

This controls the validity period of the cost estimate, quantity structure date, and the valuation date.

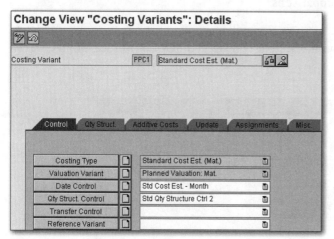

Figure 8.11 Detailing the Costing Variant for Standard Cost Estimate

The menu path for defining cost variants is **IMG • Controlling• Product Cost Controlling • Material Cost Estimate with Quantity Structure• Define costing variants**, and the Transaction is OKKN. Figure 8.11 shows how you can create a **Costing variant PPC1: Standard Cost Est. (Mat.)**. We have identified the following parameters for the costing variant:

▶ **Costing Type**

Standard Cost Est (Mat.): Because we are creating a costing variant for the estimating material cost with quantity, you need to choose a costing variant that has material as one of the parameters.

▶ **Valuation Variant**
Planned Valuation: Mat: Because we are in the process of planning the material cost, you should choose a variant that has the planned valuation for material.

▶ **Date Control**
Std Cost Est.-Month: This identifies the date control of the cost estimate and depends on the periodicity of the cost estimates.

▶ **Transfer Control**
This controls how the costing with quantity structure finds the existing cost estimate to be transferred to another cost estimate.

▶ **Reference Variant**
This allows you to access existing cost estimates for reference purposes. This allows you to create separate costing runs that improve the performance and allows you to make comparisons.

If you click on the **Qty Struct.** tab, you will reach the next screen shown in Figure 8.12. This establishes how the system will select a BOM or routing of material to be costed.

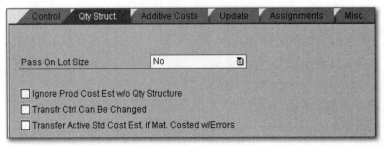

Figure 8.12 Quantity Structure

The following parameters can be maintained on this tab:

▶ **Pass On Lot Size**
This field identifies how the costing lot size is determined. Three options are available:

  ▶ **No pass**
  The highest lot size is not passed to other materials part of the BOM.

▶ **Only with individual requirement**
If the BOM contains a material that has the **Individual requirement** flag turned on, then costing uses the lot size of the highest material in the BOM structure.

▶ **Always pass**
This control allows you to pass the lot size of the highest material in the BOM. This is primarily used in sales order processing.

▶ **Ignore Prd Cost Est w/o Qty Structure**
This flag allows you to ignore production cost estimates if the costing estimate does not have a quantity structure.

▶ **Transfer Ctrl Can be Changed**
This allows you to change the transfer control at runtime.

▶ **Transfer Active Std Cost Est. if Mat. Costed w/Errors**
Setting this flag allows you to transfer the standard cost estimate even if the costing run had errors.

Figure 8.13 Additive Costs

If you click on **Additive Costs**, then you will reach the screen shown in Figure 8.13. Here you can maintain the following parameters for additive costs:

▶ **Additive Cost Comps**
You have three options here: **Include Additive Costs**, **Ignore Additive Costs**, or **Include Additive Costs and Apply Overhead**.

▶ **Include Additive Costs with Stock Transfers**
This allows you to include additive costs with stock transfers.

If you click on **Update**, you will reach the next screen which is shown in Figure 8.14.

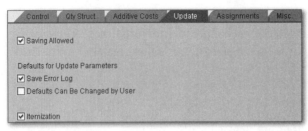

Figure 8.14 Update

Here you can maintain the parameters pertaining to saving (**Saving Allowed, Save Error Log**). If you flag **Itemization**, then itemization is saved in addition to the costing split. Clicking on the **Assignments** tab takes you to the screen shown in Figure 8.15, where you can maintain the assignments of **Cost Component Structure, Costing Version, Cost Component Split in Controlling Area Currency**, and **Cross Company Costing**.

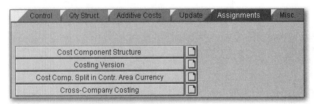

Figure 8.15 Assignments

The **Misc.** tab as shown in Figure 8.16 allows you to manage your error messages for costing variant.

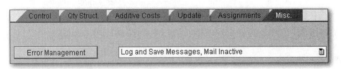

Figure 8.16 Miscellaneous Components

The following options are available:

- **Online messages**
- **Log and Save Messages, Mail Inactive**
- **Log and Save Messages, Mail Active**
- **Log messages but do not save them, Mail inactive**

If you click on **Error Management**, you can maintain the user-defined error messages for the costing variant. Now that you understand the configuration settings of a costing variant, let's take a look at how you can update the price in the material master via the costing runs.

8.2.5 Price Update

After the cost estimate for the material has been determined, you can transfer these estimates to the material master. Figure 8.17 shows how different types of cost estimates are mapped to the material master prices. You begin with a **Standard cost estimate**, which then gets adjusted to the **Modified standard cost estimate**. You can also determine the **Current cost estimate** and **Inventory cost estimate**.

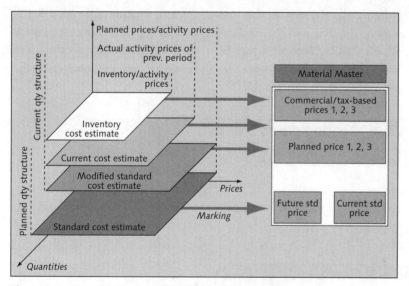

Figure 8.17 Mapping the Cost Estimates to Material Master

The following fields can be updated in the material master from costing as shown in the material master view of the figure:

▶ **Current and Future Standard Price**

▶ **Tax based prices (3)**

▶ **Commercial prices (3)**

▶ **Planned Prices (3)**

The mapping for the cost estimate to the price fields available in the material master is also shown in Table 8.1.

Cost Estimate	Price fields in the material master
Standard cost estimate	Future and current standard price
Inventory cost estimate	Commercial or tax-based prices 1-3
Modified standard cost estimate, current cost estimate, standard or inventory cost estimate	Other planned prices 1-3

Table 8.1 Mapping Cost Estimate to Material Master

After you have entered these cost estimates, you can use these in other cost estimates for planning purposes by making the material price a part of the valuation variant. For more details about *valuation variant* refer to Chapter 5, Section 5.2.2. Price Update can be maintained in the costing type that is part of the costing variant. If you click on **Costing Type** in Figure 8.11, you will see the screen shown in Figure 8.18. Here you can maintain how the cost estimate will get updated in the material master on the **Price Update** tab.

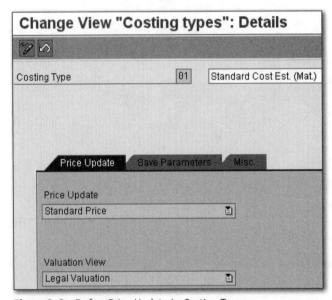

Figure 8.18 Define Price Update in Costing Type

The following options are available:

- **Standard Price**
- **No Update**
- **Tax Based Price**
- **Commercial Price**
- **Prices other than standard price**

In the Valuation view, you can choose one of the following three valuations:

- **Legal Valuation**
- **Group Valuation**
- **Profit Center Valuation**

Now that you understand the types of cost estimates, let's learn how you can tweak these in subsequent steps.

Standard Cost Estimate

You can customize the message types to suit your requirements, In addition, you can define your own message types to control the standard cost estimate. The menu path and transaction codes are shown in Table 8.2.

Parameters for Standard Cost Estimate	Menu Path	Transaction Code
Define message types for standard cost estimate	**IMG • Controlling • Product Cost Controlling • Price Update • Parameters for Standard Cost Estimate • Define Message Types for Standard Cost Estimate**	OKZZ
Define user-defined message types	**IMG • Controlling • Product Cost Controlling • Price Update • Parameters for Standard Cost Estimate • Define User-Defined Message Types**	OPR4_CKPF

Table 8.2 Menu Paths and Transaction Codes for Maintaining Parameters for Standard Cost Estimate

Now that you understand the parameters that can be configured in standard cost estimating, let's take a look at the parameters that can be controlled for inventory cost estimate.

Inventory Cost Estimate

These control the costs that go into the commercial and tax price of the material that we saw in Table 8.1. You should have flagged the cost components as relevant for commercial or tax inventory valuation in cost components (refer to Figure 8.05).

For inventory cost estimate, you can define the factors for devaluation that are not possible in standard costing. So in standard cost estimates, either a cost component is relevant for costing (Factor of 1- Indicator X) or not relevant for standard cost estimate (Factor of 0- Indicator Blank). However, for inventory cost estimate, it is possible to devalue the cost estimate by a factor (e.g., 75% relevant to costing). You will learn how to set this up in subsequent steps. First you need to define the identifiers for relevancy to costing. You can follow **IMG • Controlling • Product Cost Controlling • Price Update • Parameters for Inventory Cost Estimate• Define Relevancy to Costing**, or use Transaction OKK9. Figure 8.19 shows how you can maintain the costing relevancy factors. We have defined **Costing Relevancy** as **1: 50% Relevant to Costing**.

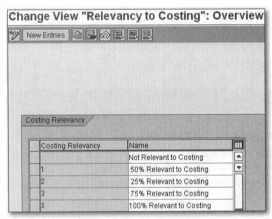

Figure 8.19 Define Relevancy for Costing

After you have defined this, you need to define the **Price Factors** for Relevancy to Costing. The menu path is **IMG • Controlling • Product Cost Controlling • Price Update • Parameters for Inventory Cost Estimate• Define Price Factors**, and the Transaction is OKK7. Figure 8.20 shows how the fixed price factor (**Fxd Prc. Factor**) and variable price factor (**Var. Price Factor**) as **0.5000** for **Costing Relevancy 1** and Valuation variant **+++**.

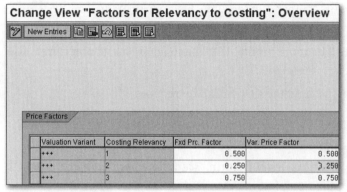

Figure 8.20 Define Factors for Relevancy to Costing

In the next section, you will learn more about the cost object controlling component of product costing.

8.3 Cost Object Controlling

The cost object controlling (CO-PC-OBJ) component is designed to answer the question: What costs have been incurred for which objects? It assigns the costs incurred during the production of company activities such as material, labor, and so on to the production process. Cost object controlling supports you in doing the following:

- Reaching make or buy decisions.
- Determining price floors.
- Performing complex cost analysis (such as target/actual analysis).
- Determining inventory values.

Cost object Controlling helps to:

- Determine whether the actual costs of an order matched or exceeded the planned costs.
- Determine the production variances between actual costs and target costs, and why these occurred.
- Decide whether to accept a particular sales order (whether the sales order will be profitable).

▶ Identify areas in your company where you have particularly low costs and, therefore, which cost objects you should concentrate on.

▶ Decide whether it will be more profitable to manufacture a cost object in-house or to outsource it.

▶ Determine whether and how the COGM can be reduced.

Cost object controlling is subdivided into the following application components:

▶ **Product cost by period**
This is used for the repetitive manufacturing scenario where the same products are manufactured in the same fashion over and over again. You might want to know the product cost at the end of the period, for example, in an assembly line manufacturing Ford trucks.

▶ **Product cost by order**
This is used primarily when you have distinct manufacturing lots with a highly flexible production environment. The focus is to control the cost of one particular set of production orders. This is especially important if you have a considerably large setup time to start production process and require full assignment of costs to production orders.

▶ **Product cost by sales order**
This is used in highly complex make-to-order production where there is a lot of customer involvement, for example, performing a turnkey installation of a power turbine at a thermal power plant. This requires that all the production specifications are tailored to the customer requirements.

▶ **Costs for intangible goods and services**
This component allows you to analyze the cost of intangible goods or services. For example, if you send a technician to service a machine at the client side, you can use this component to capture this cost and link to the overall costs for the machine.

Remember the focus of this chapter is how you can implement and optimize cost object controlling by period. Now that you understand the rationale for cost object controlling, let's take a look at how this is integrated with the other SAP ERP Financials and Controlling components.

8.3.1 Integration

The cost object controlling component integration is shown in Figure 8.21. Let's take a look at the inputs first. **Financial accounting** sends primary costs to cost object Controlling as well as overhead Controlling. **Overhead Controlling** then sends cost object Controlling secondary costs. All the MM transactions (goods issues and goods receipts) feed into cost object Controlling. **Production Planning** inputs the production confirmations to cost object Controlling.

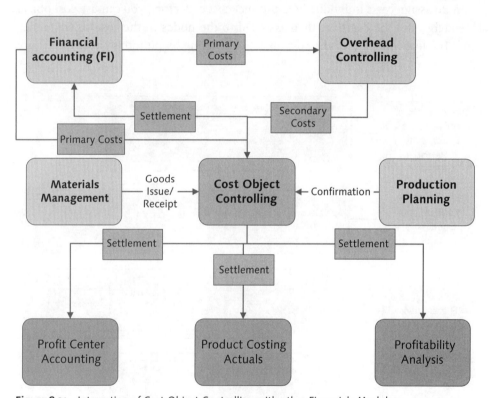

Figure 8.21 Integration of Cost Object Controlling with other Financials Modules

Now what does cost object controlling do with these inputs? It structures all this information into a format that allows you to make business decisions that we covered earlier. From cost object controlling, depending on the scenario, you can perform the **Settlement** of costs to **Profit Center Accounting, Product Costing Actuals, Profitability Analysis,** and, in some cases, back to **Financial accounting.**

The link back to financial accounting allows you to develop iterative cycles that refine the final answer regarding your cost object cost.

8.3.2 Product Cost by Period: An Introduction

Product costing by period is typically used in process industries such as chemicals or pharmaceuticals, or in repetitive manufacturing environment, which requires you to analyze the costs on the basis of production cost collectors. If you do not want to assign costs individually to product cost collectors, you can use cost object hierarchy, and the costs are then assigned to the nodes in the cost object hierarchy. The learning path of the cost object controlling by period is shown in Figure 8.22.

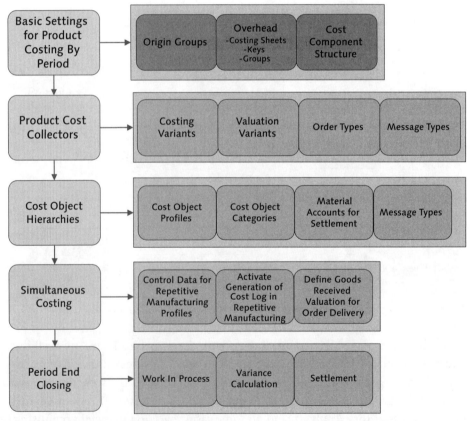

Figure 8.22 Cost Object Controlling By Period

In product costing by period, production orders or process orders are not used for cost object controlling. Rather, product cost collectors are used to perform the costing activities. Orders are just used for logistical tracking. The overall cycle for product costing by period is detailed here in case you use product cost collectors:

▶ Create product cost collector.

▶ Perform preliminary costing.

▶ Perform simultaneous costing.

▶ Perform period-end closing.

▶ Process cost and overhead allocation.

▶ Revaluate at actual prices.

▶ Understand WIP and variances.

▶ Perform settlement.

In the next subsections pertaining to product costing by period, you will learn the first four steps (the other steps are similar to what you learned in Chapter 5). First you will learn about production cost collectors, followed by an understanding of cost object hierarchies. Then you will learn how to set up costing scenarios for repetitive manufacturing. Finally you will learn about period-end closing transactions in cost object controlling by period.

You can use the following cost objects in product cost by period.

8.3.3   Product Cost by Period and Product Cost Collector

Costs by period comprises the following components:

▶ **Actual Goods Receipted Costs**
These are recorded during the period.

▶ **WIP costs**
These are assigned costs for which goods receipts have not yet taken place.

▶ **Variances**
These are calculated by using the formula *Actual Costs Posted − Goods Receipts − Work in Process.*

All of the actual costs and WIP costs are posted with reference to a production order. However, you can configure these to be assigned to a product cost collector by lots. In addition, you can assign additional overhead costs to the product cost collector. This allows you to make the product cost collector your unique master data against which you perform period-end settlement to determine the final costs by period.

Product cost collector is the first step in capturing the costs by object, which in this case, is production order. The production order lifecycle goes through the following stages: creation, scheduling, availability check, and release before you can record any actuals against the production order. You should create the product cost collector before the production order is created. When a production order is created, it will automatically get linked to the product cost collector, and then you can track the lifecycle of production order in the product cost collector from a cost perspective.

> **Note**
>
> Product cost collectors allow you to collect costs without reference to the type of production (process industry versus repetitive manufacturing) and analyze the costs by period.

Now that you understand the concept of product cost collector, let's discuss the key settings that can be made for product cost collector.

8.3.4 Product Cost by Period: Preliminary Costing Estimate

The first step in product costing by period is to create a preliminary costing estimate for the product cost collector. This initial estimate is used to valuate WIP, outline the variances, and determine the activity quantity in case of repetitive manufacturing. As you know for any costing estimate, you need to define a costing variant. So let's define a costing variant for preliminary costing.

Define Costing Variant

As you learned earlier in Product Cost Planning, the costing variant in conjunction with the valuation variant allows you to integrate the costing estimate with the quantity from either a BOM, routing, or processes. This allows you to calculate the preliminary cost estimate for the BOM, production order, and process as shown in

Figure 8.23 for the three scenarios, respectively. In each of the scenarios, **Costing variant and Valuation variant** give you the **Price**, whereas the quantity comes from **BOM**, **Routing**, or from the **Costing Sheet**.

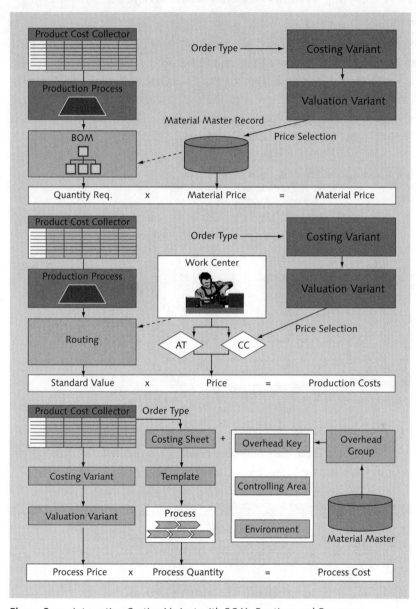

Figure 8.23 Integrating Costing Variant with BOM, Routing, and Processes

In this step, you will learn how to define the costing variant. The menu path is **IMG • Controlling • Product Cost Controlling • Cost Object Controlling • Product Cost by Period • Product Cost Controlling • Check Costing Variants for Product Cost Collectors • Costing Variants to Determine Activity Quantities**, and the Transaction is OKKN.

Figure 8.24 shows how you can define **Costing Variant PREM: Prel.Cstg Cost Collector** to determine activity quantities and link it to the product cost collector. Here you have defined the **Costing Type** as **Product Cost Collector** and **Transfer Control** as **Complete Transfer**. The rest of the parameters are the same as those you defined in product cost planning (Section 8.2). For details about the valuation variant, refer to Chapter 5, Section 5.2.2.

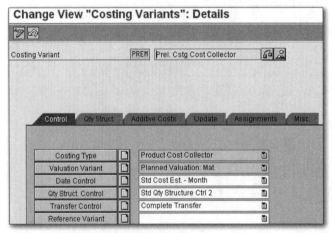

Figure 8.24 Define Costing Variants

If you click on **Qty Struct.**, you will reach the next screen as shown in Figure 8.25. Here we have checked the indicators to ignore product cost estimate without quantity structure and have allowed transfer control to be changed.

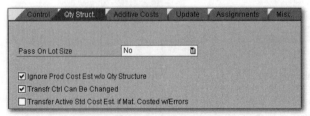

Figure 8.25 Quantity Structure

Defining a cost variant is half the battle won for configuring cost object controlling. The other half pertains to configuring product cost collectors, which is detailed next. To configure product cost collectors, you need to perform the following activities:

▶ Define the order type for the product cost collector.

▶ Define cost-accounting-relevant default values for order types and plants.

First let's recall what we've discussed about order type.

Define Order Type

Order type definition is similar to what we discussed in Chapter 5 when discussing internal orders. In this step, you will learn how order type definition is different for product cost collector. The menu path is **IMG** • **Controlling** • **Product Cost Controlling** • **Cost Object Controlling** • **Product Cost by Period** • **Product Cost Controlling** • **Check order type**, and the Transaction is KOT2_PKOSA.

Figure 8.26 shows the properties for the **Order Type RM01: Product cost collector**. You need to identify the **Order category** as **Product Cost Collector**, specify appropriate **Number range interval 700000-799999**, and identify the correct **Settlement profile PP01**. **CO Partner Update** has also been marked as **Semi-active**.

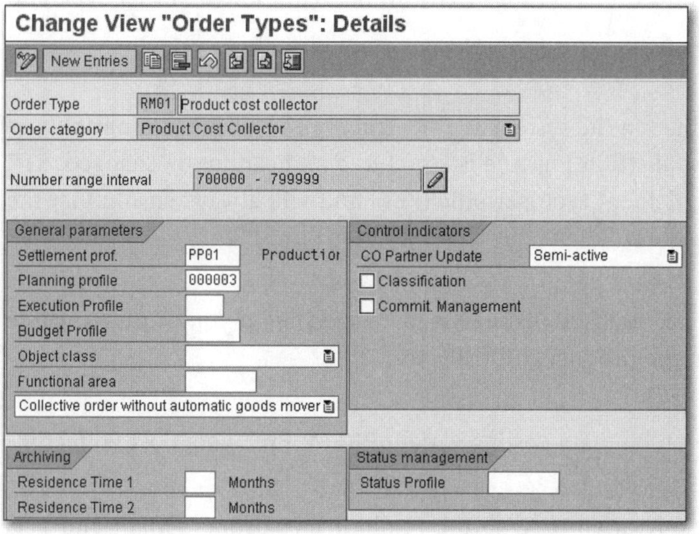

Figure 8.26 Define Order Types for Product Cost Collector

Define Cost-Accounting-Relevant Default Values for Order Types and Plants

After defining the product cost collector, you need to assign it to plants so that it can be defaulted. The integration of the preliminary costing variant and simultaneous costing variant can also be maintained by plant and order type. The menu path is **IMG • Controlling • Product Cost Controlling • Cost Object Controlling • Product Cost by Period • Product Cost Controlling • Define Cost-Accounting-Relevant Default Values for Order Types and Plants**, and the Transaction code is KOT2_PKOSA.

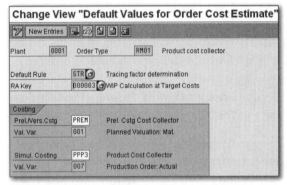

Figure 8.27 Default Values for Order Cost Estimate

Figure 8.27 shows the various settings that can be made for the order type and plant combination.

▶ **Default rule**
This is predetermined in the system as **STR: Tracing Factor determination** and represents how the distribution rule is structured and cannot be changed. STR is linked to the settlement type periodic (PER) and will always ensure that the product cost collector will have the settlement type as PER.

▶ **RA Key**
This is the results analysis key that needs to be specified if you want to include WIP calculation in the product cost collector.

▶ **Prel./Vers. Cstg**
This identifies the preliminary costing variant **PREM: Prel. Cstg Cost Collector**.

▶ **Val. Var.**
This is the valuation variant tied to the preliminary costing variant and gets defaulted automatically.

- **Simul. Costing**
  This is the costing variant for simultaneous costing **PPP3: Product Cost Collector**.

- **Val. Var.**
  This is the valuation variant tied to the simultaneous costing variant and gets defaulted automatically.

8.3.5   Product Cost by Period: Simultaneous Costing

As you learned in Section 8.3.4, you can assign the **Actual costing variant** of **Product Cost Collector** with the **Valuation variant** of **Production Order: Actual**. This allows you to record the actuals that happen against the production order (withdrawal of material, goods receipt, and confirmation of the material used).

Valuation Variant/Plant 007: Production Order: Actual is shown in Figure 8.28. Here you can see that you can maintain the material valuation according to price control in material. Material master can have the following two price controls:

- **V: Moving average price**
  The price of the material used changes as new information becomes available. This is typically set for externally procured materials. The valuation variant of delivery determines the goods receipt price.

- **S: Standard price**
  This is usually set for in-house manufactured materials. This price is derived from the standard cost estimate of the material

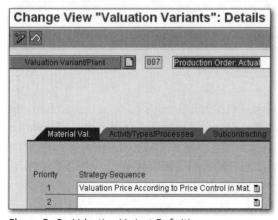

Figure 8.28 Valuation Variant Definition

In addition to recording actual values against production order, you can allocate the overhead costs to the product cost collector.

Before proceeding further, keep in mind that the period-end closing activities are common across all cost object controlling sub-modules.

8.3.6 Period-End Closing (Work in Process)

In the period-end process, before you execute the WIP calculation, you should have performed allocation, revaluation, and calculation of overhead if applicable. WIP represents the unfinished goods that have not yet posted to inventory. The most important period-end activity for cost object Controlling is to determine how WIP is valuated at month end. Table 8.3 shows the differences between the WIP calculation for cost object Controlling by period and by order. WIP is based on target costs for product cost Controlling by period. However, for product cost ontrolling by order, the basis of the WIP calculation is actual cost.

Cost Object Controlling	Cost Object	Basis of WIP	Calculation of WIP
By period	Product cost collectors with a status *other* than locked, closed, deleted, deletion flag	Target cost	Quantities confirmed at operations/reporting point multiplied by target Costs
By order	Production order	Actual cost	*Actual costs* assigned to the order (debits for material withdrawal, internal activity allocation, external activities and overhead cost) minus *actual credits* from goods receipts for delivery to stock

Table 8.3 Basis of WIP for Product Cost Controlling By Period and By Order

After you have calculated WIP, you need to transfer this to financial accounting and profit center accounting so that these can be included in the correct balance sheet account. The calculated WIP is updated in the results analysis cost element assigned to the order. The following configuration settings need to be performed for setting up the WIP that will be covered in this section:

- Define results analysis keys
- Define results analysis versions
- Define valuation method (target costs)
- Define valuation variant for WIP and scrap (target costs)
- Assignment of valuation variant for WIP
- Define line IDs
- Define assignment
- Define update
- Define posting rules for settling WIP
- Define number ranges

Define Results Analysis Keys

This controls the control parameters for WIP. An order or cost collector is only included in the WIP calculation if it has a results analysis key identified. You can then default the results analysis key for each order type and plant combination. The menu path is **IMG • Controlling • Product Cost Controlling • Cost Object Controlling • Product Cost by Period • Period End Closing• Work in Progress • Define Results Analysis Keys**, and the Transaction is OKG1. Figure 8.29 shows the results analysis keys (RA key) **000001** to **000004**, which can be maintained for a production order or product cost collector.

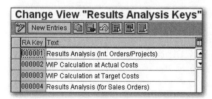

Figure 8.29 Define Results Analysis Keys

You can also maintain the valuation method by a combination of results analysis keys, Controlling area, and results analysis versions, which is discussed next.

Define Results Analysis Versions

All of the results analysis data with reference to a production order or cost collector is updated with reference to a results analysis version. This allows you the flexibility to calculate results analysis on the basis of multiple results analysis version at the same time. The menu path is **IMG • Controlling • Product Cost Controlling • Cost Object Controlling • Product Cost by Period • Period End Closing • Work in Progress • Define Results Analysis Versions**. The Transaction is OKG9. Figure 8.74 shows how you can maintain a results analysis version by Controlling area. The following parameters can be maintained for a results analysis version.

▶ Flagging **Version Relevant to Settlement** allows you to settle the results analysis results.

▶ Flagging **Transfer to Financial Accounting** allows you to transfer the costs to financial accounting. If the cost object has the link to profit center, then profit center accounting also receives the results analysis data on settlement.

▶ Initially you will only see the **Extended Control On** button. If you click on it, you will see additional parameters that can be controlled for the results analysis version, and the button will change to **Extended Control Off** as shown in Figure 8.30.

In **Extended Control,** you can maintain the following settings:

▶ **Split Creation/Usage**
Setting this allows you to maintain separate cost elements that will get depending on whether the business transaction created or used the stock (inventory, WIP, sales order stock).

▶ **Generate Line Items**
This allows you to get detailed information about how results analysis was performed.

▶ **Legacy Data Transfer**
if you check this indicator, then the version cannot be used to automatically generate results analysis

▶ **Deletion Allowed**
This flag allows you to delete the data from the version if required.

▶ **Assignment/RA key**
This allows you to assign cost element IDs separately for each result analysis key.

▶ **Update/RA key**
This should be checked if you are running results analysis on multiple objects such as WBS elements, sales orders, and so on.

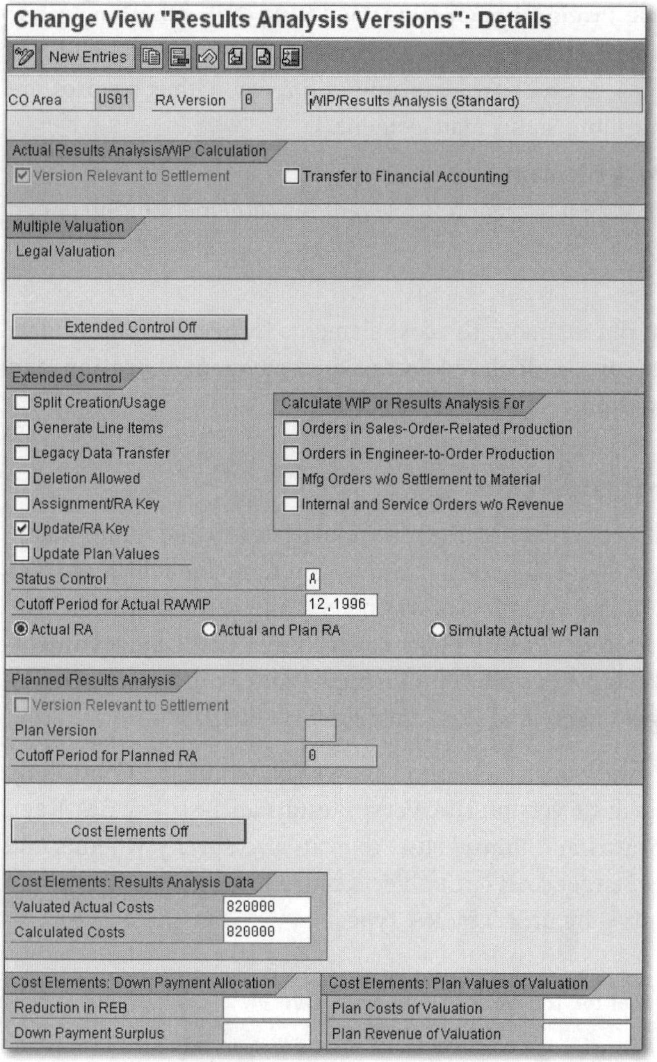

Change View "Results Analysis Versions": Details

New Entries

CO Area US01   RA Version 0   WIP/Results Analysis (Standard)

Actual Results Analysis/WIP Calculation
☑ Version Relevant to Settlement   ☐ Transfer to Financial Accounting

Multiple Valuation
Legal Valuation

Extended Control Off

Extended Control
☐ Split Creation/Usage   **Calculate WIP or Results Analysis For**
☐ Generate Line Items   ☐ Orders in Sales-Order-Related Production
☐ Legacy Data Transfer   ☐ Orders in Engineer-to-Order Production
☐ Deletion Allowed   ☐ Mfg Orders w/o Settlement to Material
☐ Assignment/RA Key   ☐ Internal and Service Orders w/o Revenue
☑ Update/RA Key
☐ Update Plan Values
Status Control   A
Cutoff Period for Actual RA/WIP   12,1996
◉ Actual RA   ○ Actual and Plan RA   ○ Simulate Actual w/ Plan

Planned Results Analysis
☐ Version Relevant to Settlement
Plan Version
Cutoff Period for Planned RA   0

Cost Elements Off

Cost Elements: Results Analysis Data
Valuated Actual Costs   820000
Calculated Costs   820000

Cost Elements: Down Payment Allocation   **Cost Elements: Plan Values of Valuation**
Reduction in REB   Plan Costs of Valuation
Down Payment Surplus   Plan Revenue of Valuation

Figure 8.30 Define Results Analysis Versions

▶ **Update Plan Values**
This allows you to update the plan values for results analysis version.

▶ **Status control**
This controls the status dependency and identifies the business transactions that affect the cost accounting. The options available are **Blank: Interpreted as A; A: Production Order: DLV (Delivered), FNBL (Final Billing); Sales**

335

Order: DLV, FNBL; B: Production Order: DLV, FNBL; C: Production Order: DLV, FNBL; and **Others: Status Change Documents**. The statuses identified for each identifier (A, B, or C) are determined directly. Other statuses are determined by Controlling Status management.

▶ **Version Relevant to Settlement**
If you flag this, then the plan version is relevant for settlement in integrated planning.

▶ **Cost Elements**
On this subtab, you can maintain the cost elements for results analysis data for **Valuated Actual Costs, Calculated Costs, Downpayment allocation,** and **Plan Values of Valuation**.

Define Valuation Method (Target Costs)

The valuation method allows you to link the results analysis key, the results analysis version and the system status together. It allows you to define which statuses will trigger the calculation and which ones will reverse the WIP calculation. The menu path is **IMG • Controlling • Product Cost Controlling • Cost Object Controlling • Product Cost by Period • Period End Closing • Work in Progress • Define Valuation Method (Target Costs)**, and the Transaction is OKGD.

As shown in Figure 8.31, the valuation method allows you to link the Controlling area (**CO Area**), results analysis version (**RA Versi**), results analysis key (**RA Key**), and the system status (**Status** and **Status Nu**). You can also specify whether the valuation is on the basis of target costs (cost object Controlling by period) or actual costs (cost object Controlling by order) by **RA Type**.

Change View "Valuation Method for Work in Process": Overview

CO Area	RA Versi	RA Key	Status	Status Nu	RA Type
US01	0	000002	REL	2	WIP Calculation on Basis of Actual Costs
US01	0	000002	DLV	3	Cancel Data of WIP Calculation and Results Ana
US01	0	000002	PREL	1	WIP Calculation on Basis of Actual Costs
US01	0	000002	TECO	4	Cancel Data of WIP Calculation and Results Ana
US01	0	000003	REL	2	WIP Calculation on Basis of Target Costs
US01	0	000003	DLV	3	Cancel Data of WIP Calculation and Results Ana
US01	0	000003	PREL	1	WIP Calculation on Basis of Target Costs
US01	0	000003	TECO	4	Cancel Data of WIP Calculation and Results Ana

Figure 8.31 Define Valuation Method (Target Costs)

An **RA Key** of **00002** ties to the actual costs, whereas an **RA Key** of **00003** ties to target costs. The following are the status codes that are applicable for WIP:

▸ **PREL**
Order is partially released with a status number of 1.

▸ **REL**
Order is released with a status number of 2.

▸ **DLV**
Order is completely delivered with a status number of 3.

▸ **TECO**
Order is technically complete with a status number of 4.

If the order status is PREL or REL, the system creates WIP on the basis of actual or target costs as specified in the RA Type depending on the RA key. If the status is DLV or TECO, then the WIP is reversed.

Define Valuation Variant for WIP and Scrap (Target Costs)

For the cost object Controlling period, you need to establish the standard cost estimate for WIP calculation. This step allows you to determine how the target costs for the valuation of WIP and scrap are calculated. You can follow the menu path **IMG • Controlling • Product Cost Controlling • Cost Object Controlling • Product Cost by Period • Period End Closing • Work in Progress • Define Valuation Variant for WIP and Scrap (Target Costs)**. Figure 8.32 shows how you can define a **Valuation Variant Z01: Valuation Variant for Scrap** that allows you to control how the standard cost estimate for WIP and scrap calculation will be determined. Here you can maintain the following parameters:

▸ **Priority**
Priority decides the sequence in which the cost will be determined.

▸ **Strategy**
This identifies the basis for the calculation of the WIP or scrap to be done.

If you want to use the plan costs as the basis, then mark **Plan Costs/Preliminary Cost Estimate** as **1**. The other options that you have are the following:

▸ **Alternative material cost estimate**
This requires that you maintain the costing variant and version on which the material cost estimate is based.

▶ **Current standard cost estimate**
If you check this as **1**, the system will use the current cost estimate as the basis for calculating WIP and scrap.

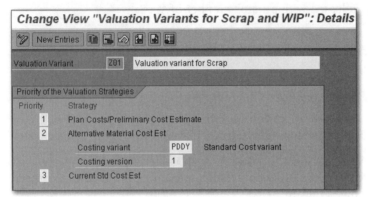

Figure 8.32 Define Valuation Variant for WIP and Scrap (Target Costs)

Assignment of Valuation Variant for WIP

In this step, you can assign the valuation variant defined in the previous step to the Controlling area, results analysis version, and results analysis key. The menu path is **IMG • Controlling • Product Cost Controlling • Cost Object Controlling • Product Cost by Period • Period End Closing • Work in Progress • Assignment of Valuation Variant for WIP**.

Define Line IDs

Line IDs allow you to group the WIP per the Financial Accounting requirements so that these can be settled to different cost elements. Typically, these are segregated as primary costs, secondary costs, revenues, and settled costs. Sometimes you can classify by the type of costs such as material overhead, external activities, internal activities, production overhead, and so on. The relevant menu path is **IMG • Controlling • Product Cost Controlling • Cost Object Controlling • Product Cost by Period • Period End Closing • Work in Progress • Define Line Ids**. Figure 8.33 shows how you can define the **Line IDs COP: Primary Costs, COS: Secondary Costs, REV: Revenues, SET: Settled Costs** by **CO Area** (Controlling area).

Change View "Line IDs for Results Analysis or WIP Calculation"

New Entries

CO Area	Line ID	Name
US01	COP	Primary Costs
US01	COS	Secondary Costs
US01	REV	Revenues
US01	SET	Settled Costs

Figure 8.33 Define Line IDs

Define Assignment

This allows you to establish the link between cost elements and line items. The menu path for defining the assignment is **IMG · Controlling · Product Cost Controlling · Cost Object Controlling · Product Cost by Period · Period End Closing · Work in Progress · Define Assignment**, and the Transaction is OKGB. Figure 8.34 shows how you can assign the **Line IDs** defined in the previous step to the masked structure of Cost elements (**Masked Co.**) with **++** being used as a wild card.

Change View "Assignment of Cost Elements for WIP and Results Analysis"

New Entries

CO A	RAV	RA Key	Masked Co	Ori	Masked Co	Maske	Business Proc	D	V	Apport	Accou	Valid-Fro	ReqToC	OptToCap	CannotBeCap	% OptToCap	% CannotBeCap
US01			00004+++++	++++				+	+		++	001.1997	REV				
US01	0		000044++++	++++				+	+		++	001.1997	REV				
US01	0		000051++++	++++				+	+		++	001.1997	COP				
US01	0		0000520+++	++++				+	+		++	001.1997	SET				
US01	0		00008+++++	++++	++++++++++	++++++		+	+		++	001.1997	COS				

Figure 8.34 Define Assignment

Define Update

This is also another coming together of different components to ensure that you can update the WIP and reserves to appropriate GL accounts. This is similar to the account determination of results analysis process. The menu path is **IMG · Controlling · Product Cost Controlling · Cost Object Controlling · Product Cost by Period · Period End Closing · Work in Progress · Define Update**, and the Transaction is OKGA. Figure 8.35 shows how you can determine the GL account (**Creation and Usage**) that will be used to capture the WIP and reserves, based on the Controlling area (**COAr**), version (**Vsn**), results analysis key (**RA Key**), line ID (**LID**), and category (next to line ID).

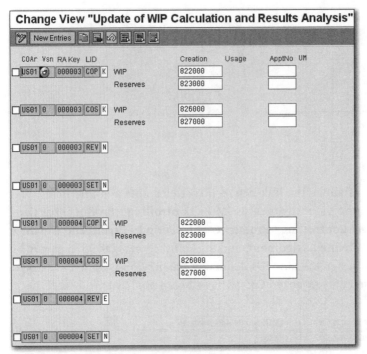

Figure 8.35 Define Update

The new element that has been introduced here is the category that allows you to group similar transactions in the results analysis process. These are also used for determining the sign (debit or credit) of the posting to WIP calculation. The following options are available for category:

▶ **A**
Settled costs

▶ **D**
Special costs

▶ **E**
Revenues

▶ **F**
Customer downpayments

▶ **G**
Direct revenues through special costs

▸ **K**

Costs

▸ **N**

Costs not to be included

▸ **P**

Costs of complaints and commissions

▸ **U**

Same as N, processing in customer enhancements possible

For example, **K: Costs** is a debit, whereas **E: Revenues** is a credit.

Define Posting Rules for Settling Work in Process

In this step, you can define how the WIP is settled ultimately to financial accounting. Posting rule is only defined for those WIPs that need to be capitalized or can be capitalized. The same holds true for the reserves. However, if you are using profit center accounting, then the posting rule also needs to be defined for settlement to financial accounting because profit center accounting gets its data from Financial Accounting. The menu path is **IMG • Controlling • Product Cost Controlling • Cost Object Controlling • Product Cost by Period • Period End Closing • Work in Progress • Define Posting Rules for Settling Work in Process**, and the Transaction is OKG8.

Figure 8.36 shows how you can define the posting rules for settling the process to financial accounting by Controlling area (**CO Ar..**), company code (**Comp....**), results analysis version (**RA Ver**), results analysis category (**RA category**), results analysis balance/creation/cancellation/usage (**Bal./Cr..**), cost element (**Cost Elem...**), and record number (**Record..**). You can maintain the **P&L account** and balance sheet account along with the accounting principle for these parameters.

CO Ar	Comp	RA Ver	RA category	Bal./Cr	Cost Elem	Record	P&L Acct	BalSheetAcct	Acc
US01	US01	0	WIPR			0	700770	132000	

Figure 8.36 Define Posting Rules for Settling WIP

Let's take a look at new term introduced here: **RA Category**. This identifies the origin of the results analysis data. For example, **WIPR** indicates the WIP with requirement to capitalize.

Define Number Ranges

You also need to define the number ranges so that Controlling documents can be created for the results analysis transactions. These can be created by following the menu path and transaction code shown and is similar to any other number creation process. The menu path is **IMG • Controlling • Product Cost Controlling • Cost Object Controlling • Product Cost by Period • Period End Closing • Work in Progress • Define Number Ranges**, and the Transaction is OKG6.

8.3.7   Period-End Closing

Cost object controlling or variance calculation needs to be performed for all the cost objects in cost object controlling (production cost collectors, production orders, and cost object hierarchies). Variance calculation allows you to understand the difference between your target costs and actual costs. This is an important input to determining the best approach to improving your processes to minimize costs. For example, if the variance is in raw material, then you need to look at your sourcing strategy. However, if it relates to labor, then you need to understand whether you can automate some of these processes. So variance calculation is an important input in trying to optimize your costing initiative. It gives you pointers and a directional approach to minimize cost and improve your productivity. Broadly it answers the fundamental question: What is the main reason for costs being higher than planned by identifying the bucket of the cost (variance category) that caused the variance?

Now lets's learn to define the control parameters for the variance calculation. First you will learn how to define a variance key.

Define Variance Keys

Variance keys establish the link between the cost object and the variance calculation. When you enter a variance key in the product cost collector master, then it becomes relevant for variance calculation. The menu path is **IMG • Controlling •**

Product Cost Controlling • Cost Object Controlling • Product Cost by Period • Period End Closing • Variance Calculation • Variance Calculation for Product Cost Collectors • Variance Calculation for Product Cost Collectors, and the Transaction is OKV1. Figure 8.37 shows how you can define the **Variance key 000001: Variance Calculation for Orders**. The following parameters can be maintained for a variance key:

▸ **Scrap**
Flagging this instructs the system to calculate scrap variances as well.

▸ **Update**
This indicator controls whether line items will be written for the variance key. Note that this is not required and generally increases the runtime for variance calculation.

Figure 8.37 Define Variance Keys

Define Default Variance Keys for Plants

This allows you to default the variance key for a production order. It happens in a convoluted fashion. First you assign the variant key to a plant. When the system creates a material master for the plant, it carries the variant key. And when you create a production order with reference to a material, the variance key is defaulted to the production order. The menu path is **IMG • Controlling • Product Cost Controlling • Cost Object Controlling • Product Cost by Period • Period End Closing • Variance Calculation • Variance Calculation for Product Cost Collectors • Define Default Variance Keys for Plants**, and the Transaction is OKVW. Figure 8.38 shows how the **Variance Keys 000001** can be assigned to Plant (**Plnt**) **US01**.

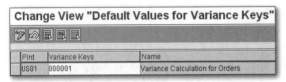

Figure 8.38 Define Default Variance Keys for Plants

Define Variance Variants

Variance variants allow you to define the variant categories that are calculated. The following variant categories are possible:

▶ **Scrap variance** indicates the percentage of scrap generated in manufacturing.

▶ **Mixed price variance** occurs if your target cost estimate is based on a standard price. However, the material is valuated at the moving average, which leads to mixed price variance.

▶ **Input price variance** is the difference between the planned prices and actual prices of the resources used.

▶ **Resource usage variance** is the variance that gets populated if you used a different resource than originally planned (having different cost).

▶ **Input quantity variance** is the difference between the planned input quantity and the actual used quantity.

▶ **Output price variance** is the difference between the planned price versus the actual price.

▶ **Lot size variance** is the difference between the planned fixed costs for the setup of production and the actual costs charged to the lot.

▶ **Remaining input variance** represents any other variances on the input that are not captured in other input variances (scrap, input price, input quantity price, and resource usage)

The menu path for defining variance variants is **IMG • Controlling • Product Cost Controlling • Cost Object Controlling • Product Cost by Period • Period End Closing • Variance Calculation • Variance Calculation for Product Cost Collectors • Define Variance Variants**. The relevant Transaction is OKVG.

Figure 8.39 shows how you can maintain the **Variance Variant** 0001: **Standard**. Here in addition to the variances that will be considered in the variant, you can also define the threshold percentage that is considered as the remaining variance (**Minor variance**).

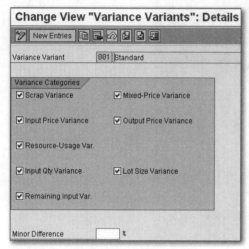

Figure 8.39 Define Variance Variants

Define Target Cost Versions

This allows you to define how the target costs calculated are used in the variance calculation by defining multiple versions and then linking them with appropriate variance variant, valuation variant for scrap, and the identifier for target costs. The menu path you can follow is **IMG • Controlling • Product Cost Controlling • Cost Object Controlling • Product Cost by Period • Period End Closing • Variance Calculation • Variance Calculation for Product Cost Collectors • Define Target Cost Versions**. The Transaction is OKV6.

Figure 8.40 shows the screen where you can maintain the target cost version (**TgtCostVsn**) **0: Target Costs for Total Variances** by Controlling area (**CO Area**) **US01**. You can maintain the **Variance Variant** defined in the earlier step **001:Standard** and the **Valuation Variant for Scrap Z01**.

You can also maintain whether the costs pertain to **Actual Costs** or **Plan Costs**. In this case, you have specified that **Current Std Cost Est** has been used as the **Target Costs**. You can also maintain the **Cost element group** that is relevant for the target cost version.

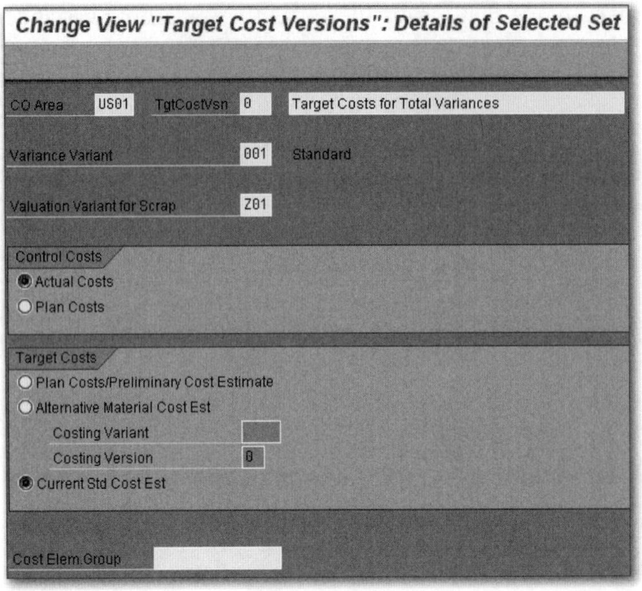

Figure 8.40 Define Target Cost Versions

Define Primary Data for Input Price Variances

In this step, you can define the percentage that will be applied as the input price variance for primary data that is getting posted. This means that the initial input should be reduced by this percentage entered. The menu path is **IMG • Controlling • Product Cost Controlling • Cost Object Controlling • Product Cost by Period • Period End Closing • Variance Calculation • Variance Calculation for Product Cost Collectors • Define Primary Data for Input Price Variances**, and the Transaction is OKA8.

Figure 8.41 shows how you can maintain the price variance for primary data by **CO Area, Fiscal Yr, Cost Element,** and a range of periods. We have maintained **10 %** as the price variance for the primary data. This completes all of the settings that can be made for configuring price variances in cost object controlling.

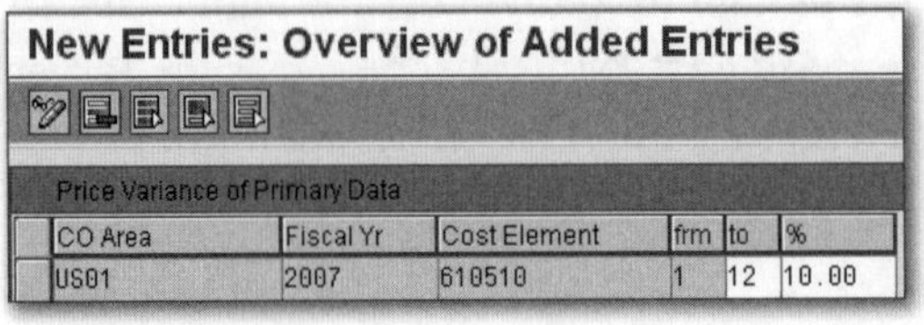

Figure 8.41 Define Primary Data for Input Price Variances

In the next section, you will learn how you can implement actual costing and the material ledger to support complex inventory costing needs.

8.4 Actual Costing/Material Ledger (CO-PC-ACT)

The material ledger is primarily used for maintaining the inventory in multiple currencies. Using the material ledger, you can carry inventory values in two additional currencies. Each goods movement in the material ledger is maintained in up to three currencies or valuations. Currency amounts are translated into foreign currencies at historical exchange rates directly at the time of posting.

Let's first understand the traditional valuation approach that can be implemented in SAP ERP. This will allow you to appreciate the significance of the actual costing or material ledger component. You can either use the moving average or the standard price for a material master as discussed in Section 8.3.5 and shown in Table 8.4.

Pricing Method	Advantages	Disadvantages
Moving average price	Material price is updated with variations from in-house as well as external procurement. Reflects the most up-to-date data.	Moving average price is heavily dependent on period timing and might be inconsistent if the invoice is posted in a different period than the goods receipt. You cannot find outliers in your production process if your material price is constantly changing
Standard price	Allows you to find out the variances in the production process as the price of the material is constant during an analysis period	Does not reflect the actual costs incurred for the material. This problem increases if there are nested BOMs that feed into each other. The cost of the finished product might be reflecting old data.

Table 8.4 Pricing Method: Comparison Between Standard Price and Moving Price

The actual costing/material ledger tries to do away with the disadvantages of each of the pricing methods by valuating all goods movements within a period at a preliminary standard price. During the month, all price differences and exchange rate differences for the material are collected in the material ledger. At the period end, the actual price is calculated. This price is then also used as a preliminary estimate of the next period. The actual price calculated at period end can also be used to revaluate your inventory at month end. Thus, now you can have the best of both worlds (standard price's stability and moving average price's up-to-date correctness and accuracy).

With that said let's take a look at how the material ledger is integrated with other financial, nonfinancial, and Controlling components.

8.4.1 Integration

Figure 8.42 shows how the material ledger is integrated with inputs from **Product Cost planning, Materials Management, Cost Object Controlling,** and **Cost Center accounting,** and outputs to **Financial Accounting and Profitability Analysis**.

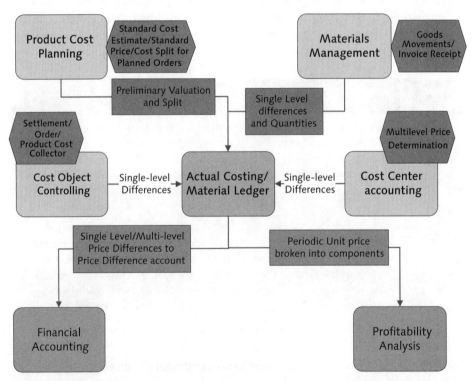

Figure 8.42 Actual Costing/Material Ledger: Integration

The preliminary valuation comes as an input to the material ledger from **Product Cost Planning** that allows you to come up with a standard cost estimate and standard price. **Material management** allows the material ledger to get the single-level price differences and quantities that have been posted. The single-level price differences also come from **Cost center accounting** and **Cost object Controlling** to the material ledger. The output of the **Actual Costing/Material Ledger** then goes to **Financial accounting** and **Profitability Analysis** with a multilevel price differences account and the unit price of the material.

8.4.2 Learning Path

Figure 8.43 shows how you can configure the material ledger to perform actual costing with more transparency about the value added processes along with multiple valuation approaches of transfer prices. First you will learn the basic settings of the material ledger, which involve activation of the valuation area for the material ledger, defining the currency types, number ranges, and so on.

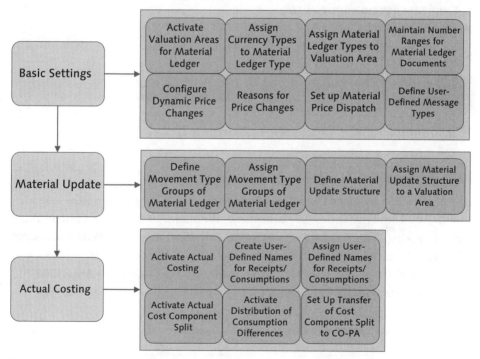

Figure 8.43 Actual Costing/Material Ledger

Then you will learn how to set up material updates in the material ledger. Finally you will be able to set up actual costing in the material ledger, which includes activation of various components and setting up the transfer of the cost component split to CO-PA.

8.4.3 Basic Settings

In this subsection, you will learn how to get started with configuring the material ledger. The following settings are covered in this subsection:

- ▶ Activate the material ledger
- ▶ Assign currency types to a material ledger type
- ▶ Assign material ledger types to a valuation area
- ▶ Define number ranges for material ledger documents
- ▶ Configure dynamic price changes
- ▶ Define reasons for price change
- ▶ Display accounts for account key UMB
- ▶ Set up material price dispatch
- ▶ Define user-defined message types

First you will learn how to activate the material ledger.

Activate the Material Ledger

In this step, you will learn how to activate the material ledger for a valuation area (plant) and company code. You can follow the menu path **IMG • Controlling • Actual Costing/Material Ledger • Activate Valuation Areas for Material Ledger • Activate Material Ledger**, or use Transaction OMX1. Figure 8.44 shows how you can activate the material ledger (by flagging **ML Act.**) for **Valuation Area 1000** and **Company Code US01**.

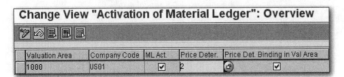

Valuation Area	Company Code	ML Act.	Price Deter.	Price Det. Binding in Val Area
1000	US01	☑	2	☑

Figure 8.44 Activation of the Material Ledger

Price Detr identifies the price determination procedure that will be used in the material ledger. You have two options:

▶ **2: Transaction based**
This is based on the price control indicator maintained in the material master. If the indicator is V in material master, then the system will use the moving average price. On the other hand, if the indicator is S, then the system will use the standard price and calculate the moving average price for information only.

▶ **3: Single-/Multilevel**
In this case, the system will keep the standard price unchanged, and the periodic unit price representing the actual price will be calculated for the closed period.

If you check the **Price Det. Binding in Val Area** indicator, the default value entered in the price determination in this step will be binding.

Assign Currency Types to the Material Ledger Type

In this step, you will learn how to assign the currency types to the material ledger type. The menu path is **IMG • Controlling • Actual Costing/Material Ledger • Assign Currency Types to Material Ledger Type**, and the Transaction is OMX2. Figure 8.45 shows the standard material ledger type (**ML Ty...) 0000,** which gets defaulted when you execute the transaction. The following currencies can be maintained in the material ledger type:

▶ **CT from FI**
Setting this currency type allows the material ledger to use the additional currencies defined in financial accounting.

▶ **CO CrcyTyp**
Setting this flag allows you to use the currency from valuation profile maintained in Controlling.

▶ **Manual**
This is checked if the currency types are determined manually if they are not taken directly from Financial Accounting or Controlling.

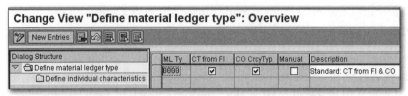

Figure 8.45 Define the Material Ledger Type

Figure 8.46 shows how we have now defined a new material ledger type **Z001**, which shows the currencies that can be manually maintained.

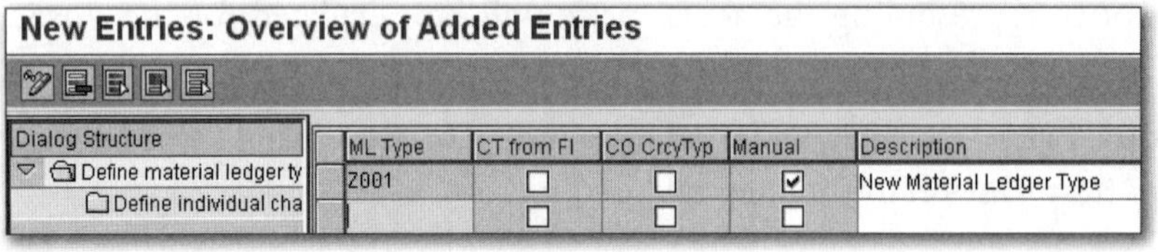

New Entries: Overview of Added Entries

	ML Type	CT from FI	CO CrcyTyp	Manual	Description
Dialog Structure					
Define material ledger ty	Z001	☐	☐	☑	New Material Ledger Type
Define individual cha		☐	☐	☐	

Figure 8.46 Define New Material Ledger Type

If you select **Z001** and click on **Define individual cha**, as seen in Figure 8.47 you will reach the next screen where you can maintain your currency types. In this case, we have maintained the currency types (**Crcy type**) **10:Company code currency**, **40: Hard currency**, and **60:Global company currency**.

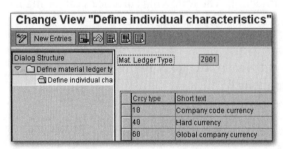

Figure 8.47 Define individual currency type and assign to material ledger type

After you save this, you will see the next screen shown in Figure 8.48 where you can see the standard **0000** and **Z001**, the new material ledger type that has been defined.

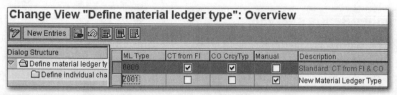

Figure 8.48 Displaying the Material Ledger Types

Best Practice

Always check the currency types from Financial Accounting and Controlling instead of defining your own manual currency types.

Assign Material Ledger Types to Valuation Area

In this step, you will learn to assign the plant/valuation area to the material ledger defined in the previous step. Follow **IMG • Controlling • Actual Costing/Material Ledger • Assign Material Ledger Types to Valuation Area**, or use Transaction OMX3. Figure 8.49 shows how you can assign the **Valuation area 1000** to the material ledger type (**Mat. ledger type**) Z001.

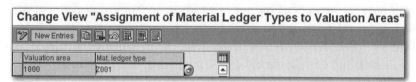

Figure 8.49 Assign Material Ledger Types to Valuation Area

Define Number Ranges for Material Ledger Documents

In this step, you will learn to define the number ranges for material ledger documents. The menu path is **IMG • Controlling • Actual Costing/Material Ledger • Number Ranges for Material Ledger Documents • Number Ranges for Material Ledger Documents**, and the Transaction is OMX4. Figure 8.50 shows how to create a seven set of number ranges valid until **Year 9999** with the **From number 1000000000** and **To number 1999999999** identified.

Maintain Number Range Intervals

	NR Object		Material ledger doc.		

Intervals

	Year	From number	To number	Current number	Ext
	9999	1000000000	1999999999	0	☐
	9999	2000000000	2999999999	0	☐
	9999	3000000000	3999999999	0	☐
	9999	4000000000	4999999999	0	☐
	9999	5000000000	5999999999	0	☐
	9999	6000000000	6999999999	0	☐
	9999	7000000000	7999999999	0	☐

Figure 8.50 Maintain Number Ranges for Material Ledger Documents

Configure Dynamic Price Changes

Dynamic price changes allow you to specify by valuation area and company code that a standard cost estimate or a planned price is activated as the valuation price whenever you post the first goods receipt or goods issue. The menu path is **IMG • Controlling • Actual Costing/Material Ledger • Configure Dynamic Price Changes**. Figure 8.51 shows how you can maintain the dynamic price release by **ValA** (valuation area) and **Co…**(company code). If you maintain the indicator **1** for **Price Release**, then the dynamic price release is activated. If you see blank, then the dynamic price release is inactive.

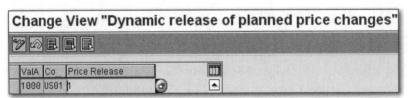

Figure 8.51 Configure Dynamic Price Changes

Define Reasons for Price Change

Here you can define the reasons for price change by transaction code. In addition, you can define the account identifier to enable you to post to the correct GL account. You can follow the menu path **IMG • Controlling • Actual Costing/Mate-**

rial Ledger • **Reasons for Price Changes** • **Reasons for Price Changes**. Figure 8.52 shows how you have maintained the **Reason VAR** for **Tcode MR21** with a blank account identifier. Here you can flag the **Default** indicator to mark the reason as the default table entry.

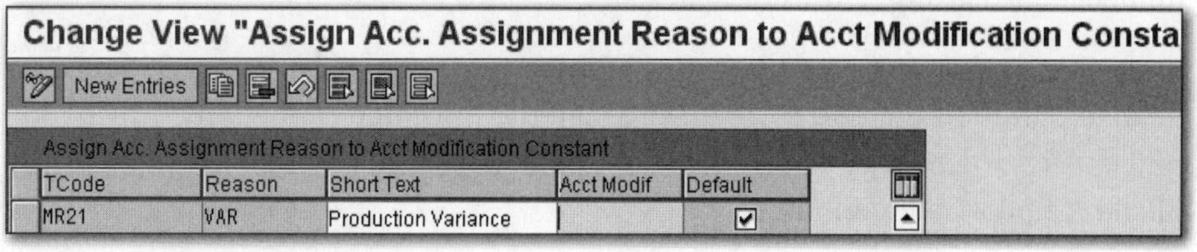

Change View "Assign Acc. Assignment Reason to Acct Modification Consta

New Entries

	Assign Acc. Assignment Reason to Acct Modification Constant					
TCode	Reason	Short Text	Acct Modif	Default		
MR21	VAR	Production Variance		☑		▲

Figure 8.52 Reasons for Price Changes

Display Accounts for Account Key UMB

The reasons defined earlier are tied to Transaction UMB, and the accounts that are tied to UMB can be displayed by using this setting. You can either follow the menu path **IMG** • **Controlling** • **Actual Costing/Material Ledger** • **Reasons for Price Changes** • **Reasons for Price Changes**, or use Transaction OMX_UMB_ ACCOUNTS. Figure 8.53 shows you the screen for maintaining the accounts pertaining to transaction key **UMB**.

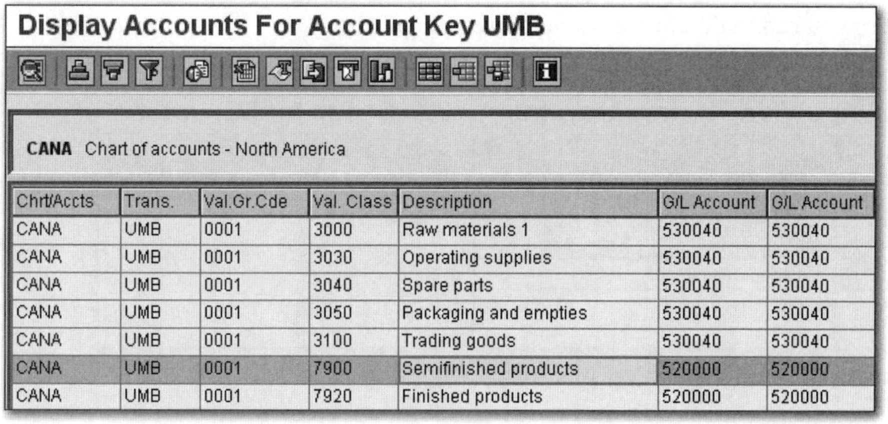

Display Accounts For Account Key UMB

CANA Chart of accounts - North America

Chrt/Accts	Trans.	Val.Gr.Cde	Val. Class	Description	G/L Account	G/L Account
CANA	UMB	0001	3000	Raw materials 1	530040	530040
CANA	UMB	0001	3030	Operating supplies	530040	530040
CANA	UMB	0001	3040	Spare parts	530040	530040
CANA	UMB	0001	3050	Packaging and empties	530040	530040
CANA	UMB	0001	3100	Trading goods	530040	530040
CANA	UMB	0001	7900	Semifinished products	520000	520000
CANA	UMB	0001	7920	Finished products	520000	520000

Figure 8.53 Display Accounts for Account Key UMB

Here you can display the parameters that can be maintained by Transaction OBYC (FI-MM Integration). For more details about this please refer to my other SAP PRESS book, *Optimizing your SAP ERP Financials Implementation*.

8.4.4 Material Update

The key in the material ledger is to understand how the various transactions map to the material ledger to arrive at the ending material price. Using the following settings, you can customize the mapping of MM transaction codes so that you can influence the closing entries of material.

In the standard system, the categories in the material update structure 0001 are so defined that the valuation price during material price determination corresponds to the weighted average price—the sum of the beginning inventory and the prices of all receipts of the period.

The system automatically uses the material update structure 0001, which allows you to valuate your material cost with the weighted average cost. You do not have to do anything if this is your requirement. If you want to modify this, you only need to configure the settings that are covered in this subsection.

Define Movement Type Groups of the Material Ledger

This allows you to define movement type groups so that you can then assign selected material movements to different categories. The menu path you will need to follow is **IMG • Controlling • Actual Costing/Material Ledger • Material Type • Define Movement Type Groups of Material Ledger**. Figure 8.54 shows the screen where you can maintain the movement type groups.

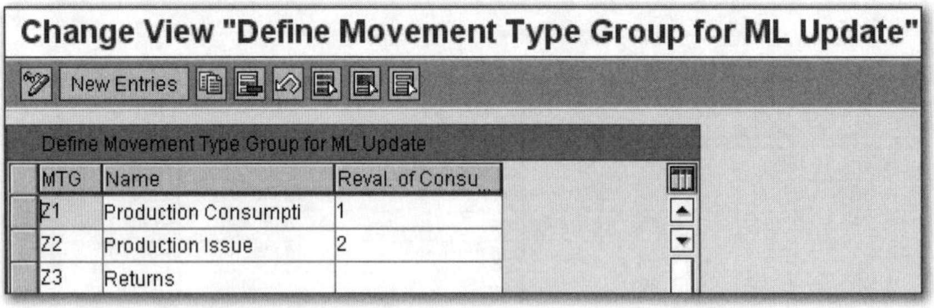

Figure 8.54 Define Material Type Group

You can maintain the following parameters for revaluation (**Reval. Of Consu...**) by movement type group:

▶ **Blank**

No revaluation.

▶ **1**

Revaluation of GL account.

▶ **2**

Revaluation of GL account and Controlling account assignment.

Assign Movement Type Groups of Material Ledger

In this step, you can assign the movement types along with their special properties to movement type groups. The menu path is **IMG • Controlling • Actual Costing/ Material Ledger • Material Type • Assign Movement Type Groups of Material Ledger**. Figure 8.55 shows you the screen where you can assign movement types to the movement type groups.

Change View "Assign ML Movement Type Groups"

Assign ML Movement Type Groups

Trans.Ty	Spe	Mvt	Rec	Cns	Movement Type Text	Movement Type Group
101		B			GR goods receipt	
101		B		A	GR for asset	
101		B		E	GR for sales order	
101		B		P	GR for sales ord.st.	
101		B		V	GR for acct assgmnt	
101		B	X		GR stock in transit	
101		B	X	A	GR st.in trans:asset	
101		B	X	V	GR st.in tr:ac.assg.	
101		F			GR for order	
101		F		A	GR for asset	
101		F		V	GR for acct assgmnt	
101	E	B			GR for sales ord.st.	
101	E	B		E	GR for sales ord.st.	
101	E	B		P	GR for sales ord.st.	
101	E	B	X		GR STO for salesOrSt	
101	E	B	X	E	GR STO for salesOrSt	
101	E	B	X	P	GR STO for salesOrSt	
101	E	F			GR for sales ord.st.	
101	E	F		E	GR for sales ord.st.	
101	E	F		P	GR for sales ord.st.	
101	K	B			GR for consgt stock	
101	O	B			GR to SC vendor	
101	O	B		V	GR to SC vendor	
101	Q	B			GR for project stock	
101	Q	B		P	GR for project stock	

Figure 8.55 Assign Movement Type Groups of the Material Ledger

Define the Material Update Structure

The material update structure controls how MM transactions are collected in the material ledger allowing you to control how the period-end prices are determined. The menu path is **IMG • Controlling • Actual Costing/Material Ledger • Material Type • Define Material Update Structure**. Figure 8.56 shows you the screen where we have maintained the **MatlUpdateStr.** (material update structure) **001**. Standard settings for the material update structure **001** correspond to the **Valuation price** of **Weighted Average Price,** which is calculated by totaling **Beginning Inventory** with the **Receipts during the month**.

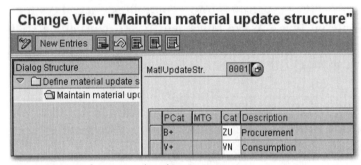

Figure 8.56 Define Material Update Structure

The following parameters can be maintained:

▶ **PCat**
This identifies the process category. **B+** indicates all the transactions relevant for Procurement, whereas **V+** indicates all the transactions relevant for Consumption.

▶ **MTG**
This identifies the material type group that is relevant for the process category.

▶ **Cat**
This identifies the category in the material update structure. There are only two types of categories: Receipts and Consumptions. All of the receipts are always considered in the final determination of the period-end price. However, you can choose to update some of the consumptions as receipts and they will be included in the final price. The following types of categories are identified in the material ledger:

- ▶ **ZU**: Receipts

- ▶ **VP**: Other Receipts/Consumption

- ▶ **VN**: Consumption

Assign Material Update Structure to a Valuation Area

After you have defined a material update structure, you need to assign it to a valuation area. Figure 8.57 shows how you have assigned the valuation Area (**ValA**) 1000 to **Matl Update Struct** (material update structure). The menu path is **IMG • Controlling • Actual Costing/Material Ledger • Material Type • Assign Material Update Structure to a Valuation Area**.

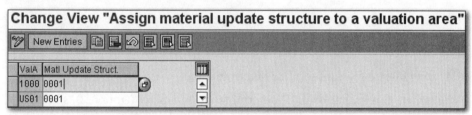

Figure 8.57 Assign Material Update Structure to a Valuation Area

In the next subsection, you will learn how to configure actual costing in the material ledger.

8.4.5 Actual Costing

The settings in this subsection allow you to modify the standard settings that the system offers for actual costing/material ledger. First you will learn how to activate actual costing and learn of its significance:

Activating actual costing allows you to use multilevel price determination. Multilevel price determination allows you to go back to the source view of all the materials. This is the last frontier of inventory costing as now you can go to the exact detail of how the actual cost of the material was determined. If you activate actual costing then the actual quantity structure is updated in the material ledger. The menu path is **IMG • Controlling • Actual Costing/Material Ledger • Actual Costing • Activate Actual Costing • Activate Actual Costing**. Figure 8.58 shows how you can activate actual costing for **Plant 1000: St Louis Mills** by flagging the **Act. Costing**.

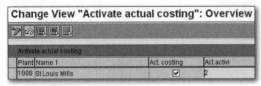

Figure 8.58   Activate Actual Costing

There are multiple options for the type of quantity structure updated in the material ledger. This can be maintained by choosing the actual activity updates (**Act. activi**):

▶ **0**

No activity update.

▶ **1**

Activity update not relevant to price determination.

▶ **2**

Activity update relevant to price determination.

If the update is relevant for price determination in a plant (Option **2**), settlement to materials are posted with a constant price throughout the period. If you want to distinguish your transactions in material, you can define your own Controlling levels. However, it is recommended that you use the standard Controlling levels. Figure 8.59 shows you the standard Controlling levels that the system already has. If you want to define additional controls, these can be defined as well. The menu path is **IMG · Controlling · Actual Costing/Material Ledger · Actual Costing · Create User-Defined Names for Receipts/Consumptions · Define User-Defined Names for Receipts/ Define User Defined Names for Consumption/ Display Controlling Level**.

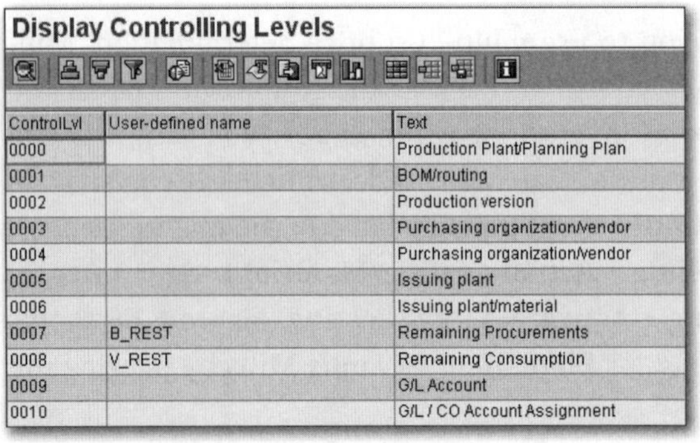

Display Controlling Levels

ControlLvl	User-defined name	Text
0000		Production Plant/Planning Plan
0001		BOM/routing
0002		Production version
0003		Purchasing organization/vendor
0004		Purchasing organization/vendor
0005		Issuing plant
0006		Issuing plant/material
0007	B_REST	Remaining Procurements
0008	V_REST	Remaining Consumption
0009		G/L Account
0010		G/L / CO Account Assignment

Figure 8.59   Display Controlling Levels

If you have defined your own Controlling levels, then you need to assign these to process categories. The standard Controlling levels already have the assignments done. Figure 8.60 shows you the assignments of standard Controlling levels (**ControlLvl**) to process categories (**Proc. Cat.**). The menu path is **IMG • Controlling • Actual Costing/Material Ledger • Actual Costing • Assign User-Defined Names for Receipts/Consumptions • Assign User-Defined Names for Receipts/Assign User Defined Names for Consumption/ Display Assignment of Controlling Levels to Process Categories**.

Display Assignment of Controlling Levels to Process Categories

Proc. cat.	Description	MTG	ControlLvl	Text
BF	Production		0000	Production Plant/Planning Plan
BF	Production		0001	BOM/routing
BF	Production		0002	Production version
BL	Subcontracting		0003	Purchasing organization/vendor
BB	Purchase order		0004	Purchasing organization/vendor
BU	Stock transfer		0005	Issuing plant
BUBM	Material tansfer posting		0006	Issuing plant/material
B+	Procurement		0007	Remaining Procurements
V+	Consumption		0008	Remaining Consumption
V++	Masked (consumption)	Z1	0009	G/L Account
V++	Masked (consumption)	Z2	0010	G/L / CO Account Assignment

Figure 8.60 Display Assignment of Controlling Levels to Process Categories

You can activate the cost component split in the material ledger, if you have used the cost component structure in product cost planning. The actual cost component split allows you to analyze actual costs at multiple production levels. You can analyze the differences of cost estimate from preliminary valuation, price differences, and exchange rate differences. The advantage of using actual cost component split is that the original identity of the costs is retained throughout, which allows you to trace the costs to the minutest level and to the source level. You can list the actual costs of the material according to cost components. This allows you to compare different production procedures and decide which procedure should be used as you can now track the costs at a procurement alternative level. At period end, you can transfer this to CO-PA where you can use the actual cost component split to revaluate the COGM. The menu path is **IMG • Controlling • Actual Costing/Material Ledger • Actual Costing • Activate Actual Cost Component Split**. Figure 8.61 shows how you can activate the cost component split (**ActCstCmpSplt Active**) for a **Valuation Area** and **Company Code.**

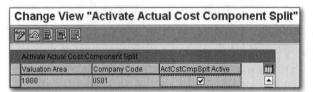

Figure 8.61 Activate Actual Cost Component Split

If you need to use the material ledger for cost component splitting, you should set this indicator. If you are activating the cost component split after you have implemented the material ledger, you need to run the program MLCCS_STARTUP, which will generate the cost component data for you.

> **Note**
>
> If you change the price determination from 3 to 2, and the cost component split was active, all the data related to the actual cost component split will be deleted.

You can choose to distribute the consumption differences that result when you perform physical inventory to orders or to subsequently debit the material. If you use this setting, then the consumption differences are posted to the material ledger. Figure 8.62 shows how you can activate the distribution of consumption differences for **Plant 1000**, **Storage location (Stor. Loc.)**, and special stock (**Spec. Stock**) by flagging **Distribution Active**. You can also specify the default distribution indicator (**Default Dis. Ind**) as either **1: Distribution Active or** blank, which connotes **Distribution is not Active**. If you flag **Binding Distr. Indic.**, the default indicator is binding and cannot be changed when you are performing physical inventory transactions. The menu path is **IMG • Controlling • Actual Costing/Material Ledger • Actual Costing • Activate Distribution of Consumption Differences**.

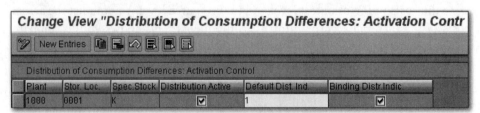

Figure 8.62 Activate Distribution of Consumption Differences

As you can see the number of configuration settings that you need to make in actual costing/material ledger component are relatively few. However, it is important that you clearly understand the significance of each of these settings.

8.5 Summary

In this chapter, you gained a detailed understanding of the components of product cost controlling. First you learned about the rationale for implementing product cost controlling as we highlighted the three pillars of product costing: *product cost planning*, *cost object controlling*, and *actual costing/material ledger*.

In product cost planning, you learned about how it is integrated with other Controlling and Financial Accounting components along with the costing sequence, which mapped product costing with the product lifecycle. Then we went into the details of defining your cost component structure along with costing variant definition. Finally you learned how you can pass on the product cost to the material master in its different views.

Then we discussed cost object controlling integration with other modules. You also learned that cost object controlling can be implemented in multiple ways in different industries: cost object controlling by period (repetitive industries), by order (process industries), and by sales order (engineer to order/turnkey installation). The overall philosophy is still the same in each of these components, although there are nuances that make them suitable for each industry. The discussion in this chapter focused on cost object controlling by period, where you learned the function of product cost collector, preliminary cost estimate, and simultaneous cost estimate. Finally you learned about the period-end activities that are common across all the subcomponents of cost object controlling. You first learned about the WIP calculation followed by a detailed understanding of the variances and how these can be calculated to support various business decisions.

This led to the final part of this chapter where you were introduced to the actual costing/material ledger. You first learned why you should implement the actual costing material ledger as we highlighted the key integration touch-points. Then you learned how you can get your material ledger installation up and running by understanding the learning path that involved the basic settings and the material update followed by a detailed understanding of the settings that can influence the way you calculate your actual costs.

In Chapter 9, you will learn how to set up profitability analysis (CO-PA) in SAP ERP which allows you to generate multi-dimensional reporting capability for analyzing the profitability of your business by segment, customer groups, division, product type and various other customizable parameters.

PART V
Reporting

Profitability Analysis allows you to measure the profitability of your organization on the basis of contribution to the sales from a market-oriented perspective. This chapter shows you how to best optimize your processes as they relate to Controlling Profitability Analysis (CO-PA).

9   Optimizing Profitability Reporting Using Profitability Analysis (CO-PA)

While implementing Controlling Profitability Analysis (CO-PA), the basic motivation is that you can analyze the profitability of your business by product groups, regions, customer groups, and various other parameters. This helps you focus your sales and marketing efforts in the right direction by identifying your growth areas along with laggards and what you can do to improve them. So it allows you to take business action based on the reporting that gets generated. Another important feature of CO-PA is to allow you the profitability reporting in multiple currencies or the currency that matters most to you.

This chapter outlines the tools and techniques to implement and optimize profitability analysis in Financial Accounting. As you learned in Chapters 4 and 5, CO-PA allows you to define customized profitability reporting to mimic your external reporting from a market-oriented perspective. The focus of this chapter is to detail the functionality of profitability analysis and implementation options available to you and then make a conscious decision to choose the most optimal solution for your reporting requirements from a margin analysis perspective.

You will first be introduced to profitability analysis, where you will learn the rationale for implementing CO-PA, highlighting the differences between costing and account-based profitability analysis and profit center accounting. You will then learn the integration touch-points of profitability analysis with other Controlling components. Let's start by getting an introduction to profitability analysis.

9.1   Profitability Analysis: An Introduction

Before proceeding further, let's understand what profitability analysis really is. In Controlling, the Profitability Analysis (CO-PA) component provides you with functions related to margin analysis for market segments. The key difference between CO-PA and Profit Center Accounting (EC-PCA) is that PA is the *external view* of the organization whereas PCA is the *internal view* of the organization for management reporting. CO-PA is an important tool to understand the company's profit and contribution margin from the market-oriented perspectives, such as customer, market segment, division, distribution channel, and so on. On the other hand, EC-PCA allows you to analyze the profitability by department, internal division, and so on.

9.1.1   Types of Profitability Analysis

Two types of PA can be implemented, which are:

▶ **Costing Based**
It groups costs and revenues according to value fields allowing you to represent a cost-based profitability margin analysis.

▶ **Account Based**
This groups costs and revenues in accounts and uses an account-based valuation approach. In this case, you will have to use cost and revenue elements for your analysis. The big advantage of this approach is that the profitability report is always reconciled with accounting.

Both of these can also be implemented simultaneously, especially if the hardware is not a constraint. Most of the companies typically implement both simultaneously and then pick and choose the reporting that they need. The only drawback in implementing both is that many tables need to be populated, which might degrade hardware performance.

9.1.2   Major Differences Between Costing-Based and Account-Based CO-PA

The main difference between the two methods is how the data related to quantities and values is stored in the system. In costing-based CO-PA, values and quantities are stored in value fields. Value fields can be considered a large grouping of cost and revenue elements. For the account based method, data is stored directly in cost and revenue elements, which are similar to the GL accounts. However, data used to be updated at different times in costing-based and accounting-based CO-PA. In standard costing-based CO-PA for a sales order, Cost of Goods Sold (COGS) is only updated at the time of billing. This ensures that when you calculate net margin, everything (sales, discounts, and COGS) is posted at the same time.

However, in the case of account-based CO-PA, COGS is updated typically at the time of post goods issue, which is before the billing process. This results in *timing differences* between the time when COGS is recorded and when sales is recorded. To take care of this problem, some companies post to an accrual account during post goods issue and post both the sales and the COGS during the billing process, which can avoid the timing difference problem. Figure 9.1 illustrates the difference between costing-based and account-based CO-PA as far as reporting is concerned.

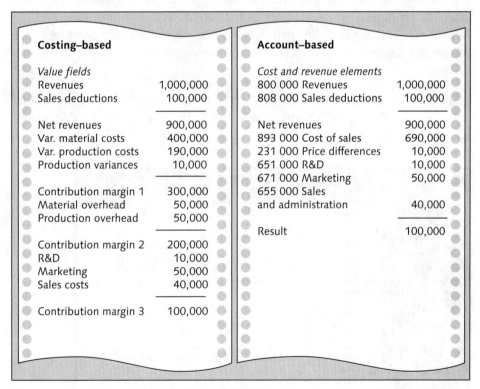

Costing–based		Account–based	
Value fields		*Cost and revenue elements*	
Revenues	1,000,000	800 000 Revenues	1,000,000
Sales deductions	100,000	808 000 Sales deductions	100,000
Net revenues	900,000	Net revenues	900,000
Var. material costs	400,000	893 000 Cost of sales	690,000
Var. production costs	190,000	231 000 Price differences	10,000
Production variances	10,000	651 000 R&D	10,000
		671 000 Marketing	50,000
Contribution margin 1	300,000	655 000 Sales	
Material overhead	50,000	and administration	40,000
Production overhead	50,000		
		Result	100,000
Contribution margin 2	200,000		
R&D	10,000		
Marketing	50,000		
Sales costs	40,000		
Contribution margin 3	100,000		

Figure 9.1 Costing-Based and Account-Based CO-PA

In costing-based CO-PA, you start with **Value fields**. So you have a **Revenues** value field totaling to **1,000,000**, whereas the **Sales deductions** value field is **100,000**. On the other hand, for account-based CO-PA, you have revenue elements **800000** and **803000**, which map to the same values used in our example. In costing-based CO-PA, you need to reduce the variable production costs and variable material costs along with **Production variances**, to calculate **Contribution margin 1**. This then needs to be reduced by the **Material overhead** and **Production Overhead** to determine **Contribution margin 2**. This is then reduced by **R&D, Marketing,** or **Sales costs** to determine your **Contribution margin 3**. The focus of the costing based CO-PA is to map your revenues to costs in a way that allows you to capture your margin analysis in a way that best represents how you want to measure the performance of your business. You essentially get the answer from a business perspective based on the cost accounting method.

For account-based CO-PA, you arrive at the same margin calculation by directly mapping your costs by cost and revenue elements as shown in Figure 9.1. The focus of account-based margin analysis is more on determining the profitability for a particular time period. In this case, you get the answer from a period accounting perspective.

Based on the discussion until now and the discussion of profit center accounting in Chapter 14, the key differences between profit center accounting (EC-PCA) and profitability analysis (CO-PA) have been outlined in Figure 9.2.

Comparison	Costing Based CO-PA	Accounting Based CO-PA	Profit Center Accounting EC-PCA
Viewpoint	External	External	Internal
Methods	Cost of Sales Accounting	Cost of Sales Accounting	Cost of Sales and Period Accounting
Key Object	Profitability Segment	Profitability Segment	Profit Center
Timing Diff. b/w COGS and Revenue	COGS & Revenue posted @Billing	COGS: PGI Revenue: Billing	COGS: PGI Revenue: Billing
Organizational Entity	Operating Concern	Controlling Area	Controlling Area
Currencies	Operating Concern, Company Code	Controlling Area, Company Code, Transaction	Profit Center, Company Code, Transaction

Figure 9.2 Comparing CO-PA with EC-PCA

Let's now take a look at the integrated view of CO-PA with other modules of SAP ERP as shown in Figure 9.3.

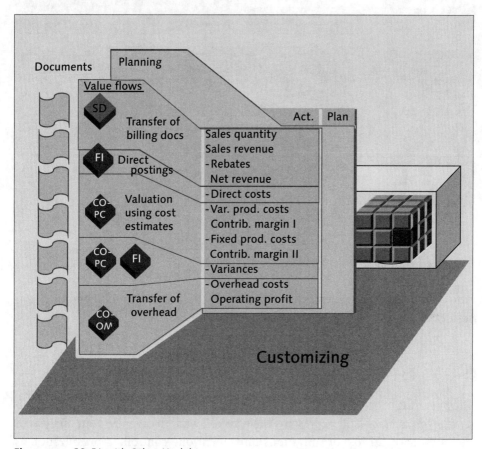

Figure 9.3 CO-PA with Other Modules

As shown in Figure 9.3, data flows into CO-PA from **SD** (Sales and Distribution), GL (**FI**), Product Costing (**CO-PC**), Overhead Costing (**CO-OM**), and other financial modules. Both actual and plan data can update the profitability segment, which is then used to map out the profitability of the organization from a marketing and sales perspective. Review Figure 9.4, which illustrates the profitability analysis structure.

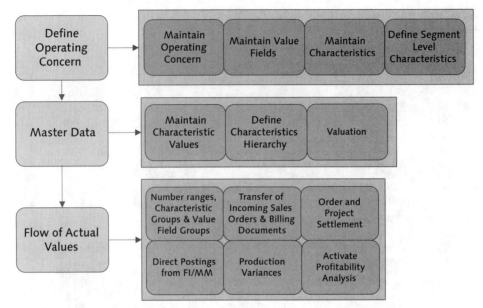

Figure 9.4 Profitability Analysis Process

Now that you have a general idea about CO-PA, let's move to the operating concern, which is the enterprise structure relevant for CO-PA only.

9.2 Operating Concern

The operating concern is the main organizational unit for implementing profitability analysis. It essentially represents the way you want to organize your analysis of the sales market. Most organizations implement one controlling organization as you learned in Chapter 3 when discussing the optimal enterprise structure. One operating concern can be assigned to multiple controlling areas to allow you to consolidate your profitability reporting.

9.2.1 Defining the Operating Concern

In this section, you will learn how to define the operating concern in the system and how you can maintain the attributes of an operating concern. You will also learn to maintain characteristics and value fields along with the definition of profitability segment characteristics for the operating concern. In the next section, you will learn to define the master data components for profitability analysis, which include characteristic values, characteristics hierarchy, and valuation attributes. Finally you will learn how to control the flow of actual values in CO-PA from the feeder modules.

Maintaining the Operating Concern

In this step, you will learn the key attributes of the operating concern definition. You will need to use the menu path **IMG • Controlling • Profitability Analysis • Structures • Define Operating Concern • Maintain Operating Concern**, or use the Transaction code KEA0. Figure 9.5 shows the screen for creating an operating concern. You need to enter the identifier for your **Operating Concern**, which is **US00**. The **Status** is automatically generated by the system.

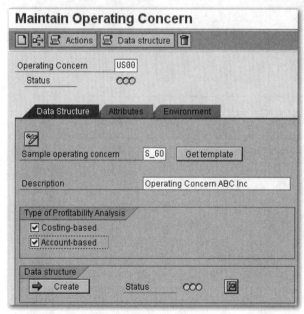

Figure 9.5 Maintain the Operating Concern

Within the **Data Structure** tab, you need to maintain the **Sample operating concern S_GO,** which will be used for copying the structures. You need to enter the

Description "Operating Concern ABC Inc" and choose whether you want to implement the **Costing-based** or **Account-based** operating concern. After you save these parameters, the **Status** of the **Data Structure** will still be red. You have to create the data structure and activate it.

When you click on the **Create** button, the screen in Figure 9.6 appears, displaying the characteristics (**Chars** tab), which are generated for the operating concern (**Data structure** in the left hand side). You can choose to add more characteristics to your operating concern by double-clicking on the characteristics maintained in the **Transfer from** pane. This highlights the characteristics in blue and moves them to the **Data structure** pane.

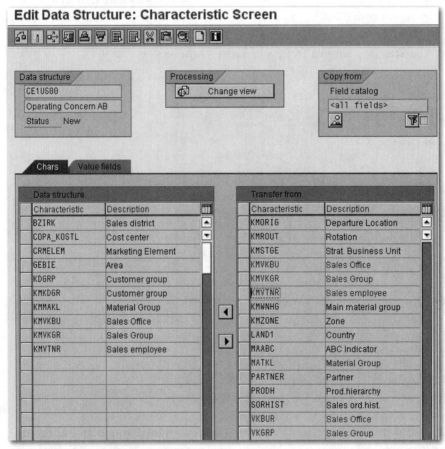

Figure 9.6 Maintain Characteristics

Figure 9.7 shows the screen for maintaining the **Value fields.** You can add more value fields if required by double-clicking on **Value fields** in the **Copy from** pane.

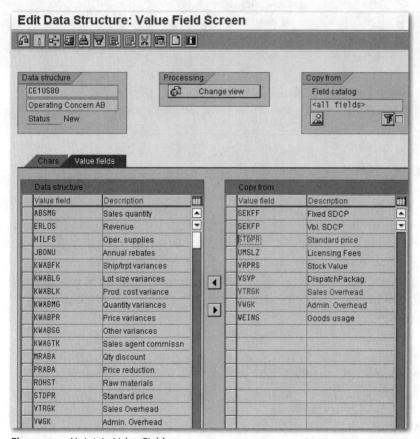

Figure 9.7 Maintain Value Fields

Let's spend some more time discussing the CO-PA tables. Review Table 9.1 to see how tables correlate with functions. Keep in mind that in the table, XXXX denotes the operating concern.

Tables in CO-PA	Data stored	Function
CE1XXXX	Actual line item data	Stores characteristics, values, value fields, and profitability segment for actuals. Can be used for drilldown reporting for actual line item tables.
CE2XXXX	Plan line item data	Characteristics, values, value fields, and profitability segment for plan. This can also be used for drilldown reporting for planning line items.
CE3XXXX	Summarized data	Stores value of value fields and profitability segment. Enhances the drilldown performance.
CE4XXXX	Summarized data	Profitability segment. Can enhance the performance tremendously if you use CE4 tables.

Table 9.1 Table 1.1: Tables and Their Functions in CO-PA

After you identify the relevant fields, you need to activate the data structure by clicking on the activation icon (the second icon from the left which looks like a lighted matchstick). This gives you a popup shown in Figure 9.8. The system asks you whether you want to generate the operating concern environment. If you click **Yes**, you will see the operating concern generated with the **Status** turning green as shown in Figure 9.9. This also allows you to define the **Attributes** of the operating concern.

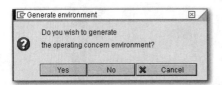

Figure 9.8 Generating the Operating Concern

Let's review what the fields shown in Figure 9.9 mean:

▶ **Operating concern currency**
Here you have to identify the operating concern currency, which is a crucial decision for an organization. It might happen that legally you are incorporated in Europe, so your group currency is **EUR**. However, your customers and market are scattered across the globe, and the majority of customers are in the United States, so you want your **Operating concern currency** to be **USD**.

▶ **Company Code Currency**
Flagging this allows you to maintain the company code currency. It is always a good practice to activate company code currency because most organizations have a dispersed geographic presence, which means different currencies. It allows you to avoid exchange rates differences.

▶ **OpConcern crcy, PrCtr valuation**, and **Comp. Code crcy, PrCtr valuation**
These allow you to maintain multiple valuation approaches from the profit center accounting perspective. Checking these two flags allow you to store values from a profit center accounting valuation perspective from both an operating concern currency and a company code currency.

▶ **Fiscal year variant**
This allows you to define the fiscal year variant of the operating concern.

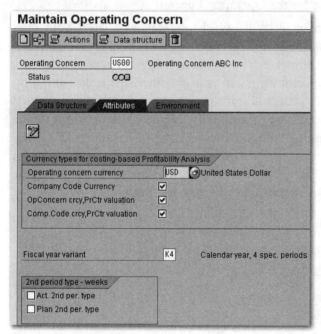

Figure 9.9 Maintain the Attributes of the Operating Concern

After you define the attributes and activate your operating concern, you will see the status for **Cross-client part** and **Client-specific part** as green on the **Environment** tab (see Figure 9.10).

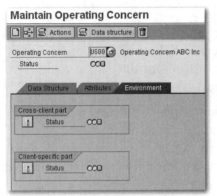

Figure 9.10 Generate the Client-Specific Part

Maintaining Characteristics for the Operating Concern

Characteristics define the parameters by which you want to analyze your sales margin and perform your profitability reporting. Some of the typical characteristics that you can use are customer, sales organization, division, customer group, material group, and so on. A combination of valid characteristics makes up a profitability segment. In this step, you will learn the key attributes of characteristics. The menu path is **IMG • Controlling • Profitability Analysis • Structures • Define Operating Concern • Maintain Characteristics**, and the Transaction is KEA5. Figure 9.11 shows the screen that can be used for maintaining characteristics for a particular operating concern. You can create a new characteristic by inputting the name of the characteristic and then clicking on **Create/Change**.

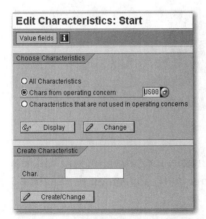

Figure 9.11 Create/Change/Display Characteristics

Clicking on the **Display** button takes you to the next screen shown in Figure 9.12 where you can maintain new characteristics by clicking on **Change** (the second icon from the left with the pencil and eyeglasses). As you can see, the important attributes other than identifier, description, short text, data type, and length are the **Origin Table** and **Origin field** name from which the characteristic is taken.

Display Characteristics: Overview

Char.	Description	Short text	DTyp	Lgth.	Origin Table	Origin field d
BZIRK	Sales district	District	CHAR	6	KNVV	BZIRK
COPA_KOSTL	Cost center	Cost ctr	CHAR	10		
CRMELEM	Marketing Element	Mrkt.Elem.	NUMC	8		
GEBIE	Area	Area	CHAR	4		
KDGRP	Customer group	Cust.group	CHAR	2	KNVV	KDGRP
KMKDGR	Customer group	Cust.group	CHAR	2	KNVV	KDGRP
KMMAKL	Material Group	Matl Group	CHAR	9	MARA	MATKL
KMVKBU	Sales Office	Sales Off.	CHAR	4	KNVV	VKBUR
KMVKGR	Sales Group	Sales Grp	CHAR	3	KNVV	VKGRP
KMVTNR	Sales employee	Employee	NUMC	8	PAPARTNER	VRTNR

Figure 9.12 Display Characteristics

You can define the following types of new characteristics to be used in an operating concern:

▶ **Characteristics created from an SAP table**
New characteristics can be defined by using the tables of customer master, material master, or general sales-related tables.

▶ **Characteristics defined from scratch**
You can also create your own characteristics that do not map to any standard tables. But this requires you to define derivation rules so that the system can determine the source of these characteristics. Custom characteristics need to begin with WW.

Next you will learn how to create your own value fields.

9.2.2 Maintaining Value Fields

Value fields represent the currency amounts and quantities that get recorded against the characteristics. These fields only need to be set up if you are implementing costing-based CO-PA and representing the costs and revenue structure. In this step, you will learn the key attributes of value fields. You can follow the menu path **IMG • Controlling • Profitability Analysis • Structures • Define Operating**

Concern • Maintain Value Fields, or use Transaction KEA6. Figure 9.13 shows the screen in which you can create, display, or change your value fields. As you can see, this is very similar to the structure for creating a characteristic.

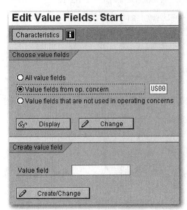

Figure 9.13 Changing Value Fields from Operating Concern

Clicking on the **Change** button brings you to the screen shown in Figure 9.14. Here you need to maintain the **Value field** identifier, **Description**, **Short text,** and specify whether the value field is an **Amount** field or a quantity (**Qty**) field. Some typical examples of value fields are **Sales quantity, Revenue, Sales Overhead**, and so on.

Change Value Fields: Overview

Value field	Description	Short text	Amount	Qty
ABSMG	Sales quantity	Sales qty	○	●
ERLOS	Revenue	Revenue	●	○
HILFS	Oper. supplies	Op. suppl.	●	○
JBONU	Annual rebates	Rebates	●	○
KWABFK	Ship/trpt variances	Shp/TrtVar	●	○
KWABLG	Lot size variances	LotSizeVar	●	○
KWABLK	Prod. cost variance	PrdCostVar	●	○
KWABMG	Quantity variances	Qty var.	●	○
KWABPR	Price variances	Price var.	●	○
KWABSG	Other variances	Other var.	●	○
KWAGTK	Sales agent commissn	AgentComm.	●	○
MRABA	Qty discount	Qty disc.	●	○
PRABA	Price reduction	Price red.	●	○
ROHST	Raw materials	Raw mat.	●	○
STDPR	Standard price	Std.price	●	○
VTRGK	Sales Overhead	Sales ovhd	●	○
VWGK	Admin. Overhead	Admin Ovhd	●	○

Figure 9.14 Display Existing Value Fields

9.2.3 Maintaining Profitability Segment Characteristics

Profitability segments allow you to combine characteristics defined earlier to build up your market segments or market representative structure that allows you to slice and dice your reporting data. In this step, you will learn how to define the profitability segments. The menu path is **IMG • Controlling • Profitability Analysis • Structures • Define Profitability Segment Characteristics (Segment-Lvl Characteristics)**, and the Transaction code is KEQ3.

Figure 9.15 shows the screen for maintaining your **Profitability Segment Characteristics**. You need to identify for each **Char.** (characteristic) whether it is used in **Costing-Based** or **CostBased+Acct.** (costing and account based). If the characteristic is not to be used, then you need to flag it as **Not Used.** For example, **Sales Order** is identified as **Not Used.** You can also use **Exceptio..** to exclude the population of profitability segments if you do not want the characteristic used in a profitability segment in specific situations. For example, you will not want to analyze customers that are not high-value customers. So you can restrict the population of **Customers** to the customers that purchased goods worth a stipulated amount.

Change View "Profitability Segment Characteristics": Overview

Operating concern   S_GO   Quickstart Template

Profitability Segment Characteristics

Char.	Description	Not Used	Costing-Based	CostBased+Acct	Exceptio
FKART	Billing Type	◉	○	○	
KAUFN	Sales Order	◉	○	○	
KDPOS	Sales Ord. Item	◉	○	○	
KSTRG	Cost Object	◉	○	○	
PPRCTR	Partner PC	◉	○	○	
PSPNR	WBS Element	◉	○	○	
RKAUFNR	Order	◉	○	○	
ARTNR	Product	○	◉	○	⇨
KNDNR	Customer	○	◉	○	⇨
BRSCH	Industry	○	○	◉	⇨
BUKRS	Company Code	○	○	◉	
BZIRK	Sales district	○	○	◉	⇨
GSBER	Business Area	○	○	◉	
KDGRP	Customer group	○	○	◉	⇨

Position...   Entry 1 of 25

Figure 9.15 Define Profitability Segment Characteristics

> **Tip**
>
> Exclude the characteristics that will occur on a frequent basis and that have a different value each time to significantly improve the performance of the system. Typical characteristics that are recommended not to be included are sales order, sales order item, order, WBS element, and cost object.

9.3   Master Data

In the previous section, you learned that you can define custom characteristics in CO-PA. Characteristic values and the characteristic hierarchy constitute the master data for profitability analysis. In this section, you will learn how to maintain values for those custom characteristics and maintain a characteristic hierarchy.

9.3.1   Characteristic Values

Whenever you define a characteristic, the system creates a check table and a text table that allow you to control which characteristic values are permitted. In this step, you will learn how to populate the check tables for user-defined characteristics. You can follow **IMG • Controlling • Profitability Analysis • Master Data • Characteristic Values • Maintain Characteristic Values** or use Transaction KES1. Figure 9.16 shows the screen that captures all the user-defined characteristics (text table).

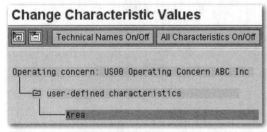

Figure 9.16   Maintain Characteristic Values

If you double-click on any characteristic, you can maintain the values of those user-defined characteristics. For example, for **Area**, you can define the regions that are allowed for this characteristic such as North, South, East, West, and so on. In the next subsection, you will learn how to maintain hierarchies for your characteristics.

9.3.2 Define Characteristic Hierarchy

This allows you to define custom hierarchical structures for your characteristics, which can then be used in your reporting. Typical characteristics that are good candidates for characteristic hierarchy definition are customers, product family, regions, and so on. In this step, you will learn to define the characteristic hierarchy for customers. The menu path is **IMG • Controlling • Profitability Analysis • Master Data • Characteristic Values • Define Characteristic Hierarchy**, and the Transaction code is KES3.

Figure 9.17 shows the characteristic table (**Char. Table**) that can be used to select characteristics for which you want to maintain hierarchy in the system. In the example shown, you have chosen to create a hierarchy **Variant "CC1"** for **Customer** characteristic (**Char.**).

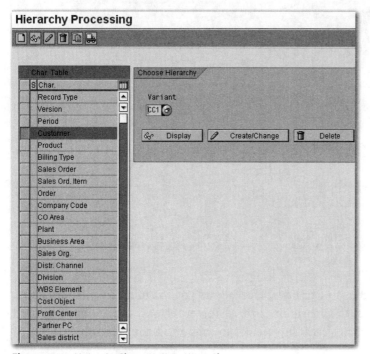

Figure 9.17 Maintain Characteristic Hierarchy

Then click on the **Create/Change** button to create a customer hierarchy. This will bring up the next screen shown in Figure 9.18.

Figure 9.18 Maintain New Hierarchy for Customers

Here you can maintain the short description **Customers** and click on the **Hierarchy** button to go the next screen shown in Figure 9.19.

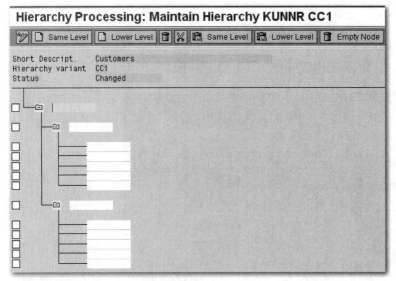

Figure 9.19 Maintain Customer Hierarchy

Creating groups at the same or lower level allows you to build a tree-like structure. Various parameters such as customer size, customer regions, and so on can be used to build multiple characteristic hierarchies to support various reporting needs.

Now let's go on to the next section in which you will learn how CO-PA is integrated with other modules from the perspective of actual data flows.

9.4 Flow of Actual Values: Integration of SD, MM, and Financial Accounting, with CO-PA

Earlier in Figure 9.3 we saw how CO-PA is integrated with other modules from a data perspective. Keeping that in mind review the following elements that get passed to CO-PA from other modules:

▶ **Sales and distribution**
Billing document detailing quantities, revenues, sales deductions, cost of goods sold, and so on.

▶ **Product costing**
Cost estimate identifying the fixed and variable cost of goods manufactured.

▶ **Direct postings from general ledger**
Rebates, delivery costs, and so on.

▶ **Cost center accounting**
Cost centers detailing administrative costs and variances.

▶ **Project systems**
WBS element or network.

▶ **Cost object controlling**
Production order with production variances.

Let's first learn how to configure the actual data flow to CO-PA from these modules.

9.4.1 Initial Steps: Setting up Number Ranges, Characteristic Groups and Value Field Groups

In this step, you will learn the basic configuration settings pertaining to setting up data flows to CO-PA. Let's proceed first with the number ranges for actual postings and then go through the remaining steps.

Define Number Ranges for Actual Postings

Let's see how we can define the number ranges for actual postings that will be used to record the document numbers for actual postings in profitability analysis. You need to define the number ranges by operating concern. The menu path for defining the number ranges is **IMG • Controlling • Profitability Analysis • Flow** of Actual Values • Initial Steps • **Define number ranges for Actual Posting**. The Transaction code is KEN1. Figure 9.20 shows how you can define number ranges for the **Operating concern US00**.

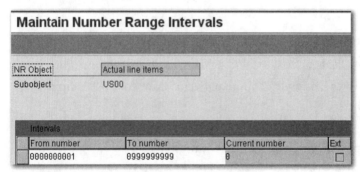

Figure 9.20 Define Number Ranges for Operating Concern

After clicking on the **(change) Intervals** button (pencil icon), you will reach the next screen where you can maintain the number range for actual line items (see Figure 9.21).

Maintain Number Range Intervals

| NR Object | Actual line items |
| Subobject | US00 |

Intervals

From number	To number	Current number	Ext
0000000001	0999999999	0	☐

Figure 9.21 Maintain Number Ranges for Operating Concern

In the next setting, you will learn to create characteristic groups.

Characteristic Groups

Characteristic groups allow you to sequence the characteristics for assigning profitability segments in different business transactions. First you need to define the characteristic group and maintain the characteristics that are part of the characteristic group. Then you need to assign the characteristic groups to business transactions and to the line items in business transactions.

- **Maintain the characteristic groups**
  Characteristic groups allow you to group characteristics along with their sequence. Use the menu path **IMG • Controlling • Profitability Analysis • Flow of Actual Values • Initial Steps • Characteristic Groups • Maintain Characteristic Groups**, or the Transaction KEPA. Figure 9.22 shows the characteristic groups that have been created for **SALE**.

Change View "Char. Groups for Actual and Planning": Overview of Select

Dialog Structure		
▽ 🗁 Characteristic groups		
🗀 Characteristics	Characteristic group	Text
	SALE	Characteristic Group 1: Customer mandatory

Figure 9.22 Define the Characteristic Group

- **Maintain the characteristics**
  If you select **SALE,** and click on **Characteristics,** you can maintain them in the right pane. You need to correctly identify the sequence and the field names for the characteristics. You can also maintain the entry status whether the field name is a **Required entry** or a **Field ready for input** (see Figure 9.23).

Change View "Char. Groups for Actual and Planning": Overview

🖉 New Entries 🗈 🖫 🖾 🖺 🖳 🖺

Dialog Structure	Characteristic group	SALE	
▽ 🗀 Characteristic groups			
🗁 Characteristics			

Row n...	Field N...	Field description	Entry status
1	KNDNR	Customer	Required entry
2	ARTNR	Product	Field ready for input
3	BUKRS	Company Code	Field ready for input
4	GSBER	Business Area	Field ready for input
5	PRCTR	Profit Center	Field ready for input
6	COPA_K...	Cost center	Field ready for input
8	KOKRS	CO Area	Field ready for input
9	KMVTNR	Sales employee	Field ready for input
10	KSTRG	Cost Object	Field ready for input
11	CRMELEM	Marketing Eleme...	Field ready for input

Figure 9.23 Maintain the Characteristics for the Characteristic Group

- **Assign a characteristic group for the assignment screen**
  Now that you have defined the characteristic group, you need to assign the same to an assignment screen. The menu path is **IMG • Controlling • Profitabil-**

ity Analysis • **Flow of Actual Values** • **Initial Steps** • **Characteristic Groups** • **Assign Characteristic Groups for Assignment Screen**, and the Transaction code is KE4G.

Figure 9.24 shows how you can assign the **BusTr..** (Business Transaction) **SD00:Billing Document** to the **Charact. Gr. SALE**. This ensures that to transfer the billing document, you need to maintain the customer and the other characteristics defined in Figure 9.23.

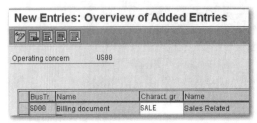

Figure 9.24 Assign Characteristic Group for Assignment Screen

▶ **Assign characteristic groups for the line item screens**
The characteristic groups can also be specified for line items. The menu path is **IMG** • **Controlling** • **Profitability Analysis** • **Flow of Actual Values** • **Initial Steps** • **Characteristic Groups** • **Assign Characteristic Groups for Line Item Screens**, and the Transaction code is KEVG2.

Figure 9.25 shows how the **RecordType A** can be assigned to the **Char.group SALE**.

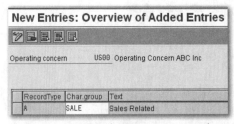

Figure 9.25 Assign Characteristic Groups for Line Item Screens

RecordType denotes the type of business transaction that can be transferred to CO-PA. The following are the typical record types that can be used to represent a group of business transactions:

- ▶ **A**: Incoming sales order
- ▶ **B**: Direct posting from Financial Accounting
- ▶ **C**: Order and project settlement
- ▶ **D**: Overhead costs
- ▶ **E**: Single transaction costing
- ▶ **F**: Billing data
- ▶ **G**: Customer agreements
- ▶ **H**: Statistical key figures
- ▶ **I**: Order-related project

Now that you understand the settings for characteristic groups, let's learn more about value field groups:

- ▶ **Value field groups**
  In this step, you will learn how to define value field groups and then assign these to line items. If you do not specify any field groups, then all the fields can be entered during the flow of actual values.

- ▶ **Maintain value field groups**
  Value field groups are used to control how a group of value fields is sequenced and then used to indicate required entries, input entries, and display only entries. You can also control the sequence in which these value fields will appear. Follow **IMG** • **Controlling** • **Profitability Analysis** • **Flow of Actual Values** • **Initial Steps** • **Value Field Groups** • **Maintain Value Field Groups**, or use Transaction KEVFG.

Figure 9.26 shows how you can create the identifier for the value field group (**Val. FldGrp**) **SALE: Sales**.

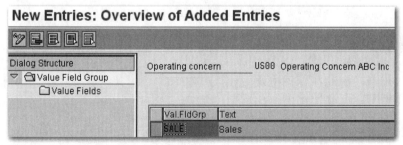

Figure 9.26 Maintain Value Field Group

If you select **SALE** and then click on **Value Fields**, you will reach the screen shown in Figure 9.27. Here you have maintained the fields along with their sequence **Row**. You also need to specify whether the status of **Field ready for input** or **Required entry**. You can also specify whether the value field can only be displayed.

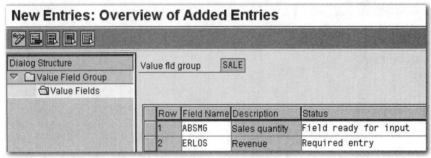

Figure 9.27 Maintain Value Fields Within the Value Field Group

Assign Value Field Groups for Line-Item Screens

In this step, you will learn to specify the value field groups to line-item screens. If you do not specify a value field group, then all the fields are available for use in the operating concern. Follow the menu path **IMG • Controlling • Profitability Analysis • Flow of Actual Values • Initial Steps • Value Field Groups • Assign Value Field Groups for Line Item Screens**, or use Transaction KEVG3. Figure 9.28 shows how you can maintain the value field group (**Val.FldGrp**) **SALE: Sales** for **Record Type F**.

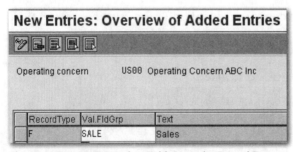

Figure 9.28 Maintain Value Field Group by Record Type

This completes the settings for value field group definition. In the next step you will learn how to summarize data during the update.

Summarize Data During Update

Summarization allows you to combine multiple entries into one line item during the transfer to CO-PA tables. This allows you to significantly reduce the data volume in CE1XXXX tables. This also speeds up the data transfer run times considerably if you are populating huge amounts of data. The menu path is **IMG • Controlling • Profitability Analysis • Flow of Actual Values • Initial Steps • Summarize Data During Update**, and the Transaction code is KE2S. Figure 9.29 shows how you can summarize documents by business transaction (**BTran**). The following are the different business transactions that can be assigned:

- **RFBU**: FI: Postings
- **RMRP**: Incoming invoice
- **RMWA**: Goods Movement
- **RMWE**: Goods receipt for purch. order
- **SD00**: Billing document

You need to check the **External** parameter if you are using BAPI (ACLREC01) or IDOCS (BILLING) for transfer of external data to CO-PA. This can only be selected for **SD00: Billing document transfer**. The **Timepoint** column allows you to perform the summarization either after the derivation or valuation (Option 1) has been completed or before the derivation or valuation has been completed (Option 2). If you choose Option 2, then the data transfer can be accomplished more quickly because your derivation rule needs to be applied to fewer items.

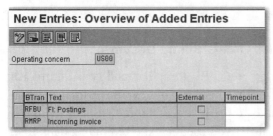

Figure 9.29 Summarize Data During Update

In this step, you will learn how to store quantities in the CO-PA standard unit of measure. The **Store Quantities in CO-PA Standard Unit of Measure** allows you to map all the quantities fields in a standard controlling order unit as well. This essentially allows you to define the base unit of measure for controlling value fields. The menu path is **IMG • Controlling • Profitability Analysis • Flow of Actual Values • Initial Steps • Store Quantities in CO-PA Standard Unit of Measure**, and the Transaction code is KE4MS.

> **Example**
>
> The sales quantity is mapped to the CO-PA sales quantity. However, you also want to store the sales quantity in BAGs for all the transactions. Using this configuration setting, you need to define a new custom value field in CO-PA and then map the same to the CO-PA sales quantity field.

Figure 9.30 shows how you can map the CO-PA sales **Quantity** field **KWSVME** to your defined field **VVIQT** and map the **Unit** as **BAG** to ensure that you maintain the sales quantity in BAGs in all the cases.

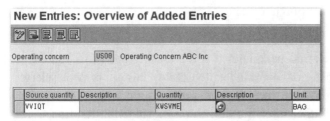

Figure 9.30 Store Quantities in CO-PA Standard Unit of Measure

Now that you understand the key settings to transfer the actual values to CO-PA, you will learn about the settings to transfer the incoming sales orders and billing documents to CO-PA.

9.4.2 Transfer of Incoming Sales Orders/Billing Documents

You can transfer incoming sales orders to CO-PA, to understand your future cash flow position. This allows you to give you a heads up of how the revenue will pan out in the near future. You can populate the revenues on the basis of the order entry date or the expected billing date. If you use the expected billing date, then it is closer to reality in terms of expected realization of the revenue.

The system automatically transfers the billing documents that have been released to accounting to CO-PA using the record type F to generate a line item in profitability analysis. Based on the SD billing, the system automatically transfers any revenue posted along with the sales deduction.

In this subsection, you will learn the key initial settings for the configuration pertaining to actual values by assigning value fields and quantity fields to CO-PA. For both incoming sales orders and billing document transfer, you need to define the condition types to be transferred to value fields and quantity in SD to CO-PA quantity fields. After you have defined the value fields, you need to activate the transfer of incoming sales orders.

Assign Value Fields

SD captures the revenue, discounts, and deductions in the form of condition types. In this step, you will learn how to assign value fields to these condition types so that these values can be transferred to CO-PA from SD. You can follow the steps given below:

1. **Maintain Assignment of SD Conditions to CO-PA Value Fields**
   You will need to follow the path **IMG • Controlling • Profitability Analysis • Flow of Actual Values • Transfer of Incoming Sales Orders • Assign Value Fields • Maintain Assignment of SD Conditions to CO-PA Value Fields** or use Transaction KE4I. Figure 9.31 shows the screen where you can maintain the condition type (**CTyp**) and the corresponding value field (**Val.fld.**) for SD condition types **PN00** and **NTRS**. These need to be maintained by controlling area. **Transfer +/-** should be used in rare circumstances when a condition type can have both negative and positive postings and appears in the same billing document as a positive and negative value. If the **Transfer +/-** indicator is checked, the system combines the positive and negative values to show the net value for a value field.

New Entries: Overview of Added Entries

	CTyp	Name	Val. fld	Description	Transfer +/-
Op. concern	US00	Operating Concern ABC Inc			
	PN00	Price (net)	KWBRUM	Gross sales	☐
	NTRS	Total Net Discounts	KWSKTO	Cash discount	☑

Figure 9.31 Maintain Assignment of SD Conditions to CO-PA Value Fields

2. **Maintain Assignment of MM Conditions to CO-PA Value Fields**
   Similarily you can assign the MM conditions to value fields in CO-PA. Follow the menu path **IMG • Controlling • Profitability Analysis • Flow of Actual Values • Transfer of Incoming Sales Orders • Assign Value Fields • Main-**

tain **Assignment of MM Conditions to CO-PA Value Fields** or use Transaction KE4IM. Figure 9.32 shows the screen where you can maintain the condition types in MM (PB00, PBXX, A002, and RB00) to value fields in CO-PA.

New Entries: Overview of Added Entries

Op. concern USOO Operating Concern ABC Inc

CTyp	Name	Val. fld	Description	Transfer +/-
PB00	Gross Price	KWMAEK	Direct mat. costs	☐
PBXX	Gross Price	KWMAEK	Direct mat. costs	☐
A002	Material Rebate	KWMAEK	Direct mat. costs	☐
RB00	Absolute discount	KWMARB	Material discount	☐

Figure 9.32 Maintain Assignment of MM Conditions to CO-PA Value Fields

3. **Assign Quantity Fields**

   This is required in the case of costing-based profitability analysis where you can assign the quantity fields in SD to quantity fields in CO-PA. This is especially important for planning because it allows you to default the quantities for planning. Follow **IMG • Controlling • Profitability Analysis • Flow of Actual Values • Transfer of Incoming Sales Orders • Assign Quantity Fields**, or use Transaction KE4M. Figure 9.33 shows how you can assign the SD quantity field (**SD qty field**) **FKIMG: Billed Quantity** to **CO-PA qty field KWSVME: Sales quantity**. This setting needs to be made by operating concern.

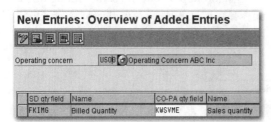

New Entries: Overview of Added Entries

Operating concern USOO Operating Concern ABC Inc

SD qty field	Name	CO-PA qty field	Name
FKIMG	Billed Quantity	KWSVME	Sales quantity

Figure 9.33 Assign SD Quantity Fields to the CO-PA Quantity Field

4. **Activate Transfer of Incoming Sales Orders**

   You can activate the transfer of incoming sales order to costing-based CO-PA. You cannot do this for account-based CO-PA because that requires the actual GL posting, which does not happen during the creation of the sales order. The menu path you will need to follow is **IMG • Controlling • Profitability Analysis • Flow of Actual Values • Transfer of Incoming Sales Orders • Activate Transfer of Incoming Sales Orders**. Alternatively you can use Transaction KEKF. Figure 9.34 shows how you can activate the transfer of incoming sales orders. You need to map the controlling area (**COAr**) and operating concern (**Op.c...**) for which you want to activate with effect from a fiscal year (**From FY**).

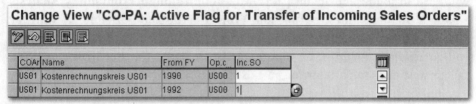

Figure 9.34 Activate transfer of Incoming Sales Order

The following options can be maintained in the transfer of incoming sales orders (**Inc.SO**) to CO-PA:

- ► **Blank**
  Inactive.

- ► **1**
  Active with date of entry.

- ► **2**
  Active with Delivery Date/Billing Plan Deadline (using KWMENG).

- ► **3**
  Active with Delivery Date/Billing Plan Deadline (using KBMENG).

This completes the discussion of transfer of incoming sales and orders and billing documents to CO-PA. In the next subsection, you will learn how to define the PA transfer structures for order and project settlement.

9.4.3 Order and Project Settlement

You can settle internal orders and projects to profitability segments as part of the settlement process to transfer the costs collected in these objects to profitability analysis so that you can calculate the gross margin. Configuring the order and project settlement to flow to CO-PA consists of two steps, which are discussed next. Remember that you learned about the settlement profile definition for internal orders in Chapter 5.

Define PA Transfer Structure for Settlement

This involves the definition of your transfer structure, whereby you divide your cost elements in groups and then assign these groups to value fields in CO-PA. You will need to follow this menu path: **IMG • Controlling • Profitability Analysis • Flow of Actual Values • Order and Project Settlement • Define PA Transfer Structure for Settlement**. The Transaction code is KEI1. Figure 9.35 shows how you can define an identifier for transfer **Structure E1:PA Transfer Structure 1**. You can create a new one by copying an existing structure.

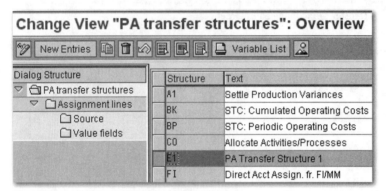

Figure 9.35 Define the PA Transfer Structure

After you select **E1: PA Transfer Structure 1** and click on **Assignment lines** in the left pane, you will reach the next screen as shown in Figure 9.36. Here you can maintain the assignment lines (**Assgnmnt**) by groups of cost elements such as 10: Personnel costs, 20: Raw/service material consumption, 30: Other costs, 40: Secondary costs, and 50: Revenues:

▶ **Qty billed/delivered**
Flagging this indicator allows you to settle the quantity billed during the settlement of sales orders or projects.

▶ **Source assigned**
This shows if a cost element has been assigned to the assignment line item.

▶ **Value field assigned**
This gets flagged if a value field is assigned to the assignment line item.

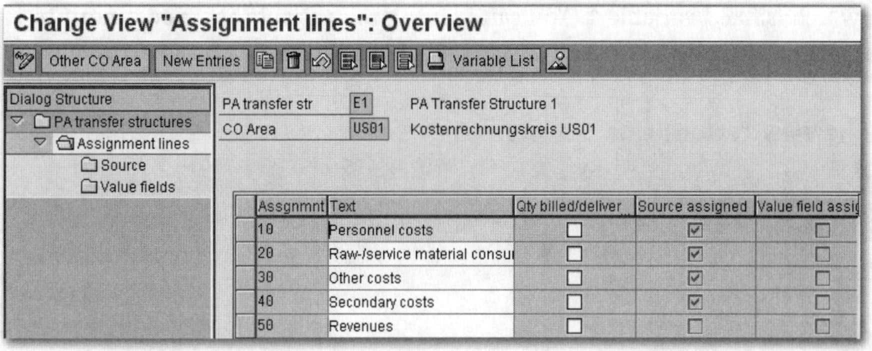

Figure 9.36 Assignment Lines

After you select an **Assignment line** in the right pane and double-click on **Source** in the left pane, you will reach the next screen as shown in Figure 9.37. Here you can maintain the range of **Cost Elements** or cost element groups. Here you can choose to identify the **Source**, whether it is **Costs/revenue**, **Variances on production orders**, or **Acct. indic. on service orders**.

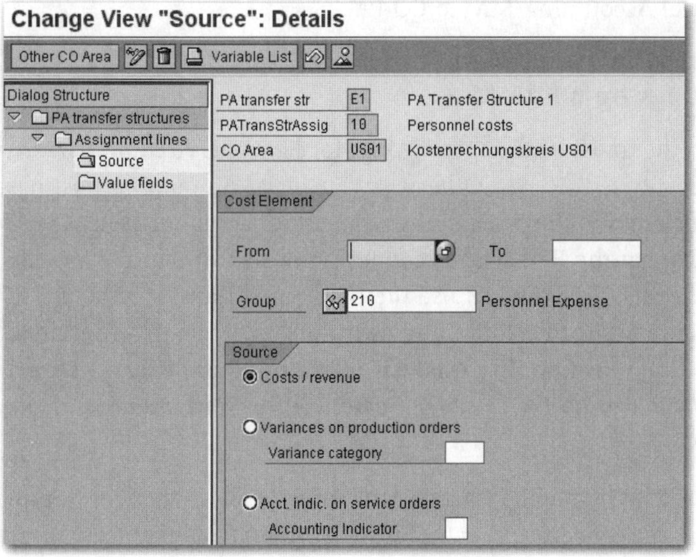

Figure 9.37 Define Source Details

If you double-click on value fields, you can maintain the value fields by clicking on the **New Entries** button and then maintaining the appropriate value fields. Figure 9.38 shows how you have maintained the **KWSOHD Sales costs** as the **Value**

field, which is fixed variable **1**. You can identify the variable as **Fixed amounts 1**, **Variable amounts 2**, and **Fixed and Variable amounts 3**.

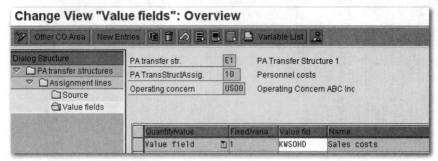

Figure 9.38 Define Value Fields

This completes the transfer structure setup for transferring the order and project settlement to CO-PA. As you learned in Chapter 5, you can always assign the PA transfer structure to the settlement profile that ties to the internal order or WBS element. In the next subsection, you will learn how to configure transfer of direct postings from Financial Accounting/MM to CO-PA.

9.4.4 Direct Postings from FI/MM

You need to maintain the transfer structure settings for Financial Accounting/MM only in the case of cost-based CO-PA. Otherwise, Financial Accounting postings are automatically transferred to the profitability segment for account-based CO-PA. The structure of setting up the Financial Accounting transfer structure is exactly the same as the previous setup. You can use the predefined transfer structure **FI** (shown earlier in Figure 9.35) to create your own transfer structure. The menu path is **IMG • Controlling • Profitability Analysis • Flow of Actual Values • Direct Postings from FI/MM • Define PA Transfer Structure for Settlement**, and the Transaction code is KEI2.

Next you will learn how to define the transfer structure for the settlement of production variances that get generated in actual costing/material ledger.

9.4.5 Settlement of Production Variances

You have to transfer the production variances recorded in actual costing by comparing against the standard costs at month end so that profitability analysis also can be correctly calculated in the system. To enable the settlement of production variances to CO-PA, you have to define a PA transfer structure that outlines the mapping of how variances will flow from actual costing to CO-PA. There are multiple ways in which you can transfer the production variances to CO-PA:

▶ **Transfer using transfer structure**
This is discussed in detail in this subsection.

▶ **Transfer the variances to FI with subsequent settlement to CO-PA**
This allows you to capture the totals to be transferred to CO-PA via Financial Accounting account assignments or postings to CO-PA.

▶ **Transfer the variance using material ledger**
Using material ledger you can perform complex allocations of production variances and assign these variances to CO-PA.

Here you will learn how to configure the transfer structure for transferring the production variances to profitability segments. For this you will need to follow the menu path **IMG · Controlling · Profitability Analysis · Flow of Actual Values · Direct Postings from FI/MM · Define PA Transfer Structure for Settlement**, or use Transaction KEI1.

Figure 9.39 shows the PA transfer structure **A1: Settle Production Variances**, which allows you to set up the settlement structure for production variances to CO-PA.

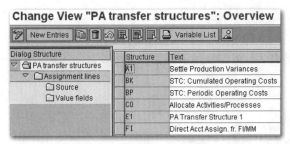

Figure 9.39 Define PA Transfer Structure for Settlement of Production Variances

If you select **A1: Settle Production Variances** and then click on **Assignment lines**, you will reach the next screen where you can maintain the relevant assignment lines. As you can see, you can maintain various types of variance ranging from **Input price variance** to **Scrap** analysis (see Figure 9.40).

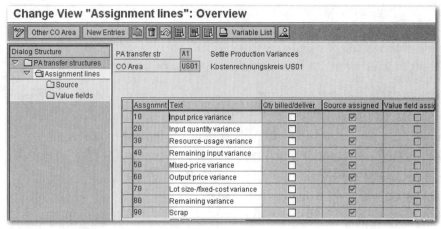

Figure 9.40 Define Assignment Lines

After you select **10**, which is the **Input price variance**, and click on **Source**, you can define the **Cost Element** ranges (from and to) or the cost element **Group**. In the **Source** subtab, you will have to choose **Variances on production orders.** Here you can define your **Variance category PRIV: Input Price Variance,** which allows you to capture the variances on input prices (see Figure 9.41).

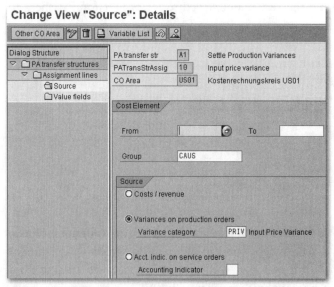

Figure 9.41 Define Source Details

After you double-click on value fields, you can maintain the relevant value fields for price variances by clicking on the **New Entries** button, which will take you to the next screen where you can maintain the **Price variances** value field for the **Input price variance** (see Figure 9.42).

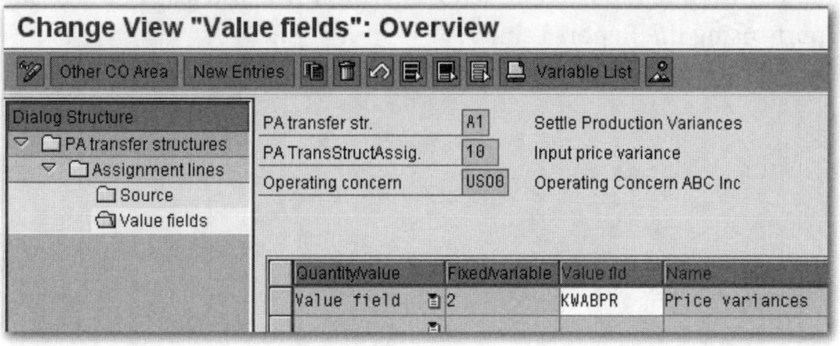

Figure 9.42 Define Value Fields

This allows you to assign the PA transfer structure defined in this step to the settlement profile for settling production variances to profitability segments.

9.5 Summary

In this chapter, you learned how you can implement profitability analysis (CO-PA) to perform margin analysis. We began the discussion with an understanding of the distinction between costing-based (cost of sales accounting concept) and account-based (period-end accounting concept) approaches to implementing CO-PA. You also learned the main purpose for implementing CO-PA and the distinction between CO-PA and profit center accounting.

You also learned how you can define your operating concerns and maintain the various attributes of operating concern such as characteristics and value fields that allow you to slice and dice your profitability segment related data. You also learned how you can define your own value fields and characteristics, which allow you tremendous flexibility to map your reporting requirements. This completed the overall structure and setup of profitability analysis from the organizational entity and master data perspective.

Finally, you were introduced to the integration component of profitability analysis and how you can optimize the flow of data from SD, MM, Financial Accounting, internal order, and PS and settlement of production variances. The integration is built on the concept of transfer structure and allows you to design multiple ways of mapping your original data to the profitability segment per your business rules.

Let's now move on to Chapter 10, where we will be discussing the Financial Accounting and Controlling reporting functionality. You will also learn how to set up custom reports using the Report Painter.

Better and more useful reporting is the reason for any new ERP implementation. Both management and statutory reporting constitute a significant portion of the overall value for implementing SAP ERP because this is what end users value the most.

10   Reporting in Financials and Controlling

Most organizations implement an SAP ERP system to improve reporting capabilities, especially from a financial perspective. The focus is to get to *one* version of truth, instead of the multiple versions that usually exist prior to an implementation of SAP ERP Financials. Because of this focus, reporting is an extremely important component of return on investment (ROI) for any new project. The goal of an SAP ERP Financials project is to arrive at common numbers that everyone agrees on and to provide business users with requisite information for informed decisions in a timely fashion.

However, when implementing an IT project, reporting typically takes a backseat to the project, which is shortsighted. It almost becomes an afterthought because the focus is on getting the configuration done and tested. Instead, reporting should drive the project, and there should always be someone responsible for delivering business-critical reports on day one of go-live.

The following are reporting-related aspects you need to consider for a successful implementation that focuses on reporting:

▸ Statutory reporting for multiple countries (if the scope is for a global implementation) must be ready for day one.

▸ Business users judge the effectiveness of the system from reporting.

▸ Training is crucial in making sure that users can get the basic reporting they were used to in the legacy systems.

▸ Testing is necessary to ensure that users have the necessary authorization to run the reports. Nothing puts off a user more than having a report available but not being able to use it.

▶ Fundamental business reports should be fast and easy to run. Therefore, it is very important that you thoroughly test the response time of the reports that you will give to power users.

▶ As we enter a collaborative era, business users are clamoring for the ability to customize the reporting per their requirements.

▶ The reporting method of delivery also needs to be identified and analyzed together with business users, so that you can capture their concerns and insights.

> **Tip**
>
> Providing users with the right reports, in the format and medium they love, allows you to accelerate the acceptance of the system and makes everyone happy. Identifying the reporting requirements will help you find any missed business requirements as well.

In this chapter, you will learn about some of the key reports available in SAP ERP Financials and how your reporting strategy can be optimized and built as a key component of ROI measurement.

Also with the advent of SAP NetWeaver Business Intelligence (SAP NetWeaver BI), portal-based reporting options, and Duet capabilities, it is very important to not only identify the data fields that need to be reported but also the medium of reporting. Therefore, in this chapter, you will learn how to make the best decisions regarding reporting structure and delivery. The following aspects of reporting will be covered:

▶ Standard reports available in SAP ERP Financials

▶ Optimizing custom reports using Report Painter

Now that you understand the importance of reporting, let's dive into understanding the standard reporting schema of SAP ERP Financials and Controlling.

10.1 Reporting in SAP ERP Financials and Controlling

To better understand reporting, it is important to first understand the SAP ERP solution map, shown in Figure 10.1, and how reporting fits into the broader scheme of things. As you can see from the figure, **Analytics** sits on top of all of the functionality that SAP ERP offers for **Financials, Human Capital Management,**

Procurement and Logistics Execution, Product Development and Manufacturing, Sales and Service, and **Corporate Services**. **Analytics** is the layer that allows you to glean the information from the transactional data that gets recorded in other sub-components of SAP ERP.

End-User Service Delivery				
Analytics	Strategic Enterprise Management	Financial Analytics	Operations Analytics	Workforce Analytics
Financials	Financial Supply Chain Management	Financial Accounting	Management Accounting	Corporate Governance
Human Capital Management	Talent Management	Workforce Process Management		Workforce Deployment
Procurement and Logistics Execution	Procurement	Inventory and Warehouse Management	Inbound and Outbound Logistics	Transportation Management
Product Development and Manufacturing	Production Planning	Manufacturing Execution	Product Development	Life-Cycle Data Management
Sales and Service	Sales Order Management	Aftermarket Sales and Service		Professional -Service Delivery
Corporate Services	Real Estate Management / Enterprise Asset Management	Project and Portfolio Management / Travel Management	Environmental Compliance Management	Quality Management / Global Trade Services

Figure 10.1 SAP ERP Solution Map

Most of the components in SAP ERP have extensive reporting capabilities. The focus of this chapter, however, is to understand the reporting capabilities available in SAP ERP Financials specifically.

Analytics in SAP ERP are broadly divided into the following categories:

▶ Strategic Enterprise Management

▶ Financial Analytics

▶ Operations Analytics

▶ Workforce Analytics

Strategic Enterprise Management focuses on the reporting for the office of the CFO, whereas Operations Analytics focuses on generating reporting for the logistics and supply chain aspects. Workforce Analytics allows you to analyze the Human Capital Management reporting. However, these will not be covered in detail in this book. We will instead focus on Financial Analytics, so let's take a closer look at its reporting capabilities:

▶ **Financial and Management Reporting**
Financial statutory reports include the following:

  ▶ Balance sheet

  ▶ Profit and loss statements

  ▶ Asset reports

  ▶ Accounts Payable and Accounts Receivable reports

Key management reports include costing reports pertaining to the following:

  ▶ Margin analysis per segment

  ▶ Costing per product

  ▶ Overhead costing analysis.

▶ **Financial Planning, Budgeting, and Forecasting**
Using standard out-of-the-box reports, you can perform operational planning for costs and revenues, as well as streamline the budgeting process.

▶ **Profitability Analytics**
Reports for profitability analysis let you slice and dice sales data by many dimensions, which in turn have drilldown capabilities that take you directly to the transaction.

▶ **Product and Service Cost Analytics**
These reports let you see costs per production process, as well as the breakdown of the costs involved in manufacturing and servicing a product.

▶ **Overhead Cost and ABC Analytics**
This set of reports helps you understand the overhead cost structure in detail and plan appropriately by providing multiple ways to allocate costs and assign them to the correct cost object.

▶ **Payment Behavior Analytics**
These reports allow you to perform an analysis of customer aging and Days Sales Outstanding (DSO). The reports can then be used to modify and optimize payment terms.

▶ **Working Capital and Cash Flow Management**
This set of reports helps identify the cash liquidity position and the cash flow analysis for long-term and short-term planning.

Now that we've covered the broad categories of analytics in SAP ERP Financials, let's review the reporting functionality by SAP components.

10.2   SAP ERP Financials Reports

You can access all of the important standard reports in SAP ERP Financials by using the information system of each area: General Ledger (GL), Accounts Receivable (AR), Accounts Payable (AP), Cost Center Accounting (CCA), and so on. Reports are also included in role-based menus. Therefore, if you have assigned someone the role of cost center manager, for example, all of the relevant cost center accounting reports will show up in the user's menu.

10.2.1   Financial Accounting Reporting

Financial accounting reporting can be divided into the following subareas:

► General Ledger (GL)
► Accounts Receivable (AR)
► Accounts Payable (AP)
► Bank Accounting
► Fixed Assets

First, let's learn about the typical reports available in GL accounting.

General Ledger

The GL is used for recording all of the financial transactions in SAP ERP and is the main source of statutory and legal reporting that is published to shareholders and external regulatory agencies

Figure 10.2 shows the menu path for financial statutory reporting using GL in SAP ERP Financials. As you can see from the figure, GL reports are divided into the following categories:

► **Financial Statement / Cash Flow**
These include the financial statements such as balance sheet and profit and loss statements, along with cash flow statements. All of these financial statements can be further divided by actual versus actual, actual versus plan, and so on, in addition to variations by country.

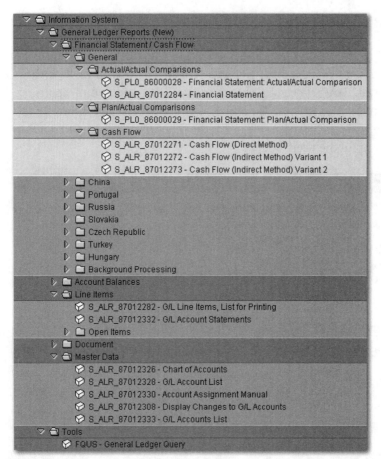

Figure 10.2 General Ledger Information System

▶ **Account Balances**

This node allows you to generate structured account balances or to simply look at the overall balances for a GL account.

▶ **Line Items**

Line item reports allow you to display the line items associated with an account balance, providing you with transaction-level data.

▶ **Document**

This category of reports allows you to audit transactions by giving you a complete listing of all transactions categorized into documents. One of the important reports in this section for the GL is the Compact document report, which shows the balance by GL account along with the customer or vendor offset.

► **Master Data**

This allows you to look at your chart of accounts, lists the changes to GL accounts, and so on.

► **Tools**

In most sub-components, you can create queries that combine two or more tables to give you information that is not available in standard reports. For this, you use the Tools node.

> **Note**
>
> Some of the reports are specific to a country. For example, there might be a particular format of Cash Journal that is required by Chile for statutory reporting. SAP ERP includes the standard report that can be used for this and many other country-specific reports.

Accounts Receivable

Accounts Receivable allows you to generate a subledger of customers that is tied to the main GL. In this section, you will learn the different ways in which you can report your customer Accounts Receivable. Figure 10.3 illustrates the reporting structure for Accounts Receivable. This follows a similar structure as the GL reports, as follows:

► **Customer Balances**

You can generate customer balances in local currency, customer sales, and other associated details.

► **Customer: Items**

The most important report in this category is the aging analysis for customers, which can help you understand how the receivables stack up in terms of number of days outstanding. This report allows you to define buckets of receivables and helps you categorize your receivables per a predefined criteria. In this category of reports, you can also generate a list of open items, due date analysis, payment history, and so on.

► **Master Data**

The reports in this category allow you to report on the customer master data. You can generate a listing of customers, display changes to key customer master data fields, and so on.

▶ **Tools**

This set of reports allows you to generate queries for customers and lets you configure your own customer information system by using evaluations (more on evaluations in a moment).

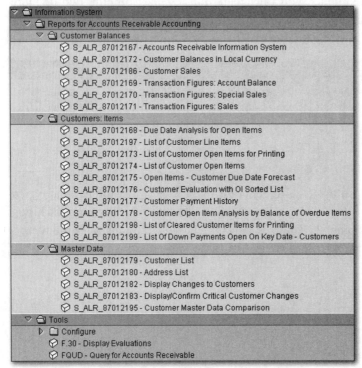

Figure 10.3 Accounts Receivable Information System

Accounts Payable

Accounts Payable allows you to generate a subledger of vendors, which is always tied to the main GL. And, Accounts Payable reporting allows you to report on your vendor balances and vendor line items, as well as perform general reporting per your requirements. Figure 10.4 shows you the reporting structure for Accounts Payable, which has a very similar structure as Accounts Receivable, except that here the reporting is for vendors:

▶ **Vendor Balances**

You can generate vendor balances and run your own vendor information system.

▶ **Vendors: Items**

This section allows you to list open vendor items, along with their due date analysis and payment history.

▶ **Master Data**

The reports in this category allow you to report on the vendor master data by generating a list of vendors and their addresses, as well as highlighting changes in key fields such as payment terms, and so on.

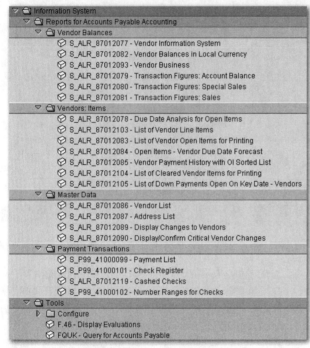

Figure 10.4 Accounts Payable Information System

▶ **Payment Transactions**

This set of reports allows you to print your check register, generate a list of payments already made, identify cashed checks, and maintain the number ranges for check lots in the system.

▶ **Tools**

This set of reports allows you to generate queries for vendors and configure your own vendor information system by using evaluations. Evaluation allows you to customize your AR and AP information system and is discussed in more detail in the box that follows this list.

Evaluation

Before moving on to the next subcomponent of reporting, we need to explain the *Evaluation* tool, which is available in Accounts Payable and Accounts Receivable to further customize the reporting structure.

Evaluation allows you to generate new nodes, which can be accessed from the SAP end user menu, and define a reporting structure, which can be customized to unique user requirements. For example, an accounting clerk who is only responsible for Accounts Receivable and collections in the United States is not interested in knowing about European customers. Evaluation allows you to define a reporting structure that only displays the Accounts Receivable information for the United States for this particular employee.

So how does this work, and what do you have to do in the system to create an evaluation in the Accounts Payable or Accounts Receivable components?

To work with evaluations, you need to define an evaluation view, identify the evaluation type, and then denote the evaluation version. You start off by creating a table entry at the evaluation view level. Each table entry at the highest level of the evaluation view creates a separate node in the standard SAP ERP user menu. Evaluation views can be used from different perspectives and help organize the views according to your needs. You can use evaluations to organize these by business areas, company codes, credit control areas, and a host of other parameters that make sense.

After you have defined your evaluation view, you need to identify the type of evaluation, such as due date analysis, payment history, and so on within an evaluation view. Finally, you define the evaluation version for the evaluation type. This can be in addition to the versions that are available in standard SAP ERP. This allows you to further segregate the evaluations you want to create.

For example, you can define an evaluation view for European customers and one for U.S. customers. Within this view, you can define the due date analysis of customers by "company code" as one evaluation type and by "business area" as another evaluation type.

Finally, you create the evaluation by activating the *Create Evaluation* checkbox. You also need to select the appropriate checkboxes in the *Evaluations Required* area so that the program can start pulling data from appropriate fields.

Tip

Always use evaluations to generate a tree-like reporting structure rather than to generate custom ABAP programs.

Bank Accounting

Bank Accounting allows you to manage your relationship with your banking partner. SAP ERP provides a lot of associated reporting in the bank accounting area, which allows you to manage your cash, check, payment advice, and bill of exchange transactions with your banking partner. Figure 10.5 shows you the reporting structure for the banking information system, which is divided into the following categories:

▶ **Information System**
Lets you print the cash book, analyze cashed checks per bank account, and also identify still outstanding checks by GL and vendor.

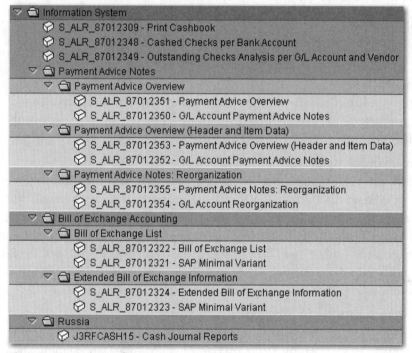

Figure 10.5 Banking Information System

▶ **Payment Advice Notes**
You can perform an analysis of payment advices, line item and header overview, and the reorganization abilities of the payment advice.

▶ **Bill of Exchange Accounting**
You can list the bill of exchanges, along with the extended bill of exchanges.

Asset Accounting

Asset Accounting allows you to manage your fixed asset processes, from acquiring to selling to retiring an asset. You can also run depreciation per the statutory requirements for tax purposes, as well as for financial statement reporting.

SAP ERP provides you with a lot of standard reporting related to the asset history sheet and other statutory reports, which can also be modified to suit your specific requirements. Figure 10.6 shows you the reporting structure for Asset Accounting, which is very different from the Accounts Payable and Receivable structure. The focus is more on statutory reporting of assets and support for reporting of financial statements pertaining to fixed assets. The following categories of reports are available in the Asset Accounting Information System node:

▶ **Individual Asset**
You can display an individual asset with all of the details related to the master data, transaction data and associated depreciation, and net book value.

▶ **Asset Balances**
This shows the list of balances for the assets along with the inventory list and list of leased assets. You can perform an analysis for more than one asset using a grouping criterion.

▶ **Notes to Financial Statements**
This allows you to generate the asset history sheet, which is the most important report in Asset Accounting. It allows you to see the Opening balance of an asset, the transactions that happened on the asset (e.g., acquisition, retirement, etc.), and the Closing value of the asset after depreciation has been run. You also have country-specific asset history sheets for Germany, Austria, and Italy. These reports help detail the fixed assets portion of the balance sheet and form the appendix or explanation to financial statements.

▶ **Explanations for P&L**
In this section, you will find a series of reports that provide detail about depreciation. You can run reports for Ordinary Depreciation, Total Depreciation, Special Depreciation, Unplanned Depreciation, Transfer of Reserves, Write ups, Depreciation Comparison, and Manual Depreciation. You also have country-specific reports for Singapore (Capital Allowance Report) and the United States (Group Asset Balances).

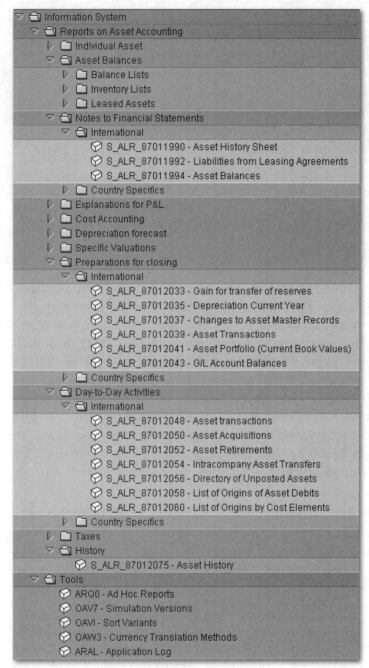

Figure 10.6 Asset Accounting Information System

▸ **Cost Accounting**
This allows you to see specific details about the depreciation that has been posted by cost centers, by period, and by asset. In addition, you can run the revaluation, depreciation, and interest-posting calculation reports.

▸ **Depreciation forecast**
You can run a simulated version of depreciation for the current year and for the capitalized assets to generate a depreciation forecast for your company codes. These forecasts can then be used to plan out your profit and loss statement figures.

▸ **Specific Valuations**
You can run net worth valuation and insurance valuation reports to analyze the net worth tax and insurance values, respectively. You can also run specific reports for Japan and Portugal.

▸ **Preparation for closing**
You can run the various reports that help you get ready for month-end and year-end closing. You can run the gain for transfer of reserves report to analyze changes in reserves for intangible assets. Changes in asset master records can be run to identify if there were any changes in the useful life or other important parameters that might affect the depreciation value or the net book value of the asset. You can simulate running the depreciation for the current year and then compare the information against the depreciation that was posted for the current month. You can also run the asset transactions report, the asset portfolio report, and the GL account balances report to analyze whether your assets are synchronized with the GL. You also have some specific reports by country for Korea, Poland, Thailand, and the United States.

▸ **Day-to-Day Activities**
These reports allow you to manage the daily activities that have happened in the fixed assets area, so you can track asset acquisitions, retirements, intercompany asset transfers, the directory of unposted assets, the list of origins for asset debits, the list of origins by cost elements, and other asset transactions. You also can run specific reports for Singapore and France, which give you more insight into managing your assets on a daily basis.

▸ **Taxes**
In Asset Accounting, you have to follow a different procedure for calculating depreciation and asset value for tax purposes, which can be done by creating a depreciation area for taxes. This section contains reports on the statutory tax-

related calculations, which allow you to separate out the depreciation for tax purposes. In addition to the general reports, there are specific reports for the United States, India, and Korea.

▶ **History**
The asset history report shows the activities that have taken place on an asset throughout the month or fiscal year, showing you the details per the financial accounting standards.

▶ **Tools**
These allow you to define ad-hoc reports using queries, define your own simulation versions, and sort variants and currency translation methods for asset balances in a currency different from the local currency.

This covers the typical reports that come standard in financial accounting. Next you will learn about the management reporting structure available in Controlling.

10.2.2 Controlling Component (CO) Reporting

As you learned earlier in this book, Controlling is focused on providing management with information that allows them to make key decisions based on relevant information. Reporting in Controlling can be divided into the following subareas:

▶ Cost element accounting

▶ Cost center accounting

▶ Internal order accounting

▶ Profit center accounting

▶ Product cost planning

▶ Product cost by period and sales order

▶ Actual costing and material ledger

▶ Profitability analysis

▶ Consolidation

First, we will take a look at cost element accounting.

Cost Element Accounting

Cost element accounting is the component that replicates the profit and loss GL accounts in Controlling. This was explained in detail in Chapter 5. Figure 10.7 shows the cost element reporting structure, which can be broken down into the following categories:

▶ **Overview**
You can run a listing of cost elements by company code.

▶ **Document Display**
This allows you to look at the actual costs that are recorded in controlling by cost elements.

▶ **Master Data Indexes**
You can list the cost elements, cost centers, and internal orders.

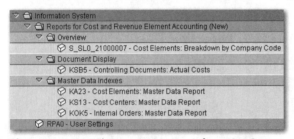

Figure 10.7 Cost Element Accounting Information System

Cost Center Accounting

Cost center accounting allows you to manage your costs per the responsibility areas/cost centers. This was explained in detail in Chapter 5. Figure 10.8 shows the **Cost Center Accounting** information system structure. The different types of reports that can be run are as follows:

▶ **Plan/Actual Comparisons**
You can run the cost center report for actual values and compare it against planned values. The report allows you to generate variance listings by cost center and by period. In addition, you can run these reports with *additional characteristics* and *additional key figures*, further allowing you to break the information down by partner, business transactions, activity types, statistical key figures, WBS elements, and commitments and projections.

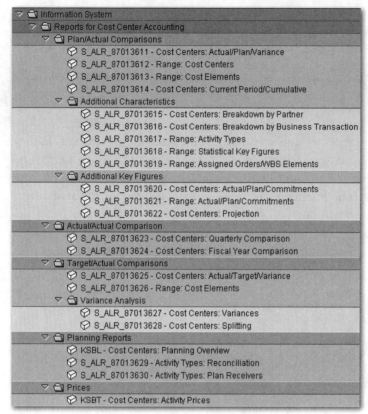

Figure 10.8 Cost Center Accounting Information System

▶ **Actual/Actual Comparison**
You can run the cost center report for the actual values and compare it against the actual values of the previous quarter or previous fiscal year.

▶ **Target/Actual Comparisons**
In addition to setting plan values, you can set target values in cost center accounting. This set of reports allows you to compare target values against actual expenses or revenue recorded in the system. You can do a variance analysis by cost centers and use cost elements as a range for the report execution parameters.

▶ **Planning Reports**
These reports allow you to review the plan values for a range of cost centers and analyze their variances. In addition, you can perform reconciliation of the activity types that have been planned.

▶ **Prices**
These reports allow you to review the activity prices that will be used during cost center planning and for recording actuals for cost center accounting.

Figure 10.9 shows the additional cost center accounting reports classified in the following headings:

▶ **Line items**
You can run the cost center line item reports that detail the transactions as they occurred in the Financial Accounting component and other components, and that were transferred to controlling. You can run actual values, commitment values, and plan value line items. In addition, you can display the actual costs and plan costs for controlling.

▶ **Master Data Indexes**
This set of reports allows you to display the cost centers, cost elements, activity types, and statistical key figure reports.

Figure 10.9 Cost Center Accounting Information System

▶ **More Reports**

These reports cater to the new and extended functionalities that have been added in cost center accounting. Examples include the cost center rolling year report, average costs report, currency translation report, and so on.

Internal Order Accounting

Internal order accounting allows you to plan and manage your mini projects, which are created in SAP ERP as internal orders. For more details refer to Chapter 5. Figure 10.10 shows the structure for *internal order* reporting. The categories of reporting follow the same structure as cost center accounting, with some additions as follows:

▶ **Plan/Actual Comparisons**

You can compare the plan costs to actuals and find out the variances between the two. You can run this for the current period or cumulatively from the beginning of the fiscal year.

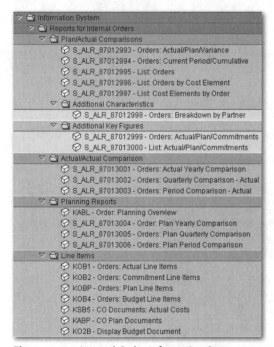

Figure 10.10 Internal Order Information System

In addition, you can list the orders, detail the orders by cost elements, or list the cost elements by order. These items can also be broken up by partners. In addition, you can compare the actual values and plan values against the commitments that have happened against the internal order.

▶ **Actual/Actual Comparison**
You can compare the actual costs to the actual costs of the previous quarter, the previous period, or a previous fiscal year.

▶ **Planning Reports**
These reports allow you to develop an overall internal order planning strategy by providing plan values for the year, quarter, or particular plan period.

▶ **Line Items**
You can run reports that show the actual line items, commitment line items, plan line items, and budget line items. In addition, you can display the controlling documents for actual costs, plan values, and budgets.

Figure 10.11 shows additional reports available in internal order accounting, as follows:

▶ **Master Data Indexes**
You can run a list of internal orders, settlement rules, cost elements, and statistical key figures.

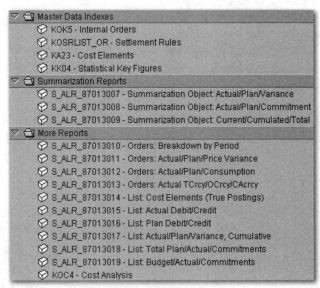

Figure 10.11 Internal Order Information System

▸ **Summarization Reports**
Summarization allows you to provide another layer of reporting by summarizing attributes such as order type, responsible cost center, plant, and so on to combine the reporting parameters. This allows you to generate reports for actual values, plan values, and commitment values, and compare them against the current, cumulated, or total values.

▸ **More Reports**
You have access to additional reports that allow you to analyze the breakdown by period and in different currencies such as order currency, transaction currency, and controlling area currency. In addition, you can list the transactions that have occurred for the internal order, and perform a cost analysis for the internal order.

> **Note**
>
> Define your own reports for internal orders by using the following tables and libraries:
>
> ▸ **Cost related reports**: Table CCSS, Library 601
> ▸ **Budgeting reports**: Table RWCOOM, Library 602
> ▸ **Summarization reports**: Table KKBC, Library 701

Profit Center Accounting

Profit center accounting is used to manage your cost and revenue aspects per the profit centers. This was also discussed in detail in Chapter 5. Figure 10.12 shows the reporting structure for profit center accounting, which is divided into the following groupings:

▸ **Interactive Reporting**
This set of reports allows you to perform drilldown analysis on plan, actual, and variance values for a profit center group or a range of profit centers. You can compare the values for the current period, cumulated value of for the entire fiscal year, or for specific quarters. In addition, you can run a profit center comparison report for ROI.

▸ **List-Oriented Reports**
These reports are similar to interactive reporting in terms of output parameters. However, you cannot drill down into these reports. You can run reports for statistical key figures associated with profit center assessments.

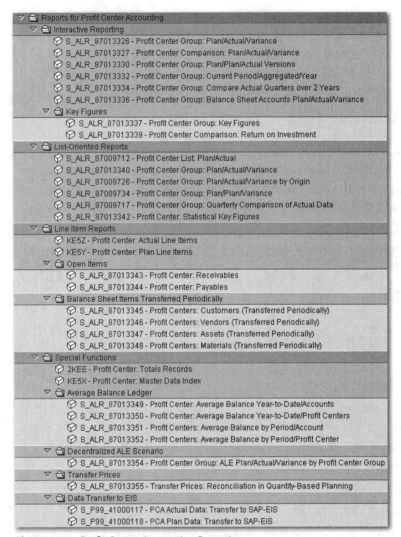

Figure 10.12 Profit Center Accounting Reporting

▶ **Line Item Reports**

These reports allow you to view the actual and plan line items. In addition, you can display the open payables and open receivables for a particular profit center. You can also find out which balance sheet items have the profit centers populated from customers, vendors, assets, and materials. Transfers from these reports allow you to generate the balance sheet for a particular profit center.

▶ **Special Functions**

These reports allow you to analyze the totals records and master data index for profit centers. If you have activated the Average Balance Ledger, you can run the reports detailing average balances for year to date, and by period, for profit centers and GL accounts. You will also be able to run various reports that can help you reconcile transfer pricing based on quantity-based planning. Furthermore, you can run reports that show how data is transferred from profit center accounting to the executive information system, which is a structure of reports that can be configured to meet the unique reporting requirements of CxO level executives.

Product Cost Planning

Product cost planning allows you to answer your key questions related to product costing and was discussed in detail in Chapter 8. Most of the reports in this section are common across all of the product costing components. Figure 10.13 shows the reporting structure for product cost planning, which is divided into the following headings:

▶ **Summarized Analysis**

These reports are used to analyze the results of the costing run. In addition, you can perform price and cost estimates. You can also run reports to figure out the variances between costing runs.

▶ **Object List For Material**

These reports allow you to analyze and compare the material cost estimates according to various selection criteria such as plant, material, costing variant, costing version, and costing date. In addition, you can display materials that are being costed and the materials for which no cost estimates exist in the system.

▶ **Object List For Base Planning Object**

This allows you to generate a list of existing base planning objects according to the selection criterion such as name, sorting field, base object group, entered by, last changed by, and so on. In addition, you can find out where a particular base planning object is used.

▶ **Detailed Reports For Material**
This allows you to generate reports for materials based on the material cost estimates already existing in the system. You can analyze costed multilevel bills of materials, cost components, partner cost component splits, cost element breakup of materials, and itemization.

▶ **Detailed Reports For Base Planning Object**
You can generate reports for costed multilevel bills of materials for the base planning object and itemization.

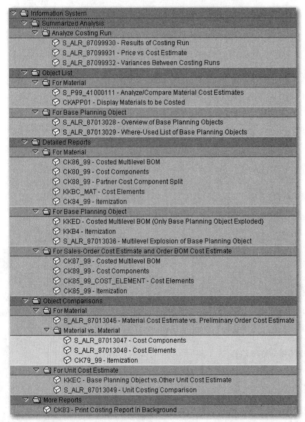

Figure 10.13 Product Cost Planning Information System

▶ **Detailed Reports For Sales Order Cost Estimate and Order BOM Cost Estimate**
You can also generate detailed reports for sales orders with costed multilevel bills of materials, cost components, cost elements, and itemization.

▶ **Object Comparisons For Material**
These reports allow you to compare the material cost estimate to a preliminary order cost estimate. In addition, you can compare materials by cost components, cost elements, and at an item level.

▶ **Object Comparisons for Unit Cost Estimate**
This section allows you to prepare the unit cost estimate by comparing the base planning object estimate with other unit cost estimates, and unit cost comparisons in general.

▶ **More Reports**
These reports allow you to print the overall costing report in background mode.

Product Cost by Period, By Order, and By Sales Order

Figure .14 shows you the reporting structure for the Information System node of Product Cost by Period:

▶ **Summarization Analysis**
This category contains other report categories that let you show aggregated data. You can choose to define your own summarization hierarchy, which allows you to define the appropriate structure in the desired format. You can also choose to execute reports with product drilldown, which allows you to perform target versus actual versus production variances, which can be cumulative or for a particular period. In addition, you can execute reports for variance categories, work in process, and actual costs.

▶ **Object List**
This allows you to perform order selection and display an overview of summarization and cost object hierarchies.

▶ **Detailed Reports**
You can run detailed reports for product cost collectors and for cost object hierarchies.

▶ **Object Comparisons**
In this section, you can compare the orders' plan and actual values in addition to comparing the summarization hierarchy attributes of plan and actual values.

► **Line Items**

This category of reports allows you to display the variances, results analysis/ work in process, and actual costs for product cost collectors and different cost objects.

The reporting structure for product cost by order and sales order also follows a similar structure, so we won't discuss it in further detail at this point.

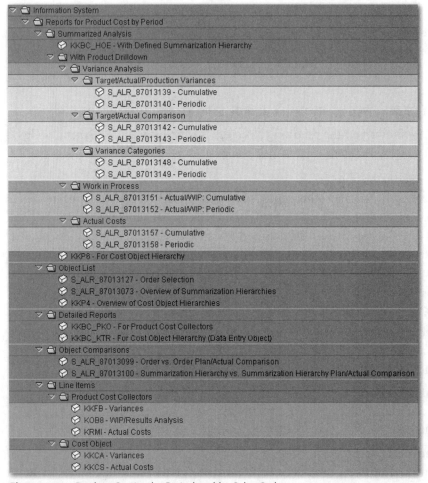

Figure 10.14 Product Costing by Period and by Sales Order

Actual Cost and Material Ledger

Figure 10.15 shows you the Information System structure for the actual cost and material ledger functionality. The broad categories are listed here:

▶ **Object List**

These reports allow you to perform specific analysis for understanding price and inventory values. You can choose to identify the materials with the largest moving price difference, and the materials with the highest inventory value. In addition, you can analyze the materials by period status (new material, price change completed, quantities and values entered, values entered, price determined single level, price determined multi level, etc.). The value flow monitor allows you to understand the "Not Distributed" and "Not Included" differences that were not allocated to higher levels of costing. You can detail these differences by valuation area, plant, and material.

▶ **Detailed Reports**

These reports allow you to analyze material prices by performing a price and inventory analysis over several periods, detailing the cost components for price, finding the transaction history for material, understanding valuated multilevel quantity structure, and displaying actual cost component splits.

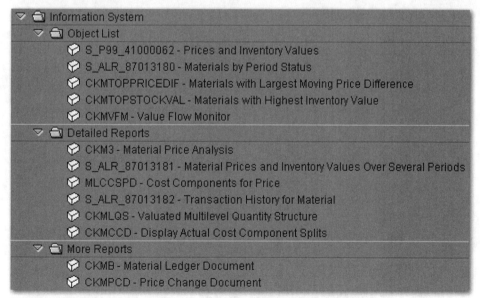

Figure 10.15 Actual Costing/Material Ledger Information System

▶ **More Reports**

These reports allow you to display documents posted in the material ledger and to display price change documents.

Profitability Analysis

Figure 10.16 shows you the Information System structure for profitability analysis, as follows:

▶ **Display Line Item List**

You can run reports that display a line item list for actual and plan values that have posted in profitability analysis.

▶ **Define Report**

Profitability Analysis reporting is primarily created using Report Painter and Report Writer. This group of reports also allows you to create a profitability report, change the report, display the report, and split the report, if necessary.

▶ **Current Settings**

You can define variables for reports, create and assign forms for profitability reports, and maintain line item layouts for the reports. In addition, you can define variants and variant groups, and schedule variant groups for background processing of these reports.

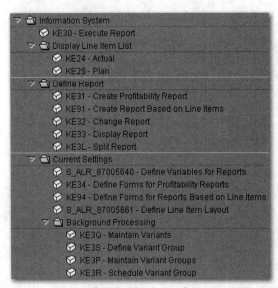

Figure 10.16 Profitability Analysis Information System

Consolidation

▶ Consolidation allows you to generate consolidated financial statements for legal and management reporting. Figure 10.17 shows you the Information System structure for consolidation reports. Consolidation reports are segregated into *drilldown reports* and *master data*. Drilldown reports are classified as follows:

▶ **Standard Reports**
You will find the balance sheet report that shows the details of the consolidated financial statements for the current year in a percentage form.

▶ **Comparisons**
These reports are the annual comparisons of the current year financial statement data with the previous year data and the variances between them. You can also run quarterly and period comparisons, version comparison, local and group currency comparisons, and currency translation key comparisons. Furthermore, you can compare consolidation units and groups (or both) across different years.

▶ **Changes in Values**
These reports can be used to figure out the changes from local values to consolidated values, and quarterly changes in an income statement or a balance sheet. You can also analyze monthly changes.

▶ **Further Reporting Functions**
You can also run the following reports to support your consolidated statements: Sales by Region, Profit and Loss by Functional Area for Cost of Sales Reporting, Changes in Investee Equity, and Asset History Sheet.

The Master Data section of reports allows you to maintain, display, and change consolidation groups, consolidation units, financial statement items, and subitems.

This completes our overview of the standard reporting structure for Controlling. Now that you have a good idea about the breadth of the reporting functionality across SAP ERP Financials and Controlling, let's take a look at some of the important features that allow you to speed up your reporting, such as defining variants and variables for reporting, which allows you to access the information you want faster.

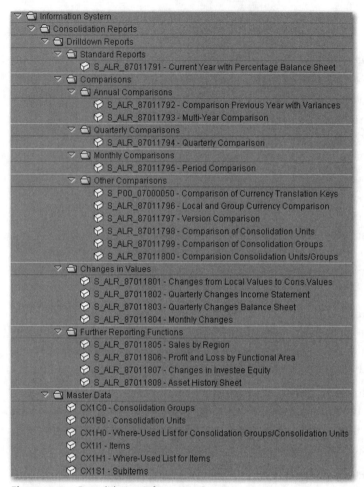

Figure 10.17 Consolidation Information System

10.3 Variants and Variables in Reporting

In this section, you will learn how to use variants and variables in reporting. First you will learn to create variants.

10.3.1 Variants

Variants allow you to execute a report with different selection criteria in different variants. That is, instead of entering values for a report repeatedly, you can enter them in a variant and then save the variant. The next time you want to execute the report, you can just select the variant and all of the selection parameters are automatically correctly populated. Variants are especially useful when you have to execute a report in batch mode month after month. So let's say that we are executing a Financial Statement (from the GL Information System) with the parameters shown in Figure 10.18.

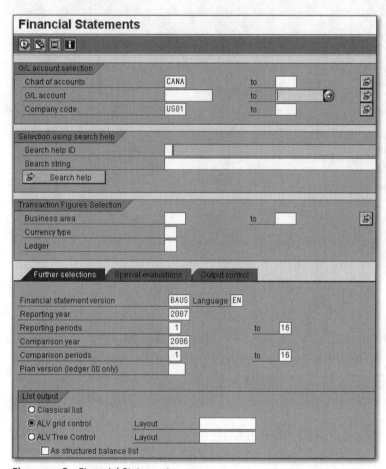

Figure 10.18 Financial Statements

By clicking on the Save button, a variant for this report is created that you can use later. You are then taken to the next screen, as shown in Figure 10.19.

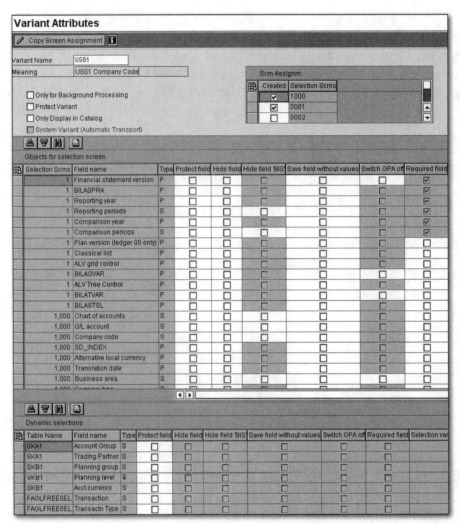

Figure 10.19   Define a New Variant

You can specify some of the key attributes of a variant definition:

▶ **Only for Background Processing**
Ensures that the variant can only be executed in the background.

▶ **Protect Variant**
Makes sure that only you can change the variant.

▶ **Only Display in Catalog**
Ensures that the variant does not appear in F4 Input help.

At field level, you can protect a field, hide a field, or make a field a required entry. After you save this variant, when you come back to execute this report again, you just need to select the variant by clicking the second button from left as shown earlier in Figure 10.18 (to the right of the clock button), and your saved variant becomes available to be chosen. If you do so, all of the parameters you saved will be pre-populated.

The values you pre-populate for a variant are static. To make them dynamic, you use variables, which is explained next.

10.3.2 Variables in Reporting

If you want to call up a report using a particular variant but want to change the display values through the current day, you can use variables. Three types of variables are available:

- Table variables from TVARV
- Date specific
- User specific

Values can be maintained in Table TVARV by going inside a variant and then clicking on **Environment • Maint. Sel. Variables**. Figure 10.20 shows you the screen for maintaining the values in **Table TVARVC**.

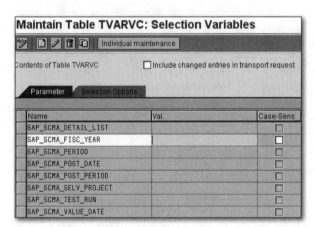

Figure 10.20 Maintain Table TVARC with Appropriate Variables

After you have defined these variables in TVARVC, they can be used in variants, as variables rather than fixed values, which allows you to schedule and run these programs at the beginning of a month without any ABAP coding. On the **Parameter** tab of Figure 10.20, you can maintain the following dynamic date selection fields:

▶ Current date

▶ From month start to today

▶ Current date +/- certain number of days

▶ First day of next month/previous month

▶ Current month/previous month.

Now that you've learned about variants and variables, let's take a look at the drilldown reporting capability in SAP ERP Financials, which can be used to further enhance the user's ability to interact with the system.

10.4 Drilldown Reporting in SAP ERP Financials

In this section, you will learn about the architecture of drilldown reporting and the process of creating a new drilldown report using utilities such as Report Painter and Report Writer.

In most of the financial reporting in a transactional ERP scenario, you always want to access the source document or data that made up the numbers. For example, if you are looking at cost center actual, and you get an abnormally high number, you will want to investigate what made up that number. Being able to just drill down from the number, rather than running another report for the detailed analysis.

Drilldown reporting allows you to create a dialog-oriented information system that can be used for combining data from the Financials and Controlling databases. It lets you analyze the overall numbers for profit center accounting in Controlling and then drill down to the actual sales order that created the posting in the first place.

Figure 10.21 shows you the architecture of drilldown reporting, which displays the different elements that come together to allow you to execute a drilldown report.

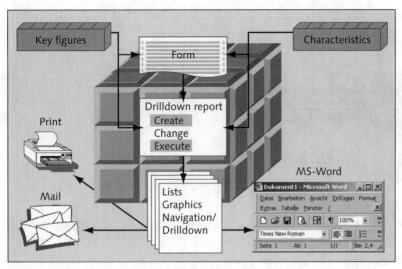

Figure 10.21 Architecture of Drilldown Reporting

With drilldown reporting, first you need to define the **Characteristics** and **Key figures** of the report. These are tied together using a **Form** that outlines the layout of the report. After you execute the report, you can process the report interactively with various built-in printing functions of SAPGraphics and SAPmail together with Microsoft Word and Excel.

> **Note**
>
> This structure is very similar to the SAP NetWeaver BI reporting schema.

Creating a Report with Report Painter

Report Painter is an interface you use to define the following:

- Report Writer reports
- Drilldown report forms
- Planning layouts

We will now examine how you can create a drilldown report. Start by using Transaction FXI1, which brings you to a screen where you need to select a **Report type**. In this case, select **003: Reporting for Table FAGLFLEXT.** Then, double-click on the selected report type to be taken to the screen shown in Figure 10.22 Once there,

you need to enter the **Report** name "ZFIRSTGLRPT: Your First GL Report" along
With form "ZFIRSTFORM".

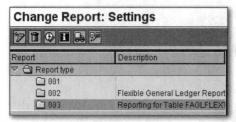

Figure 10.22 Create Drilldown Report: Initial Screen

You can enter a **Report** in the **Copy from** section if you are changing an existing
report's layout. After you click on Execute (the clock icon), you will reach the
Report Painter: Create Form screen shown in Figure 10.23. This screen allows
you to define a new form. You can configure the **Lead column** as **Financial Statement** and also maintain other details.

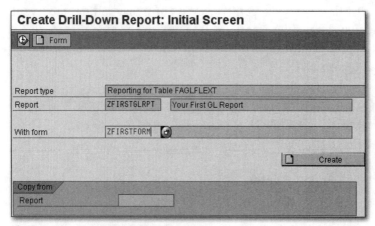

Figure 10.23 Report Painter: Create Form

If you double-click on a row, you are taken to the **Element definition** screen for
the row, as shown in Figure 10.24. You can define the **Characteristic values** as **Fin.
Stmt Vers, Currency, Company Co.**, and so on by selecting the appropriate item
from the **Available characteristics** lists on the right side and bringing them to the
left by clicking on the left arrow buttons in the middle.

Report Painter: Create Form

Form	ZFIRSTFORM	Your First GL Report		

Lead column	Column 1	Column 2	Column 3	Column 4
Financial Statement	XXX,XXX,XXX	XXX,XXX,XXX	XXX,XXX,XXX	XXX,XXX,XXX
Row 2	XXX,XXX,XXX	XXX,XXX,XXX	XXX,XXX,XXX	XXX,XXX,XXX
Row 3	XXX,XXX,XXX	XXX,XXX,XXX	XXX,XXX,XXX	XXX,XXX,XXX
Row 4	XXX,XXX,XXX	XXX,XXX,XXX	XXX,XXX,XXX	XXX,XXX,XXX

Figure 10.24 Define Characteristic Values in Rows

Similarly, you can define the key figures by first clicking on the columns shown in Figure 10.24, and then providing configuration parameters, as shown in Figure 10.25 for the **Key figure Balance Carryforward**. You can configure the **Chart of Accts**, **Account Num**, **Profit Center**, and **CO Area**, which together further refine your selection parameters.

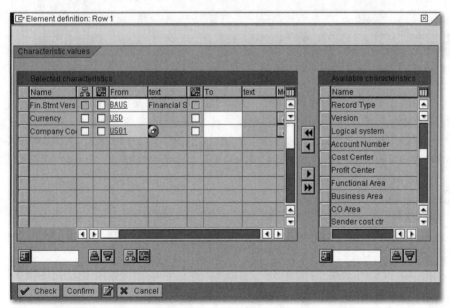

Figure 10.25 Define Characteristic Values in Columns

439

After you have saved the key figures and characteristics, the form will appear as shown in Figure 10.26.

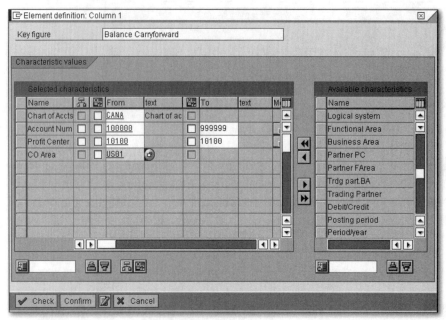

Figure 10.26 Create and Generate the Form

If you return to the report by clicking on the back button, you will reach the original report for which you created this form. You can see this in Figure 10.27. You can see the characteristics that will be visible in the report: **Currency Type**, **Account Number,** and **Ledger**. You can select additional characteristics if required.

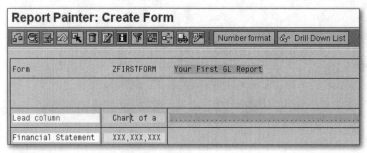

Figure 10.27 Specify Characteristic Values

If you select the **OutputType** tab shown in Figure 10.27, you will reach the next screen as shown in Figure 10.28.

Create Drill-Down Report: Specify Characteristic Values

Report	ZFIRSTFORM	Your First GL Report
Form	ZFIRSTFORM
Report type	Reporting for Table FAGLFLEXT

Characteristics | OutputType | Options

Sel. characteristics

Char.			V.	Name
Currency Type	☐	☐	10	Company code currenc
Account Number	☐	☐		
Ledger	☐	☐	0L	Leading Ledger

Char. list

Characteristic
ADB Period From
ADB Period To
Altern. account
Base Unit
Business Area
Cost Center
Debit/Credit
FS Item
FS Item/Account
FS Item/Acct/FA Long

Figure 10.28   Configure the Output Type

You can configure the parameters related to how the output will appear. You can specify Graphical report-output, Classic drilldown, Object list (ALV), and XXL (spreadsheet). In addition, you can specify that these options be Available on selection screen when you run a report.

If you select the **Options** tab, you will reach the next screen as shown in Figure 10.29. You can configure the parameters for **Print Setup** related to **Mass print settings**, **Drilldown List** for **Totals lines,** and any **Extras** such as **Maintain comment** and **Report assignment.** Report assignment allows you to attach multiple reports within a report, which can be called depending on the type of analysis being done. For example, if you want to analyze changes on a year-to-year basis, you can set up a report that has the year-to-year format built in. However, if you need month-to-month details, then you can set up a report that displays month-to-month details.

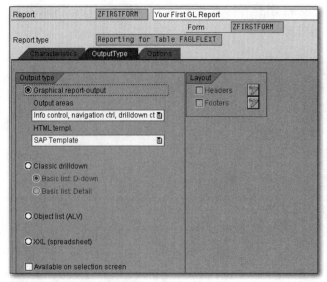

Figure 10.29 Specify Report Options

After you save this report and generate it, you can execute (run) it. On executing the report, you will reach the screen shown in Figure 10.30.

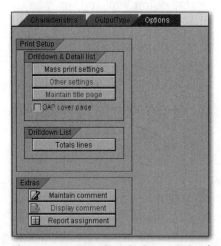

Figure 10.30 Your First GL Report Is Ready

Now that you see how the report actually looks, let's review what we did to create it. First we identified the key figures and characteristics that make up the rows and columns of the report. Then we created a form that allows you to create the layout for the report. After we created the form, we assigned the key figures and characteristics to the report and the form, and customized the layout per our requirements. We also restricted the report to run for specific values of characteristics and customized the output types and printing parameters. Finally, we generated the report and then executed it to see how it looks from a selection parameter perspective.

10.5   Summary

In this chapter, you learned about the standard reporting functionality available in SAP ERP Financials. First you learned about the available statutory reports in the Financial Accounting component, and then you were introduced to the management reporting available in the Controlling component. Next, you learned about the function of variants and variables, and then we covered the drilldown reporting architecture in SAP ERP Financials by using a real-world example of creating a financial report.

The future direction of reporting lies in combining disparate sources of data (SAP and non-SAP) in one system to help you get the maximum benefit out of your existing applications. This can be accomplished by using SAP NetWeaver BI as a common platform for reporting both financial as well as non financial data. Currently, it is also important to integrate SAP with Office (Duet), which allows you to disseminate information to a wider audience who can make effective decisions on the basis of the available information.

11 Concluding Remarks

This book has given you the tools you need to start thinking about Controlling business processes from a process perspective, and you should now be at a point where you understand the bigger picture. This, in turn, will help you focus your efforts on optimizing these processes to suit your requirements. For example, having read this book, you might decide to implement the entire product costing component, along with actual costing or the material ledger, or you might decide to get a standard cost estimate using product cost planning. It all depends on your needs, and you now understand which Controlling tools will best address those needs.

In parting, I would like to say that the only thing that is constant is change and then, more change. Therefore, it is very important for you to understand how your business is evolving and then design a Controlling solution that addresses these changing needs. This, however, might sound almost impossible in the current world, where everything is new and different every other month, so how can you implement a solution that can survive the onslaught of changing market conditions, be in line with the business vision, and also meet the ROI needed for the investment?

The answer is actually not that difficult: You have to prioritize what is most important, get started, and make the project happen in as short a period of time as possible. Otherwise, you might end up implementing a system that, by the time it's in place, is already outdated. After you've built a base that forms the core of your organizational IT system landscape, you also need to continuously optimize it, always thinking about the future direction and how you can get there quickly. With that, I wish you the best of luck in all of your SAP ERP Financials endeavors!

Appendices

A Glossary and SAP Abbreviations

ABAP Advanced Business Application Programming, the SAP programming language.

Account determination System function that determines automatically the accounts in financial accounting to which the postings occur during any posting transaction.

ALV ABAP List Viewer allows you to sort, filter, subtotal, find, and customize the line layout of the report in a way that makes the most sense to you.

AM/AA The Asset Management module/Asset Accounting is used to manage your fixed assets.

ALE Application Link Enabling supports the creation and operation of distributed applications, and application integration is achieved via synchronous and asynchronous communication, not via a central database.

APO Advanced Planner and Optimizer allows you to run optimization routines on demand planning, supply network planning, and global available to promise (GATP), which allows you to make decisions regarding the supply chain processes.

ATP Available-to-promise is the quantity of a material or part still available to MRP, which could be used for new sales orders.

BAPI Business Application Programming Interfaces are SAP supplied data modification routines. You should use many BAPIs rather than custom ABAP code whenever possible

because they are supported by SAP for future releases.

BDC Batch Data Communication is used to define the processing mode for a batch input session, such as displaying all records, displaying error dialogs, displaying process sessions in the background, and so on.

BW Business Information Warehouse is used to manage your business intelligence reporting.

CRM Customer relationship management is used to manage your interactions with your customers.

Company code The smallest organizational unit for which a complete self-contained set of accounts can be drawn up.

Controlling SAP ERP module that controls and monitors internal transactions or reporting processes for nonexternal parties.

Debit and credit (D/C) This identifies the debit and credit indicator for an account posting.

EDI Electronic data interchange is the mechanism by which you can communicate with your external partners.

ERP Enterprise Resource Planning is the philosophy of integrating all your enterprise applications into one, which helps you in supporting your organizationwide efforts at collaboration and integration.

Financial Accounting   SAP ERP module that organizes and controls the financial accounting processes and transactions of an organization and mostly oriented toward external parties.

Financial Supply Chain Management (FSCM)   SAP ERP module that deals with financial processes such as contract accounts payable and receivable, electronic bill payment and presentment, credit limit management, and working capital management.

GI   Goods issue refers to the issue of goods to a cost object so that they can be used for processing.

GL   General ledger refers to the general ledger master record that is used to structure your balance sheet and income statement.

GR   Goods receipt refers to the receipt of goods with reference to a cost object. Typically, GR refers to the stockable materials and increases the inventory that can then be used in various processes.

GT   Goods transfer allows you to move goods from one location to another location.

GUI   Graphical user interface by which you can access SAP ERP. You can also access SAP via a thin client that does not require any GUI to be installed on the desktop. However, it is recommended that you use the GUI for heavy users.

HR   The human resources SAP ERP module that helps you manage HR function.

IDOC   Intermediate document is the data container for data exchange between SAP systems or between a SAP system and a non-SAP system.

IR   Invoice receipt refers to the recording of invoice in the system with reference to a purchasing document.

IS   Industry specific solutions are SAP supplied solutions to meet the unique needs of an industry-specific problem. For example, IS Oil & Gas for handling petrochemicals industry unique requirements.

LES   Logistics Execution System is the SAP component that allows you to manage your transportation and shipping processes.

LIFO   Last In First Out is an inventory valuation procedure according to which the stocks of a material that were last received are the first to be used or sold.

MM   Materials Management is one of the logistics modules designed to manage and control the material flow of information inside a company such as purchase requisition, bills of material, inventory management, purchasing and supplier information, and others.

KPIs   Key performance indicators are identified at the highest level of aggregation and are of strategic significance for the managers of the process or business unit. However, you can define KPIs for any process area.

MAP   Moving average price is the price indicator that allows you to capture the changes in materials price as these are recorded in the system.

MM SRV   Material Management External Services Management allows you to manage the process of requesting an external service, actual execution of the service, and payment of the service in an integrated fashion.

MPS Master production scheduling takes care of those parts or products that greatly influence company profits or that take up critical resources.

MRP Material requirements planning takes into account and plan every future requirement during the creation of order proposals (independent requirements, dependent requirements, and so on).

OLAP Online analytical processing is used to refer to the BW and SEM, which are primarily used for decision making.

OLTP Online transactional processing is the traditional ERP architecture, which is based on recording transactions and avoiding duplicate data entry.

PLM Product lifecycle management refers to a product suite of SAP ERP, which allows you to manage your portfolio of products along with their entire lifecycle from launch to growth and then decline and replacement of the product line

PP The Production Planning module in SAP ERP is used to manage your production order planning and execution.

PS The Project Systems module allows you to manage your projects and integrates with financials to capture costs and revenues.

RFC Remote Function Call allows you to call and process predefined procedures/functions in a remote SAP system.

QM Quality Management is the logistics module, which is used to measure and record quality attributes while processing materials and services.

RFQ Request For Quotation is used in the context of requesting a quotation from the vendor before the purchase order is created for the vendor.

SOA Sarbanes-Oxley Act, which is a U.S. regulatory governance model that increases operational controls and assesses the effectiveness of independent auditors and corporations to guarantee proper financial reporting. This act was introduced in the aftermath of the Enron debacle.

SAP IDES The SAP Training platform that is available as a separate system with preconfigured objects and loaded data, which allows users to train and practice with predefined business content.

SAPScript SAP's word processing system that allows you to design your forms for communicating with your business partners or forms for internal processing. However, this is something that is now increasingly being replaced by Smart Forms and PDF-based forms.

SAPmail Electronic mail system in SAPoffice that allows you to transmit messages between SAP and an external messaging system.

SAPoffice The electronic mail system and folder structure in the SAP ERP system that allows you to send documents internally or externally.

SCM Supply Chain Management refers to all the supply chain components such as PP,

APO, capacity planning, consumption-based planning, logistics execution, and purchasing functions. This is the umbrella term for all the logistics functions that allow you to manage your supply chain better.

SD Sales and Distribution is the logistics module that allows you to manage your sales processes from sales inquiry to billing. Only cash collection is part of financials. The rest of the sales-related processes are part of SD or CRM.

SOP Sales and Operations Planning is a flexible forecasting and planning tool with which sales, production, and other supply chain targets can be set on the basis of historical, existing, and/or estimated future data.

SRM (SEM component) Stakeholder Relationship Management is the component in SAP SEM that allows you to manage your relationship with external stakeholders and shareholders

SRM (Purchasing) Supplier Relationship Management (Purchasing) is the component in procurement that handles the integration with your suppliers allowing you to achieve significant cost savings in terms of invoice reconciliation and provides you with increased visibility to your purchasing process.

WBS The Work Breakdown Structure element is the lowest level master data element in PS, which breaks down the project work into manageable chunks so that you can assign these and track the costs on WBS elements.

WF Business Work Flow tool for automatic control and execution of cross-application processes.

B   Bibliography

B.1   Internet Resources

http://help.sap.com/erp2005_ehp_02/helpdata/en/80/ea89395eb58c4f9d-0c3e837cf0909d/frameset.htm

http://www.sap.com/community/pub/events/2007_04_SAPPHIRE_US/solutions.epx#mySAPERPFinancials

http://www.sap.com/community/pub/showdetail.epx?itemID=8866

B.2   Conference Resources

Simplify, Optimize, and Innovate with SAP ERP: 2007_04_sapphire_us_GE1859

Back to School: A Dual Strategy for Innovation, Speed and Success: Hasso Plattner: Creating Roadmaps with SAP Value Engineering, 2007_04_sapphire_us_GE1621.

Benchmarking Study Model: 2006 ASUG SAP Benchmarking Study: SAP Insight, Katherina Mullers-Patel

B.3   Customer Success Stories and Best Practices

Top 100 SAP ERP: Customer success stories: http://www.sap.com/solutions/pdf/CS_100_Customer_Successes.pdf

Best Practices Baseline Package: http://help.sap.com/content/bestpractices/baseline/index.htm

Best Practices by SAP ERP Solution: http://help.sap.com/bp/initial/index.htm

C   The Author

Shivesh Sharma, PMP, is an MBA and certified project management professional and has worked on multiple end-to-end SAP ERP implementation and upgrade projects for IBM (formerly PwC Consulting), Computer Sciences Corporation, and Fujitsu Consulting.

Shivesh's consulting background combines different ERP team lead positions and project and program-management experiences for multiple Fortune 500 clients. His domain areas for SAP ERP consulting include business process design, change management, project management, and hands-on configuration of SAP ERP Financials (GL, accounts receivable, bank accounting, asset management, Funds Management, special purpose ledger, cost center accounting, profit center accounting, Investment Management, Profitability Analysis, and consolidation using ECCS).

Shivesh is currently based out of St Louis, Missouri, and can be reached at *shivesh. sharma@gmail.com*. In his free time, Shivesh enjoys traveling, reading, writing, and playing with his son.

Index

Understand and implement strategies for maximizing Financials reporting capabilities

Learn and apply best practices for simplifying, streamlining, and automating financial and management reporting

668 pp., 2008, 79,95 Euro / US$ 79.95
ISBN 978-1-59229-179-3

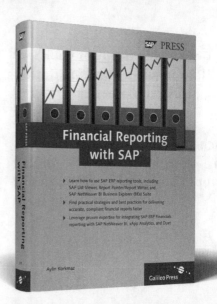

Financial Reporting with SAP

www.sap-press.com

Aylin Korkmaz

Financial Reporting with SAP

This book provides finance and IT teams with best practices for delivering financial reports faster, more accurately, and in compliance with various international accounting standards. Featuring step-by-step coverage of all major FI reporting functions (including Sub-Ledger, Corporate Finance Management, and Governance, Risk & Compliance), this timely book will help you streamline and simplify financial business processes and automate financial and management reporting in SAP ERP Financials. It includes coverage of integrating FI reporting with Business Intelligence, xApp Analytics, and Duet™.

Get the most out of your SAP ERP Finacials implementation using the practical tips and techniques provided

Achieve operational efficiencies by adopting the process-driven approach detailed through out the book

675 pp., 2008, 79,95 Euro / US$ 79.95
ISBN 978-1-59229-160-1

Optimize Your SAP ERP Financials Implementation

www.sap-press.com

Shivesh Sharma

Optimize Your SAP ERP Financials Implementation

The real work in SAP Financials begins after the implementation is complete. This is when it's time to optimize and use SAP Financials in the most efficient way for your organization. Optimization entails understanding unique client scenarios and then developing solutions to meet those requirements, while staying within the project's budgetary and timeline constraints. This book teaches consultants and project managers to think about and work through best practice tools and methodologies, before choosing the ones to use in their own implementations. The variety of real-life case studies and examples used to illustrate the business processes and highlight how SAP Financials can support these processes, make this a practical and valuable book for anyone looking to optimize their SAP Financials implementation.